Created and Directed by Hans Höfer

INSIGHT GUIDES

ITALY

Project Editor by Katherine Barrett

Managing Editor: Dorothy Stannard

Editorial Director: Brian Bell

HOUGHTON MIFFLIN COMPANY

APA PUBLICATIONS

ABOUT THIS BOOK

Höfer

his is a completely updated and expanded edition of one of Apa Publications' most popular guides to Europe. It refines further the Insight Guides approach of inspiring and informing the serious traveller with a solid background of history and current information, stunning photography, good writing and honest reporting of destinations, warts and all.

Insight Guides' award-winning formula, which has produced books on nearly 200 destinations, was created in 1970 by **Hans Höfer**, who is still the driving force behind Apa Publications. Two further series, Compact Guides and Insight Pocket Guides, have since been added to make Apa Publications the most prolific guidebook publishers in the world.

Italy certainly suits Apa's approach, for it is one of the world's great destinations. Henry James decided it was "of a beauty (an interest and complexity of beauty) so far beyond another that none other is worth talking about." Lord Byron called it "my Magnet". Italy has it all: beautiful cities steeped in history, a vibrant street life, a rich culture, snowy mountains, green valleys and backwater villages. Never far away is a great meal with a choice of memorable wines. In one direction is the deep blue Mediterranean and the other the green Adriatic sea.

Stannard

ow, then, can one describe, explain – indeed, simply cover adequately – a subject that has inspired poets, novelists and composers for centuries? The task fell to managing editor **Dorothy Stannard**, who juggled the assignment with that of editing a new title, *Insight Guide: Jordan*.

Catling

To help make a good book even better, she enlisted the expertise of Italy specialists, including several Insight regulars: **Christopher Catling**, author of *Insight Pocket Guide: Florence*, who expanded and updated the chapters on Florence, Tuscany and Umbria and The Marches, and brushed up the feature on Renaissance art, a subject close to his heart; **Ginger Künzel**, a Munich-based writer who wrote about the Italian Alps and the Trentino-Alto Adige region, an area which, in her own words, she

Boulton

Gerard Sharp

"quite simply adores"; **Susie Boulton**, who updated and expanded the sections on Venice, a city she has already revealed to Insight readers in *Insight Pocket Guide: Venice*; and **Lisa Gerard Sharp**, who took time off from writing *Insight Pocket Guide: Sicily* to advise on the content of this guide and cast her eye over the Sicily chapter.

Among those contributing brand-new chapters to the book were wine writer **James Ainsworth**, whose abiding passion for Italian wines developed while he was conducting wine-lovers' tours to Italy, and Rome-based **Bruce Johnston**, who writes about the Mafia, a subject that has occupied much of his time and talents as a journalist for *La Stampa* and London's *Sunday Times*.

Also providing input and on the ground in Italy was travel writer and editor **Jane Shaw**, who, having just travelled through the south of the country, updated the chapters on Apulia, Calabria and Basilicata, plus Abruzzo and Molise. **Susan Stacey**, **Janette Jongepier** and **Karen Phillips**, three representatives of the tour operator Magic of Italy, helped update the fact-packed Travel Tips section.

Much of this new edition builds on the work of **Katherine Barrett**, editor of the original edition of *Insight Guide: Italy*. Like so many Americans, Barrett first saw Italy from the window of a bus. A student at Harvard, she was intrigued by the possibility of becoming an archaeologist and signed up for a semester in Rome. She was attracted by all of Rome's layers: from its antiquities and its churches to its shop windows. After graduating, Barrett spent a year living in Rome and travelling around Italy. The editorship of *Insight Guide: Italy* presented the perfect opportunity for her to combine her interests in Italy, travel writing and journalism. She wrote the chapters on Rome and Famous Travellers.

McHugh

The most prolific writer in this volume, **Clare McHugh**, wrote the chapters on Italian history through to the beginning of the 20th century and the chapters on the northern provinces for the Places section.

Rossatti

It is to **Alberto Rossatti** – a latter-day Renaissance man (he has worked as a lawyer, teacher, actor, director and translator of literature) – that the book owes much of its native expertise. As well as assisting Clare McHugh in her research, Rossatti interpreted Italian manners and customs in "The Italians" and celebrated their unrivalled sense of style in a chapter on fashion.

Swett

Other contributors to the original guide included New Yorker **Benjamin Swett**, who wrote about the south; **Jacob Young**, a political journalist who, as well as writing about Italian history in the 20th century, took time out from his job as associate editor of *Newsweek International* to research Florence and Tuscany; **Claudia Angeletti,** who abandoned the elegant arcades of home town Turin to explore Sicily and compiled the all-important, nuts-and-bolts Travel Tips ; **Kathleen Beckett**, a fashion journalist who turned her aesthetic eye to Renaissance art; **Melanie Menagh**, another New Yorker, who "forsook the grey canyons of Manhattan for the green hills of Umbria and the Marches"; **Peter Spiro**, who recounted the fascinating history of the Vatican, and **George Prochnik**, a New York writer, who wrote about food.

Angeletti

Viesti

Like all Insight Guides, this book owes a lot to its photographs much of which is the work of New York-based **Joe Viesti**. The subject matter was undoubtedly rich, but Viesti brought humour, sensitivity and a great aesthetic sense to his images. An American of Italian descent, Viesti had an opportunity to discover his roots during the six weeks that he spent taking pictures of people and places all the way from Milan to Palermo.

Peter Namuth, a freelance photographer based in New York, did the archival photography. His work for animated films and award-winning documentaries has also been seen on Public Television. Additional photographs were contributed byold and new hands **Albano Guatti**, Rome-based **Susan Pierres**, and Florentine **Gaetano Barone, Catherine Desjeux, Lyle Lawson, Thomas Schöllhammer, Mike Newton, Steve Day** and **Bill Wassman**.

Martine Singer applied her precise eye to the maps. Amilia Medwied of the Ente Nazionale per il Turismo in New York and her colleague Signora Lantini in Rome offered assistance in planning itineraries and arranging accommodation.

This edition was proofread and indexed by **Pam Barrett**.

CONTENTS

Introduction

The Eternal Seductress 21

Travellers 23

History

Beginnings 31

Rome Rules the World 35

Life in the Empire 41

The Middle Ages 43

The Renaissance 49

Renaissance Art 55

Birth of a Nation 61

The 20th Century 65

The Mafia 70

People & Culture

The Italians 79

The Italian Look 89

Food 95

Wine 101

Opera 107

Italian Film 113

The Vatican 121

Places

Introduction 135

Rome 139

Rome Environs 162

Abruzzo and Molise 169

The North 181

Milan and Lombardy 183

The Lakes 193

<u>Preceding pages</u>: handywork from the Renaissance; bronze door of San Zeno Maggiore church, Verona; Limone, Lake Garda.

CONTENTS

Piedmont, Val d'Aosta
and Liguria 197

Venice 207

Venice Environs 218

Trentino-Alto Adige 225

Friuli-Venezia Giulia 232

Emilia-Romagna 234

Florence 247

Tuscany 259

Umbria and the Marches .. 273

The South 289

Naples 291

Environs of Naples 300

Apulia 309

Calabria and Basilicata 317

Sicily 325

Sardinia 334

Maps

Italy 134
Rome 136
Central Italy 162
Northern Italy 178
Milan 184
Venice 208
Bologna 234
Tuscany, Umbria and
the Marches 244
Florence 248
Southern Italy 286
Naples 290
Bay of Naples 300
Sicily 326
Sardinia 335

TRAVEL TIPS

Getting There

By Air 338
By Road 338
By Rail 338

Travel Essentials

Visas & Passports 339
Money Matters 339
Tipping 339
Customs Regulations 339
Animal Quarantine 340
What to Wear 340

Getting Acquainted

Government & Population .. 340
Weights & Measures 340
Time Zones 340
Climate 340
Electricity 340
Business Hours 340
Holidays 341
Festivals & Seasonal
Events 341

Communications

Postal Services 341
Telephone & Telegram 341

Emergencies

Security & Crime 342
Medical Services 342

Getting Around

Domestic Travel 343
City Transport 344
The Metro 344
Taxis 345
Water Taxis & Gondolas 345
Private Transport 345

Where to Stay

Hotels 346

Food Digest

What to Eat 351
Where to Eat 351

Things to Do

National Parks 358

Culture Plus

Museums 359
Theatres 360
Concerts 360

Nightlife

Where to Go 360

Shopping

Shopping Areas 361

Sports

Spectator 362

Useful Addresses

Tourist Information 363

Further Reading

Bibliography 363
Other Insight Guides 364

Art/Photo Credits 365

Index 366

THE ETERNAL SEDUCTRESS

Italy, like the sorceress Circe, tantalisingly beautiful and at the same time treacherous, has attracted kings, scholars, saints, poets and curious travellers for centuries. The spell of the "Eternal Seductress", as men have dubbed her, which once drew people across stormy mountains and seas, now leads them into hardly less turbulent airports and train stations.

Italy has always seemed somewhat removed from the rest of Europe: physically by mountains and sea, spiritually by virtue of the Pope. In the eyes of outsiders, the Italians themselves are characterised by extremes: at one end of the spectrum, the gentle unworldliness of St Francis, and, at the other, the amoral brilliance of Machiavelli; on the one hand, the curiosity of Galileo or the genius of Michelangelo, on the other, the repressive dogmatism of Counter Reformation Jesuits. There have been those who thought the Italians were unworthy of Italy, and others, such as the English novelist E. M. Forster, who considered them "more marvellous than the land".

This book believes that Italy and the Italians are equally worthy of attention. It explores the land and its people, from Calabrian villagers to Milanese sophisticates and delves into their justly famous treasures, from Etruscan statues to Botticelli's radiant *Birth of Venus*. Special features celebrate Italian passions – films, fashion, opera and food – while the history section threads its way through a tumultuous past, from the legendary founding of Rome by Romulus and Remus to the Renaissance, reunification, Mussolini and the Mafia.

In Italy the past is always present; a housing development rises above a crumbling Roman wall; ultra-modern museums display pre-Roman artifacts; old people in tiny mountain villages preserve customs which are centuries old while their grandchildren roar into the future on shiny new Vespas.

This is the country which inspires imagination in the dull, passion in the cold-hearted, rebellion in the conventional. Whether you spend your sojourn in Italy under a brightly coloured beach umbrella on the Riviera, shopping in Milan or diligently examining churches and museums, you cannot be unchanged by Italy. At the very least, you will receive a highly pleasurable lesson in living. Whether you are struck by the beauty of a church facade rising from a perfectly proportioned piazza, the aroma of freshly carved *prosciutto*, or the sight of a stylish passer-by spied over the foam of your *cappuccino*, there is the same superb sensation: nowhere else on earth does just living seem so extraordinary.

Preceding pages: Pisa's leaning tower; Venice carnival-goer in the guise of Janus, the Roman God of the New Year (who looks both backwards and forwards); St Peter, Rome; artistic endeavours at Piazzale Michelangelo, Florence; welcome to Venice. <u>Left</u>, in the Piazza San Marco in Venice.

Between 40 and 50 million foreigners visit Italy each year, their reasons as various as the attractions they come to see. The one thing these travellers tend to share is a dislike of their fellows. "Though there are some disagreeable things in Venice," wrote Henry James in 1882, "there is nothing so disagreeable as the visitors."

For centuries, Europeans and Americans have been crossing mountains and oceans in search of what Keats called "a beakerful of the warm south". Their numbers have included a fair proportion of the world's greatest writers and painters. Italy features in so many journals, poems, letters, paintings and novels that Italy-through-the-artist's-eye has become almost as tangible as the geographical reality.

Pilgrims' progress: The first peaceful visitors to Italy were pilgrims. Their destination was Rome where they found, along with the shrines of St Peter and St Paul, much of the imperial city still standing. By the 12th century there was a guidebook to the Eternal City called the *Mirabilia Urbis Roma*. Rome, despite her declining state, was still considered to be the centre of civilisation: "While stands the Colosseum, stands Rome; when falls the Colosseum, falls Rome and also falls the world."

The first major deluge of foreigners occurred in 1300 when Pope Boniface VIII established a jubilee (Holy Year). For this special year only he granted plenary indulgences (previously preserved for those who made the more arduous trip to Palestine) to pilgrims who visited the shrines of St Peter and St Paul. One contemporary historian reported that there were never fewer than 200,000 visitors in Rome at any time during the year. The total number of visitors that year was estimated at 2 million. "In the streets and churches," wrote Edward Gibbon, "many persons were trampled to death by the eagerness of devotion." One unfortunate English monk had his leg crushed while he was admiring the famous relic of St Veronica (still in the Vatican today).

Left, the heroine of Nathaniel Hawthorne's *The Marble Faun* has an assignation in Perugia.

Pope Boniface VIII was probably motivated more by the need to replenish Rome's coffers than by any real desire to save the souls of the faithful. The dramatic influx of hungry, tired foreigners was an economic boon to the citizens of Rome, who discovered a thousand ways to make money. They sold religious trinkets – cheap metal pins with pictures of St Peter and St Paul, not unlike the gew-gaws found in the Vatican today. A number of edicts were passed against greedy innkeepers who, in their eagerness to attract business, would forcibly remove guests from the inns of competitors.

The humanists, starting with the poet Petrarch in the 14th century, applied their knowledge of ancient texts to the ruins they saw. As well as taking a scholarly interest, they began to respond imaginatively to the ruins. A 15th-century scholar, Poggius, wrote a dialogue called *De Varietate Fortunae* (On the Varieties of Fortune) that reveals an early tendency to view Rome as a symbol of the mortality of man's creations and the supremacy of God, a theme later picked up by the Romantics. Inspired by the ruins of the Capitoline, Poggius wrote: "The spectacle of the world, how it is fallen! How changed! How defaced! The path of victory is obliterated by vines, and the benches of senators are concealed by a dunghill."

One of the most significant journeys to Italy for the history of Western civilisation was made by a young German monk, Martin Luther, in 1510. In his eagerness to see Holy Rome, Luther rushed through Milan, Bologna and Florence. Arriving at Rome, he found Pope Julius II on the throne of St Peter, a war-like Renaissance prince more interested in military conquest than in celebrating Mass. "I would not for a hundred thousand florins have missed seeing Rome," wrote the disillusioned Luther many years later. "I should have always felt an uneasy doubt whether I was not, after all, doing injustice to the Pope. As it is, I am quite satisfied on that point."

Between the 16th and the 17th centuries gentlemen of means considered an extended trip to Italy to be the final step in their education both as humanists and as courtiers.

Italy, wrote one 17th-century traveller, "hath always been accounted the nurse of policy, learning, music, architecture and limning [painting], with other perfections which she dispertheth to the rest of Europe."

Others, however, felt differently. For them Italy was less the cradle of civilisation than a centre of papist corruption and court intrigue. "The art of atheisme, the art of epicurizing, the art of whoring, the art of poisoning, the art of sodomitrie," were some of the "fine arts" which the early English novelist Thomas Nashe found in Italy. In the popular imagination of Elizabethan England, the Italian political theorist Machiavelli was linked with the devil. English national-

Gothic romance set in Italy. Edward Gibbon claims to have received the inspiration for his mammoth *The Decline and Fall of the Roman Empire* while musing amid the ruins of the Capitoline in Rome.

Travel during the days of the Grand Tour lacked the comforts of even the cheapest expedition today – to describe a hotel as "lousy", for example, had an uncomfortably vivid meaning. The English novelist Tobias Smollett found 18th-century travel difficult: "The house was dismal and dirty beyond all description; the bedclothes filthy enough to turn the stomach of a muleteer; and the victuals cooked in such a manner, that even a Hottentot could not have beheld them with-

ists bridled at the influence of sophisticated Italian manners and fashions. In Shakespeare's *Richard II*, one of the king's uncles speaks contemptuously of the Italian pretensions of the royal court: "Proud Italy/Whose manners still our tardy, apish nation/Limps after in base imitation."

Despite such hesitations, the list of well-known visitors to Italy before the French Revolution is impressive: the essayist Montaigne, the diarist John Evelyn, the poet Milton, painters Reubens and Velasquez. Horace Walpole travelled with the poet Thomas Gray, a journey which inspired *The Castle of Otranto*, Walpole's bloodcurdling

out loathing… here I took my repose, wrapped in a greatcoat, if that could be called repose which was interrupted by the innumerable stings of vermin."

By the end of the 18th century the "Proud Italy" of the Renaissance had been humbled by foreign invasions and repression of the Counter-Reformation. Travellers still admired the Italians' aesthetic sensibility, but the respect was tempered by a sense of their own political superiority. Visitors came to view Italy as a storehouse of the past – a past unconnected to the living, breathing inhabitants they met. John Ruskin, though enamoured by Italy's marvellous works of art, often said that he loathed modern Italians.

The romance of ruins: By the 19th century the interests that brought visitors to Italy were quite varied. The Colosseum, to Dickens, was an inspiring spot for "moralists, antiquaries, painters, architects, devotees". The number of visitors increased dramatically, since travel was no longer only open to aristocrats. Every visitor of note felt inspired to publish his thoughts on Italy. Superlatives swelled and proliferated: "Sister land of paradise", "the promised land", "the land that holds the rest in tender thrall", "the whole earth's treasury", and "men's mother, men's queen".

The northern enthusiasm for Italian ruins was well underway by the 18th century. English gentlemen were busy building ruined temples to make their gardens look more picturesque. Giambattisa Piranesi, dubbed "the Rembrandt of the ruins", had familiarised thousands with his fantastic images of the Italian landscape. Goethe became one of Italy's most devoted fans.

The pathetic charm of greatness brought to its knees attracted the Romantics, such as Shelley and Byron. Shelley contended that the Colosseum was more sublime in its ruined state, half-fallen, wreathed with weeds and flowers, than it had been during the days of the Roman empire when it glistened with marble. Where more pious visitors had seen the hand of God in the ruins, the Romantic Shelley saw the triumph of nature: "Rome has fallen, ye see it lying/ Heaped in undistinguished ruin;/ Nature is alone undying."

For Shelley, and his close friend Lord Byron, Italy provided a necessary retreat from the repressive morality of England. Shelley's belief in free love and the abandonment of his wife had caused a scandal, while Byron was forced to flee England following the discovery of his incestuous relations with his half-sister. Both men felt alienated in their native land and spent years wandering through Italy, which was an escape from persecution to art and sunshine. Byron captured his impressions most vividly in his poem *Childe Harolde*. With its lengthy and evocative descriptions of Italy's most famous sights, the poem became a standard guidebook for visitors to Italy. In fact, by the middle of the century, most of the famous passages were being quoted in the standard guidebooks. For Byron's hero the journey to Italy became nothing less than the journey to his own soul. The spiritual pain of the Romantic exile, misunderstood and despised by his own country, he sees reflected in the mighty ruins of Rome. Childe Harolde cries "Oh, Rome! my country! City of the Soul!/ The Orphans of the Heart must turn to thee."

Neither Byron nor Shelley ever returned to England. Byron went on to Greece where he died at the age of 36; Shelley drowned off the coast of Liguria while sailing to Lerici in his boat *The Don Juan*. Their compatriot John

Keats, another romantic poet, also died in Italy, in a little room overlooking the Piazza di Spagna in Rome.

Two other imaginative works used to inform the average traveller were Mme De Stael's *Corinne* (1807) and Nathaniel Hawthorne's *The Marble Faun*. The former, although little known today, was enormously popular in the 19th century. The novel tells the story of the love affair between an Italian poetess called Corinne and a brooding Scot, Lord Nevil. In the course of their relationship, Corinne instructs Nevil – and the reader – in the beauties of Italy. Chapters with such titles as "On Italian Character and Manners",

Left, Piranesi's fanciful drawing of Hadrian's Villa at Tivoli. **Right**, Mme de Stael, author of *Corinne*, a popular 19th-century novel.

"The Statues and Pictures" and "The Tombs, Churches and Palaces" reveal this romance to be a thinly disguised guidebook. De Stael was highly esteemed for her sympathetic portrait of the Italian character, so often maligned as superficial, immoral or faithless. In fact, it is the proper, duty-bound Nevil who proves to be faithless.

Like so many northerners, Nevil goes to Italy to develop his "taste". Corinne gently shows him how to appreciate things sensuously rather than intellectually. But once back in Scotland "his thoughts begin to steady from the Italian intoxication which had unsettled them". With Nevil as the stiff northerner and Corinne as the southern tempt-

inspiration". Despite a distaste for the baroque aspects of Italian culture, Hawthorne appreciated the rich history and mysterious atmosphere that Italy offered. His own country, he admitted, lacked an intriguing presence of the past. *The Marble Faun*, like *Corinne*, contained extensive descriptive passages in such chapters as "A Stroll on the Pincian" or "A Moonlight Ramble".

The problem with all the publicity – the novels, poems, guidebooks, lithographs – showered on Italy in the 19th century was that it often led to disappointment once the traveller was actually there. Ruins rarely looked like Piranesi etchings, and few people were capable of feeling that Rome was

ress, the novel was read as an allegory of England and Italy, highlighting the contrasts between reason and passion, art and duty, society and the individual, the intellect and the senses.

An American response: Hawthorne's *Marble Faun* reveals the ambivalent response of a 19th-century New Englander. The novelist is openly hostile to Catholicism, a religion depicted as seducing its followers with a "multitude of external forms". He sees a similar superficiality in Italian paintings which "show a marvellous knack of external arrangement instead of the live sympathy and sentiment which should have been their

truly the city of their soul. The escalating numbers of uneducated tourists didn't have the grounding in the Italian language, history and classical culture traditionally recommended by earlier travellers. Thus Henry James's Daisy Miller, the personification of silly American girlhood, was unabashedly bored by antiquities. But she also fell into a tourist trap: her eagerness to see the Colosseum by moonlight, a must on any tourist's itinerary, led to malaria and her eventual death in Rome.

One of the most entertaining expressions by an American of impatience with the cult of Italy is Mark Twain's *The Innocents*

Abroad (1869). Though Twain did poke fun at American smugness as well as at the pretensions of Italophiles, he also defended American common sense. "But isn't this relic matter a little overdone?" he asked. "We find a piece of the true cross in every church we go into, and some of the nails that held it together… I think we've seen as much as a keg of these nails." Admiration for Michelangelo he also found excessive: "Enough! Say no more! Lump the whole thing! Say that the creator made Italy from designs by Michelangelo!"

It is hard to think of a 19th-century American writer of any importance who didn't go to Italy and leave some record of their impression: James Fenimore Cooper, Melville, Hawthorne, James, Washington Irving, William Dean Howells. Most of the painters and sculptors went as well.

Many artists stayed on for inspiration, for an environment more conducive to creativity than the hard-nosed business world back home, and for the cheap marble and skilled craftsmen. The neoclassical sculptor William Wetmore Story rented out a suite of 50 rooms in the Palazzo Barberini in Rome. There he hosted receptions for the many American and British expatriates living in or around the Piazza di Spagna. In Florence, Casa Guidi, home of Robert and Elizabeth Barrett Browning (the latter an invalid whose health and happiness in Italy is put down to a Chianti cure), was the nucleus of a community of artists, writers and musicians. Elizabeth loved Florence and never tired of praising Italy at the expense of England. She spent many hours on her balcony, and the view from "Casa Guida Windows" slipped neatly from reality into her most famous poem.

Some scrimped and saved to make their one trip to the "promised land". It was the dream of a lifetime for many small-town school teachers and clergymen. For others, like James's Millers, it was a way of acquiring culture, of rubbing off some of their provinciality and new money. Europeans tended to be less hostile towards them than the upper-class society in New York or San Francisco. Many American millionaires, advised by such connoisseurs as Bernard Berenson, would purchase Italian art. It is thanks to many of them that America is so well endowed with Italian masterpieces.

Modern travellers: At first glance, modern travellers may seem to have little in common with their predecessors. Most visit Italy for only a week or two and few have a Classical education (how many feel these days, as Byron did, that the Forum "glows with Cicero"?). Yet certain attitudes and behaviour persist. First time visitors still feel impelled to go to Rome, Venice and Florence, just as they did in the days of the Grand Tour in the 19th century. The puritanical distaste

that Hawthorne felt for the baroque is shared by many of his spiritual descendants today. And many, like Shelley and Lord Nevil before them, feel that in Italy they can at last let loose. And as for religious pilgrimages, the oldest type of Italian travel, one only has to go to the pope's public audiences in Piazza S. Pietro to see that not since the Middle Ages have the devout swarmed to Rome in such numbers.

Above all, however, Italy is romantic. As Harold Acton, the grand old man of English letters, said when asked what made life worth living: "Writing a book, dinner for six, travelling in Italy with someone you love."

As school children have noticed for years, Italy looks like a boot. The long, narrow peninsula sticking out of Europe's underbelly is perpetually poised to kick Sicily westward. This peculiar shape made Italy a natural site for early civilisation. The Alps, which cut across the only land link with the rest of Europe, protected the peninsula from the barbarians who roamed the plains of Northern Europe, while the Mediterranean, which surrounds the three remaining sides, served as a highway, first to bring civilisation to the peninsula and later to export it.

The land itself encompasses two separate regions: the northern continental, and the southern peninsular. Together the two parts cover an area of about 146,500 sq. km (91,000 sq. miles). The smaller, northern section is a plain, bordered on the north and northwest by the Alps and on the south by the Apennines. Once a vast bay of the Adriatic, this plain was gradually filled with silt from the Po, the Adige and other rivers. The deposits were rich in nitrates and the plain became the most fertile region in Italy.

The Apennine range, the so-called backbone of Italy, dominates the peninsular section of the country. These mountains zig-zag down the peninsula from the French Alps and the coast of Liguria in the northwest, through northern Tuscany and southeast to the Adriatic coast, and veer west again to the Strait of Messina, between Sicily and the toe of the boot. They reach their greatest height in the central province of Abruzzi where the peaks of the Gran Sasso d'Italia soar as high as 2,912 metres (9,700 ft).

It is no coincidence that the early inhabitants of Italy flourished in the west, on the lowland plains north and south of Rome. Here there are a few natural harbours and long rivers. The Tiber, Arno, Livi and Volturno are easily navigated by small craft, and their valleys provide easy communication between the coast and the interior. What's more, the plains of Tuscany, Latium and

Campania comprise fertile farmland, thanks to a thick layer of ash and weathered lava from the many once-active volcanoes.

Around 200,000 years before the founding of Rome, only cavemen lived on the Italian peninsula. These early inhabitants hunted and gathered for food. Italy became more fully populated when, with the Indo-European migrations (2000–1200 BC), tribes of primitive peoples poured into Italy from Central Europe and Asia.

Archaeological evidence suggests that these tribes lived in round huts clustered in small villages. The Villanovans, as the tribesmen are called, were farmers who could make and use iron tools. They cremated their dead and placed the ashes in tall, clay or bronze urns.

Villanovan culture spread from its original centre around Bologna south to Tuscany and Latium. Nowhere, however, did Villanovan settlements grow to the size of towns; Italian life at this time centred on primitive villages. Nor were the artistic achievements of the Villanovans particularly great. Their funerary urns, for example, were shaped crudely, and no tomb or wall paintings have ever been found.

The Greeks in Italy: The transformation of Italy from a primitive backwater to the centre of the ancient world was due to the Greeks and the Etruscans. Both sailed across the sea in search of rich new land. They sowed the first seeds of civilisation on the peninsula in the early 8th century BC.

Greek colonists settled in Sicily and on the west coast near modern-day Naples. Most came in search of land to farm, for Greece had insufficient arable land to feed the entire population. Others were political refugees: when a Greek king was overthrown, all his followers were required to flee.

On arriving in Italy, Greek settlers formed independent cities, each of which was loosely linked to the city on the Greek mainland from which the settlers had originated. One of the earliest colonies was at Cumae, on the shores of the Bay of Naples. Greeks from Euboea, a large island northeast of Athens, settled there in approximately 770 BC. Other Euboeans founded Rhegion (modern Reggio-

Preceding pages: 18th-century map of Italy, which was then a collection of separate states. Left, an Etruscan statue of the god Apollo wears a mysterious smile.

Calabria), at the tip of the boot, a few years later. The Corinthian city of Syracuse on Sicily ultimately became the most powerful of the Greek colonies.

The colonists farmed the land around their cities, and engaged in trade with mainland Greece. They soon prospered and made important contributions to Italian agriculture. They were the first people to cultivate the vine and the olive – plants that had previously only grown wild.

In the 5th century both Syracuse and Athens tried to establish rival empires out of the Greek colonies in Italy. Numerous battles were fought. Many Italian natives were forced to participate as drafted soldiers. But after

The civilising influence of the Greeks went beyond the visual arts. The natives adapted the Greek alphabet for their own Indo-European tongues and each native group soon had its own letters. By example, the Greeks also taught the Italian natives about modern warfare, lessons that they were eventually to use against their Greek teachers. The Italians learnt how to fortify towns with high walls of smooth masonry, and the value of shock troop tactics with armoured spearmen.

But exceptional wealth and knowledge didn't enable the Greeks to control Italy. Civil wars left the Greeks little time for expansion and conquest. They were willing to trade with the natives, but not able to unify

years of fighting neither side achieved total victory, and eventually the Greek leaders gave up the struggle.

The colonists continued to argue among themselves, which prevented them from becoming a dominant political power in Italy. They did, however, become the major cultural and artistic force. Italian natives were eager to trade for Greek luxury goods, the like of which they had never seen before. Soon Greek bronze and ceramic ware was dispersed throughout Italy and provided natives with new and sophisticated art patterns to imitate. The sculpture and architecture in the Greek cities also served as models for the Italians.

them under Greek leadership. This left great political opportunities wide open.

The Etruscans: In approximately 800 BC, Etruscans settled on the west coast where Tuscany (Etruscany) and Lazio are today. Questions about the origins of the Etruscans still puzzle scholars. The Greek historian Herodotus claimed that they came from Asia Minor, and that revolution and famine at home had driven them to seek new lands. However, recent archaeological evidence casts doubt on this theory and suggests that a small group of Phoenicians from Palestine may have landed in Italy, imparted to the natives the knowledge they had brought from the East, and Etruscan culture was the result.

Wherever they came from, there is no doubt that the Etruscans were a highly civilised people. Little is known about the details of their lifestyle because their language is incomprehensible to modern scholars, but archaeological remains reveal a hearty appetite for life. Hundreds of Etruscan tombs have survived, many of them decorated with wall paintings depicting dancing, dinner parties and music-making. Other paintings show battle and hunting scenes.

The Etruscans were also skilled craftsmen. Their speciality was metal working. Italy was rich in minerals, and trade in metal goods became the basis of an active urban

Indeed, long after Etruscan power had been eclipsed by Rome, the Etruscans' reputation for religious devotion lived on. Indeed, young men in imperial Rome were often sent to Tuscany to learn how to read the entrails of animals for signs from the gods.

Each Etruscan city supported itself by trade. The Etruscans were eager to obtain luxury goods from the Greek colonists and they developed overland routes to reach the Greek cities. These cut straight through Latium, the plain south of the Tiber occupied by Italian natives called Latins.

One of their trading posts on the route south was a Latin village called Rome, originally no more than a cluster of mud huts.

society. Etruscan cities sprang up where previously there had been only simple villages.

Each Etruscan city (there were 12 in all) was independent, but they were grouped in a loose confederation for religious purposes. Representatives of the cities would gather at regular intervals to worship the 12 Etruscan gods, but that was the extent of their political unity. Their fascination with religion far surpassed their desire for political power.

Left, an ancient Greek dives gracefully into the hereafter in a fresco from a tomb at Paestum. **Above**, an Etruscan statue of the she-wolf that raised Romulus and Remus.

Under the influence of the Etruscans, the settlement flourished. They drained the swamp that became the Roman Forum and built grand palaces and roads.

For 300 years, starting in the late 8th century BC, Etruscan kings ruled Rome and directed its growth. But by the 5th century BC, their power was fading. In the north, Gauls overran Etruscan settlements in the Po Valley. Next, Italic tribesmen from the Abruzzi threatened the main Etruscan cities. Then, in the south, the Etruscans went to war against the Greeks. The Romans took advantage of this moment of weakness to rebel against their Etruscan masters.

The historians of ancient Rome wrote their own version of events leading to the overthrow of the Etruscan kings. They drew upon accepted legends about Rome's past and claimed that the city had only fallen under Etruscan rule temporarily. According to legend, Rome was founded by the descendants of gods and heroes.

Romulus and Remus: In his epic the *Aeneid*, Virgil tells how Aeneas, a hero of Homeric Troy, journeyed west after the sack of Troy to live and rule in Latium. In the 8th century one of his descendants, the Latin princess Rhea Silvia, bore twin sons, Romulus and Remus, fathered by the god Mars. Her uncle, King Amulius, angry because the princess had broken her vow of chastity as a Vestal Virgin, locked her up and abandoned the boys on the river bank to die. They were found there by a she-wolf who raised them.

The story goes on to tell how, as young men, the brothers led a band of rebel Latin youths to find a new home. As they approached the hills of Rome, a flight of eagles passed overhead – a sign from the gods that this was an auspicious site for their new city.

Rome was ruled by Etruscan kings until 509 BC when the son of King Tarquinius Superbus raped a Roman noblewoman, Lucretia. She killed herself in shame and Roman noblemen used the incident as an excuse to revolt against the Etruscans.

The leader of the Roman revolt, Lucius Junius Brutus, may have been an actual historical figure. In Roman legend he's larger than life: the founder of a republic, a vigorous leader, and a puritanical ruler. The historian Tacitus wrote that Brutus was so loyal to Rome that he watched without flinching as his two sons were executed for treason.

In the war against the Etruscans, Rome was also aided by a talented soldier named Cincinnatus. The legend "merits the attention of those who despise all human qualities in comparison with riches, and think there is no room for great honours but amidst a profusion of wealth," wrote the Roman his-

Left, Augustus of Prima Porta shows a youthful emperor looking to Rome's future of *Imperium sine fine* (rule without end).

torian Livy. Cincinnatus was a simple Roman farmer who left his plough to help his city. He was so able that he rose quickly to the rank of general. But once the fight was won, he surrendered his position of power and returned to his life as a plain citizen.

These stories of Rome's early heroes reveal a lot about the Roman character. For the Romans, nothing was as important as *pietas* – dutiful respect to one's gods, city, parents and comrades. They used the heroes of legend as propaganda tools.

Upon the overthrow of the Etruscans, Rome's leaders declared that no more kings would rule Rome. A republic based on the Greek model was founded and the Senate, a group of Rome's leading citizens who had previously had advisory roles in government, took control of the city.

During the next 200 years Rome conquered most of the Italian peninsula. But Carthage, a city in North Africa founded by the Phoenicians, controlled the western Mediterranean. If Rome was ever to expand its borders across the Mediterranean, Carthage had to be defeated.

The Punic Wars: The initial clash between the two cities, the First Punic War (264 BC), began as a struggle for the Greek city of Messina on Sicily. By the time it was over, in 241 BC, the Romans had driven the Carthaginians out of Sicily completely. The island became Rome's first province. Three years later Rome annexed Sardinia and Corsica as well, and further military triumphs followed. When Rome conquered Cisalpine Gaul (northern Italy) and extended its borders to the Alps, it alleviated the threat of invasion by the Gauls.

War broke out again in 218 BC when the brilliant Carthaginian general Hannibal, who from the age of nine had dedicated his life to the destruction of Rome, embarked on an ambitious plan to attack Rome from the north via Spain, the Pyrenees and the Alps. Rome eventually counterattacked Carthage, and Hannibal was forced to return and defend his homeland. He was defeated in 202 BC at the battle of Zama 100 km (80 miles) from Carthage.

The Third Punic War was almost an afterthought. Carthage had been stripped of many of its possessions 50 years before, but had recovered much of its commercial power. When the Carthaginians challenged Rome indirectly, the Romans took the opportunity to rid themselves of their bitter rival forever. The city of Carthage was razed, and salt was ploughed into the soil. The Carthaginians themselves were sold into slavery.

Revolution at home: The blessings of peace were mixed. Rome was now more prosperous than ever before, but only the middle class and the rich benefited. For the common people, many of whom had served their city faithfully during the wars, peace meant greater poverty. The menial jobs they had

depended on for their livelihood were now filled by slaves. Independent farmers, a group that traditionally formed the backbone of the Roman state, sold their land to the owners of great estates, who used slaves to work it. These displaced farmers joined the Roman mob or wandered Italy in search of work.

The Senate's usual way of dealing with potentially explosive situations was to feed the masses bread and entertain them with circuses. But eventually one man from the patricians' ranks challenged the exploitative system. His name was Tiberius Gracchus, and in 133 BC he was elected tribune. He campaigned for the reintroduction of an old

law limiting the size of the great estates, and proposed that farming and grazing land owned by the state should be distributed among the poor. The Senators, many of them wealthy landowners who did not want to see their influence curtailed, objected. The Senate blocked Tiberius's plan, and when he persisted and ran for re-election as tribune it engaged hired assassins to murder him and his supporters.

But Tiberius's spirit did not die with him. Eleven years later, his younger brother, Gaius, was elected tribune. A volatile personality and an effective speaker, Gaius was even more popular than Tiberius with the Roman masses. Once in office, he called for sweeping land reform. Again the Senate struck back viciously. The Roman people were incited to riot, and Gaius was blamed. He was either killed or forced to kill himself (the records are not clear), and his followers were thrown into prison.

The power of the army commanders now became the determining factor in Roman politics. The heroic general Gaius Marius, son of a farmer, returned to Rome from triumphant campaigns in Africa determined to smash the power of the despised Senate. To the Roman people, Marius was a god-like figure who had transformed the Roman citizen legions into a professional army. He and his supporters butchered the senatorial leaders and thousands of aristocratic Romans.

This fateful action, done in the name of liberty, opened the way to dictatorship. The Senate turned to Silla, a rival general and a patrician by birth, who answered Marius's violence with a blood bath of his own. After Marius's death in 86 BC, Silla posted daily lists of people to be executed by his henchmen. He proceeded to conduct equally bloody campaigns abroad.

He returned to Rome to rule as absolute dictator. The Senate could put no check on him, for they had opened the door for him to take power. The Republic was dead, the victim of three centuries of empire building.

Enter Pompey the Great: For two years the streets of Rome ran with blood. But in 79 BC Silla grew tired of ruling and retired to his estate near Naples. Civil war broke out once more. The eventual successor to Silla was another general, Gnaeus Pompeius, called Pompey the Great. He restored many of the liberties that Silla had suspended, but he failed to go far enough for the rioting masses.

Pompey's solution was to join forces with two other military men, Crassus and Julius Caesar, and form the Triumvirate, a ruling body of considerable power and influence. This arrangement was successful at first but did not last. When Crassus died in 53 BC, the two remaining leaders quarrelled. For several years Pompey and Caesar eyed each other warily, then Caesar took a fateful step. Against the orders of the Senate he led his army across the flooded Rubicon River (the border between Cisalpine Gaul and Italy). With Caesar heading toward the capital, Pompey quickly left for Greece taking his own army and most of the Senate with him.

content. Caesar's monarchical tendencies made them nervous. This did not stop factions within the Senate from heaping honours on the new ruler, as they hoped for favours in return, but many patricians watched suspiciously as Caesar had statues of himself raised in public places and his image put on coins. A conspiracy formed against him.

Beware the Ides of March: An Etruscan soothsayer had warned Caesar to beware of misfortune that would strike no later than March 15th, 44 BC. On that day – the Ides of March – Caesar was scheduled to address the Senate. As he travelled from his house to the Senate chamber he passed the soothsayer. Caesar laughed and remarked that the Ides

Pompey had planned to strike back at Caesar from Greece, but Caesar moved first. He attacked Pompey's allies in Spain and then in Greece, forcing Pompey to flee to Egypt where he was eventually killed.

Caesar returned to Rome in triumph. The masses believed that his victories proved he was divinely appointed to rule Rome. For the first time in decades there were no riots in the capital. But the upper classes were less

Left, Julius Caesar raised patrician eyebrows when he put his face on a coin. **Above**, Emperor Augustus built the monumental *Ara Pacis* to celebrate peace.

had come safely. The Etruscan replied that the day was not yet over.

In the chamber, Caesar was surrounded by the conspirators and stabbed 23 times. When he saw that Marcus Junius Brutus, a patrician he had treated like a son, was among his murderers, he is said to have murmured, "*Et tu, Brute?*" ("You too, Brutus?") and died.

After Caesar's death, Mark Anthony, Caesar's co-consul and Octavian, his grandnephew, joined forces to pursue and murder the conspirators. Despite their cooperation, the two were never the best of friends. Initially they collaborated with an army leader called Lepidus to form an uneasy Second

Triumvirate, but the arrangement faltered when Anthony fell in love with the Egyptian queen Cleopatra and rejected his wife, Octavian's sister, to marry her. Octavian got his revenge by turning the Senate against Mark Anthony, and then declared war on his former partner. When defeat was imminent, Anthony and Cleopatra committed suicide.

Augustus and the Pax Romana: Octavian's triumphant return to Rome marked the beginning of a new era. He called himself simply "Augustus" meaning "the revered one", but in actuality he was the first emperor of Rome. But unlike his grand-uncle before him, he took care not to offend the republican sentiments of the Romans and therein lay his

the result. Augustus met this challenge by creating a personal bureaucracy within his household. Not only did he have footmen and maids working for him, he also had tax collectors, governors, census takers, and administrators as his "servants". He allowed this personal civil service to grow to a size sufficient to run the empire, but always kept it under tight control. At first, many members of the nobility refused to join because they believed that any office in the household, however influential, was too close to personal service. But poor men of talent joined Augustus readily, and throughout his reign the Empire ran smoothly.

With peace, art and literature flourished.

success. He was not interested in the trappings of power; he lived and dressed simply. The Republic was allowed to function outwardly as it always had, while he ran the show, very effectively, from behind the scenes. The competence and sensitivity with which Augustus reigned made for a period of peace and prosperity, the like of which Rome had never seen. Indeed for 200 years after Augustan reform, the Mediterranean world basked in a Pax Romana, a Roman peace.

Before Augustus had assumed power, the republican institutions had been unable to administer the vast territories Rome now controlled. Military dictatorship had been

The poet Virgil, who had lived through the civil wars and military dictatorships, was so impressed by Augustus's achievements that he paid tribute to them in the *Aeneid*. Another poet, Horace, likened the emperor to a helmsman who had steered the ship of state into a safe port.

Augustus himself took part in the artistic resurgence and set about rebuilding the capital. He claimed that he had found Rome a city of brick and left it a city of marble. He also worked to rebuild the character of the people, outlawing drunkenness and prostitution, and strengthening the divorce laws.

Augustus reigned for 41 years and set the

tone of Roman leadership for the following 150. None of the men who succeeded him had the same breadth of interests nor the same ability. Some were merely adequate rulers, others were quite mad. But the institutional and personal legacy of Augustus did much to preserve peace in the flourishing Roman world.

The mad and the bad: The Emperor Tiberius had none of his stepfather's sense of proportion, nor his steadiness. He began his reign with good intentions, but he mismanaged many early problems. He spent the last 11 years of his reign at his villa on Capri, from where he issued a volley of execution orders. Svetonius wrote, "Not a day, however holy,

pressures of high office. He insisted that he was a god, formed his own priesthood and erected a temple to himself. He proposed his horse be made consul. Finally a group of his own officers assassinated Caligula, and Rome was rid of its most hated ruler.

The officers took it upon themselves to name the next emperor. Their choice was Claudius, the grandson of Augustus, who they found hiding behind a curtain in the palace after the assassination. Many people thought Claudius a fool, for he stuttered and was slightly crippled, but he turned out to be a good and steady ruler. He oversaw the reform of the civil service, and the expansion of the Roman Empire to include Britain.

passed without an execution; he even desecrated New Year's Day. Many of his men victims were accused and punished with their children – some actually by their children – and the relatives forbidden to go into mourning." (Translator Robert Graves.)

Rome was relieved when Tiberius died, only to find that there was worse to come. Caligula, his successor, ruled ably for three years, then ran wild. His derangement may have been the result of illness, or simply the

Left, a reconstruction of the Colosseum. **Above**, the philosopher emperor Marcus Aurelius rears above Rome's Campidoglio.

Claudius was poisoned by his ambitious wife Agrippina, who pushed Nero, her son by a previous marriage, onto the throne. Like Tiberius before him, Nero started out with good intentions. He was well-educated, an accomplished musician, and showed respect for the advice of others, especially senators. But the violent side of his nature soon became apparent. He poisoned Brittanicus, Claudius's natural son, and tried to do the same to his mother, but she had taken the precaution of building up an immunity to the poison. In the end Nero accused her of plotting against him, and had her executed.

Nero's excesses caused alarm among

Rome's citizens. When a fire destroyed the city in AD 64, Nero was accused of setting it. He was actually away from the city at the time and stories of him fiddling while Rome burned are probably untrue.

Nero lost his throne after the Roman commanders in Gaul, Africa, and Spain rebelled. When the news reached the capital riots broke out and the Senate condemned him to death as a public enemy. With no hope left, Nero killed himself in AD 68. His suicide threw the empire into greater turmoil. He left no heir. The commanders who had risen against Nero fought among themselves for a year until a legion commander named Vespasian Flavius emerged as emperor.

Vespasian proved to be a wise emperor, and his rule ushered in a period of peace. There was a short time of troubles when Vespasian's younger son, Domitian, became emperor; but, by the time he died, the Senate was powerful enough to appoint its own Emperor, Nerva, a highly regarded lawyer from Rome.

Nerva was the first of the "five good emperors" who reigned from AD 96 to 180. Trajan, Hadrian, Antoninus Pius and Marcus Aurelius ruled in turn after Nerva. All of these five were educated men, interested in philosophy and devoted to their duties. Not only were they loved by the people of Rome,

but all over the Empire their names were spoken with reverence. They administered their vast territories efficiently and built up a successful defence of the Empire's borders.

Decline and fall: During the period between the death of Marcus Aurelius and the sack of Rome in the 5th century, it became more and more difficult to defend the Empire from barbarians. Between AD 180 and 285, Rome was threatened in both the east and the west by barbarian tribes. The Empire doubled the size of the army. The drain on manpower and resources caused an economic crisis, and the increased power of the army meant that it could place emperors on the throne and remove them at will. Most of these "barracks emperors" served for less than three years and never even lived in the capital.

Plague also struck Rome, which weakened the Empire and made it more vulnerable to enemy attack. On all sides wars raged. In the east the revived Persian Empire threatened Syria, Egypt and all of Asia Minor. Franks invaded France and Spain.

Major political reform was undertaken by Emperor Diocletian in 286. He believed the Empire could no longer be ruled by one man, so he divided it into an eastern and western region. He chose Nicomedia in Asia Minor as his capital and appointed a soldier named Maximinus to rule the west from Milan.

Unfortunately this arrangement did not end quarrels about the succession. Constantine marched on Rome in 311 to assert his right to the throne. While on the road, however, he claimed he had a vision. The sign of the cross appeared in the sky with the words "By this sign win your victory." As a result, when Constantine emerged as the sole Emperor in 324, he ruled as a Christian. This established Christianity, which had been spreading through the empire since the time of Nero, as the religion of the Roman state and thus the Western world.

Despite the conversion to Christianity the Empire continued to deteriorate. In 324 Constantine decided to move the capital east, and make a fresh start in his new city of Constantinople. Back in Italy, the barbarians gradually moved closer. The city of Rome was sacked in 410.

Left, one of the late "barracks emperors", probably Valentian. **Right**, a fresco in the Casa dei Vettii in Pompeii.

LIFE IN THE EMPIRE

In more than 60 treatises on morality, Plutarch (AD 46–126) laid down what was expected of a Roman gentleman. It was a damnable luxury to strain wine or to use snow to cool drinks. It was "democratic and polite" to be punctual for dinner; "oligarchical and offensive" to be late. Conversation over dinner ought to be philosophical, like debating which came first, the chicken or the egg. Salt fish was scooped up with a single finger, but two could be used if the fish was fresh. There was only one permissible way for a Roman gentleman to scratch himself.

It would be naive to think that Romans universally obeyed Plutarch's strictures. Life was as diverse as in any modern capital, with an elegant high society at one end of the scale, vicious louts at the other, and every permutation in between. If there was one common factor, it was probably a passion for bathing. With elaborate underground furnaces heating the water, the baths got bigger and bigger. The well-preserved Caracalla baths could disgorge 1,600 glowing Romans per day.

In the early days of Rome, relations between patricians and plebians were codified, as were family matters. Patricians were the source of "tranquillity", mainly by lending an ear to plebians' personal problems and dispensing advice. In return, plebians had to stump up money when the patrician was held to ransom or could not settle his debts. Money made available in such circumstances was not a loan but a plebian's privilege, for which he was grateful, or supposed to be. On the other hand, plebians were not enslaved and could switch allegiance from an unsatisfactory patrician to one more suitable.

Divorce was introduced comparatively late. At first, marriage was permanent and wives automatically acquired half the conjugal property. Nevertheless, husbands exercised the ultimate sanction in that they were legally entitled to murder wives for serious offences, such as poisoning the children or making duplicates of their private keys. Fathers were prevented from selling sons into slavery once the boys were married.

Citizens bombarded bureaucrats with complaints about the quality of life in Rome: disgraceful traffic congestion and refuse collection; preposterous fashions like men experimenting with trousers; galloping inflation; homosexuals getting too big for their boots; the filthy habit of smoking dried cow dung, and so forth. The most castigated men in Rome were unscrupulous property developers who first set fire to a building they wanted and then, as the flames went up, offered a pittance to the uninsured owner. As soon as the deal was struck, the developer summoned a private fire brigade parked around the corner.

In a spiritual context, the lives of the Romans were wrapped up in astrology and mysticism. The spread of Bacchic rites in republican Rome alarmed the government which described them as: "This pestilential evil… this contagious disease." Senators "were seized by a panic of fear, both for the public safety, lest these secret conspiracies and nocturnal gatherings contain some hidden harm or danger, and for themselves individually, lest

some relatives be involved in this vice."

The social decadence supposedly behind the downfall of Rome was not without its own decorum. Petronius Arbiter, author of the *Satyricon*, orchestrated the lascivious side of Nero's orgies. He eventually fell out with the emperor and received orders to take his own life. Petronius invited friends to a farewell banquet where he sat with bandages wrapped around wrists which he discreetly slashed as the evening progressed. The controlled bleeding enabled him to sustain repartee right up to the moment when his head slumped. It is not known whether he expressed any parting thoughts on the interesting question of the chicken and the egg. ∎

POPE GREGORY. *Frontispiece.*

For four centuries after the sack of Rome in 410, barbarian invaders, including the Goths and the Lombards, battled with local military leaders and the Byzantine emperors for control of Italy. Under these conditions, the culture and prosperity that had characterised ancient times faded. The Roman Empire had unified Italy and made it the centre of the world, but after its demise Italy became a provincial battlefield. Since none of the rival powers was strong enough to control the whole of Italy, the land was divided. Italy wasn't unified again until the 19th century.

The Dark Ages began with a series of Visigoth invasions from northern and eastern Europe. The emperors in Constantinople were still in theory the rulers of Italy, but in reality for many decades they accepted first the Visigoth and later the Ostrogoth leaders as *de facto* kings. Justinian I, who became emperor in Constantinople in 527, had dreams of reviving the earlier splendour of the Empire and sent the brilliant general Belisarius to regain direct control of Italy. But although Belisarius met with initial success – he captured Ravenna from the Goths in 540 – a new group of barbarians soon appeared on Italy's borders: the Lombards.

The Lombards were German tribesmen from the Danube valley. They swiftly conquered most of what is now Lombardy, Venetia and Tuscany, causing the inhabitants of the northern Italian cities to flee to the remote eastern coastal regions where they were protected by the Byzantines, who still controlled the seas. Many of them settled around the lagoon of Venice.

Meanwhile the Lombards altered the system of government. They replaced the centralised Roman political system (which previous barbarian invaders had respected) with local administrative units called "duchies" after the Lombard army generals who were known as *duces*. Within each duchy a *duce* ruled as king. The land was distributed to groups of related Lombard families. Each family was headed by a free warrior, who owed limited feudal allegiance to his king

Left, the 6th-century Pope Gregory the Great was one of many early popes to be canonised.

but was allowed a free hand on his own land. This, plus the fact that the Byzantines continued to control many provinces, meant that Italy was effectively divided.

The rise of the popes: The radical changes that the Lombards brought to Italy's administration did not affect the Church. Indeed, in Rome the bishopric rose to new prominence because the emperors in Constantinople were too far away to exert any temporal or spiritual authority.

Greatest among the early popes was Gregory I (589–603), a Roman by birth and a scholar by instinct and training. (He instituted many liturgical reforms – the Gregorian chant is named after him.) He was also a great statesman. He persuaded the Lombards to abandon the siege of Rome, and helped achieve peace in Italy. He sent missionaries to Northern Europe to spread the word of God and the influence of Rome and sent the first missionaries to the British Isles.

Gregory's successors reorganised the municipal government of Rome, and effectively became rulers of the city. It was inevitable that the popes would eventually clash with the emperor in Constantinople. In 726, Emperor Leo decreed that veneration of images of Christ and the saints was forbidden and that all images were to be destroyed. The pope opposed his decree on the grounds that the Church in Rome should have the final say on spiritual matters, and he organised an Italian revolt against the Emperor. The Lombards joined the revolt on the side of the popes and used it as an opportunity to chase the Byzantines out of Italy.

After the imperial capital, Ravenna, fell to the Lombard army in 751, the popes realised they were more directly threatened by the powerful Lombards than an absent emperor, so they sought a new ally from across the Alps. Since Gregory's time, they had sent missionaries to the Frankish kingdom in Northern Europe to convert the people to Christianity. Now the Franks answered the popes' cries for help.

Pepin, king of the Franks, invaded Italy in 754. He reconquered the imperial lands but he gave them to the pope not to the emperor. Twenty years later, Pepin's son, Charlemagne, completed his father's work by defeating and capturing the Lombard king, confirming his father's grant to the papacy, and assuming the crown of the Lombards.

A new empire is formed: After Charlemagne had conquered the Lombards, he returned to the north and campaigned against the Saxons, the Bavarians and the Avars, making himself ruler of a large part of Western Europe. In recognition of these accomplishments, and in an effort to unify his vast territories under Christian auspices, he had Pope Leo crown him Holy Roman Emperor at St Peter's in Rome on Christmas Day 800.

Charlemagne was an extraordinary man who used his position to promote religion,

became a base for raids on the Italian mainland, and Charlemagne's great-grandson, Louis II, who was emperor for 25 years, tried but could not raise an organised defence against them. The Lombard dukes in the south, whom Charlemagne had not conquered completely, allied themselves with these invaders against the Carolingian emperor. What success Louis had was overshadowed by Pope Leo IV's defence of Rome and the naval victory against the Saracens at Ostia.

The Normans in the south: In the early 11th century small groups of Normans arrived in southern Italy. They were adventurers and skilled soldiers who were seeking their fortunes in a sunny land. They found a ready

justice and education. But he lived only 14 years after his coronation, and none of his successors matched him in ability. After his death, authority fell into the hands of Frankish counts, vassals of Charlemagne who had accompanied him south and been granted land of their own. As representatives of the crown they were required to raise troops from among the population. But the counts often used these troops to fight among themselves for more land and power.

This period of feudal anarchy was also marked by invasions. In the south the Saracens invaded Sicily in 827, and for the next 250 years Sicily was an Arab state. Sicily also

market for their skills in southern Italy. They would fight for anyone who would pay: Greek, Lombard and Saracen alike. In return they asked for land.

Soon landless men from Normandy arrived to fight, settle and conquer for themselves. The papacy lost no time in allying themselves with this powerful group of Christians. In the 1050s the Norman chief, Robert Guiscard, conquered Calabria in the toe of Italy. Pope Nicholas II "legitimised" Norman rule of the area by calling it a papal fief and then investing Guiscard as its king.

Robert's nephew, Roger, conquered Sicily. He was crowned king in Palermo in 1130 and ruled over the island and his uncle's mainland possessions. He was an efficient and tolerant ruler, and his court became a magnet for Jewish, Greek and Arab scholars. Still visible today are the architectural achievements of this sophisticated culture. Brilliant examples of Arab-Norman architecture can be seen in Palermo (San Giovanni degli Eremiti, the Zisa and the Cuba), and at the cathedrals of Monreale and Cefalú.

Despite some external opposition (from both the eastern and western emperors) and occasional domestic rebellions, Roger's son and grandson were able to preserve the regime. Only when William II died in 1189, leaving no legitimate male heir, did civil war

perors started a trend that would later cost them more than they anticipated.

In the 11th century, the popes strove to reform the church further by organising a strict clerical hierarchy. Throughout the Holy Roman Empire, bishops were to be answerable to the pope, and priests to bishops. A single legal and administrative system would bind all members of the clergy together. These reforms immediately angered all lay rulers from the emperor down.

The struggle reached a climax when Emperor Henry IV invested an anti-reform candidate as archbishop of Milan in 1072. As a result, Pope Gregory VII decreed in 1075 that such investiture by a non-cleric was

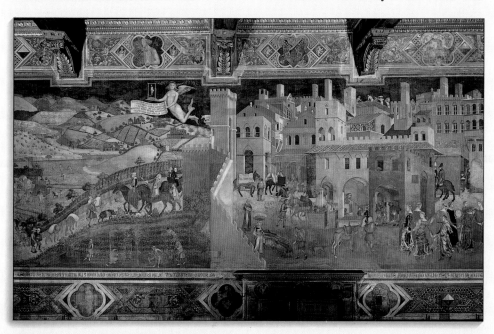

break out and Norman control of southern Italy end.

Church and emperor clash: During the 9th and 10th centuries, the papacy was completely controlled by Roman nobles. The men they picked for office were often corrupt. After the Emperor Ottoue I arrived in Rome in 962, he insisted that no pope could be elected until the emperor had named a candidate. But by reforming the papacy, the em-

Left, glittering mosaics, such as this one of the Emperor Justinian, are reminders that Ravenna was once the capital of Byzantium. <u>Above</u>, fresco in Siena's town hall.

forbidden. At the same time the Pope excommunicated Henry IV. For three days in the cold winter of 1077, the humbled emperor stood in the courtyard of a Tuscan castle where Gregory was staying, and pleaded for a reconciliation with the pope.

Henry was forgiven, but Gregory had no way of knowing whether he would keep his promise to recognise the claims of the papacy. As it turned out Henry did not, and a new civil war broke out. Gregory's supporters were defeated initially and he was carried off to Salerno and death, but the years that followed witnessed the triumph of his cause. The men who succeeded him worked gradually for the reforms Gregory died fighting for. The emperors were forced to give up their rights of investiture in 1122.

The city-states: During the years of the investiture controversy and the ensuing civil wars, the cities of northern and central Italy grew rich and powerful. The emperors were too distracted to administer them directly. Simultaneously, Mediterranean commerce was revived. With new wealth at their disposal, the cities forced the nobles in the countryside to acknowledge their supremacy. The Italian city-states were born.

The maritime republics of Venice, Genoa, and Pisa were foremost among the Italian cities, but inland cities also prospered on

account of their positions on rich trade routes. Milan and Verona lay at the entrance to the Alpine passes, Bologna was the chief city on the Via Emilia, and Florence had a route to the sea via the river Arno and controlled two roads to Rome.

The growing political power of the city-states was an important factor in renewed conflict between emperor and pope during the 13th century. Emperor Frederick II (1197–1250) tried to build a strong, centralised state in Italy. The cities that supported him kept their rights of self-government, but were forced to join an imperial federation. The cities that opposed him, which wanted com-

plete political autonomy, found an ally in Pope Gregory IX who secretly had imperial designs of his own for Italy. Northern Italy became a battlefield for civil war between the Guelfs, supporters of the Pope, and the Ghibellines, allies of the emperor.

By the time Frederick died in 1250 without instituting his reforms, the Guelf cause had won. The alliance of pope and the city states had ruined imperial plans for a unified Italy. Frederick's heirs, his illegitimate son Manfred and his grandson Conradin fought on for 15 years, but they could not defeat the combined forces of pope and townspeople.

The age of Dante: The Guelfs beat the Ghibellines decisively, but a feud broke out between two factions in the Guelf party: the Blacks and the Whites. This split was especially severe in Florence where the Blacks defended the nobles' feudal tradition against the Whites, rich magnates who were willing to give merchants a voice in government.

Pope Boniface VIII sided with the Blacks and worked to have all the prominent Whites exiled from Florence in 1302. Among the exiles was Dante Alighieri, who went on to write the *Divina Commedia* (the *Divine Comedy*), a literary masterpiece that promoted Tuscan Italian to the status of a national tongue. The *Divine Comedy* also reveals much about the politics of the period.

"Rome used to have two suns, which lighted the roads of the world and of God. Now one has extinguished the other...Christ has been made captive in the person of his Vicar," Dante wrote.

Dante believed that Italy needed a new form of political unity. He put his faith in the weakened Holy Roman Empire, convinced that it could and should usher in a new period of cultural and political prominence for Italy.

When Henry VII became Holy Roman Emperor in 1308 an opportunity arose for testing Dante's scheme for Italian salvation. Henry wanted to revive imperial power in Italy and establish a government that was neither Guelf nor Ghibelline. But when he came to Italy, the cities refused to support him. Dante's home town of Florence was the centre of the resistence to imperial plans.

Left, one in a series of illuminated manuscripts made for the wealthy Dukes of Milan in the late 14th century. Right, Dante Alighieri, as painted by Andrea del Castagno.

The constant fighting in Northern Italy subsided in the early 14th century when both the popes and the emperors withdrew from Italian affairs. After Henry VII's demise, the emperors turned their attention to Germany. Meanwhile the influence of the papacy declined following a quarrel between Pope Boniface and King Philip of France in 1302. The pope insisted that Philip had no right to tax the French clergy; the king's response was to send his troops to capture the pope. French pressure ensured that the next pope was a Frenchman, Clement V, and he moved the papacy from Rome to Avignon, where it stayed until 1377.

As a result of these events, the people of Italy were free from outside interference during the 14th century and the Italian cities grew stronger, richer and bigger than any in Europe. Against the political background of the supremacy of the city-state, a new culture bloomed and new ideas flourished. Rulers were able to try new methods of administration. Scholars were allowed to rediscover and explore the pagan past. Merchants were rich enough to become lavish patrons of the arts. Through their commissions, artists experimented with a new, more realistic style.

Not even the Black Death – the terrible outbreak of bubonic plague that ravaged Europe in the 14th century – could smother the new cultural awakening. But the plague did cause enormous human suffering and a prolonged economic depression. During several months of 1347 the death rate was 60 percent in some Italian cities. The merchants' solution to the declining profits of the period was to change the way they did business. Their innovations included marine insurance, credit transfers, double-entry book-keeping and holding companies – all of which eventually became standard business practice.

The birth of humanism: To be a good businessman in the early Renaissance required a basic education: reading, writing and arithmetic. But the more complicated business became, the more knowledge was needed,

Left, Michelangelo's *David* is a splendid illustration of Renaissance Italy's rediscovery of the beauty of the human form.

including an understanding of law and diplomacy, and a general appreciation of the ways of the world. Thus the traditional theological studies of the Middle Ages were replaced by the reading of ancient authors and the study of grammar, rhetoric, history and moral philosophy. This type of education became known as *studia humanitatis*, or humanities.

Humanism developed partly out of the need for greater legal expertise in the expanding world of Mediterranean commerce. To learn how to administer their new, complex societies, lawyers looked back at the great tenets of Roman law. As they struggled to understand the codes of the ancients they grew to appreciate the cultural riches of that long-buried classical civilisation. All aspects of Italian life were re-examined in the light of this new humanism. One way of life was thought to be ideal – that of the all-round man based on classical models. The Renaissance man was a reincarnation of rich, talented Roman philosophers.

Despots and republics: Italians of the 14th century considered themselves citizens of particular cities, not members of a large national unit. They revered local saints, believed myths that explained the origin and uniqueness of their city, and feuded with other cities. The competition between the city states even played a role in art patronage. Rulers encouraged artists and writers to glorify their towns.

There were a few experiences and conditions that many cities shared. As the authority of the popes and the emperors declined, life in the cities became increasingly violent. Leading families fought each other constantly, and often came into conflict with groups lower on the social ladder which wanted a role in the political life of the city. The remedy to this bloody civil strife was the rule of one strong man. The pattern was repeated over and over again in Northern Italy. Traditional republican rule which could not keep order was replaced by a dictatorship. Sometimes a leading faction would bring in an outsider, known as a *podestà*, to end the chaos – for example, the lordship of the Este Family in Ferrara was established in this way. More often, the future despot was originally a *capitano del popolo*, in other words, the head of the local police force and citizens' army. Over time, this captain would extend his powers until he controlled the entire city. Then he was in a strong enough position to make his office hereditary. This was how the della Scala family in Verona, the Carrara in Padua, the Gonzaga in Mantua and the Visconti in Milan came to power.

Once established, a despot would centralise all agencies of the government under his personal supervision. His power would only be threatened if he overstepped what his subjects could tolerate.

Some cities, including Venice and important cities in Tuscany (Florence, Siena, lands they gained a new regional state. These larger states greatly increased the economic resources a city had to draw upon, but they tended to be costly in military terms, for the citizens of the absorbed towns resented outside rule and were likely to revolt at any time. Furthermore, the new territory had to be constantly defended from encroachment by the other states.

The Visconti: Of the Italian city states, the most successful and the most powerful, was Milan. During the 14th century, the authoritarian Visconti family led the city to innumerable military and political victories until it was the largest state in northern Italy. The famous historian of the Renaissance, Jacob

Lucca, and Pisa) did not succumb to despotism until quite late in their history. In these places, the merchants were so powerful that rulers such as the Medici only survived by winning their support. In these cities republicanism flourished briefly, but even so the merchants dominated the organs of the republican government.

During the 14th and 15th centuries northern and central Italy changed from an area speckled with innumerable, tiny political units to one dominated by a few large states. Both republics and despots were expansionist in outlook. They would conquer their smaller neighbours, and construct out of the

Burckhardt, admired Visconti's Milan for its "strict rationalism". He considered the Milanese government "a work of art".

The Visconti regime may have been, in its efficiency, unlike anything Europe had seen for centuries, but for the Milanese people it had great drawbacks. The personal brutality of the Visconti controlled Milan. The regime could not rely on the loyalty of the populace for its survival. When the Visconti line died out in 1447, the Milanese took the opportunity to declare a republic. Unfortunately this republic was not strong enough to rule over all the restive towns Milan now controlled. When, in 1450, Francesco Sforza, a famous general who had served the Visconti, overthrew the republic and became the new duke, ruling with his wife Bianca Visconti, many Milanese were relieved.

The Republic of Florence: The spectacular transformation of Florence from a small town in the 1100s to the commercial and financial centre it had become by the end of the 14th century came about because of the profitable wool trade. The wool guild of Florence, called the *Arte della Lana,* imported wool from Northern Europe and dyes from the Middle East. Using its own secret weaving and colouring techniques guild members produced a heavy red cloth that was sold all over the Mediterranean area. Profits from the wool trade had provided the initial capital for the banking industry of Florence. Since the 13th century Florentine merchants had lent money to their allies, the pope and other powerful Guelf nobles. This early experience led to the founding of formal banking houses, and made Florence the financial capital of Europe.

The leading merchant guilds of Florence spent their wealth on art. The city was a showcase of the best of Renaissance sculpture, painting and architecture. In the second half of the 13th century a building boom began with the construction of the Bargello, the Franciscan church of Santa Croce, and the Dominican church of Santa Maria Novella. Arnolfo di Cambio designed the cathedral and the Palazzo Vecchio. The *Arte della Lana* paid for the construction and decoration of the cathedral. The city hired Giotto to design the Campanile which is named after him, and in 1434 they had Brunelleschi finish the great dome.

The rich men of Florence controlled the city government through the *Parte Guelfa.* With membership came the right to seek out and persecute anyone with "Ghibellistic tendencies". Other political non-conformities were also not tolerated. When members of lesser guilds demanded a greater share of power, or joined with the lower classes to fight the *Parte Guelfa,* they were met with quick and effective annihilation. However, in the early 15th century the violence of class

Left, Italian city-states were constantly at war with one another. **Right**, Cosimo the Elder established the Medici family as rulers of Florence.

war escalated. The unenfranchised artisans struck back repeatedly. At this point the rich merchants allowed Cosimo de' Medici to rise to the leadership of Florence.

The 15th century was the golden age of the Renaissance. All the economic, political and cultural developments of the previous century had set the stage for a period of unprecedented artistic and intellectual achievement. To live in Italy at this time was to live in a new world of cultural and commercial riches. Italy was truly the centre of the world.

The political history of the century divides into two parts. Until 1454 the five chief states of Italy were busy expanding their borders, or strengthening their hold on territories they

already, in name, possessed. These developments required fighting many small wars. The soldiers who fought them were for the most part *condottieri* (mercenaries). After 1454 there was a period of relative peace, during which the states tried to further their own interests through alliances rather than war. These later years witnessed the greatest artistic achievement, when Italian states of all sizes became cultural centres.

Italian wars of the Late Middle Ages and Early Renaissance had traditionally been fought by foreign mercenaries, but by the 15th century the mercenaries were more likely to be Italian. Men of all classes and from all parts of Italy joined the ranks of the purely Italian companies to fight northern wars for rival nobles. The *condottieri* looked upon war as a professional, technical skill. In battle the object was to lose as few men as possible but still win. Soldiers were too valuable to be sacrificed unnecessarily. The countryside, however, suffered heavily as village after village was given over to plunder. The *condottieri* did not hesitate to take what they could get in the field despite the fact that they were very well paid. They were bound by no patriotic ties, only by a monetary arrangement, which meant that an important captain could always be bought by the enemy.

Among the *condottieri*, one of the greatest was Francesco Sforza. Sforza had inherited the command of an army upon his father's death in 1424. He fought first for Milan and then for Venice in the northern wars until Filippo Visconti sought to attach him permanently to Milan by marrying him to his illegitimate daughter Bianca.

Visconti died in 1447 leaving no heir, and Milan declared itself a republic. Sforza was expected to be the captain of the new republican forces. Instead he went into exile. But when the republican government proved incompetent he turned his forces on the city and was able to starve Milan into surrender. The chief assembly of the republic invited him to be the new duke of the city.

Peace and the Italian League: Sforza, the great soldier, was instrumental in bringing peace to northern Italy. He signed, and encouraged others to sign, the Treaty of Lodi, which led to the Italian League of 1455. This was a defensive league between Milan, Florence and Venice that the king of Naples and the pope also respected. The League was intended to prevent any one of the great states from increasing its powers at the expense of its weaker neighbours, and to present a common national front against attack.

The smaller states of Italy benefited most from the new arrangement. Previously they had spent vast resources, human and monetary, on maintaining a defence against the larger, more aggressive states. "This most holy League upon which depends the welfare of all Italy," wrote Giovanni Bentivoglio, a leading citizen of Bologna in 1460.

During the decades of peace in Italy, Florence experienced its own Golden Age under the rule of the Medici family. When the historian Guicciardini later wrote about the Florence of Lorenzo de' Medici, where he had spent his childhood, he described it thus: "The city was in perfect peace, the leading citizens were united, and their authority was so great that none dared to oppose them. The people were entertained daily with pageants and festivals; the food supply was abundant and all trades flourished. Talented and able men were assisted in their careers by the recognition given to arts and letters. While tranquillity reigned within her walls, externally the city enjoyed high honours and renown."

In part, the success of the Medici was a

public relations coup. They allowed the Florentines to believe that the city government was still a great democracy. Only after Lorenzo's death, when Florence was briefly ruled by his arrogant son, did the citizens realise that their state, for all its republican forms, had drifted into the control of one family. They then quickly exiled the Medici and drafted a new constitution. Until that time, both Cosimo and Lorenzo de' Medici had managed to dominate Florence whilst never appearing to be more than prominent private citizens. They did this partly by manipulating the elections for the *Signoria* – Florence's city council – but the real base of their power lay in their complete acceptance by the city's leading citizens.

The Medici did more than simply rule and successfully keep the peace. They promoted art and culture in Florentine life. When the famous humanist Niccolo Niccoli died, Cosimo acquired his book collection and attached it to the convent of San Marco, creating the first public library in Florence. Cosimo also had Marsilio Ficino trained to become head of the new Platonic Academy and make Florence a centre of Platonic studies. He supplied Donatello with classical works to inspire his sculpture. Lorenzo de' Medici grew up in the atmosphere his grandfather had created and when he became leader

of Florence he also was a great patron of the arts. For his employees he was a peer as well as a patron. His poetry was widely admired.

When the political theorist Machiavelli wrote *The Prince*, his famous handbook for rulers, he was inspired by Lorenzo's example when he named the qualities that a successful ruler must have. "A ruler must emulate the fox and the lion, for the lion cannot avoid traps and the fox cannot fight wolves.

Left, **Francesco Sforza married the natural daughter of the last of the Visconti rulers of Milan and became despot of Milan. Above, his beloved wife Bianca.**

He must be a fox to beware of traps and a lion to scare off wolves."

When Lorenzo de'Medici died in 1492, the fragile Italian League that had successfully kept Italy at peace and protected her from foreign attacks died with him. Ludovico il Moro, the lord of Milan, immediately quarrelled with the Neapolitan king and proposed to the king of France that he, Charles VIII, conquer Naples and the surrounding states. Ludovico offered financial assistance and safe passage through the north of Italy. Charles readily accepted the offer and so began one of the most demoralising chapters of Italian history.

The internal disarray in Italy at the time was so great that the French troops faced no organised resistance. The new leader of Florence, a Dominican friar named Girolamo Savonarola, went so far as to preach that Charles was sent by God to regenerate the Church and purify spiritual life. Other Italians also welcomed the French. They believed that the invaders would rid Italy of decadence and set up governments with natives in the principle posts. Only when these ideas proved illusory could Italian patriots recruit an army and challenge the French.

The French and Italians met near the village of Fornovo on 6 July, 1495. At first it appeared that the Italians, led by General Francesco Gonzaga, would be certain victors: they outnumbered the French two-to-one, and they could launch a surprise attack against their enemy. But in the pitch of battle, the Italian strategy fell apart. Crucial troops could not cross the river to the French position. General Gonzaga entered the fiercest fighting and did not direct the battle as a whole. Some soldiers were distracted by the sight of the French king's booty and left the battle to capture it. When the battle ended, Charles escaped with what was left of his troops. Four thousand men had died – the majority of them Italian.

"If the Italians had won at Fornovo, they would probably have discovered then the pride of being a united people… Italy would have emerged as a respectable nation… a country which adventurous foreigners would think twice before attacking," wrote Luigi Barzini in his book *The Italians*. Instead, Fornovo broke the Italian spirit and opened the way for 30 years of foreign interventions, bloody conflicts, civil wars and revolts.

Italian art shone brightest during the Renaissance when, as in most disciplines, a revolution took place. The Early Renaissance (1400–1500), the *Quattrocento*, introduced new themes that altered the future of art. Ancient Greece and Rome were rediscovered and with them the importance of man in the here and now. As a consequence, the human body surfaced as a new focal point in painting and sculpture. The discovery of perspective changed architecture.

The Early Renaissance centred on Florence. The city wanted to be seen as "the new Rome" and public works flourished. First was Lorenzo Ghiberti's commission for sculpting the gilded bronze north doors (1403–24) of the Baptistry, won in a competition with Filippo Brunelleschi in 1401. Ghiberti's later, more famous, east doors (1424–52) are so dazzling that Michelangelo called them "the Gates of Paradise".

It was Filippo Brunelleschi (1377–1466) who championed the new classically inspired architecture. After losing the Baptistry door competition, he set off for Rome to study the proportions of ancient buildings. His studies led him to design such masterpieces as the dome of Florence cathedral, the arcade fronting the Innocenti orphanage, the church of San Lorenzo (1421–69), the Pazzi Chapel of Santa Croce (begun 1430–33), and Santo Spirito, all in Florence. You need not get out your yardstick to appreciate the refined use of mathematical proportions. The overriding impression is of harmony, balance and calm.

If Brunelleschi was the most noted architect, Donatello (1386–1466) ruled the realm of sculpture. His work expresses a whole new attitude about the human body. The figure of St George, made for the church of Orsanmichele, (now in the Museo del Bargello) is not only a realistic depiction of the human form, but also a work of psychological insight. His *Gattamelata* (1445–50) in Padua was the first equestrian statue cast in bronze since Roman times. Similarly his bronze *David* (1430–32), in the Museo del

Bargello, was the first free-standing nude statue since antiquity.

Seminal influence: The groundwork for the revolution in painting was laid a century earlier by Giotto (1267–1337). His frescoes – in Florence's Santa Croce, in Padua's Cappella degli Scrovegni, and, most notably, in Assisi's Basilica di San Francesco – depart from the flat Byzantine style and invest the human form with solidity and volume, and the setting with a sense of space and depth. His breakthrough was carried further by the Early Renaissance's most noted painter, Masaccio (1401–28). His Florentine frescoes of *The Holy Trinity with Virgin and St John* in Santa Maria Novella (1425), and *The Life of St Peter* in the Brancacci Chapel of Santa Maria del Carmine (1427), display all the traits characteristic of the Renaissance: the importance of the human form, distinct under its clothing; the display of human emotion; and the use of perspective.

Domenico Veneziano moved to Florence in 1439 and introduced a new colour scheme: pastel greens and pinks awash in cool light. The palette was picked up by his assistant, Piero della Francesca (1416–92), for his frescoes at San Francesco in Arezzo (1466) – marvels of pale tone as well as mathematics: heads and limbs are variations of geometric shapes; spheres, cones and cylinders.

The artistic revolution in Florence soon spread to other parts of Italy. Leon Battista Alberti (1404–72), an author of noted treatises on sculpture, painting and architecture, introduced the tracing of classic motifs (columns, arches) on the exteriors of buildings, for example on the Palazzo Rucellai in Florence (1446–51) and the Malatesta Temple in Rimini (1450).

Giovanni Bellini (1430/1–1516) triumphed in Venice. In his *Madonna and Saints* in San Zaccaria (1505), the grandeur of Massacio's influence is tempered by a newer concern: Flemish detail and intimacy.

Detail most delicately expressed is the hallmark of Sandro Botticelli (1444/5–1510). The Uffizi Gallery houses the enchanting, allegorical *Primavera* (1480), and the lovely *Birth of Venus* (1489).

The High Renaissance (1500–1600) was

the heyday of some of the most famous artists in the entire history of art: Leonardo da Vinci, Michelangelo, Bramante, Raphael, and Titian. Unlike their predecessors, who were thought of as craftsmen, they were considered to be creative geniuses capable of works of superhuman scale, grandeur and effort. Their extravaganzas were made possible by a new source of patronage – the papacy. Having returned to Rome from exile in Avignon, the popes turned the Eternal City into a centre of culture. The art of the High Renaissance is marked by a move beyond rules of mathematical ratios or anatomical geometrics to a new emphasis on emotional impact. The increasing use of oil

painting. *Chiaroscuro* (literally, light and dark) – the use of light to bring out and highlight three-dimensional bodies – is vividly seen in the whirl of bodies in the *Adoration of the Magi* (1481–82) in the Uffizi. Another invention was *fumato*, a fine haze that lends paintings a dreamy quality, enchancing their poetic potential.

In 1503 Pope Julius II, an important patron of the arts, commissioned the most prominent architect of the day, Donato Bramante (1444–1514), to design the new St Peter's. Bramante had earlier made his mark with the classically inspired gem, *The Tempietto* (1502) in the courtyard of Rome's San Pietro in Montorio. The pope's directive for the new project was

paints, introduced to the Italians in the late 1400s, began to replace egg tempera and opened new possibilities for richness of colour and delicacy of light.

Leonardo da Vinci (1452–1519) was born near Florence but left the city to work for the Duke of Milan, primarily as an engineer and only secondarily as a sculptor, architect and painter. In Milan, da Vinci painted the *Last Supper* (1495–98), in Santa Maria delle Grazie. The mural – an unsuccessful experiment in oil tempera, which accounts for its poor condition – is nonetheless a masterpiece of psychological drama.

Da Vinci also exploited new techniques in

to create a monument which would surpass any of ancient Rome. Working with a stock of classic forms (domes, colonnades, pediments) Bramante revolutionised architecture with his revival of another classic technique: concrete. Used by the ancient Romans and abandoned in the Middle Ages in favour of brick or cut stone, concrete enables greater flexibility and monumental size.

Bramante died before his design was realised. It was not until 1546, when Michelangelo was put in charge of the project, that St Peter's gained its present form.

Michelangelo Buonarroti (1475–1564) first astounded the world with his sculpture:

human figures with a dignity, volume and beauty inspired by Hellenistic precedents, yet given new emotional impact. It has been said that Michelangelo sought to liberate the form of the human body from a prison of marble: an allegory for the struggle of the human soul, imprisoned in an earthly body, and a condition ripe for themes of triumph and tragedy. The resulting tension imbues his most famous works: *David* (1501–04) in Florence's Galleria dell' Accademia; *Moses* (1513–15) in Rome's San Pietro in Vincoli, and the beloved *Pietà* in St Peter's.

Julius II commissioned Michelangelo to paint the Sistine Chapel ceiling. The result, which was completed in only four years

design outweighs many functional considerations. Michelangelo's architectural genius culminates in his redesign of Rome's Campidoglio (1537-39). This open piazza, flanked by three facades, became the model for modern civic centres.

While Michelangelo was busy on the Sistine Chapel ceiling, another artist was working nearby, decorating a series of rooms in the Vatican Palace. This artist would soon be known as the foremost painter of the High Renaissance: Raphael (1483–1520). His masterpiece in this series is the *School of Athens* (1510–11). The dramatic grouping of philosophers around Plato and Aristotle suggests the influence of Michelangelo; the

(1508–12), is a triumph of human emotions unleashed by the human condition: man's creation, his fall, and his reconciliation with the Lord.

Michelangelo returned to the Sistine Chapel in 1534 to paint the spectacular *Last Judgement*. In the intervening years he went to Florence to complete the Medici Chapel of San Lorenzo (1524–34) and the Laurentian Library (begun 1524) where the drama of the

Left, Botticelli's ethereal *Venus* rises modestly from the sea. Above, Titian's goddess of love, painted a hundred years later, has a more earthy sensuality.

individualised intention of each recalls da Vinci's *Last Supper*.

In Venice, the paintings of Giorgione da Castlefranco (1476/8–1510) have all the delicacy and charm of Bellini's. In addition, they favour poetic mood over subject matter (*The Tempest* [1505] in Venice's Galleria dell'Accademia is a perfect example), prefiguring the romantic movement of later centuries.

Also looking ahead to the freer brushwork and shimmering colours of the Impressionists is the Venetian Titian (1488/90–1576). Titian mastered the technique of oil painting, and left behind him a legacy of opulentlycoloured and joyously-spirited religious pictures as well as masterful portraits.

The Mannerists: The drama of da Vinci, the theatricality of Michelangelo, the poetic moodiness of Giorgione, set the stage for the Mannerist phase of High Renaissance art, when the serenity and calm classicism that characterised the works of Raphael were abandoned. In Mannerism the human form is paramount yet it is usually depicted in strained, disturbing poses and violent colours. Mannerist artists include Bronzino Pontormo and Rosso Fiorentino who revelled in the use of bold and unnatural colours, dramatic poses and heightened emotions.

This highly unnatural look grew directly out of the work of artists such as Michelangelo, who had already begun to exaggerate human features to create tension and drama (consider the overlarge head and hands of David, for example, or the contorted pose of the Virgin in his famous *Doni Tondo*, now in the Uffizi in Florence).

Expression of an "inner vision" at the expense of reality was vital to Mannerism. In a work typical of the new movement, Rosso Fiorentino's *The Descent from the Cross* (1521) in Volterra's Pinacoteca, the angularly draped figures bathed in an unreal light stir feelings of anxiety and tension. His friend, Pontormo (1494–1557), is also known for works of unexpected colour, unnaturally elongated figures and disquieting mood.

Agnolo Bronzino (1503–72), Pontormo's pupil and adopted son, epitomises Mannerism's achievements in his remarkable psychological portraits of Cosimo I and his wife Eleanora of Toledo and her son Giovanni de' Medici (1550) in the Uffizi Gallery.

The work of Parmigianino (1503–40) is Mannerism taken to excess, where the painter distorts merely for effect, rather than to convey tension and heightened emotions. In his *Madonna with the Long Neck* (1535) in the Uffizi, the figures are elongated beyond any reality, the setting is fantastical, and the inspiration for the work – Raphael's fluid grace – is exaggerated beyond recognition.

In Venice, Jacopo Tintoretto (1518–94) combined the bold style, rich colours and glowing light inspired by Titian with a mystical inclination. His attempt to depict one of religion's greatest mysteries – the transubstantiation of bread into the body of Christ – results in the haunting *Last Supper* (1592–94),

San Giorgio Maggiore, Venice, with its swirling angels created out of vapors.

In architecture, Andrea Palladio (1518–80) stands out. Like his predecessor Alberti, Palladio wrote theoretical studies of ancient architecture. His own designs – the Villa Rotonda, Vicenza (1567–70); San Giorgio Maggiore, Venice (1565) – are based on a repertoire of classic forms and concepts, and influenced later architects from Inigo Jones to Thomas Jefferson.

The baroque: Mannerism was succeeded by a return to vitality and nature. The baroque (1600–1750) was born in Rome, and nurtured by a papal campaign to make the city one of unparalled beauty "for the greater glory of God and the Church". One artist to answer the call was Caravaggio (1573–1610). A stormy individual, Caravaggio was at odds with society in his personal life as well as his art. His early secular portraits of sybaritic youths revealed him to be a painfully realistic artist. His later monumental religious painting entitled *The Calling of St Matthew,* in Rome's San Luigi dei Francesi, shocked the city by setting a holy act in a contemporary tavern. Many other Caravaggio paintings were criticised for indecorum.

The decoration of St Peter's interior by Gianlorenzo Bernini (1598–1680) was more acceptable to the Romans: a bronze tabernacle with spiralling columns at the main altar; a magnificent throne with angels clustered around a burst of sacred light at the end of the church; and, for the exterior, the classically simple colonnade embracing the piazza (1657).

Bernini's rival was Francesco Borromini (1599–1667), whose extravagant, eccentric, romantic designs were the opposite of Bernini's classics. Many of Borromini's most famous designs hinge on a complex interplay of concave and convex surfaces, seen in the undulating facades of San Carlo alle Quattro Fontane, Sant'Ivo, and Sant'Agnese in Piazza Navona (1653–63).

The influence of the Italian baroque spread quickly to Germany and Spain and soon eclipsed the classical style of the Renaissance, though that style, rediscovered in the 19th century, continues to excite the entire world to this day.

Right, Caravaggio's *Bacchus* raises an ample glass to the good life.

After the battle of Fornovo, all the armies in Europe came to Italy. An international free for all resulted as they fought among themselves for a share of the spoils.

Spain, the most powerful nation in Europe at the time, eventually emerged as the clear master of Italy. The pope crowned King Charles V of Spain Holy Roman Emperor in 1530. Charles and his descendants ruled Italy with a heavy hand for 150 years. This period has often been called the dullest in Italian history. The burden of high Spanish taxation and the exploitation of Italy's resources by petty Spanish officials killed all native energy. The papacy was no less oppressive; the rules of the Inquisition, the Index and the Jesuit Orders forced many Italians to flee.

Under the oppressive rule of the Spaniards and later (after the 1713 Treaty of Utrecht) under the equally oppressive Austrians, Italy lost its reputation as a cultural centre. But the French Revolution inspired many Italians, and the ideals of republicanism spread like wildfire. Patriots dreamt of an independent Italian republic modelled on France.

When Napoleon invaded Italy in 1796, the people rose against the Austrians and a series of republics were founded. For three years the whole peninsula was republican and under French domination. But in March 1799, an Austro-Russian army expelled the French from Northern Italy and restored many of the local princes. In Naples, the republicans held out for a few more months, but eventually they too had to surrender. They suffered for their brief resistance. The British Lord Nelson had the republican Admiral Caracciola hung from the yardarm of his flagship.

To work against the foreign oppressors and their local sycophants, Italian patriots joined clandestine organisations, including the famous Carbonari. In their love of ritual they resembled the Freemasons, but they had a deadly serious goal: to liberate Italy.

The Risorgimento: In 1800, Napoleon managed to win back most of Italy. The kingdom that he founded lasted only briefly, but by

Left, Giuseppe Garibaldi, a prominent leader of the Risorgimento. **Right**, Camillo Beuso Count of Cavour, Italy's first great statesman.

proving that the country could be a single unit it gave Italian patriots new inspiration and direction. From the time of the Congress of Vienna in 1815, which reinstated Italian political divisions, until Rome was taken in 1870 by the troops of King Victor Emmanuel II of Savoy, the history of Italy was one continuous struggle for reunification.

The period is a complex one. Many northern and southern Italians wanted the peninsula to become one nation but there was no agreement as to who would rule or how its

CAVOUR.
(From a contemporary print in Bianchi's *Cavour*.)

creation was to be achieved. Some believed in peaceful evolution. Others, like Mazzini, wanted to revive the Roman republic. Still others were for a kingdom of Italy under the House of Savoy. A writer-priest, Vincenzo Gioberti, argued in his book *The Moral and Civil Primacy of the Italians* for a federated Italy, with the pope as president.

In 1848, a year of revolt all over Europe, the first Italian war for independence was fought. First, rebellions in Sicily, Tuscany and the Papal States forced local rulers to grant constitutions to their citizens. In Milan, news of Parisian and Viennese uprisings sparked the famous "five days" when the occupying Austrian army was driven from the city. A few days later, Charles Albert of Savoy sent his army to pursue the Austrians, and the revolution began in earnest.

Charles Albert was soon supported by troops from other Italian states and the war was going well. The tide turned when the pope refused to declare war on Catholic Austria. With that, the Austrians regained confidence and drove Charles Albert's army back into Piedmont. After Charles Albert's abdication a few months later, the House of Savoy signed a peace treaty.

Garibaldi: Venice and the Roman Republic continued the fight. In Rome, Mazzini led a triumvirate that governed the city with a true

with the House of Savoy kept them out of that region, so it was now the only Italian state with a free press, an elected parliament, and a liberal constitution.

Piedmont-Savoy was also blessed, from 1852, with a brilliant prime minister – Count Camillo Cavour – who was devoted to the cause of Italian unity. Cavour went to England and France to raise money and support for the Italian cause. He contributed Piedmontese troops to the Crimean War, and thus won a seat at the peace conference, where he brought the Italian question to the attention of Europe's most important statesmen. Although Cavour made no tangible gains at this meeting, he won moral support.

democratic spirit despite the siege conditions. The commander of the city's armed forces was the colourful Giuseppe Garibaldi, a life-long Italian patriot, who had honed his fighting skills as a mercenary in the revolutions of South America, where he had fled after being convicted of subversion in Piedmont. Now he and his men faced the combined strength of the Neopolitans, the Austrians and the French. It was French forces that entered the city on 3 July 1849, the day after Garibaldi escaped into the mountains. The following month the Venetians succumbed to an Austrian siege.

The peace treaty the Austrians had signed

Europe was thus not surprised when France and Piedmont went to war with Austria three years later. The French king, Napoleon III and Cavour had agreed in secret that after the expected victory an Italian kingdom would be formed for the Piedmontese king, Victor Emmanuel, and Nice and French Savoy would be returned to France. The people of the Italian dukedoms rushed to proclaim their allegiance to Victor Emmanuel.

Unfortunately, the French soon tired of fighting and decided to make a quick peace with Austria. The Austrians agreed to let Lombardy become part of an Italian Federation (with Austrian troops still in its garrisons), but the Veneto region went back to Austria and the dukes of Modena and Tuscany were reinstated.

In Italy, everyone was outraged. Cavour resigned in protest, although first he arranged plebiscites in Tuscany and Modena. Citizens refused to have their dukes back and voted to become part of Piedmont.

Garibaldi and 1,000 volunteers sailed for Sicily from Quarto near Genoa on 5 May 1860. Shortly after landing on the island, Garibaldi declared himself dictator in the name of Victor Emmanuel. He and his troops had to fight hard, but with the help of Sicilian rebels Garibaldi entered Palermo in triumph. Inspired by his success, men from all over

wanted to take the city by force; the conservative majority wanted to negotiate.

Finally, in 1870, after the French were weakened by a defeat in the Sudan, Italian troops fought their way into the city through Porta Pia. The pope barricaded himself in the Vatican. For half a century, no pope emerged to participate in the life of the new Italy.

The new government of all Italy was a parliamentary democracy with the king as the executive. The most powerful men in the early days of the Italian state were the sober, loyal Piedmontese parliamentarians who were largely responsible for its creation. They designed the administration, and established standard weights and measures for the

Italy now came to help him and, on 7 September, Naples fell to the patriots.

Meanwhile, Victor Emmanuel gathered troops and began marching south to link up with Garibaldi. The two groups met at Teano, and the kingdom of Italy was declared. However, one gaping hole remained – Rome. The pope preached against the patriots, and the French garrisoned troops there to protect the city. The victorious nationalists were divided on how to deal with Rome. One group

Left, Garibaldi and Victor Emmanuel II of Savoy join forces at Teano. **Above**, celebration of Italian liberty in Turin.

whole peninsula. But once the government moved down to Rome, this group began to splinter. The left came to power under a new prime minister, Agostino Depretis.

Depretis had been a skilled legislator and manipulator when he was a member of the parliament, but once he became prime minister he was less effective. He could not organise his party or set forth a coherent programme for the nation. His rivals on the right had done no better, but their opposition made it hard for Depretis to accomplish much. This was the beginning of the breakdown of the party system in Italy, the effects of which are discernible today.

As governments so often do during times of rapid change and relative instability at home, the young republic began to look abroad for confirmation of its hard-won independence. Relations with France had already cooled during the final fight for unification; when France occupied Tunisia, a traditional area of Italian influence, they became positively chilly. Italy's response was to sign the Triple Alliance with Germany and Austro-Hungary, providing for mutual defence in the event of war.

Under the conservative governments of Francesco Crispi (1887–91, 1893–96), Italy also joined the scramble for colonies in North Africa. Crispi successfully pushed into Eritrea, but when he tried to subdue Ethiopia, the Italian army suffered a humiliating loss at Adwa. The defeat immediately brought Crispi's second administration crashing down. Italy's only other unqualified success at colonisation came during the Italo-Turkish War (1911–12), which ended with Rome's victory and the occupation of Libya and the Dodecanese Islands.

At home, the years leading up to World War I were already marked by the division that still plagues the country today: relative wealth in the north and extreme poverty in the south. The economy was overwhelmingly agricultural, and the government's staunchly protectionist policies left Italy increasingly isolated from other European markets. The industrial boom of the late 1800s, mostly in textiles and refining, was confined to the north. The crushing economic conditions in the south fuelled an ever-increasing wave of emigration. In the last years of the century, nearly half a million people a year set out for the New World.

When World War I began with Austria's attack on Serbia in July 1914, Italy was caught almost completely unaware. Prime Minister Antonio Salandra reasoned that since his government had not been consulted before the Austrian advance, Italy was not bound by the terms of the Triple Alliance. On 2 August, he declared Rome's neutrality. If

Left, Benito Mussolini, in 1928, making one of his fiery speeches.

anything, public opinion began to swing away from the Germans and Austrians in the direction of the Allies. To help win Italy over, the Allied governments dangled the possibility of territorial gains: among other things, Rome was offered the chance to gain *Italia irredente*, the "unrecovered" provinces of Trieste and Trentino, long held by the Austro-Hungarian Habsburg Empire. In addition, Italy would receive the upper valley of the Adige River, plus various north African and Turkish properties. Finally swayed, in April 1915 Italy signed the secret Treaty of London. A month later, the government broke the Triple Alliance and entered the war on the Allied side.

Seldom had an army been so ill-prepared for battle. The armed forces were poorly equipped, and Austrian troops had already dug into defensive positions in Alpine strongholds along the 480-km (300-mile) border the two countries shared. For the Italian army, the war turned into a stalemate, albeit a costly one; of the 5.5 million men mobilised, 39 percent were either killed or wounded.

Unfortunately, the war's true end came not on the battlefield but at the conference table. Although Prime Minister Vittorio Emmanuele Orlando sat with the victors, he was hardly regarded as an equal. Despite Orlando's protests, which at one point included storming out of the conference and returning to Rome, the Treaty of London was ignored. In the end the Treaty of St Germain (10 September 1919) gave Italy Triento and the Alto Adige, as well as Trieste. But Fiume, Dalmatia and the other promised territories were negotiated away by the Allies.

The rise of fascism: The disappointments at the peace table, combined with the social and economic toll of the war, produced chaotic domestic conditions. Soon there was talk that Italy had won only a "mutilated victory" despite its wartime sacrifice. Inflation soared. Urban factory workers regularly took to the streets, and rural peasants clamoured for land reform. All the government could do was try to keep a semblance of public order.

Into this power vacuum marched Benito Mussolini and his Fascist Party. When he founded the party in 1919, Mussolini's philosophy was more one of opportunism than anything else. He played on the worst fears of all Italians. To those who fretted over the "mutilated victory", he was a chest-thumping nationalist. To placate the wealthy, he denounced Bolshevism, although he himself had once been an ardent socialist. To the frightened middle classes he pledged a return to law and order, and a corporate state in which workers and management would pull together for the good of the whole country.

By mid-1922, fascism had become a major political force. The *borghesía* class longed for relief from the almost constant turmoil. When workers called for a general strike, Mussolini made his move. On 28 October, 50,000 members of the fascist militia converged on Rome. Although Mussolini's supporters held only a small minority in parliament, the sight of thousands of menacing fascists flooding the streets of the capital was enough to topple the already tottering government of Prime Minister Luigi Facta. Refusing to sanction a state of siege, King Victor Emmanuel II instead turned the reigns of government over to Mussolini, the 39-year-old son of a schoolteacher and a blacksmith-cum-socialist-revolutionary.

Once in control of Italy, Mussolini quickly rammed through an act assuring the Fascists a permanent majority in the parliament. After questionable elections in 1924, he completely dropped the pretence of collaborative government. Italy was now a dictatorship. At Christmas of that year, he declared himself head of the government, responsible only to the king. Fascist fronts took over all the rights once held by unions and management organisations, lockouts and strikes were banned, and national corporations were set up to supervise every phase of the economy.

Within two years, Mussolini had completely co-opted his political opponents. All parties except the fascists were banned, and opposition activists were jailed and forced into exile or the underground. Anyone Mussolini could not subject by will or law was crushed by force. He would haul "offenders" before a political crimes tribunal or dispatch bands of thugs to do his dirty work.

Despite its ugly underbelly, on the surface fascism seemed to work. Weary of inflation, strikes and street disturbances, Italians eagerly embraced their severe new government and its charismatic *Duce*, or leader. This spontaneous response to fascist rule was reinforced by a relentless propaganda campaign. Mussolini promised to restore to Italy the glories of ancient Rome, and for a time promises were more than enough.

Soon, however, the government could show some results. The economy firmed, the trains, so they said, ran on time, massive public works projects were launched, and Mussolini even managed to make up with the Vatican, hammering out the Lateran Treaty (1929), which ended the 50-year rift between Rome and the Catholic Church. He also set out on an ambitious imperial campaign, restoring control over Libya, which had been ignored during World War I and its immediate aftermath. In October 1935, Italian troops crossed the border of Eritrea and headed for the Ethiopian capital of Addis Ababa. The League of Nations howled in protest, but took no real action to stop Mussolini's advance. Six months later, *Il Duce* announced to an hysterical Piazza Venezia crowd that, finally, Rome had begun to reclaim its empire.

World War II: The international outcry over the Ethiopian occupation left Rome badly isolated. The one government willing to overlook Mussolini's expansionism was in Berlin, where Adolf Hitler's Nazis had held power since January 1933. Both Germany and Italy had supported Generalissimo Francesco Franco's nationalist troops in the Spanish Civil War (1936–39), and this cooperation on a foreign battlefield led eventually to the signing of the Pact of Steel between Berlin and Rome in May 1939.

Three months later, Hitler invaded Poland. Within days, Britain and France declared war on Germany.

At first the Rome government held back, as it had during World War I, arguing that Berlin's surprise attack on Poland did not require an automatic military response. In any case, most Italians opposed intervention, and the army, again, was poorly prepared for war. But as Hitler racked up victory after victory – in Denmark, Norway and Belgium, and with France near collapse – the lure of sharing the spoils of war finally proved irresistible. On 10 June 1940, Italy entered the war, just in time for the fall of France. From the start, however, it was obvious even to Mussolini that he was definitely

Hitler's inferior in their alliance. To make matters worse, the security-obsessed Germans kept their specific combat plans secret, for fear they might leak out through the Italian officer corps.

Eager to pull off his own battlefield coup, in autumn 1940 Mussolini set his sights on Greece, in his estimation an easy target. But the Greeks fought back fiercely. The prospect of a total Italian defeat was eliminated only after the Nazis came to the rescue, steamrolling through Yugoslavia to back the Italians up. The war was also going badly for the Axis in North Africa, and eventually even the battlefield genius of General Erwin Rommel could not prevent the collapse.

dered his arrest and Mussolini was taken on the steps of the Villa Savoia immediately following a royal audience. Well aware that the Nazis would try to rescue Mussolini, the new prime minister, Marshal Pietro Badoglio, organised his removal to a resort high in the Abruzzi Mountains. There, despite all predictions that the prisoner was untouchable, a crack team of German air commandos did manage to get to Mussolini and spirit him off to Munich.

Chaos broke out in the final days of the war. To placate the Germans, who would otherwise have occupied the entire country, Badoglio publicly declared that Italy would fight on. In secret, however, he entered nego-

Heartened by their desert victories, in the summer of 1943 American and British troops captured Sicily. The beginning of the end was in sight.

From their base in Sicily, the Allied forces began bombing the Italian mainland, and the already slumping Italian public morale sunk even lower. On 25 July 1943, the Grand Council of Fascism voted to strip *Il Duce* of his powers. In keeping with his character, Mussolini refused to step down. The next day, however, King Victor Emmanuel or-

Above, Enrico Berlinguer was head of the Italian Communist Party (PCI) from 1972 to 1984.

tiations with the Allies, who by then had fought their way as far north as Naples. Above that line was the hastily organised *Repubblica Sociale Italiana,* headed by the liberated *Duce.* But the Italian Social Republic was nothing more than a puppet regime under the thumb of Berlin, and a morose Mussolini spent most of his time brooding about the judgement that history would pass on him.

As the Allies fought north, the Italian Resistance, or the Corps of Volunteers for Liberty, finally felt safe enough to begin widespread activities. Combined, the forces managed to liberate Rome on 4 June 1944;

Florence followed on 12 August. The Germans and Mussolini managed to last out the winter behind the so-called "Gothic line" in the Apennines, but by spring 1945 that effort too had collapsed. Mussolini, only a few months before the supreme leader of the entire country, tried to sneak into Switzerland disguised as a German soldier. Italian partisans found him, however, and the next morning he was shot. His body was hauled into Milan and hung by a rope for the passing public to see.

Recovery and resiliency: In the immediate post-war period, Italy suffered greatly. This time there was no representative from Rome at the meetings that dictated the terms of

the Socialists and Communists, Christian Democrat leader Alcide de Gasperi gained control of government, booting out his leftist partners. For more than a decade after that, centrist coalitions of one sort or another ran the country. The rift between right and left was not healed until the *apertura a sinistra*, or opening to the left, in the early 1960s, under which the Christian Democrats, Socialists, Social Democrats and Republicans formed a coalition government. The combination proved remarkably durable, ruling, in various combinations, until 1968.

Marx but no Marx: One of the most distinctive features of Italian politics – at least by Western standards – has been the influence

peace. All of the Italian colonies, won at such great cost, were taken away. Reparations had to be paid to the Soviet Union and Ethiopia. The political system was in need of a complete overhaul. In elections in June 1946, voters decided 54–46 in favour of making the country a republic, thus formally ending the days of the monarchy. The economy was in a shambles, although Italy's inclusion in the European Recovery Programme, otherwise known as the Marshall Plan, helped ease the burden from 1948 on.

The first order of business was to get a government going again. After the June 1946 elections, and a brief alliance that included

of the Italian Communist Party (PCI). In the immediate post-war years, the PCI cleaved to the political line set by the Soviet Union, and the centrist government that sat in Rome kept the Communists at arm's length. But under the leadership of Enrico Berlinguer, who became PCI secretary in 1972, the party's orientation changed dramatically. Under the charismatic Berlinguer, the PCI often led the so-called Eurocommunism movement, which advocated a greater independence from Moscow. Under Berlinguer, the PCI scolded the Soviets for human rights abuses and for the invasion of Afghanistan in 1979. On economic issues, it grew ever more centrist, prompting some to dub it a "Marxist party without Marx". By 1981, this platform had attracted nearly 2 million members, and could regularly count on about a third of the vote in elections. That made it the largest communist party in Western Europe and second largest political group in Italy after the Christian Democrats. In 1984, Berlinguer collapsed at a political rally and died shortly thereafter. He was replaced by Alessandro Natta, one of his long-time lieutenants.

Fuelled by the availability of cheap labour, there was an economic surge at the end of World War II. Throughout the 1950s there was a steady migration from rural areas to the cities and from south to north, especially into the big manufacturing centres of Milan, Turin and Genoa. Heavy industry such as chemicals, iron, steel and autos took off. In 1958, Italy became one of the founding members of the European Community. By the mid-1960s, manufacturing overtook agriculture as the major source of GNP, and observers hailed the Italian "economic miracle".

Only a few years later, however, the boom had gone bust, and Italy was dubbed the "sick man of Europe". As the bloom faded from the "miracle", inevitable social ills set in. By far the worst was terrorism: from the late 1970s on, kidnappings, knee cappings and murders became an all too common fact of life. The most horrifying incident was the kidnapping in March 1978 of former Christian Democratic prime minister, Aldo Moro, by the left-wing *Brigate Rosse*. The Red Brigade wanted a group of their comrades released from jail, but the government refused to negotiate any deals with the terrorists. Nearly two months later, Moro's body was pulled from the trunk of a car parked on a Rome street. The murder spurred a new round of anti-terrorist measures, and eventually 32 Red Brigade members were convicted and sentenced to life imprisonment for the deaths of Moro and 16 others.

Meanwhile, neo-fascist terrorism also plagued the country, culminating, in 1980, in a bomb blast at Bologna station which killed 84 people. And crime of another sort gripped the nation in May 1981, when there was an attempt on the life of Pope John Paul II as he rode through a crowd-packed St Peter's Square. Turkish-born Mehmet Ali Agca was convicted and sentenced to life for shooting the much-loved pope. In rambling testimony in the months after his conviction, Agca implied that he had had help in his plot to assassinate the pope, and relations between Rome and Bulgaria, whose agents Agca said had assisted him, became strained.

Dogged effort helped cut inflation, and in 1985 the Craxi government pushed through tightened tax-collection regulations. Though inflation remained in the high single digits, and the lira proved unsteady, the national economy continued to grow and the term *Il Sorpasso* (signifying Italy's overtaking of France and Britain in the economic league) became the catch-phrase of the decade.

Corruption scandals: But troubles were in store. The last few years have proved to be one of the most turbulent periods in Italian politics since the war. In the early 1990s a wave of corruption scandals rocked the state. In 1992 it was alleged that in what was dubbed "the mother of all bribes" some £67 million (US$100 million) was shared out among the leaders of the five parties governing Italy in coalition in 1990. Two former prime ministers, the ex-Socialist Party leader Bettino Craxi, and the ex-Christian Democrat leader Arnaldo Forlani, were accused of being chief recipients. Meanwhile veteran prime minister Guilio Andreotti, the other member of the triumvirate governing Italy at the time, was linked with the Mafia. In the wake of the politicians' fall from power several leading Italian businessmen committed suicide, including Raul Gardini, once the boss of the industrial giant Ferruzzi.

The scandals shook Italy to the core and unleashed a volley of reforms. In the hope of altering the pattern of coalition governments that had allowed corruption to spawn, the system of proportional representation was changed to include an element of the first-past-the-post system. Measures were taken to prune Italy's bloated and unaffordable public sector and determined efforts were made to confront organised crime, in spite of retaliatory terrorism attacks in Milan, Rome and Florence. On the negative side, the political turmoil has strengthened calls for separatism in Northern Italy, especially in Milan and the Lombardy region, the country's industrial powerhouse.

Left, feminist protest march in Rome's Piazza Venezia. Their banner proclaims "I accuse the society of males".

To many people in Northern Italy, the notion of the Mafia conjures up images of *lupara*, the shotgun used by the Sicilian underworld; corpses dripping with blood; and onlookers standing by, helpless, and resigned. The Mafia may affect the majority of Sicilians directly or otherwise, but local attitudes are now changing profoundly, and represent the biggest threat yet to the Mafia.

The revulsion of Sicilians over the 1992 murders of Mafia-fighting judges Giovanni Falcone and Paolo Borsellino helped weaken the Mafia's grip on public opinion, previously its greatest weapon, and in turn badly dented the age-old code of silence, known as *omerta*. This, coupled with tougher laws, greater police determination, and a parallel moral revolution, has isolated and exposed organised crime as never before.

Pentiti ("the penitents"), a curious local word for Mafia turncoats, swelled from a handful in May 1992, when Falcone was killed, to 500 in August 1993. Dozens of important dons, including the "boss of all Mafia bosses", Salvatore "Toto" Riina, the Godfather of Corleone, were jailed. For years they ruled in "hiding" – often completely openly in Palermo – protected by the now shamed power brokers in return for votes.

The Mafia, previously obsessed with tradition, is also changing its spots, however. As the old Mafia guard languish in their prison cells, their women, once tied to the home, are often forced to take up the "family business". If they still do the laundering, it is more likely to be of money than their husband's shirts. Women, even children, are no longer immune to Mafia violence.

The younger generation of gangster is as ruthless on the stock exchange floor as he is on the streets of Palermo, and is as likely to be in Milan or Prague, armed with a computer. Upwardly mobile *mafiosi* are girding themselves for new determined attempts by the state to seize their assets; also imminent is the expected struggle – possibly all-out clan warfare – to fill a power vacuum created by the capture of Riina and other bosses. Riina is thought to have created a secret and parallel Mafia; alongside it, and also vying for supremacy, are the *stidde* ("stars" in local dialect), new maverick Mafia groupings which are pitted against the organisation.

Added to drugs, extortion and property speculation, the trading of arms, nuclear and conventional, between Eastern European and Middle Eastern and other embargo-covered countries has been added to Mafia activities. Investment features as much in Moscow as it does in Palermo. Mafia violence, which was once limited to the vendetta, then to campaigns targeting public figures, is now aimed at ideas as well as people, and at emblematic

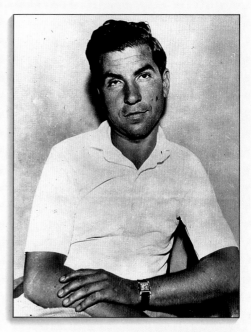

objects such as Italy's art treasures.

Medieval origins: Romantic treatment of what is arguably Italy's biggest blight and its second largest private company (its estimated annual turnover is £5 billion/US$7.5 billion), pins its origins to medieval times and a mysterious religious sect, the Beati Paoli, whose hooded members lurked, armed with pikes and swords, in underground passages below Palermo. Some say the word Mafia first appeared in the mid-1600s, and was used to mean a witch; others maintain it derives from any of a number of dialectical or Arabic words meaning "protection", "misery", or "hired assassin". What is certain is that the Mafia as we know it began to take shape in the early 19th century, in the form of brotherhoods, formed ostensibly to protect miserable Sicilians from corruption, foreign oppression and feudal malpractice, especially in connection with the land. Criminal interests quickly seeped in, corruption became the preferred milieu, and soon the brotherhoods were feeding on the misery from which they pretended to defend their members.

Judges were soon said to be secretly protecting them; nobles, to be backing them; the

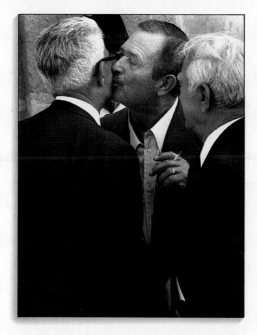

double-dealing fraternities offered to return stolen property to people who had been robbed. The brotherhoods' most important manifestation was as the *gabelotti*, organised minders of the land holdings of a bored and often absent nobility, who distributed jobs and land, and policed the countryside.

When Garibaldi set off from Sicily with his redshirts, he did so thanks to the efforts of the brotherhoods, which lent the support of some 20,000 men. Many were said to be

Left, a young Lucky Luciano, who forged links between the Sicilian and American Mafia. **Above**, "the kiss of death", often used as a sign.

cutthroats, whose aim was to cash in on the spoils of a successful campaign. Turned back by the troops of Turin, they reorganised to oppose the redistribution by statute of nearly half a million acres of Church land in Sicily to an ambitious class of private landlords. These were known as the "agrarian mafiosi".

As early as 1838, the brotherhoods – first mentioned in court documents in that year – infiltrated every walk of Sicilian public life. After 1863 the word Mafia became common parlance thanks to a comedy on prison life – *I Mafiusi della Vicaria* – which filled the theatres of the day. By 1875, the Mafia had infiltrated the Bourbon household in Palermo. Any investigator who delved too deeply into the brotherhoods was likely to find himself stripped of his case, then his job. The same year, the word Mafia was first mentioned in a Parliamentary Committee Report.

The American connection: Cardinal to the so-called "Southern Question" was severe economic misery. Between 1872 and World War I, poverty and the defeat of agrarian trade unions forced 1½ million Sicilians to emigrate. Most went to the Americas. There, many joined brotherhoods based on those back home in a bid for solidarity in a new, hostile environment, and the foundations of Cosa Nostra were laid. Elements willing to cash in on every form of illegal activity found a springboard with prohibition. American bootlegging marked the Mafia's graduation from rural bands to a sophisticated urban gangster organisation.

Back home, Mussolini was appalled at the Mafia's new importance as a surrogate state, and in 1925 set out to bring it to its knees. He sent his special prefect, Cesare Mori to Sicily, investing him with almost unlimited powers. By 1927, victory was already proclaimed for Mori's heavy-handed tactics. Called the "surgical precision of fascism", they entailed throwing thousands of people into prison on flimsy grounds, and laying siege to towns (even their water was cut off) to flush out the bosses. Politicians may have needed their votes but Mussolini did not.

But Mori was a threat to a greater form of mafioso than the kind he had flung in jail – the powerful agrarian variety. Soon Sicily's landed interests struck a deal with the fascists, and Mori left the island. In return, the agrarian mafiosi saw to it that the more criminal Mafia elements in Sicily were almost wiped out.

They won a reprieve in 1943, when the members of organised crime were given the job of clearing the way for the Allied invasion. Fearful of the consequences which war between the US and Italy would have on their interests, Italian and American mobsters such as Lucky Luciano had struck a deal with US authorities in 1940. In return for their help they were to be left alone. The operation overseen by Don Vito Genovese, a Naples thug wanted for murder in the US, went so

the site of Italy's first heroin refinery. In Sicily, organised criminals began supporting the pre-separatist movement backed by agrarian interests. Together with the authorities, the Mafia joined in the suppression of banditry, which had made inroads into its territory during the fascist siege. Always conservative (the Mafia would later ally itself closely to the Christian Democrats, by far the most popular post-war party on the island), it spared Sicily's folk-bandit hero, Salvatore Giuliano, until 1950, when he espoused the Communist cause and embarked on a series of outrages.

"Americanised" and emerging from its rural roots, Sicily's Mafia achieved its quan-

well that the Allies hardly fired a shot.

Mafia mayors: Local mafiosi, rearmed with weapons taken from Italian forces, and their dons – such as Don Calogero Vizini (39 murders, six attempted murders) – were installed by the Allies as mayors of key Sicilian towns. In the peace treaty, Italy promised to spare 10,000 people who helped the Allied cause, including 1,000 mafiosi.

Changing fortunes brought Sicilian and American Mafia elements to hitherto virgin cities such as Milan and Naples; Naples, ruled by the less organised local Mafia, the Camorra, became a fiefdom of Cosa Nostra, and was chosen by American gangsters as

tum leap in the late 1950s with the introduction of drugs. In 1957, after a crackdown in the US against organised crime, American bosses entrusted to their Sicilian counterparts the importation of heroin into America.

The move was built on roots laid down by Lucky Luciano before his death in 1962, and is thought to have given the Sicilian end its present-day organisation. Frank "Three fingers" Coppola, claimed to have been at the centre of the new Sicilian-US connection, was expelled from the US to Italy, and reha-

Above, a threatening gesture is made against a photographer during one of the "maxi-trials".

bilitated close to Rome as a "builder". But he concentrated more on constructing the first important ties between the Mafia and politicians in Rome. His protégé was Luciano Liggio, an ambitious mobster from Corleone who had won his stripes by black marketeering during the war.

Clan warfare: Liggio launched his Corleonese family to the top of the heroin trade and to the pinnacle of the Cosa Nostra pecking order by breaking almost the entire codex of Mafia laws. Jailed in 1974 – he now amuses himself in prison by painting pictures of his home town – he continued to run the Mafia as a tyranny through his lieutenants, Toto Riina, called the Wild Beast, and Bernardo "the tractor" Provenzano.

The tactics of the Corleonesi, whom Riina wrested from Liggio's control five years after he was jailed, were simple: the systematic blowing away of any mafioso who coveted power, caused trouble, or those who, like the old guard who baulked at such tactics, simply differed. The Mafia clan war of the early 1980s left Palermo's streets strewn with blood and the Corleonesi the undisputed victors. Riina's name has been linked to some 1,000 murders.

Not all concerned mafiosi. In response to the drugs trade which had prompted the carnage, a parliamentary anti-Mafia committee had been set up; in response, the Mafia, led by the Corleonesi, instituted a campaign of terror in which top officials, the police and politicians were targeted.

The gruesome list of illustrious corpses began with Palermo's chief prosecutor Pietro Scaglione in 1971, allegedly murdered by Liggio, Riina, and Provenzano. In answer to the 1982 killing, together with his wife, of General Carlo Alberto Dalla Chiesa, the *carabiniere* who had vanquished terrorism before being sent to Palermo as chief prefect, the government pushed through the La Torre law to get at Mafia assets. The law had been proposed by Pio La Torre, Sicilian regional Communist Party leader, gunned down 100 days before Dalla Chiesa.

Dalla Chiesa had begun digging into the island's huge construction industry, an easy area in which to invest profits from drugs, and is thought to have stumbled on a minefield: the "Third Level" question of who in the country's highest political circles protected, or possibly also issued orders to, the Mafia. The Mafia's most important supergrass, Tommaso Buscetta, claimed in 1993 that Giulo Andreotti, seven times prime minister, ordered the mob to kill Della Chiesa and a journalist, because he knew too much. Buscetta was earlier responsible for the "Buscetta theorem" claim that the Mafia was not a fictitious invention or collection of individuals, as many bosses and politicians maintained, but a solid organisation with a hierarchy, rules, and a concrete overall plan.

Buscetta's evidence after his arrest in Brazil in 1982 led to several "maxi-trials" in the 1980s, where hundreds of mafiosi sat in the dock, and effectively launched Giovanni Falcone, a young Mafia-fighting Sicilian magistrate to whom Buscetta gave evidence, on the road to success. Falcone, a firm believer in the Buscetta theorem, became the most conspicuous of a group of magistrates who became known as the "anti-Mafia pool". Despite its success at bringing the Mafia almost to its knees – some would say because of it – the pool was disbanded by authorities jealous of its autonomy and fame. Former pool members, especially Falcone, were frequent victims of damning, anonymous information circulating in the palace of justice, redubbed "the palace of poison". Falcone, ostracised and left with few important cases, later abandoned Palermo for a top job in Rome's Justice Ministry.

Failure to use his weight to overturn a guilty verdict concerning the same "maxi-trial" in a supreme court decision in February 1992 is believed to have been the reason for Salvo Lima's killing by the Mafia in March of that year. Lima, a former Palermo mayor, an MP and a Euro MP when he died, was the most powerful Christian Democrat in Sicily and the island's representative of the party faction headed by Giulio Andreotti. He was later named as a mafioso.

His murder was the first in a new campaign of terror which included the Palermo airport motorway bomb attack in May 1992 which killed Falcone, his wife, and three bodyguards, and the car-bomb killing of Judge Paolo Borsellino. The campaign continued in 1993, this time aimed at the country's artistic patrimony, with bombs devastating Florence's Uffizi Gallery, Milan's Royal Villa and art gallery, and Rome's San Giorgio in Velabro and San Giovanni in Laterano churches.

And don't, let me beg you, go with that awful tourist idea that Italy's only a museum of antiquities and art. Love and understand the Italians for the people are more marvellous than the land.

—E.M. Forster

It has been said that the Italians do not exist, that those who are thought of as Italian consider themselves Piedmontese, Tuscan, Venetian, Sicilian, Calabrian and so on. No one has ever been able to classify the Italians convincingly: to be born in Palermo, Sicily or in Turin, Piedmont is a classification by itself. And sometimes fellow-countrymen can seem like foreigners. In Germi's movie, *Il Cammino Della Speranza* (The Path of Hope), a peasant woman says: "There's bad people in Milan, they eat rice."

According to the writer Ennio Flaiano, being Italian is a profession – except that it doesn't require much studying, one just inherits it. Generations of Italians have learned the complex art of *arrangiarsi*, of getting along in all kinds of difficult situations. Having to deal with and adjust to quick political changes and foreign conquerors has produced a flexible mentality and a detached attitude towards political institutions and regimes, all of which are considered ephemeral. The forest of rules, statutes, norms, regulations, some of them hundreds of years old, others of obscure interpretation, some forgotten but lying there ready to be revived suddenly for the benefit of one group against another, has engendered distrust of the state. The popular saying *fatta la legge, trovato l'inganno* (a law is passed, a way past it is found) is practically a national motto.

North versus south: Since the very first years after Italian unification, the problem of the south vexed political thinkers. Camillo Cavour, one of the architects of Italian unity, turned his political thinking to the problem of the *mezzogiorno* and the "poor Neapolitans". He attributed the region's corruption

to the previous rule of the Bourbons, and exhorted his successors to bring morality, education and liberty to the area. Since that time, pouring money into the region in an attempt to solve its problems has been a constant feature of government policy. Yet the gap between the two Italies still exists. At the turn of the century, hundreds of thousands of southerners fled hunger and underdevelopment by moving to New York and South America. During the 1960s even more southerners (2½ million) migrated to north-

ern Italy. The causes of underdevelopment in the south have been attributed to a variety of factors, from the region's history of oppression to its distance from markets and lack of sources of energy and raw materials.

Conditions in the south are complicated by the presence of the Mafia. *Gli amici* as Mafia men call themselves, are concentrated in Western Sicily, where nothing happens without their approval, in particular any kind of progress. Northerners resent their taxes being spent on alleviating southern problems and tend to see such aid as pouring their hard-earned money into Mafia pockets.

At election time, a higher proportion of

Preceding pages: street games in Naples' back streets; a woman in Positano. **Left**, a Sardinian beauty decked out in native costume. **Right**, a Neapolitan man.

people go the polls in Italy than in most of the other European countries. Yet the average man in the street, when questioned, expresses a total revulsion for politics: *La politica è una cosa sporca* (politics is a dirty thing). He believes all parties are the same, and that politics work only for politicians – not an unjustified accusation in view of the political scandals that have rocked Italy recently.

The history of the young republic is riddled with sensational thefts against the community and gigantic tax evasions, sometimes with the help and complicity of the Vatican banks. The Italian courts have acquitted Mafiosi of international renown, corrupt politicians, and terrorists plotting with the

ture, even members of the Marxist parties, has given up on ideology. As for the man in the street, he believes that things would be better if everything were left to the commonsense and free initiative of those "who work and produce".

Behind such opinions there is often an unrestrained individualism that denies social responsibility. Yet, hand in hand with such entrepreneurship, you will often find a nostalgic yearning for "the strong man" whose power and will is stamped in his face, whose gestures command and direct, whose voice captures the needs and desires of the nation as it carries over the loudspeakers. It was a wave of such nostalgia that swept

national intelligence services. During recent years, Italian citizens have seen drastic curbs placed on their liberties. They can be sent to jail for years without being tried (some have languished in prison for as many as nine years without trial). A simple confusion over names, or an accusation made by someone already in jail who is aiming to reduce their own sentence, can be enough to land an Italian in prison.

It's no wonder then that the Italians remain sceptical of the state. It's no surprise that the Italians cannot conceive of abstract solutions to their problems or put their trust in ideologies. Everyone in Italian political cul-

Alessandra Mussolini, granddaughter of Benito, into the Italian parliament in 1992. Similarly, in northern Italy, in the wake of the political scandals of the early 1990s, many Christian Democrat supporters were won over by the oratory of Umberto Bossi, the leader of the Northern League, a right-wing autonomy movement.

The Italian look: Contrary to popular notions, the Italian look defies easy definition. The Mediterranean type may prevail, but there are innumerable variations: the Latin strain (the Julius Caesar type which is seen in the faces of statues at the Capitolium Museum) can still be found, especially in the remoter regions of the mountains around Rome. Sicily was once an Arab kingdom, and Semitic features are still noticeable among the population there, as are those of the Normans, who succeeded the Arabs in Sicily and southern Italy. The peasants of the Veneto near the border with the former Yugoslavia have strong Slav traits; the Gothic, Lombard and other Germanic conquerors of the period following the fall of the Roman Empire, though relatively few, left faint traces of their physical characteristics, especially in the people of Lombardy and Piedmont.

Today there are Albanian and Greek areas in Calabria and Sicily; the region of Friuli-Venezia Giulia has a very large Slavic popu-

The language: The Italian language is the closest to Latin of any of the so-called Romance languages. It's the official language at public occasions, in parliament and in the media. It is taught to foreigners and supposedly in schools. It's a result of the ideas and labours of various writers from the 14th to the 19th century, from Dante Alighieri to Alessandro Manzoni. These authors assumed as their standard the educated language of Tuscany, and the best form of speech is said to be *la lingua toscana in bocca romana* (the Tuscan tongue in the Roman mouth).

The vocabulary comes mainly from Latin, and the grammar is also clearly derived from that ancient tongue. Italian is said to be the

lation, and there is a former German province – South Tyrol – within the frontiers of the Republic. Even in areas south of the Tyrol – in Treviso for example – you can see a variety of blond that you may easily meet punching your ticket at Düsseldorf railway station. But the blond Germanic type represents only about 2 percent of the Italian population. Generally, in the eyes of a foreigner, Italians are dark, with abundant black hair, olive skin and brown/black eyes.

From left to right: a quizzical nun in Rome; mounted police patrol; a modern-day gladiator teaches fencing in a studio in Rome.

most musical language in the world: Emperor Charles V is supposed to have used Spanish with God, French with men, German with his horse, but Italian with women. The Italian language is capable of expressing many subtleties of thought and feeling in a delicate manner. It can be as precise as any other language, yet it is opaque and often falls victim to verbosity. The style of newspaper editorials, art criticism and political speeches in particular is often abstract, obscure and boring. In Italian, lack of ideas may be easily disguised by elegantly ambiguous prose.

This non-communicating style has an ancient origin: it was introduced by learned humanists in the courts of the 15th century. It was taken up by the subtle preachers of the Counter-Reformation in the following century, and then revived by the later theoreticians debating the significance of the student protests of the 1960s. Among Italians, talking about concrete things, *pane al pane e vino al vino,* always sounds a little shocking.

Until recently, over 1,500 dialects existed side by side with the official Italian language, most of them virtually incomprehensible outside their own village.

Many of the dialects contained a large number of foreign words imported by foreign occupiers. The dialects of northern Italy,

Calabria and Sicily. Sardinia has its own language, and Catalan is spoken at Alghero in Sardinia.

You can still hear dialect spoken among the old people in the countryside, but among the younger generations dialects are fading away as a combined result of school, radio, television and military service.

Regional differences: Until 50 years ago in Italy, differences between classes and towns were very noticeable. They were there not only because of geography or gaps between the social classes, but because of a long historical process of separatism. It was possible to observe marked differences – from the pronunciation of vowels to the cooking

for example, contain German elements, while Spanish, French, and German words are common in Neapolitan. Piedmontese was strongly influenced by the French, and Spanish, French and Arabic enrich the dialects of Sicily. In addition, French is spoken widely in Val d'Aosta; the population of South Tyrol speaks German; about half a million people in Friuli-Venezia Giulia speak Slovene and other Slav tongues, and Slav dialects are also found in the Molise region to the south of Rome. Ladin, a direct descendant from Latin, related to the Romansh language of Switzerland, is spoken in some valleys of the Dolomites; Greek and Albanian are spoken in

of pasta – by simply moving from one town to the next. Clothes and haircuts also differed, and some even claimed there were differences in the way of making love. "Oh, those unforgettable years on the Autostrada del Sole [the main highway from Milan to Calabria] when at each exit and every toll booth you could experience a different way of making love," sighs the writer Alberto Arbasino. Gore Vidal, who chose Italy as his second home, has complained: "Towns that were once different to the point of hostility are now all unified by TV, Fiat, festivals and soccer matches."

These two writers may be right to complain of the progressive disappearance of many unique features of Italy, but deep cultural divisions between various areas can still be observed today, and will probably continue to exist for years to come. The Venetian with his mild manners, sweet talk and respectful fear of authority is a quite different creature from the more aggressive Roman; the Piedmontese maintains a dignified, reserved, slightly conceited attitude betraying traces of French influence; the Milanese are renowned for their commercial instincts; the Florentines continue to exhibit a cool, classical snootiness; and the Neapolitans are as superstitious as they ever were. And, when speaking of general national char-

party procession with white carnations stuck in the bonnets of the cars and in the hair of the womenfolk.

Another shared characteristic is individualism. Centuries of political and religious authoritarian structures, which oppressed the values and needs of individuals, forcing people to fall back on cunning self-reliance, have produced an over-blown ego. The strong sense Italians have of their own existence is even evident in the way they line up (or rather don't) at the windows of government offices, at the bus stop, or in the tobacconist.

Self-regard is reflected in the way the Italians dress. They are consistently elegant. Shoes, ties, beautiful fabrics, and liberty of

acteristics, one can be sure that, be it virtue or flaw, its intensity changes and increases as one moves south.

Natural ebullience: The lively temperament of the Italians may seem, to the ear of a foreign listener, decidedly over the top. Simply put, the Italians are noisy, ebullient, expressive. A chorus of car horns beneath your window could be the joy of football fans celebrating a victory, the mourning of policemen remembering a recently fallen colleague, or the enthusiasm of a wedding

Left, cyclists in Calabria. **Right**, young Italians take time out in the sun.

the imagination all contribute to the "costume". The same fastidious care is lavished on cars and even motorcycles, which are widely seen as extensions of the personality. Similar care is not lavished on homes or on the landscape.

Sex and the family: The image of the Italian man as the great Latin lover – passionate, impetuously sentimental, and powerful in bed – is a myth. The principal male characteristic is an attachment to his mother. The bond goes far beyond the natural tie to a parent, and its residue is always there, even late in life: the need to feel loved and understood, the wish to receive affection while giving little in return. The Italian mother herself, tender, anxious and generous, often does much to reinforce the phenomenon.

The mother image is carried like an icon when an Italian man searches for a wife. The ideal woman is tender, sweet, willing to give up anything for him and always puts his wishes first. The search is the first step in the development of the family morality, or amoral familism (as the British sociologist E. Bumfield called it in the 1960s) which cannot see beyond the family into the community and which strengthens arrogant individualism at the expense of the state.

Female virginity is still one of the pillars of official morality. In the south the Christian

ideal of virginity has been reinforced by the influence of Islam. Virginity for southerners is part of the honour and wealth of a family. And when a women marries, faithfulness is the natural extension. If the codes of virginity or faithfulness are violated and dishonour falls on a family, it can only be repaired by a crime of passion. During the 1970s, about 1,500 such crimes were reported each year. A less drastic solution is to marry the shamed girl to her seducer.

Southern Italians tend to divide women into two groups: those who have to be respected and those who don't (the latter category often includes blonde foreigners, who

in the fertile imagination of young Italian males, represent all that is attractive about sex and sin). In the south men talk frequently about sex, often in an obsessive way. At the bar, while sipping coffee, standing on a street corner or at work the talk is of either sex or soccer. Tales of real or imaginary adventures are swapped, evoking visions of extraordinary future pleasures in younger listeners.

As if to make up for women's limited role in society, within the home the wife is often a tyrannical figure, imposing her will through hysterical scenes, heavy silences and constant nagging. In many cases men end up fearing their wives, and go out to find companionship with male friends, soccer, cards, and sex. It is estimated that more than half of Italian men have had extra-marital affairs. Though most men get along with their wives, and imagine they could never do without them, male adultery is a habit.

In the 1970s, under pressure from the feminist movement, Italy's archaic sexual and family morality started to give way. Italian women rejected the traditional roles subscribed to them and claimed economic and sexual independence. Old taboos were overturned. The 1980s, however, saw a backlash, and women are still most frequently portrayed in the media as beautiful, semi-naked and young.

How can one judge the national life of the Italians? Many would say that Italian life is a failure because of the persistence of many seemingly insoluble problems. There are so many things, from the traffic in Rome to the cumbersome paperwork that is attached to the simplest official action, which restrict and frustrate. And Italians seem unable to believe in the possibility of constructive change. For them, life is not about work and progress, but survival and individualism. On the other hand, and perhaps for that reason, Italian life sparkles with a brilliance unmatched anywhere else in Europe. The Italians have perfected a style of life that may be short on efficiency but is long on enjoyment. Simple things, such as eating a meal, taking a walk, watching the world go by, become special in Italy. Life is enjoyed to the fullest, with a flair gained over centuries of practice.

Left, a Sardinian patriarch preserves traditions at the Cavalcata festival. Right, veiled lives in Palermo, Sicily.

Italy's clothing, textile and footwear industry is the country's biggest employer and export earner. Yet at the dawn of the Italian look one finds not a group of refined stylists of international renown but a bunch of patriots fighting for Italy's independence and unity. Over 150 years ago, when Milan was still under the firm thumb of the Austro-Hungarian empire, these patriots launched a programme of National Fashion. Their idea, inspired by economics and political ideology rather than aesthetic considerations, was to put an end to the importation of German cloth and at the same time to revive Italian traditions in design and fabrics, which had been eclipsed by the prevailing fashion of the French style. Why waste money abroad, they reasoned, when corduroy was still being produced in Genoa according to an ancient tradition of craftsmanship?

At the time women still wore crinolines and fashion meant ladies' fashion, for by the early 19th-century men's fashion had made its great "renunciation", giving up colour and ornament and limiting itself to the dull uniform of the three-piece ensemble of jacket, trousers and waistcoat. The only possible expression of originality was in the excellent quality of the material and in the cut, which at that time followed English styles.

One of the most striking garments of the day was the flaming red shirt of the *Garibaldini*, the 1,000 men (*i mille*) of the army of the revolutionary leader Giuseppe Garibaldi. These red shirts – actually a sort of tunic – were originally designed for Argentinian butchers, but owing to trade difficulties between Buenos Aires and Montevideo, Uruguay, where the shirts had been made, they had not been sold. Garibaldi snapped them up for a song. The red colour fitted his Republican cause, the red flag being the banner of revolution.

Italian fashion takes off: In Milan in 1906 a seamstress called Rosa Genoni renewed the attack on the influence of French *couture* in Italy. Finding inspiration in medieval and

Preceding pages: billboard in Milan, fashion capital of Italy. **Left,** catwalk model wears Valentino couture.

Renaissance paintings, and in Greek and Egyptian art, she put together a whole series of patterns which brought her the admiration of the French themselves. She borrowed ideas from Botticelli's *Primavera*, works by Giotto, Pisanello, Fra Angelico and even from frescoes in the catacombs. Actress Lyda Borelli, later to become Countess Cini, and other elegant ladies wore Genoni's dresses for cocktail parties, outings to the theatre and to horse races. Signora Genoni also influenced the trend towards simplicity by launching her *robes fourreau* (sheath dresses).

After World War I a less happy contribution was made to Italian style – the fascist black shirt, worn by Mussolini and his followers. Inspired by the *Arditi*, a sort of storm trooper employed by the Italian army during the war, it was later teemed with *orbace* (a fabric from Sardinia) black trousers and shining black boots.

Fascist fashion for women was more varied. In 1930 Mussolini's beloved daughter Edda married the handsome Count Galeazzo Ciano and Maria Jose of Belgium married the Crown Prince, Umberto di Savoia. Both brides wore Italian wedding-dresses, and Maria Jose, in line with Mussolini's dictum that Italian home-made products should be chosen in preference to "perverse Parisian chic", never opened her 80 trunks full of fabulous French lingerie and parures.

Wealthy Italian ladies were forbidden to buy French dresses or Italian imitations of French dresses. Instead they were encouraged to copy Renaissance portraits of *belle dames* or the peasant costumes unique to the various regions of Italy. The rich embroidery, jewels and contrasting primary colours – black, red and white – were especially attractive, though the rural style of the dresses looked rather out of place in Milan and Rome.

The working-class women of the period were not slim, nor could they diet, since their first duty to their country was to procreate. They wore dresses made from new synthetic fibres such as rayon and a loathsome fabric called lanital, which was Mussolini's answer to Italy's wool shortage. In order to reverse Italy's negative balance of trade, Il Duce encouraged the development of lanital as a wool substitute. Unlike other synthetics, it was not made from vegetable substances, but from an animal product, casein, the milk residue left behind when butter is made. Lanital had many unfortunate qualities: it smelled rancid, and when damp it expanded and then stiffened.

However, fascist fashion had its high points. When Italy occupied Ethiopia, a shopkeeper in Milan hit on the idea of printing Mussolini's speech marking the occasion on a scarf. Fashion critics were delighted. The American magazine *Harper's Bazaar* said: "These days, women want to carry their faith right up front where everyone can see it."

cess Giovanna Caracciolo – with her exquisite, aristocratic outfits; Princess Simonetta Colonna who, with the help of the sculptor Alberto Fabiani, revolutionised the feminine figure; the Fontana sisters, whose white, full skirts and little straw hats were soon seen as far away as Hollywood; and Germana Marucelli, whose creations were to a great extent inspired by Florentine art.

The reaction of the American buyers and journalists convinced Giorgini that the moment had come to launch the Italian style throughout the world. Upper-class women dropped the French look and the middle classes soon followed suit. They presented their seamstresses with the latest fashion

Post-war turning point: On 12 February 1951, Florentine Marquis Giovanni Battista Giorgini, who had operated as an antique dealer on the American market during the war, organised a fashion show of Italian *haute couture* in his beautiful house in Florence. This event was a turning point in the history of modern Italian fashion. Instead of inviting representatives of well-known Italian houses who were working on French lines, he assembled a team of adventurous young stylists, enticing them with the promise of rich American buyers: Jole Veneziani, with her gorgeous fur coats and strange gold and embroidered eyeglasses; Carosa – Prin-

magazines showing the Florentine models: sloping shoulders, floating coats, rows of buttons, scarves, knots, ribbons and collars up to the chin, high stiletto heels and tiny cloches which made the head look small and shrunken.

Soon *Life* and *Time* magazines were demanding tickets for the Italian shows and calling up in advance to find out what the voltage was for their lighting equipment. By 1952 Italian fashion was in demand in the United States, especially the colourful designs of Florentine aristocrat, Emilio Pucci, passionate sportsman and much-decorated war pilot. His shirts and scarves, generally gorgeously patterned abstracts, were fashion landmarks (signed Pucci shifts have since become collector's items). His aim was to take women from city clothes into sports clothes.

In 1953 the fashion show moved to the Sala Bianca of Palazzo Pitti, the famous palace designed by Brunelleschi in 1440 for the magistrate Luca Pitti. The new stage was a 30-metre (98-ft) platform covered with light beige moquette. It was flanked by the world's leading fashion editors and buyers, who were enticed not just by the fashions and designers but by the opulence of the setting and the chance to rub shoulders with local aristocrats. The show was a triumph. Bold an economic boom. Italy's new prosperity spread wealth through the population, and suddenly women working in factories and offices, whose numbers were multiplying fast, wanted to look more stylish. Designers and textile managers worked together to meet the new demand for fashion, and the industry was revolutionised. *Prêt-à-porter* (ready-to-wear) was invented to meet the demands for designed clothes at more affordable prices than *haute couture*.

But there were blows to come. In the 1960s fashion's spotlight switched to England. In 1966, the mini-skirt, soon followed by hot pants, arrived in Italy from London. Italian men of every age were flabbergasted by the

printed shirts teamed with Capri pants and bare, brown legs were hailed as young, sexy and a totally new departure from the structured fashions of the French.

The roaring sixties: In 1960 London's *Financial Times* awarded the lira an "Oscar" for its fine performance. Cheap labour in the post-war period (especially compared with labour costs in the rest of Europe) had led to

<u>Far left</u> to <u>right</u>: Garibaldi's red shirt; Sorelle Fontana's black dress, modelled here by Ava Gardner, was worn by Anita Ekberg in Federico Fellini's *La Dolce Vita*; ruffled feathers look; and Pucci bathing suit.

new look. Then, in the second half of the 1960s, student riots erupted in California, Paris, Milan and Rome. In search of a new ideology, young men rejected the tie and the grey flannel suit of their fathers and adopted the costumes of the rebel: blousons, psychedelic shirts, tight jeans, red scarves, and leather jackets. They dressed casually (or they pretended to), claiming that fashion was not fashionable any more. They believed in self-expression and urged everyone to create his or her own image. "To dress oneself must be a fact of self-security and self-knowledge, not an adjustment or an act of obedience imposed by others," said

Fiorucci, the most celebrated Italian designer of the decade. No longer could one fashion prevail; instead, many different styles co-existed.

In the 1970s stylistic trends fragmented. The power of *haute couture* diminished. The mini-skirt was seen alongside the midi and the maxi. Youth was the only consistent theme in fashion. More than any other designer, Fiorucci rode the wave of the young style. A parallel phenomenon in fashion was "revivalism", whereby the looks of past decades were tried on once again.

The liberalisation of morals continued to have an effect, and the revolution in men's fashion continued. Now it was not only teenagers who were rejecting grey-suit conformity and rediscovering colour, ornament and originality. Meanwhile the mini-skirt, the hippy style and the gypsy look, which reflected looser mores, gave way to the nude look. Garments were designed to show off the body. Towards the end of the decade unisex came to the fore.

The year 1973 saw the arrival of Giorgio Armani, whose softer tailoring for both men and women changed the modern way of dressing for good. He had no money (he sold his Volkswagen to get started) but had served an apprenticeship with Nino Cerruti. Together with his then partner, Sergio Galeotti, he bought up lengths of linen, cut them out and covered them in polka dots with a felt-tip pen. He tried out the results on the female staff in his office. Just over 20 years later Armani's business is worth almost £400 million (US$600 million), and has expanded into restaurants and cafés as well as into the more usual territory of perfumes and toiletries. An Armani jacket is one of the most coveted items of clothing in the world.

Revival in the 1980s: The 1980s saw the return of high fashion and the resurrection of couture. Suddenly fashion designers were being wooed by other artists, such as film and theatre directors and painters. The Fendi sisters designed the costumes for Fellini's films and the furs for Ken Russell's *Boheme*; Krizia entertained Michelangelo Antonioni, Francesco Rosi (her brother-in-law), and Andy Warhol at intellectual soirees and sponsored a tour of the most prestigious Italian State theatre (the Piccolo Teatro di Milano) to Los Angeles for the 1984 Olympics. Gianni Versace designed (and still does) costumes

for the ballet company Bejart; a big textile concern from Turin sent Lorin Mazeel to conduct on the podium in Bologna; Renato Guttuso, the charismatic interpreter of Italian socialist realism and the official painter of the Italian Communist Party, designed scarves and fabrics for the stylist Nicola Trussardi; the Missoni husband and wife team, whose sweaters are displayed in the Metropolitan Museum of Modern Art in New York, designed Luciano Pavarotti's costumes for *Lucia di Lammermoor*; the University of Parma organised a retrospective exhibition of Sorelle Fontana; and Valentino promoted a "Valentino's award" to men of culture.

When the Revlon Research Centre produced an atomic-proof time capsule which will remain sealed until the year 2453, it included among the 50 items selected for prosperity a tie made by Gucci and a purse made by Fendi.

The 1990s: Italian fashion is a leader among Italian exports, boasting higher figures than either cars or chemicals. Krizia and Missoni clothes sell best in the United States. Valentino (*the* top designer in the opinion of most Italians), Coveri, Nino Cerruti, Versace and Armani make important contributions to the Paris fashion scene.

But what is the essence of Italian fashion today? No simple answer to that question exists, not because Italian fashion is currently in crisis but because it is going in so many different directions at once.

Today's fashion is highly tuned to street trends and developments in the arts, yet at the same time the Italians have succeeded in industrialising the manufacture of high-quality, ready-to-wear designer clothes. While Benetton has tapped into a worldwide mass market by decentralising production and sales and developing a trademark rainbow range of knitwear, the partnership Dole e Gabbana, the *wunderkinder* of Italian fashion, is one of the most inventive forces on the world's catwalks.

One thing is clear: the Italians have a wonderful ability to play with materials and forms. Italy's pastry-cooks and bakers, ice-cream makers and greengrocers, the Neapolitan crib makers and the marzipan confectioners of Sicily all share the same special gift.

Right, blue velvet: Versace couture.

Halfway through dinner with Trimalchio the Roman satirist Petronius received the final main course: "A calf was brought in on a two-hundred pound plate: it was boiled whole and wearing a helmet. Following it came Ajax, slashing at the calf with drawn sword like a madman. Up and down went his arm – then he collected the pieces on the point of his sword and shared them among the surprised guests... I looked at the table, already there were trays of cakes in position, the centre of which was occupied by a Priapus made of pastry, holding the usual things in his very adequate lap – all kinds of apples and grapes... every single cake and apple needed only the slightest touch for a cloud of saffron to start pouring out... naturally we thought the dish must have some religious significance to be smothered in such an odour of sanctity."

Today's visitors to Italy will find it difficult to replicate the gustatory experience immortalised by Petronius in *The Satyricon*, a picaresque account of the licentiousness of Roman society. Nonetheless the Italians' all-consuming passion for food, its preparation and eating is as important today as it was in the 1st century BC.

The Italians preserve a sense of food as theatre, and at even a quite simple meal each dish is afforded its due appreciation. Dinner is at once a drama to be witnessed in stages with mounting surprise and delight, and a sacrament to be shared in affirmation of bonds of blood or love. For the Italians, the meal is a celebration of life itself – less of man's art, than of nature's wondrously bountiful providence.

One of the secrets of Italian cuisine, impossible to replicate elsewhere, lies in Italy's soil. After making pulp of Mexico, the Spanish conquistador Hernando Cortés returned to the Old World laden with strange new fruits and vegetables, among them a humble, fleshy yellow sphere smaller than a ping-pong ball which, in 1554, the Italians dubbed the *pomo d'oro* (golden apple). Two hundred years on, thanks to the rich Italian soil,

these jaundiced cherries had metamorphosed into huge, lush tomatoes in deep ruby hues; moreover, their relatively demure taste (the contemporary writer Felici had described the original fruit as "more good-looking than good") had been transformed into a piquant yet tantalisingly sweet sensation.

These days, as well as being a key ingredient in many more elaborate Italian dishes, tomatoes are stuffed with beans or rice, or served as an *antipasti* with alternating slices of fresh mozzarella cheese, or simply served

lightly dressed in olive oil and topped with sprigs of basil.

A savoury past: Until the Renaissance, the history of Italian cooking largely corresponded with Italy's military fortunes. In the 9th century the Arabs invaded Italy, introducing Eastern sherbets and sorbets, originally served between courses to refresh the palate. The region where Arab influence was most entrenched, Sicily, is still noted for its sorbets and sumptuous sweets, including *cassata siciliana*, sweet sponge filled with ricotta cheese or pistachio cream and decorated with almond paste and candied fruit. Two hundred years after the Arabs left main-

Left, a cat looks for scraps at an outdoor restaurant in Positano. **Right**, fireside dining.

land Italy, the Italians set off on their own holy wars to the east. Their return was sweetened by the presentation of sugar-cane which they had discovered in Tripoli. They referred to it as "Indian Salt" and initially used it as simply one more condiment for meat and vegetables, not suspecting for almost another whole century its natural affinity with dessert.

Sometime in the late Middle Ages pasta appeared. Nobody knows exactly how it was invented, but the legend of Marco Polo bringing it back from Cathay is firmly refuted by Italians. The Roman gastronome Apicus describes a *timballo* (a sweet or savoury pie made with pasta). Later, in the Middle Ages,

invented macaroons, *frangipane* (filled with cream and flavoured with almonds) and *panettone* (a spicy celebration brioche incorporating sultanas). Conquistadors bombarded the Old World with its first potatoes, pimentoes and, of course, tomatoes. When Catherine de' Medici, a keen gourmet, married Henry II of France, she took with her to France her Italian cooks, thus laying the foundations for French cuisine. Until then, France had no cuisine of its own. Even *Larousse Gastronomique* honours Italy as the mother cuisine

Regional flavours: The concept of an Italian national cuisine is highly treacherous. Italy offers the world 23 regional cuisines, a di-

Boccacio recommended the combination of macaroni and cheese.

It was during the Renaissance that cooking became a fine art and evolved along the lines familiar to us today. Bartolomeo Sacchi, a Vatican librarian, composed a highly sophisticated cookbook entitled *De Honesta Valuptate ac Valetudine* (Concerning Honest Pleasures and Wellbeing); within three decades the volume ran through six editions. Florentine merchants spent huge sums on establishing schools for the promotion of culinary knowledge.

Consolidation of the Venetian Spice Route led to fragrant innovations. New pastry cooks

versity reflecting the country's pre-unification history and the importance of locally available produce (for example, hare, boar, rabbit and chestnuts in Tuscany; pork and truffles in Umbria; mozzarella, squid and *polpo* – octopus – in Naples). Distinctive culinary identities evolved as naturally as particular painting styles or costumes. Even more influential than political boundaries were natural variations in soil type, climate and proximity to the sea.

But the single inescapable territorial distinction is that between the north and the south. There are two important culinary differences between the two regions. Firstly, northerners eat flat pasta shaped like a ribbon while southerners eat round pasta shaped like a tube. Northern pasta is usually prepared at home with eggs and eaten almost immediately, often *alla Bolognese*, the classic pasta sauce made with lean veal and tomatoes and seasoned with carrot, celery, *prosciutto*, lemon zest and nutmeg. Southern pasta, on the other hand, is manufactured in factories (the first factories opened in the 19th century), does not contain eggs and is purchased dry, a tradition stemming from the days when it was dried in the warm sea breezes around Naples The classic sauce in the south is *Napoletana*, based on pork.

The second difference between north and

rived from the Latin *gobius pagenellus* (little pagans). It is said that when St Anthony of Padua came to Rimini in 1221 he preached a sermon for which all the fish, save the gobie, lifted themselves from the water.

Zuppe di pesce, which is more of a stew than a soup, is a stalwart of every menu and usually served in an enormous tureen. Luxury versions include *buridda alla Genovese*, incorporating octopus, squid, mussels, shrimps and clams.

Anchovies and sardines are classic Mediterranean fish. *Pasta con sarde*, a speciality of Palermo, combines *rigatoni* with a sauce of wild fennel, pine nuts, raisins and fried sardines. A more intricate dish, often found

south concerns the lubrication used for cooking. North of Emilia-Romagna, Italians butter almost all pots and pans, but south of Bologna olive oil sets the pans sizzling.

Between the Adriatic and the Tyrrhenian seas, Italy hauls in well over 700 million pounds of fish a year. Wonderful fish abound in Emilia-Romagna. Alpine streams make the Adriatic significantly less salty than most oceans, making it an ideal habitat for rombo, "the pheasant of the sea", and gobies, de-

Left, preparing to cleave an enormous tuna in Palermo, Sicily. **Above**, Venetian shoppers pick the freshest fish from an outdoor market.

as an *antipasto*, is sardines stuffed with capers, pine nuts, pecorino cheese (from Sardinia), bread and eggs.

Italy also produces some of the finest meats in the world, which may explain why the Italians, unlike the French, don't find it necessary to add sauce to their national specialities. Tuscany's Chianina cattle are pure alabaster in colour and grow to weigh 1,814 kg (4,000 lbs). Chianina beef is used to best advantage in *bistecca alla fiorentina* – a recipe in which the steak is marinated in a little olive oil, wine vinegar and garlic, then rapidly grilled. Baby lamb and kid is popular in hilly regions. Game birds are also used extensively (Italians are widely attributed with eating anything which flies, however small), and warbler, bunting, lark, quail and pheasant are favourites on regional menus. Thrushes and larks are eaten whole, bones as well. *Piccioni* (wild pigeon), served fresh rather than hung, attains new gustatory heights in Italy. Look out for *piccioni alle olive*, pigeons wrapped in bacon, roasted and served with green olives.

Of all Italy's provinces, Rome has the most festivals. And Rome's cuisine comes nearest to sustaining a feast atmosphere. Suckling pigs and suckling lambs are mouth-watering specialities. And the justly famous *saltimbocca alla Romana* (a thin slice of veal

wrapped around a slice of *prosciutto* and a leaf of fresh sage, browned in butter and simmered in white wine) lives up to its name – "jump into the mouth". Romans also thrive on *gnocchi* – feathery dumplings incorporating butter, eggs, nutmeg and Parmesan – while their poor relation, *polenta*, is popular in Lombardy.

Emilia-Romagna has splendid natural resources. Moreover, the entire province has always had one of the world's best road systems ensuring rapid distribution of ingredients. *Prosciutto* (air-cured ham) is synonymous with Parma, though Tuscany and Umbria also produce a good *prosciutto*

rubbed with a garlic and pepper mixture before curing. It is often served with sliced melon or figs. Emilia-Romagna is also the place for sausage. Bologna, the capital of Italian cuisine, lies in the heart of Emilia-Romagna. It is from here that *mortadella*, described by one connoisseur as "the noblest of pork products", originates. *Mortadella* is made from finely hashed pork, generously spiced, then forced into a casing made from suckling pig skin.

Bologna is also the home of *tortellini,* rosebud shaped pasta filled with spinach and ricotta cheese. "If the first father of the human race was lost for an apple, what would he not have done for a plate of *tortellini*?", goes a local saying. Legends as to tortellini's origins abound. The favourite version gives credit to a young cook of a wealthy Bolognese merchant who modelled the curiously shaped pasta on the navel of his master's wife whom he had seen sleeping naked.

As well as being *polenta* country, Lombardy also boasts the most modern methods of food production in Italy. It produces more rice than any other European region and the famous *risotto alla Milanese*, seasoned with saffron, does justice to the native grain, which, as the great cook and writer Elizabeth David pointed out, is ideally suited to slow cooking. Variations on the risotto theme, in which rice is cooked in a broth to absorb its flavour, include *risotto nero*, in which the rice is coloured black by cuttlefish ink. One of the ways of transforming a plain risotto into a dish fit for a king is to shave a little truffle over the top. Truffles, a superior type of mushroom which grow beneath the soil around tree trunks, are prized for their unique fragrance and flavour. White truffles are found in Piedmont, where they are sniffed out by specially trained dogs. Black truffles are associated with Umbria.

Bread and pizza: Naples is the place to eat pizza baked over wood in a brick-lined oven, traditionally pizza Napoletana (tomatoes, mozzarella, anchovies and oregano), pizza Margherita (topped with mozzarella, tomatoes and basil leaves) and pizza marinara (topped with tomatoes, garlic, clams, mussels and oregano). A good pizza should be moist and fragrant with a raised rim known as *ilcornicione* (large frame).

Bread, eaten without butter, accompanies every meal and is used to mop up juices and olive oil. Every region, even every town, in Italy has its own varieties and the different shapes alone are said to number 1,000. In Tuscany, bread (rough, white and with a floury top) is saltless to counteract the saltiness of the food; in the south bread comes in large crusty wheels. Favourite speciality breads include *pane alle olive* (a Genoese bread incorporating olives) and *focaccia*, a flat bread drizzled with olive oil and sprinkled with salt, or, in a more elaborate version similar to pizza, topped with olives or onions. Sardinia is noted for its *carta da musica* (music-paper bread), a wafer-thin unleavened bread, which is crunchy and long-lasting. Shepherds traditionally took it with them

of the day, the time when families swap stories and adventures.

Though the specialities differ greatly, all regions eat their particular dishes in a remarkably similar order. The first course (*il primo*) invariably consists of a pasta or rice dish (especially in the north) or soup. (Generally antipasti is served only in restaurants or at banquets.) The second course (*il secondo*), comprising meat or sometimes (especially on Friday) fish, complements or elaborates the theme begun by the first. For example, if the first course was *tortellini* filled with parsley and ricotta, the second would probably be something light – such as a sautéed chicken dish with lemon and a little

when they went off on long expeditions into the hills with their flocks.

Wherever you are in Italy the rituals surrounding food and eating remain the same. Devotion to any repast, however humble the content, is evident in the time Italians spend at the table. In most regions of Italy work still stops for a full two hours at midday. During this time everyone, from the poorest to the richest, is expected to go home and eat. Often the midday meal is the most important event

Left, proprietor of 12 Apostoli in Verona gingerly lifts a pastry lid off a salmon. **Above**, the interior of 12 Apostoli is decorated with frescoes.

more parsley to recall and resonate the first course's theme. The second course is usually enhanced by at least one, and sometimes two or three vegetable side dishes, such as *funghi trifolati* (mushrooms sauéed with garlic and parsley), *fave in salsa di limone* (broad beans in lemon sauce) and *cicoria all'aglio* (chicory with garlic sauce).

Afterwards, a light green salad is ordinarily served to cleanse the palate, and prepare the taste buds for the grand finale – anything from an exotic pastry (*dolce*) to one of Italy's many cheeses, perhaps served with fruit. Needless to say, each course is washed down with ample quantities of wine.

In Italy, wine is part of the cultural furniture. It goes on the table along with salt, pepper, olive oil and cutlery. If you meet three people in Italy, the chances are that two of them will make wine, or live next door to somebody who does, or have a cousin who does. The doorman at the hotel, the taxi-driver, the restaurant proprietor, can all take you to a vineyard, not five minutes away from where you are standing, that produces one of the 12 best wines in Italy. They are able to do this because nearly all Italian wines, if their proud makers are to be believed, make it easily to the top dozen.

Italians have a reputation for being individualists, and their wine only confirms it. A pride in what they make, and a less than deferential attitude towards officialdom and bureaucracy, combine to produce a situation that in some regions – Tuscany during the 1980s, for example – can verge on chaos. Never mind, for the visitor it is all good fun. Wine in Italy is rarely accorded the reverence it is in, say, France or California. It exists to turn ordinary everyday meals and family get-togethers into hugely enjoyable social occasions.

Vine-growing echoes the north-south divide, largely for climatic reasons. Most Denominazione di Origine Controllata or DOC wine (which accounts for one in every eight bottles) is produced north of Rome: as one travels south the grape varieties, and the tastes, become increasingly exotic. Italy grows more grape varieties, and makes more wine (nearly a fifth of the world's total) than any other country. Not all of it is good, but much of it is exciting. Drinkers who prefer the safety and security of Chardonnay or Cabernet Sauvignon will find them, but those who are prepared for adventure will be amply rewarded. If in doubt, take a risk.

Light but quaffable: Soave and Valpolicella illustrate a useful principle. These light white and red wines are produced on a vast industrial scale. The Veneto region – from Venice to Lake Garda, from the Yugoslavian Alps to the flat Po Valley – is the largest producer of

<u>Left</u>, Umbrian wines for sale. <u>Right</u>, hand-made methods in Tuscany.

DOC wine; Soave, by far the country's biggest selling dry white DOC, can be as memorable as muzak or waiting-room wallpaper. But for those who are prepared to pay a little more, for wine made on a small scale by first-rate producers, it can be very good indeed. Looking at three Soaves on a wine list, and picking the most expensive, may seem perverse, but those from Pieropan, Anselmi or Tedeschi (and Valpolicellas from Allegrini, Quintarelli or Le Ragose) will be a significant step up from much of the competition.

Any Valpolicella billed as *ripasso* will have more character than a straight Valpolicella. Recioto Amarone and Recioto Amabile (made from dried grapes) are stronger versions, the former dry (*amaro* means "bitter"), the latter sweet and reminiscent of port. Recioto Soave is the white equivalent, a golden, gently honeyed wine. Alternatively, for even lighter versions of straight Valpolicella and Soave, it is worth hunting down a cherry-red Bardolino or white Gambellara, Lugana, or Bianco di Custoza from a producer such as Boscaini, Masi, Portalupi or Podere Co'de Fer.

To the north and east of Venice, Friuli-

Venezia Giulia is a source of much crisp and fresh white wine (from a long list of grape varieties that includes Tocai, Pinot Bianco, Pinot Grigio, Chardonnay, Sauvignon Blanc, and Riesling). Collio and Colli Orientali are among the best DOCs. Jermann, Schiopetto, Gravner and Russiz Superiore are first rate producers.

Up above Lake Garda, where the Adige and Isarco rivers (or the Etsch and Eisach for German speakers) tumble down from the Austrian Alps, is the delightful region of Trentino-Alto Adige. It is officially Italian, but the oompah-pah bands and *lederhosen* give the game away: this, the South Tyrol, was once part of Austria. White wines (from Chardonnay, Muscat, Riesling, Müller-Thurgau and Gewürztraminer) are as crisp and fresh as the mountain air, and range from feather-light to ethereal.

Among producers who make the best of this cool sub-alpine region's resources are Lageder and Tiefenbrunner. Reds vary from hefty Teroldego Rotaliano through plummy, chewy Lagrein Dunkel and juicily fresh Marzemino to lighter, gulpable, strawberry-flavoured Lago di Caldaro (or Kalterersee, to give it its German name).

Piedmont, Italy's other sub-alpine wine region, is a wonderful place to visit in autumn, when the early morning fog that hangs over the vineyards clears slowly, and the streets of Alba smell of white truffles. The fog, or *nebbia,* gives its name to the main red grape variety, Nebbiolo, which ripens very late, and has a thick skin to enable it to survive the humidity and rot that would threaten thinner-skinned varieties.

The thick skin is also responsible for the wine's deep colour, and for mouth-puckering tannins that make Barolo and Barbaresco such big, powerful, chewy, long-lived wines. They are both DOCG (the G stands for *garantita*), a step up from DOC. Alcohol can also be a hefty 13 percent. Mature Barolo and Barbaresco from a good producer can be a sublime amalgam of black cherries, plums, damsons, roses, woodsmoke, chocolate, liquorice and tobacco. Among producers to look for are Castello di Neive, Cavallotto, Conterno, Gaia, Giacosa, Mascarello, Produttori del Barbaresco, Ratti, Vietti and Voerzio; some (including Ascheri, Chiarlo and Ceretto) make Barolo in a more approachable style. As with Valopolicella, there are lighter alternatives (made from the same grape) in and around the region: Gattinara, Carema, Valtellina, Nebbiolo d'Alba and Nebbiolo delle Langhe.

There is more to Piedmont than just Nebbiolo, though. The Dolcetto grape makes vivid, beetroot-purple, softish but invigoratingly fresh wines, while Barbera (the country's most widely planted grape variety) produces all styles from light and slightly frothy to seriously oak-aged. Then there are the whites. Gavi (from the Cortese grape) is both fashionable and expensive, but Asti Spumante and its cousins (Moscato d'Asti, Moscato Spumante) are wonderful value: gloriously aromatic, frothily inconsequential, irresistibly quaffable.

Chianti country: Tuscany challenges Piedmont as producer of the country's most aristocratic wines. Some of the families in the business today (Antinoris and Frescobaldis, for example) have been making wine since before the Renaissance, so they should be good at it by now. Chianti is the staple, Italy's best known red wine, made mostly from the Sangiovese grape. The "blood of Jove" manifests itself in varying forms – there is no single style of Chianti that is easy to pin down – but most of it is gratifyingly better than it used to be, even a decade ago.

Brunello di Montalcino and Vino Nobile di Montepulciano, both Sangiovese-based DOCGs, have traditionally represented the heights to which Tuscan reds could aspire. But Super Tuscans, a loose-knit family of brilliant but quirkily named wines that burgeoned during the 1980s, have thrown up more excitement. Some are Sangiovese-based (Ceparello, Fontalloro, Tignanello), some rely more on Cabernet Sauvignon (Sammarco, Sassicaia, Solaia), and most are pricey. They have given Tuscan producers a new confidence, and drinkers an old problem: trying to remember the names.

Dry white wines from Tuscany are less exalted. Galestro is a brave attempt to show that Italy's ubiquitous, high-yielding and rather boring Trebbiano grape can turn into something tasty, especially when blended with Sauvignon Blanc, Chardonnay and others. Vernaccia from the medieval turreted town of San Gimignano is made in more traditional style. Tuscany's classiest whites however are sweet, made from dried grapes, and called Vin Santo.

Food and drink contribute significantly to the strong sense of regional identity to be found throughout Italy. In Emilio-Romagna, where dishes are gloriously rich and sticky, Lambrusco is the natural partner. Most of it is red, some is dry, and the bubbles vary from a mere prickle to a full-blown sparkle. Much of it, too, is an improvement on the coloured sweet pop that floods the export market. Look for Lambrusco di Sorbara to get a taste of the real thing. Look also for Albana di Romagna, a rare DOCG white wine.

If Frascati did not have Rome on its doorstep, it might not have achieved the fame it has. Most is Trebbiano-based and quaffable, but the better producers – Fontana

Castelli di Jesi) from the Marches on the eastern flank; Nuragus and Vernaccia (different from Tuscany's) in Sardinia.

Southern riches: Sweet whites are often made from Muscat or Malvasia, and are invariably worth a punt. Moscato di Pantelleria (from an island closer to Tunisia), or Carlo Hauner's Malvasia from the island of Lipari, plus those from Sardinia, echo the wines of classical times.

The best red grape of southern Italy is Aglianico, which makes meaty, plummy Taurasi in Campania. Among the softer and more supple reds, Montepulciano (made in Abruzzo, the Marches and Molise) is a spicy delight. Rosso Conero (with a dash of

Candida and Colli di Catone (especially Colle Gaio) among them – use Malvasia.

The story is much the same throughout Italy. Rather bland whites (if no grape variety is mentioned you can bet it is Trebbiano) are the norm, often enlivened with a faint refreshing prickle; what they lack in character they more than make up for in being versatile partners for a wide range of dishes. Umbria's Orvieto is more flexible still, since it comes dry, medium dry (*abboccato*) and sweet (*amabile*). Elsewhere, other white grapes ring the changes: Verdicchio (the best is

Above, a taste of Tuscany.

Sangiovese) and Rosso Piceno (with even more) are the Marches' best red wines; look for producers Umani Ronchi and Villa Pigna.

Torgiano is virtually a one-man Umbrian DOC run by the Lugarotti family; Rubesco di Torgiano Riserva, made principally from Sangiovese, is first-class. Umbria's most curious wine is made from dried Sagrantino grapes; a rich, densely fruity red, sometimes dry, sometimes sweet with a passing resemblance to Recioto Valpolicella. The DOC is Sagrantino de Montefalco, and the best producer is Adanti. Cannonau grapes are dried and used to similar effect in Sardinia, while Sicily's best red is rich and plummy Regaleali.

"These are the laws of the musical theatre," the composer Giacomo Puccini said of his art, "to interest, to surprise, to move." Of himself, he once commented, "I have more heart than mind." In these characteristics lies the tremendous appeal of Italian opera. The form is sensual and lush, appealing more to the emotions than the intellect. Subtleties exist, especially in Verdi's later, more difficult works, yet opera's overriding effect remains emotional and sensual.

Rossini, Donizetti, Bellini, Verdi and Puccini head the list of composers whose music is constantly performed throughout the world. The bookends of Italian opera's golden age stand clear: on the one side the 1815 production of Rossini's classic *opera buffa* (comic opera), *Il Barbiere di Siviglia*; on the other, the posthumous 1926 opening of Puccini's last and unfinished opus, the romance of *Turandot*. Between the two lies more than a century of operatic triumphs. The course of 19th-century Italian opera marked a tremendous cultural flowering.

Yet there is much more to the story of Italian opera than the few dozen classics which contributed to the razzmatazz surrounding the 1990 World Cup. Hundreds of other operas lie lost or forgotten, their makers relegated to the backroom of music history.

Opera's origins: For an art form that is popularly conceived of as "classical", opera is a relatively new phenomenon. It stems from the traditional Italian mystery plays, the *maggi*, and from the madrigal comedies of the early 16th century. An intellectual rationale for the new form emerged when scholars discovered that Greek drama had been set to musical accompaniment.

In the early 1580s composers and the literati gathered in the Florentine salon of the Count of Venio to discuss the potential for musical reform. The new style of composition was first put to the test by Jacopo Peri with a 1597 private production of *Dafne*, the score of which no longer survives. Peri also staged the very first public showing of an *opera in*

musica (literally, work in music), a performance in Florence of *Euridice* to mark the marriage of Maria de' Medici to Henry IV of France in 1600.

These first works amounted to little more than dramatic recitals with a skeletal musical accompaniment, but the operas of Claudio Monteverdi (1567–1643) exploited the new medium more fully by employing an orchestra of 39 brass, wood, and stringed instruments. Monteverdi's *Arianna* "visibly moved the entire theatre to tears" at its first performance in 1608; but it is his *La favola d'Orfeo* (1607) that is generally acknowledged to be the first operatic masterpiece.

Opera was soon being performed throughout the Italian peninsula, and in major cities all over Europe. The first public opera house, the Teatro di San Cassiano, opened in Venice in 1637. By 1700 Venice had 17 theatres in which opera was performed. At that point opera's popularity exploded. Almost 2,000 original compositions were first (and sometimes last) produced in 18th-century Italy.

With that level of output it was impossible to maintain the standards we are accustomed to in opera today. Many agreed with the French intellectual Charles di Saint-Evremond, who found opera "a bizarre thing consisting of poetry in music, in which the poet and the composer, equally standing in each other's way, go to endless trouble to produce a wretched result". To satisfy demand, Italian composers were resorting to clichéd musical formulas and conventions.

Rowdy audiences: If the quality of operas had fallen to an abysmal low, most 18th-century Italians didn't seem to mind, for they flocked to the houses night after night for hours of social frolicking. "Every small town, every village has a theatre," remarked one contemporary. "The poor may lack food, the rivers may lack bridges, the sick unprovided with hospitals… but we may be sure the idle will not want for a Coliseum of a kind." The comparison to the ancient Roman circus seems altogether apt. In the theatres the middle and upper classes gathered to eat, drink, and gamble. The operas themselves were often mere sideshows.

Opera houses were all constructed on the

Preceding pages: a glittering gala at Milan's La Scala Opera House. **Left**, a portrait of Verdi in the Museum of La Scala, Milan.

model of the early Venetian theatres. A horse-shoe of box tiers rose over the *platea* (the pit or orchestra). The original San Carlo in Naples, for instance, was 27 metres (30 yds) long and almost 18 metres (20 yds) high, with a stage covering some 929 sq. metres (10,000 sq. ft). "The King's Theatre," wrote Englishman Samuel Sharp of San Carlo, "upon first view is, perhaps, almost as remarkable an object as any man sees in his travels."

Theatre boxes, which one could buy, sell, mortgage, or sublet as with any other piece of property, were much sought after by city socialites. Each box enjoyed a private dressing room and often a balcony curtain which

which Italians might publicly display a playful exuberance; it was no coincidence that attendances peaked during the carnival season. In theory, unruliness was illegal – the various governments of the politically fragmented peninsula enacted statutes against everything from curtain calls to excessive applause – but the boisterous audiences carried on regardless.

In Milan, for example, a law against clapping before the sovereign, was circumvented by choruses of coughs or nose-blowing. Fearing, with some justification, that outbursts would turn into riots, the authorities in Rome had a flogging block installed outside the Teatro Valle.

provided complete privacy (or refuge from a bad performance). The grandest patrons ordinarily opted for the second tier, where the royal box, if there was one, would be situated; the higher one went, the lower the prestige. As a rule, however, boxes were held only by members of the nobility.

The pit was occupied by middle-class merchants and professionals. "Cultured ladies did not sit there," wrote the English singer Michael Kelley, noting that box holders were inclined to spit and throw litter into the *platea* below.

Opera goers were a generally rowdy bunch. The theatres provided the only forum in

Some performers would have liked firmer enforcement of such laws. When opera patrons had a spare moment to look up from the roulette or dining tables in their box, they were not famed for their generosity. Charles Dickens, after a stay in Genoa, noted the "uncommonly hard and cruel character" of Italian audiences, who seemed "always to be lying in wait for an opportunity to hiss". Listeners seated in the *platea*, known to follow librettos closely by the light of their own candles, would yell out "*brava, bestia*" ("bravo, you beast") upon catching a singer in a botched line. Overworked *prima donnas* might be showered not with roses and flattering sonnets jotted on handkerchiefs but with radishes and leeks, traditional symbols of ridicule. After a bad opening night, a local theatre organiser (the *impresario*) was likely to go home and find his windows smashed out with stones. Even the premiere of Puccini's *Madama Butterfly* (1904) met with catcalls and whistles of derision.

Opera's golden age: In the 19th century, when Giocchino Rossini, Gaetano Donizetti, and Vincenzo Bellini dominated the scene, Italian opera moved dramatically towards the idea – "to interest, to surprise, to move". They took a hackneyed form and infused it with vitality, and Europe once again looked towards Italy for operatic innovation. All

Puritani. These operas are part of standard repertories everywhere.

The three shared a small-town background. Rossini and Bellini were sons of provincial musicians, and though Donizetti was not, he was exposed to song and composition in his childhood. They all enjoyed tremendous success at an early age; if a laggard is to be found it would be Bellini, who made his operatic debut when he was 22 years old. Each faced the voracious demands of impresarios and the finicky tastes of leading performers, and they were all able to respond with remarkable speed, producing new works in the space of a few weeks.

They acquired gold and glory all over

three (born within a decade of one another) shared much in style, and their meteoric careers followed similar paths and detours.

Rossini is probably most celebrated for his productions of *Il Barbiere di Siviglia* and *Guillaume Tell*, while Donizetti's masterpieces are *Lucia di Lammermoor* and the *Daughter of the Regiment*. Bellini's best work is usually considered to be his *semi seria* works, *La Sonnambula*, *Norma* and *I*

Europe, including Paris, but finally, and tragically, all three burnt themselves out. Bellini and Donizetti died young, the latter a crazed syphilitic, and Rossini's last triumph came before he turned 40.

Not surprisingly, there was a fierce and jealous rivalry between the three. Upon hearing that Signor Rossini had composed *Il Barbiere di Siviglia* in 13 days, Donizetti shrugged proudly and concluded, "No wonder – he is so lazy." At one point, Bellini accused the other two of a devious plot to subvert his artistic opportunities. Speaking of engagements the other two had together in Paris, Bellini claimed: "Rossini decided to have Donizetti commissioned also because in that way, set up against me, he would suffocate me, exterminate me, with the support of Rossini's colossal influence." As the three faced decline, they were reconciled, and it is only fitting that they should have been followed by the brightest light in Italian opera: Giuseppe Verdi.

Verdi was born in 1813 (the same year as Richard Wagner) in Le Roncole, a small village 17 km (12 miles) from Parma. His father was a semi-literate peasant, and the Verdis had no history of talent, musical or otherwise, but young Giuseppe made a mark as the local church organist. His talents almost went to waste when, in 1832, he was

Italy, Verdi was a composer of true international stature.

It was a reputation well deserved. His sharp, almost brutal dynamism freed Italian opera from the lingering vestiges of empty conventions. His productions, refined yet fresh, "had nothing to do with theories," wrote one critic, "it is the voice of nature speaking in the idiom of art". The English composer Benjamin Britten sang his praises most eloquently: "I am an arrogant and impatient listener, but in the case of a few composers, a very few, when I hear a work I do not like I am convinced it is my own fault. Verdi is one of those composers."

In at least two important respects, the

denied admission to the prestigious Milan Conservatory. But the young Verdi was persistent, and although his first two productions, *Oberto* (1839) and *Un giorno di regno* (A One-Day Reign, 1840), met with lacklustre receptions at La Scala premieres, rave notices for the epic *Nabucco* (1842) marked the beginning of a long and distinguished career. From then on, Verdi saw success after success, highlighted by *Rigoletto* (1851), *Il Trovatore* (1853), *La Traviata* (1853), *La forza del destino* (1862), *Don Carlo* (1867), *Aida* (1871), and *Otello* (1887). With premieres in London, Paris, St Petersburg and Cairo, along with those in the theatres of

context in which Verdi thrived was more conducive than those in which his predecessors had laboured. Composers were no longer subject to the whip of their *impresari*; their fortunes now hinged on commissions from large publishers such as Ricordi and Lucca, who were much less interested in volume than in quality. Late in his life, Verdi looked back on the 1840s and 1850s, during which he had produced one or two scores a year, as his "time in the galleys", although that workload would have been a holiday to an 18th- or early 19th-century composer. Secondly, Verdi refused to tailor his works to the whims of individual singers, something no com-

110

poser had dared do in the past. Verdi's independence extended to his personal life. In a very conservative and religious society, Verdi openly lived with his mistress, the soprano Giuseppina Strepponi, for more than a decade before taking her to the altar in 1859.

If Verdi was permitted artistic and personal freedom, he was still constrained by the political realities of his day. Censorship was a constant impediment in an Italy dominated by foreign powers. Dictated revisions were often trivial, as when the exclamation *Dio!* (God) had to be replaced with the less offensive *Cielo!* (Heaven). Other times, the censor tried to rip the heart from a work with scores of senseless changes. Scrutinising an

of Count Cavour, Verdi briefly served in the new chamber of deputies after unification. On his death in 1901, Verdi was mourned not only as a composer but also as a patriot.

Although operas of fine quality continue to be composed today, the golden age of Italian opera drew to a close with the career of Giacomo Puccini. Others contended for the mantle of Verdi, but Puccini had the advantage of the blessing of the old man himself. "Now there are dynasties, also in art," lamented rival Alfredo Catalani, "and I know that Puccini 'has to be' the successor of Verdi... who, like a good king, often invites the 'crown prince' to dinner!" A dynasty it may have been, but one clearly

early manuscript of *Rigoletto* butchered by the Austrian authorities, in which names and localities were changed and the title character was not allowed to be a hunchback, Verdi exclaimed: "Reduced in this way, it lacks character, importance, and finally the scenes have become very cold."

Verdi was himself an ardent nationalist. His historical works were charged with analogies of the Italians' plight – allusions not lost upon native audiences. A dear friend

Far left to **right**: the famous 20th-century tenor Enrico Caruso (right) on stage; Giacomo Puccini; curtain call at La Scala, Milan.

based more on merit than on anything else. *La Bohéme* (1896), *Tosca* (1900), and *Madama Butterfly* (1904) are among the best loved works of opera.

From Monteverdi to Puccini, Italy remains, of course, the best place to sample the operas of the great Italian composers. Such grand old houses as La Scala in Milan, San Carlo in Naples, the Teatro Comunale in Florence, and La Fenice in Venice, and the many others that maintain an old-world elegance – provide an incomparable backdrop to sublime music. No visitor should miss the opportunity to enjoy the art of opera where it began and flourished.

Italian cinema has always flickered between monumental spectacles and unabashedly intimate emotions. Before the outbreak of World War I, Italian directors had already filmed *The Romance of a Poor Young Man* and several versions of Bulwer-Lytton's monumental novel *The Last Days of Pompeii*. Roberto Rossellini, patriarch of neo-realism, launched his career by filming for Benito Mussolini a patriotic panegyric on dashing navy pilots. Paolo Pasolini documented nihilist delinquents demolishing one another atop heaps of Roman ruins in *Accattone* (1961), then scripted the pious *The Gospel According to St Matthew* (1964).

When the Alberini-Santoni production company released *La Presa di Roma* in 1905 the Italian feature film was born. The subject is the 1870 rout of the pope by Garibaldi's troops. In its most famous scene, Bersaglieri rallies his forces to breach the wall at Rome's Porta Pia. Because so much of it was shot on location, *La Presa di Roma* anticipates the two dominant currents in Italian film history: realism and historical spectacle. Indeed, many of the films made before 1910 anticipated the themes occupying Italian cinema to this day.

A cerebral cinema: However, unlike America or France, Italy produced nothing of lasting merit until the 1920s. As a result, Italian cinema skipped several steps in the development of international cinema. In England, America and France, early directors associated themselves with vaudeville and music halls and so motion pictures tended to be classed as "low entertainment". Since Italian cinema missed this stage, film-makers did not risk being labelled as "fairground mentalities". Italy's first feature film-makers were the most learned and aristocratic in the world, create what was dubbed a "cerebral cinema". At a time when most other countries still saw film as an amusing novelty, Italy was using it to express the meaning of life.

Early extravaganzas: In the first decade of the 20th century two directors, Enrico

Left, Marcello Mastroianni, Italy's most sophisticated leading man, in Fellini's *8½*. Right, an early Italian heart-throb, Maciste, had a cruder appeal for audiences.

Guazzoni and Piero Fosca, revolutionised Italian films. The historic and melodramatic tastes of the two directors perfectly complemented Italy's burgeoning nationalism. Both men thrived on glorifying the martial exploits of ancient Rome.

But Guazzoni's significance derives as much from his commercial innovations as from his conceptual ones. *Quo Vadis?* (1913), which established his reputation, was promoted as enthusiastically for the quantity of its footage as for the quality of its scenes.

Rolling in at a full 10 reels, *Quo Vadis?* ran for two hours and used the world's first gargantuan sets. Guazzoni shrewdly limited distribution to first-class theatres, and in New York *Quo Vadis?* received the first personality-spangled premiere. Such glamorous openings helped Guazzoni to initiate the star system. What's more, his shrewd marketing enabled future producers to command unprecedented financial backing. However, *Quo Vadis?* masks any complexity of character with extra busy sets and costumes; and escapist addiction to costume drama haunts Italian cinema to this day.

Piero Fosco's contribution is more aesthetic and, ultimately, more influential than that of Guazzoni. His grand opus, *Cabiria* (1913), details the adventures of virtuous maidens, strong men, gruesome villains and romantic generals during the Punic Wars, the conflict between ancient Rome and Carthage. Elephants dextrously career down Alpine *piste*; virgins weep; muscle men bend iron bars; armies pursue; dictators gesture; crowds scatter; lovers unite. Fosca originated a number of techniques which advanced the effectiveness of film, including panning cameras across vast scenes and introducing live orchestras at screenings.

Most importantly, *Cabiria* showed it was possible to include subtle characterisation

potential. Industrialists saw opportunities of making money. Also intrigued was the aristocracy, the source of many of Italy's filmmakers and patrons. (Luchino Visconti, first generation neo-realist, was the heir of an aristocratic Sicilian family; a Roman countess provided Rossellini with the money to begin filming *Roma Città Aperta*.)

The support of the nobility is one explanation for the high production standards of early Italian cinema. While directors in France and the United States were still pinning up painted backdrops, Italians hired the nation's finest architects to design and construct full-scale sets. Furnishings in historical dramas were often borrowed from the personal col-

within the epic form. Though many of its characters are based on stock types, astounding details save them from being mere ciphers. Maciste – prototype for all future film strong men – tempers his pectoral flexes with a silly sense of humour; Scipio, the romantic hero, is capable of prolonged sulking fits. D.W. Griffith, the American director whose 1915 epic *Birth of a Nation* had a profound influence on the development of the cinema as an art form, was directly influenced by *Cabiria*. It was from Italy that Hollywood drew inspiration for its own epics.

After the successes of *Quo Vadis?* and *Cabiria*, the world woke up to film's great

lections of actual descendants of the depicted heroes. Actor butlers had been acting as actual butlers since boyhood. When a film included aristocrats, authentic aristocrats were invited to make the grandest guest appearance of all time.

This so-called Golden Age of Italian cinema hardly had time to blossom before the fascists came to power. Mussolini instituted several organisations to regulate cinema, so convinced was he of the power of the medium. The Direzione Generale per la Cinematografia became an official department of the Ministry of Popular Culture. In addition, the Banco del Lavoro helped provide finance for politically agreeable films. Directors who established their ideological credibility were eligible for up to 60 percent state financing. Particularly patriotic endeavours, like *Scipione Africano*, often received total backing from the government. If the government was pleased with the final film, producers were excused from making any repayment.

The final blow to creative competition was dealt by the new Ente Nazionale Importazione Pellicole Estere (National Body for Importation of Foreign Films). It decided which films could be imported, then insisted they be dubbed into Italian. Unable to compete economically, Italy's better directors went into hibernation. Motion pictures metamor-

rough visceral throb that was revolutionary for the time. Some sequences seem to be documentary footage; the camera jerks and twists; shots break off suddenly without conventional aesthetic purpose.

Despite the unprecedented, relentless immediacy, *Roma Città Aperta* has a complex symbolic structure. Each character represents a larger element in contemporary Italian society while at the same time coming over as a complete individual. *Roma Città Aperta* elevates squalid drug addicts, priests, German lesbians and Austrian deserters to levels of wider symbolic import without sacrificing their unique personalities. Pina (Anna Magnani), for example, an agonised mother

phosed into military cheerleading.

Neo-realism: In 1944, when the Germans were still in the process of departing from Rome, Roberto Rossellini made *Roma Città Aperta*, a film whose unflinching confrontation with truth unnerves audiences to this day. The film follows the lives of several resistance workers. Every scene, except for those set in the Gestapo headquarters, was shot on location. *Roma Città Aperta* has a

Left, Roman orgy in one of the early historical spectacles, *Quo Vadis?* <u>Above</u>, Anna Magnani as a housewife who resists Nazis in neo-realism's masterpiece, Rossellini's *Open City*.

leading a mob of matriarchs to plunder exploitative bakeries in the neighbourhood, is utterly convincing on a personal level, yet she also symbolises the desperate plight of Italian housewives during the war.

Federico Fellini, who helped Rossellini write the script for *Roma Città Aperta*, summarised the atmosphere following World War II that produced neo-realism: "We discovered our own country… we could look freely around us now, and the reality appeared so extraordinary that we couldn't resist watching it and photographing it with astonished and virgin eyes."

For the next six or seven years, Rossellini,

along with Visconti, Vittorio de Sica and Alberto Lattuada, developed a cinema characterised by rapid, seemingly spontaneous juxtaposition. Neo-realism remains the core of what is considered modern in film. The movement was a result of the remarkable homogeny Italy achieved just after World War II. Confusion concerning the future did not undermine the almost unanimous conviction that fascism was wrong. Neo-realist directors spoke from and for an Italy which could confess, if not to chaos, at least to contradictions.

But, as the Cold War set in, Italian cinema came under fire. The government accused the best neo-realists of purposefully black-

tials, is also responsible for its worst failing, a heavy-handed use of generalisation.

The numerous epics on Scipio Africanus by Mussolini's film-makers sought only to satisfy the nationalist desire to glorify Italy's contemporary African invasions. Scipio was interesting only as a type for Mussolini. But the fascist directors raiding history for examples of Imperialist gusto were no worse than some neo-realists plundering the slums' heartbreak. Fat matrons gathering laundry from endless lines while men in vests beat bare tables with hairy fists in between swigs from straw-covered Chianti jugs are no more inherently real than stalwart legions wading into apish Carthaginians waving spears from

ening Italy's image to encourage communism. The worst neo-realists focused only on the quainter aspects of Italian poverty, such as washing clothes and eating pasta, which traditionally found substantial audiences abroad. Most directors returned to making motion pictures about how much fun it was to have money.

Because Italy always takes its cinema so seriously, all films have some political responsibility. Even the silliest costume drama implies an advocation of escapism and hence support of the *status quo*. Thus, Italian cinema's greatest virtue, a faith in the power of film to communicate human essen-

above the swirling trunks of elephants.

Following the Cold War, new economic prosperity triggered a resurgence of Italian film. This time the directors were Federico Fellini, Michelangelo Antonioni and Francesco Rosi. Because the moral crisis facing these directors was an international crisis of faith rather than the specifically Italian experience of fascism, their films seem less dependent on a particular time period than those of De Sica and Rossellini. Questions of belief in God eclipse debates about finite political systems.

In many ways Fellini can be viewed as the triumphant culmination of neo-realist philosophy. His characters are constantly torn between the desire to realise their true selves and the urge to conform to society. His heroes swing wildly between the desire to be like no one and the need to be like everyone. They don't hesitate to remember being bathed by their mothers or to confess a desire to be an emperor hosting a gaudy sex orgy.

Fellini's most autobiographical work, *8½*, stars Marcello Mastroianni (Fellini's favourite male actor) as a director about to begin his greatest opus. Gradually it becomes apparent that Guido has no idea what his grand opus should be about, despite the fact that he has hired Europe's most prestigious stars to act in his film and has promised all of them

ised films, made on surprisingly low budgets, became the Italian movie industry's most successful exports since Gina Lollobrigida, Sophia Loren and Claudia Cardinale.

Fading star: After the glorification of the art film in the 1960s and '70s, when directors came close to being deified, the Italian cinema of the 1980s reflected the mood of the country, with political commitment going out of fashion and the emphasis shifting to entertainment. The chief beneficiaries of this were American movies which, as elsewhere in Europe, came to dominate the market. The frequency of cinema-going fell more steeply in Italy than elsewhere, a fact not unrelated to the astonishing number of films shown on

the roles of their lives. Full of ambiguity, oscillating drunkenly between reality and dream, spontaneity and steady linear narration, *8½* celebrates the fact that life can be loved even though it can't be controlled. This effort to represent the whole of life without reducing it has always been the object of Italy's best film-makers.

In 1967, with *A Fistful of Dollars* and *The Good, the Bad and the Ugly*, Sergio Leone presented world cinema with a new genre: the spaghetti western. These witty and styl-

Left, Federico Fellini on the set. <u>Above</u>, Giuseppe Tornatore's 1988 hit *Cinema Paradiso*.

television – more than 5,000 a year on the eight main networks alone.

Hopes were raised in 1988 when Giuseppe Tornatore's *Cinema Paradiso* scored at the Cannes Film Festival and then won an Oscar. Although the film hadn't made much impact in Italy before the awards, critics were soon talking of its Sicilian director as a great storyteller and the natural heir to Sergio Leone. But Tornatore's next film, *Stanno tutti bene* (*Everybody's Fine*) was a disappointment. Whether the Italian cinema's current doldrums are symptomatic of a wider crisis in the European cinema as a whole continues to divide the critics.

THE VATICAN

If size were the only measure of a nation's power or importance, the Vatican would warrant hardly any attention at all. Yet the Vatican serves as an exception to the rule that postage-stamp sized nations are famous for little more than their postage stamps.

For centuries the Vatican was the unchallenged centre of the Western world. Its symbolic significance, both past and present, and its enduring international role, as both a religious and a diplomatic force, have put this tiny city-state on a par with nations many million times larger. No matter how secular our world has become, divine authority seems still to count and to make the Vatican much more than a geographic oddity, much more than the academic footnote it might otherwise be.

Covering a total area of slightly more than 40 hectares (100 acres), Vatican City is by far the world's smallest independent sovereign entity. What other nation is as small as New York's Central Park? What other nation can lock its gates at midnight, as the Vatican's doorkeepers do each night, opening them only at the ring of a bell? What other nation can be crossed at a leisurely pace in well under an hour?

Ancient origins: In imperial Roman days, the lower part of what is now Vatican City was an unhealthy bog, famous among caesars and consuls for its vinegary wine, snakes and diseases. But in the 1st century AD, the dowager empress Agrippina had the Vatican valley drained and planted with tranquil imperial gardens. Under Caligula and Nero, the area was turned over to the circus. Chariot racing and executions – including that of St Peter – were regular events on what later became St Peter's Square.

The Lateran Treaty of 1929, concluded between Pope Pius XI and Benito Mussolini, established the present territorial limits of the Vatican. The city is roughly trapezoidal in shape, bounded by medieval walls on all sides except on the corner, where the opening of St Peter's Piazza marks the border

with Rome and the rest of Italy. Of the six openings to the Vatican, only three are for public use: the Piazza, the Arco delle Campane (south of St Peter's Basilica), and the entrance to the Vatican Museums. Pius XI had a special Vatican Railway station built in the early 1930s, a facility which no paying passenger has ever used (even popes use it very infrequently). A heliport has been built on a spot where British diplomats, restricted to the confines of the city, whiled away their days during World War II.

Aside from an impressive array of palaces and office buildings, there is also a Vatican prison, a supermarket, and the printing press, which churns out the daily *L'Osservatore Romano* and scripts in a wide range of languages, from Coptic to Ecclesiastical Georgian to Tamil. In short, the Vatican is much more than an oversized museum.

Subjects of the Holy See: Like other states, the Vatican protects its citizens – though there are only about 400 of them. To hold a Vatican passport is to belong to one of the world's most exclusive clubs. Vatican citizens either live or work permanently in the city or are abroad on diplomatic missions for

Preceding pages: the Vatican library. **Left**, Pope John Paul II, the first Polish pontiff. **Right**, St Peter's Basilica.

the Catholic Church. The privilege of citizenship hinges on a direct and continuous relationship with the Holy See. When ties are severed, the privilege is lost.

There is one person for whom severance ordinarily comes only with death: the pope himself. He carries passport No. 1 (although he is unlikely ever to have to use it); he rules absolutely over Vatican City and he holds ultimate authority within the Catholic Church. Within the Vatican and Catholic hierarchies, his power is unchallenged. A glance at his official titles, as listed in the *Annuario Pontificio*, the official Vatican directory, dispels any doubt of this supremacy: Bishop of Rome, Vicar of Christ, Successor of the

onstrated by a benevolent concern for the advancement of humanity, occasionally by stern warnings against theological or spiritual deviation. John Paul II, elected in 1978, the year of three popes, has asserted his moral authority vigorously. His 1993 encyclical (a letter sent to all Roman Catholic bishops in the world), which was six years in the making and part of a concerted plan to purge dissident theologians, denounced contraception, homosexuality and other infringements of the Catholic faith as "intrinsically evil".

John Paul II's 262 predecessors did not always show such integrity. In briefly considering the history of the papacy, it is impor-

Prince of the Apostles, Supreme Pontiff of the Universal Church, Patriarch of the West, Primate of Italy, Archbishop and Metropolitan of the Roman Province, Sovereign of the State of Vatican City, Servant of the Servants of God.

The pope's role is best characterised by the root of the word "pope". In Greek *pappas* meant simply "father" – in this case the spiritual father of all mankind. Although the papacy's claim to universality has undoubtedly eroded in the two millennia since St Peter assumed the mantle as a heavenly representative on earth, the pope's image remains decidedly paternal, ordinarily dem-

tant to remember that its powers were for many centuries more temporal than spiritual. The pope until modern times was a mighty piece on the chessboard of European politics; and just as there have been good and bad kings, there have been good and bad popes.

The facts and figures: The shortest reign of a pope was that of Stephen II, who died four days after his election in March 752. At the other extreme, the 19th-century's Pius IX, famous for his practical jokes and his love of billiards (he had a table installed at the Vatican Palace), headed the Holy See for 32 years. The youngest pope on record, John XI, was just 16 when he took the helm in 931;

the oldest, Gregory IX, managed to survive 14 years after his election in 1227 at the age of 86. While the great majority have been of either Roman or Italian extraction, Spain, Greece, Syria, France and Germany have all been represented, and there has been at least one of African birth (Miltiades, 311–314), and one hailing from England (Hadrian IV, 1154–59). John Paul II is the first Pole to lead the Catholic Church.

At least 14 popes abdicated or were deposed from office (Benedict IX in the 11th century was elected and then deposed three times). Ten popes met violent deaths, including a record three in a row in the 10th century. Popes have been arrested, imprisoned, and otherwise humiliated by various lay leaders, and many have never ruled from Rome at all.

Some 80 popes have been canonised by the church, most recently Pius X (1903–14). Some of the others are unlikely ever to climb out of the inferno. The decidedly unchristian Stephan VII (896–897) exhumed the body of his predecessor, Formosus (891–896), dressed it in papal vestments and put it formally on trial on charges of usurping the throne. In what became known as the Synod of the Corpse, Formosus was predictably convicted on all counts, his body stripped, dismembered, and thrown into the waters of the Tiber. Stephan got his just desert, however, when a Roman mob rose up and strangled him.

But more scandalous, if less gruesome, is the case of Alexander VI (1492–1503), the infamous Borgia pope. Even before the Spaniard won election to the throne, gained by means of powerful family connections, Alexander had a reputation as a womaniser and profligate. He flaunted a dalliance with the lovely Vanozza de' Cataneis. A party he hosted in Siena in 1460 provoked an angry rebuke from Pius II: "We leave it to you to judge if it is becoming in one of your position to toy with girls, to pelt them with fruits… and, neglecting study, to spend the whole day in every kind of pleasure."

Alexander improved little during his tenure as Holy Primate, casting papal favours in the direction of his mistresses and 10 illegitimate children. One son, Cesare Borgia, was made a cardinal even though he had never been ordained. Other progeny openly frolicked in the mire of Italian court escapades. The family's only saving grace was Alexander's great-grandson Francisco, who became head of the Jesuit order and went on to sainthood.

For all the popes remembered for unseemly deeds, there are, of course, many more of undoubted virtue. The popedom of St Peter himself, crucified upside down by the Emperor Nero in AD 64, was the first in a long line of papal reigns characterised by distinguished leadership. For example, St Gregory the Great (590–604) emptied the Vatican treasury to feed thousands of starv-

ing refugees from the Lombard wars. Likewise St Leo IX (1049–55) reversed a steep decline in the Church by cleaning up rampant corruption among the clerical ranks, including the common practice of trading in holy offices. More recently John XXIII (1958–63) transformed the papacy into a more caring and humane institution simply through his warm personality. "We are not on earth to guard a museum," he once said of the Church, "but to cultivate a garden." Pope John also addressed the Vatican's tendency towards pomposity: where the *L'Osservatore Romano* used to write, "following is the allocution by his Holiness as we have gath-

Left, a public Mass draws thousands to St Peter's Square. **Right**, the Vatican's Swiss Guards are responsible for the safety of the Holy See.

ered his words from his lips," John ordered a simple "the Pope said".

Picking the pontiff: The process of electing a new pope is unique. The papacy is the world's only elective monarchy. The Sacred College of Cardinals, a largely titular body of 120 bishops and archbishops appointed by the pope, assumes responsibility for the selection, convening for a conclave from points the world over soon after the death knell tolls in the Vatican Palace. The electors are sealed into the Sistine Chapel – no cameras or tape recorders are allowed – and cannot leave until a new successor has been chosen. Voting can proceed by any one of three methods: by acclamation, whereby divine inspiration

nate Matteo Rosso Orsini forced the electors to enjoy the company of the dead pope's corpse. Gregory X (1271–76) ordained that the cardinals should be reduced after five days to a diet of bread and water.

Paper ballots are burned after each tally, and onlookers eagerly await the tell-tale smoke from the chapel's chimney: dark smoke indicates an inconclusive vote while white plumes denote a winner (electors are provided with special chemicals labelled *bianco* and *nero* so that there can be no mistake). The cardinal dean announces to the faithful, "*Habemus Papam*", and the chosen cardinal appears in one of three robes (sized small, medium and large) kept on

provokes the cardinals all to shout the same name at the same time; by scrutiny, in which four ballots are cast daily until one candidate has captured a two-thirds majority plus one; or, as a last resort, by compromise, entrusting a small group of perhaps two dozen members to hammer out a resolution.

All modern popes have been selected by the second method. The process is usually relatively speedy (John Paul II was elected after two days; his predecessor, the short-lived John Paul I, after only one), though outside authorities have occasionally hurried the cardinals along. After the death of Innocent III (1216), for example, local mag-

hand for the occasion. The coronation takes place on the following day.

Although popes have absolute legislative, executive, judicial and doctrinal authority over both Vatican City and the Church as a whole (they were declared infallible in matters relating to faith by the First Vatican Council in 1870), the immensity of their responsibilities obviously necessitates substantial assistance.

Governance of the Vatican itself is handled by the Pontifical Commission for the state of Vatican City, which consists of seven cardinals, and a lay official, who directs the city-state's administrative affairs. But it is the task of shepherding the spiritual deportment of more than 800 million Catholics worldwide, and of managing a global religious bureaucracy composed of 4,000 bishops, 400,000 priests, and at least 1 million nuns, that occupies the great majority of those who work within the Vatican walls. This highly organised body of institutional supervisors, known collectively as the Roman Curia, directs everything from the Church's diplomatic and missionary affairs to the interpretation of Catholic marriage law.

Of the 4,000 or so employed in Vatican City, most operate within the Curia, the Vatican civil service. Once plump with sinecures, this organisation has been markedly

As well as criticising wasteful practices, the Curia has reformed its policy of elevating lay officials within its ranks. As late as 1860, the Vatican and Church governments employed almost 200 laymen for every priest; today, the proportion is reversed.

Most prominent among the remaining non-initiates are the Swiss Guards, who are exclusively charged with protecting the Holy See. This corps of 120 men, all Catholic, all Swiss, all brightly dressed in blue, red and yellow uniforms allegedly designed by Michelangelo himself, may seem no more than an ornamental regiment. In fact, the Guards have a history of military prowess dating back to the early 16th century. Today

pared in recent times. However, the tightening up could go further still. The position of Secretary of Briefs to Princes and of Italian Letters, for instance, is responsible primarily for adapting the dead language of Rome for such new words as "telephone" and "airport". A standard joke about the Vatican's extravagance is that the city's "SCV" licence plates stand not for *State della Citta del Vaticano* but rather for *Se Cristo Vedesse* ("if Christ could see...").

Left, the Vatican Museum – seemingly endless corridors of artistic treasures. **Above**, view from the Vatican dome over the Tiber.

their function is not unlike that performed by the Secret Service in America.

So the Vatican is distinguished by much more than the artistic masterpieces it shelters. Though the powers of the pope and the Church would undoubtedly survive without Vatican City, its existence helps ensure the continued respect and deference of the world's other leaders. Supported by centuries of tradition and history, the Vatican is unlikely to be incorporated into the rest of Italy. Some would argue it is best that a body of the spirit maintains this small perch against the onslaught of governments answering to less thoughtful authorities.

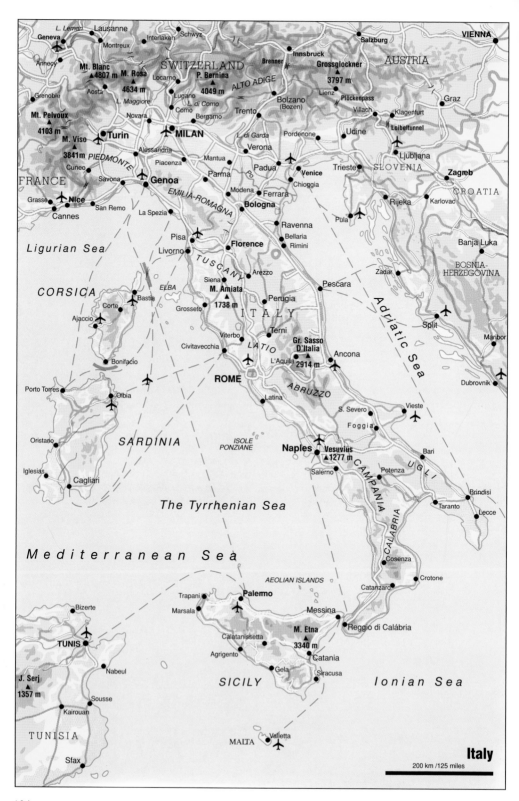

Italy

200 km /125 miles

PLACES

Negotiating the tangle of one-way streets in an Italian city takes years of experience. Often a helpful native will point the way, even take you personally to your hotel, restaurant or museum. But if no-one materialises, don't panic, simply follow the tourist signs for *Centro Storico* (historic centre) and *Duomo* (cathedral), and remember that *senso unico* means one way. Then find the first *parcheggio* (car park) and abandon your car, for most Italian cities are best explored on foot. If you arrive by train, the station will invariably be in the seedier part of town, so leave it behind for the greener pastures of the Centro Storico.

Modern life has stamped even small villages with a bar and a large population of motor-cycle-riding youths. Every town has its Duomo, but how different is the austere Romanesque cathedral of Apulia from the lavish baroque of the one in Turin. Every town has at least one piazza: in the south they are crowded with men smoking and playing cards; in the north, the men are still there, but so are the women and the tourists.

Our favourite places in Italy include many spots less frequented than the tried and true trio of Rome, Florence and Venice. We suggest that, after visiting Rome, you take an excursion east into Abruzzo or Molise, those hitherto remote regions whose architecture, parks, mountains and beaches rank among the most refreshing vacation spots in the country. Or, if you happen to be exploring the Bay of Naples, rent a car and continue down to Italy's heel and toe – Apulia, Basilicata, Calabria.

The north has Florence and Venice, of course, but also Milan and Turin, two very modern cities packed with art and history. You could follow the path of generations of travellers who, with Dante and Ariosto in hand, toured the cities of Lombardy, Venetia, Emilia-Romagna and Tuscany. If you want to catch your breath and relax, retreat into the green hills of Umbria, home of Italy's beloved St Francis of Assisi.

Preceding pages: the snow-covered Dolomites; view over Bologna; St Peter's, Rome; walking through a marble maze.

Rome

800 m / 0,5 miles

136

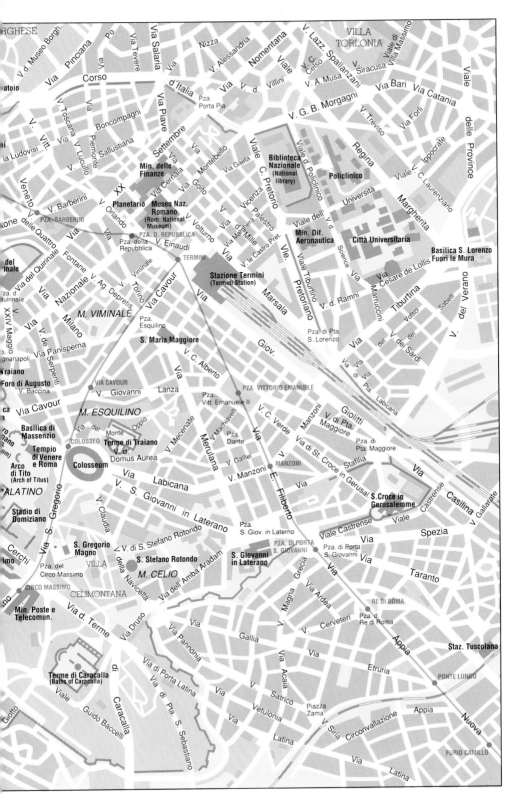

ROME

"City of the Soul" was the epithet Lord Byron gave to Rome (Roma). Poetic hyperbole perhaps, but the description still strikes a chord in visitors to the city. Though less efficient and sophisticated than Milan, less picturesque and well-preserved than Florence or Venice, Rome remains, in Thomas Hardy's words, "Time's central city". More than any other city, it helps us understand ourselves, our "petty misery" (Byron) and the fragility of the world.

The Palatine Hill: The best introduction to Rome is not Piazza Venezia, the terrifying roundabout at the centre of the modern city, but the more pastoral **Palatine Hill**, believed by the ancients to be the home of Rome's mythical founder, Romulus. On a more prosaic level, its claim to be the site of the original settlement is supported by the remains of early Iron Age dwellings in the southwest corner of the hill.

Close by are the remains of the **Tempio di Cibele**, picturesquely planted with an ilex grove. The cult of the eastern goddess of fertility, also known as Magna Mater, was introduced to Italy during the Second Punic War (218–201 BC). Though its mystical rites – throngs of frenzied female worshippers, self-mutilation of priests, sacrifices of bulls – were distasteful to old-fashioned Romans, the cult spread widely in the imperial era.

The name Palatine, said to be derived from Pales, the goddess of shepherds, is the root of the word palace. In Roman times this hill was celebrated for the splendour of its princely dwellings. Earliest, and simplest of these was the **Domus Augustana**. A portion of it, erroneously called the **Casa di Livia** (Livia was Augustus's wife), is renowned for its *trompe l'oeil* wall paintings.

To the north, alongside the **Palazzo di Tiberio** (now mostly covered by the Farnese Gardens) runs the **Cripto-porticus**, a cool underground passage with a delicately stuccoed vault, built by Nero to connect the palaces of Augustus, Tiberius and Caligula to his own sumptuous Golden House on the Esquiline Hill. To the southeast of this passage extend the remains of the **Palazzo dei Flavi**, built at the end of the 1st century AD by the Emperor Domitian. An infamous sadist, who took pleasure in torturing everything from flies to senators, Domition suffered from an obsessive fear of assassination. According to the ancient historian Suetonius, an entertaining if not entirely trustworthy source, the emperor covered the walls of the peristyle (the room with an octagonal maze) with reflective moonstone so that no assassin could creep up on him unobserved. Next to the peristyle lie the remains of a splendid banqueting hall, hailed by contemporaries as "the dining room of Jove". Its buckling pavement, still covered with pink and yellow marbles, gives some sense of its former grandeur. To the south lie the extensive remains of the **Domus Augustana** and the **Stadium**.

Following the fortunes of the city as a whole, the imperial palaces fell into disuse during the Middle Ages; monks made their home among the ruins; the powerful Frangipani family built a fortress here. Then, during the Renaissance, when there was a surge of new building throughout the city, Cardinal Alexander Farnese bought a large part of the Palatine and laid out the gardens on the slope overlooking the Forum. The lush **Orti Farnesiani** are delightful. They offer symmetrical landscaping, soothing sounds of fountains and birds and good views over Rome.

For lovers of the picturesque, the ruins of the Palatine are hard to beat. Even archaeologists' excavations cannot deprive this location of its wild charm. It is the last remaining place in Rome where you can find a landscape as it might have been drawn by Piranesi or Claude Lorraine. Roses, moss, bright poppies growing amidst the crumbling bricks and shattered marble give this location a romantic rather than an imperial splendour. It is the perfect place in which to wander, sketch or picnic.

The Roman Forum: The **Clivus Palatinus** leads from the domestic ex-

Left, view from the Vatican.

travagances of the emperors down into the **Forum**, the civic centre of ancient Rome. This area, once a swamp used as a burial ground by the original inhabitants of the surrounding hills, was drained by an Etruscan king in the 6th century BC. Until excavations began in the 19th century, the Forum, buried under 8 metres (25ft) of dirt, was known as the "Campo Vaccino" because *contadini* tended their herds among the ruins. Today it reveals a stupendous array of ruined temples, public buildings, arches and shops. The overall effect is impressive, but identifying individual buildings can be hard work. We will wander through, stopping at only the most interesting sights.

At the bottom of the Clivus Palatinus rises the **Arco di Tito** which commemorates that emperor's destruction of Jerusalem and its sacred temple. This event marked the beginning of the Diaspora and the shift from the temple to local synagogues as the focus of Jewish worship. Until Israel was founded in 1948 and the return to Palestine became possible, pious Jews refused to walk under the arch.

The **Via Sacra** leads past the three remaining arches of the **Basilica di Constantino**, a source of inspiration for Renaissance architects. Bramante said of his design for St Peter's: "I shall place the Pantheon on top of the Basilica of Constantine." **The Tempio di Antonino e Faustina**, also known as **San Lorenzo Miranda**, is a superb example of Rome's architectural layering. Originally a temple erected in AD 141 by the Emperor Antoninus Pius, it was converted into a church in the Middle Ages. During the 17th century a baroque facade was added, as was the case with so many Roman churches.

Across the Via Sacra is the lovely, round **Tempio di Vesta** (goddess of the hearth), where the six vestal virgins took turns tending the sacred fire. The punishment for allowing the fire to die down was a whipping by the priest. Service was for 30 years and chastity was the rule. Few patricians were eager to offer their daughters and the Emperor

Classical, medieval and baroque coexist around the Roman Forum.

Augustus had to pick girls by lot. Laxity about vows was common and the Emperor Domitian resorted to the traditional punishment of burying errant virgins alive and stoning their lovers to death in the comitium. The lovely **Casa delle Vestali** was some compensation for this demanding life. The ruined buildings and their garden remain a rose-scented haven.

Rather like 20th-century Americans, the ancient Romans were keen litigators. Walk past the three elegant columns of the **Tempio dei Castori** to the **Basilica di Guilio** (on the left of the Via Sacra), where trials were held, as many as four at one time. The acoustics were terrible and on one occasion the booming speech of a particularly loud lawyer was applauded by audiences in all four chambers. In cases where an advocate wanted a little extra help, professional applauders, called "supper praisers", could be hired. When not employed, these claqueurs would loiter on the steps of the basilica and play games. Their roughly carved boards can still be seen.

The senate met across the way in the **Curia**, the best preserved building in the Forum. Its sombre, solid appearance fits the seriousness of its purpose – though there too, as in the basilica, conditions could be overcrowded.

At the western end of the Forum rises the famed **Rostra**, where the orator Cicero declaimed to the Roman masses. After his death, during Octavian's anti-Republican proscriptions, Cicero's hands and head were displayed here. Opposite the rostra is the single **Colonna di Foca**. For centuries the symbol of the Forum, it was described by Byron as the "eloquent and nameless column with the buried base". Unburied and named, it is still, as the Italians say, *molto suggestivo*. To the right is the **Arco di Settimio Severo**.

At the end of the Via Sacra, in the shadow of the Capitoline Hill, rise the eight ionic columns of the **Tempio di Saturno**. The god's festival, called the Saturnalia, marked the merriest occasion in the Roman calendar, when gifts were exchanged and distinctions between

A fragment of a glorious past.

master and slave forgotten. Behind the temple are, from left to right, the graceful **Portico degli dei Consenti**, the **Tempio di Vespasiano e Tito** and the **Tempio della Concordia**.

Outside the Forum excavations, across from Pietro da Cortona's **Chiesa di SS Luca e Martina**, is the **Carcere Tulliano** (Mamertine Prison), home of some of Rome's most famous prisoners. A plaque on the wall lists how they met their unhappy ends: strangling, starvation, torture, decapitation. According to Catholic legend, this dank, gloomy dungeon was where St Peter converted his pagan guards. Miraculously, a fountain sprang up so that he could baptise the new Christians.

From the Capitoline Hill the Temple of Jupiter Capitolinus (dedicated 509 BC) watched over the city. It was also here that modern Italians raised their tribute to Italy's unification after 1,400 years of fragmentation. The **Vittoriano** (Victor Emmanuel monument), completed in 1911 and dedicated to Italy's first king, captures the neoclassical bad taste of the 19th century. Natives and visitors alike claim to despise this "typewriter" or "wedding cake".

Throughout Rome's history hopes for Italy's future have centred on this hill. In 1300, the poet Petrarch was crowned here; in 1347 Cola di Rienzo roused the Roman populous to support his shortlived attempt to revive the Roman Republic; in the 16th century Michelangelo planned the elegant Campidoglio, thus restoring the Capitoline's status as the architectural focal point of the city; and it was here that the historian Edward Gibbon drew inspiration for *The Decline and Fall of the Roman Empire*.

If you're feeling energetic, climb the 124 steps to the medieval **S Maria a' Aracoeli** (if you happen to be here at Christmas, come for the midnight mass). The weak-kneed will probably prefer Michelangelo's regal staircase (known as **La Cordonata**), flanked at the top by monumental statues of Castor and Pollux. In the back of the **Campidoglio** the **Palazzo Senatorio** surmounts the ancient **Tabularium** dating from Re-

The Campidoglio designed by Michelangelo.

publican times. On the left rises the **Palazzo dei Conservatori**, on the right, **the Palazzo del Museo Capitolino**, each housing art collections. For insight into ancient Roman character, study the busts of emperors in the **Sala degli Imperatori** in the Museo Capitolino. Realistic portraiture was Rome's greatest contribution to the art of sculpture.

Mussolini's legacy: Piazza Venezia, at the foot of the Vittoriano monument, marks the centre of contemporary Rome. You may feel you risk your life by crossing its wide expanse but usually the torrents of traffic will part to allow a pedestrian passage. The **Palazzo Venezia** dominates one side. Rome's first great Renaissance palace (built 1455), this was Mussolini's headquarters from 1929 on. Some of his most famous speeches were delivered from this balcony. The light burning in his bedroom at all hours of the day and night reassured the Italians that the "sleepless one" was busy solving the nation's problems (though according to Luigi Barzini the light was often left on

when Mussolini was not there). Now the palace contains the **Museo del Palazzo Venezia** with its collection of paintings, sculptures and tapestries.

"Ten years from now, comrades, no one will recognise Italy," proclaimed Il Duce in 1926. One of the most dramatic changes the fascists wrought on Rome was the **Via dei Fori Imperiali**. Mussolini cut down old neighbourhoods (reminders of Rome's decadent period) in order to excavate the fora and build the road. Thus he made a symbolic connection between Rome's glorious, distant past and his regime.

Westernmost of the Imperial fora is **Trajan's Fora**, dominated by its famous **Colonna**. Behind are the splendidly preserved **Mercati Traiano**, a favourite haunt of Rome's ubiquitous *gatti*. In ancient times the five storeys of the market were abundantly stocked with exotic fare. The top floor contained two fishponds, one of which received water from an aqueduct, while the other held sea water brought all the way from Ostia. Cunning vendors attracted customers

The *Dying Gaul*, Capitoline Museum.

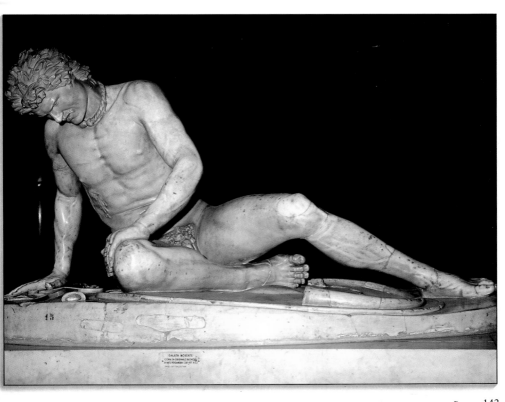

by displaying monkeys whose clever antics proved to be an effective magnet.

Augustus and Nerva both built their fora to accommodate Rome's growing population and passion for litigation. Statues of the emperors stand opposite their fora.

Finally, at the end of all this ruined splendour, rises the **Colosseum**, stripped of its picturesque wildflowers and weeds, surrounded by buses and snack stands, encircled by a swirling moat of traffic. This symbol of the Eternal City is less splendid than it was in its marble-clad, imperial days, less picturesque than in its tumble-down Romantic period; but, scientifically excavated, much of it roped off to ensure the safety of both visitor and building, it remains one of the key sights of Rome.

The Colosseum was built in AD 79 when the Emperor Vespasian drained the lake of Nero's **Domus Aurea** (Golden House). The message was clear: where Nero had been profligate, emptying the coffers of the empire to construct his own personal pleasure palace, the Flavian prince built a public monument.

Now the public can also enjoy Nero's domestic extravaganza on top of the **Esquiline Hill**. Upon completion of the Domus Aurea, the emperor is said to have remarked "At last I can begin to live like a human being!" Also near the Colosseum is the **Arco di Constantino**.

Architectural layer cake: From the Colosseum, Via San di Giovanni Laterano brings you to **San Clemente**, one of Rome's most interesting churches. There are three levels of building. A 12th-century basilica descends to a 4th-century basilica, which in turn leads to a 1st-century Roman *palazzo* and an apartment building containing, in its courtyard, a Mithraic temple honouring one of the popular cults of imperial Rome. The excavations are extremely well documented in a little booklet called *St Clement's Rome*, on sale here.

A little further along, Via di San Giovanni opens up into the piazza of that name, containing some of the most important buildings in Christendom. The **Obelisk** is the tallest and oldest in Rome

Far left, **Trajan's Column**. **Right**, *in restauro*.

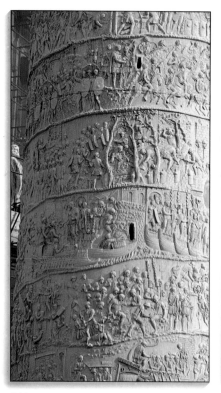

and a suitable marker for the Church of Rome, **S Giovanni in Laterano**, founded by Constantine the Great. Not surprisingly, such an important church is a hodge-podge of building styles, from the exquisite 4th-century baptistry (custodian will show mosaics) to the peaceful medieval cloister, to the majestic baroque interior. The **Palazzo Laterano** was the home of the popes until the Avignon exile in 1309. The pious may want to ascend the nearby **Scala Santa** (on their knees of course), said to be the steps Christ walked down after being condemned by Pontius Pilate. Constantine's mother, St Helena, retrieved them from Jerusalem.

The ghetto: Rome's old **ghetto** lies on the other (west) side of the Capitoline Hill, near the ruins of the **Teatro di Marcello**. The city has had a Jewish community since the Republican era, but its isolation dates from the Counter-Reformation and Pope Paul IV (1555–59). From then on, the gates to the ghetto were locked from sunset to sunrise, Jewish men had to wear a yellow hat, the women a yellow scarf, and most professions were closed to Jews. "The iron of persecution and insult is every day driven into their souls," wrote one outraged 19th-century American. At that time the Jews were forced several times a year to listen to a tirade from a Dominican friar in **S Angelo in Pescheria**.

Wandering through the narrow streets or visiting the **Synagogue** on the Tiber, one gets little sense of those years of confinement. A plaque on **Via Portico d'Ottavia**, however, is a reminder that just 50 or so years ago more than 2,000 Roman Jews were deported to a concentration camp.

The Via del Teatro Marcello leads to **Piazza Bocca della Verità**, which yokes together two Roman Temples (**Tempio di Portuno** and the round **Tempio d'Ercole**), a baroque fountain and the medieval **S Maria in Cosmedin**. In the portico of the Byzantine rite church is the **Bocca della Verità**, a marble slab resembling a human face and considered to be one of the world's oldest lie detectors. If a perjurer puts his hand in

Enduring and immutable, the Colosseum today.

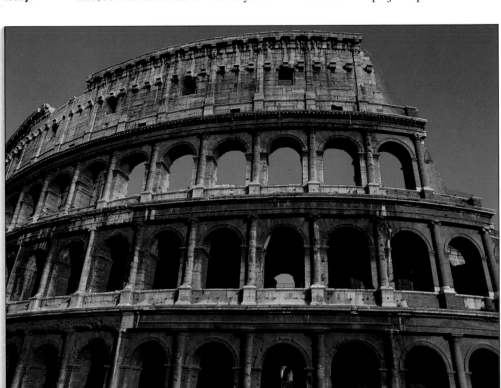

the mouth, so the legend goes, it will be bitten off. In fact, the slab's origin is sadly prosaic: it once covered a drain.

The oldest and largest of the famed Roman circuses, the **Circus Maximus**, lies in the valley between the Aventine and Palatine Hills. It once seated 250,000 people. In addition to the main event, vendors, fortune tellers and prostitutes plied their trades beneath the arcades.

If the circus has earned the ancient Romans a bad reputation, their public baths have inspired great praise. The **Terme di Caracalla** boasted, in addition to the three pools (hot, warm and cold), exercise rooms, libraries and lecture halls, for the improvement of mind and body. But less salubrious activities also went on here, especially when mixed bathing was permitted. Some took their cleanliness to an extreme. The Emperor Commodus is said to have taken eight baths a day. But for the most part, the baths represent a triumph of the Roman public spirit. Cleanliness was not limited to those rich enough to have private facilities.

The Terme di Caracalla are now used for opera in the summer.

The affluent Aventine: For a contrast to the dusty and barren remnants of the circus and baths, visit the **Aventine**, one of modern Rome's most desirable residential neighbourhoods. As you climb the **Cliva dei Pubblici** the smell of roses wafts down from the pretty garden at the top of the hill. The Via Sabina leads to **Santa Sabina**, a perfectly preserved basilican church of the 5th century. Inside shafts of Rome's golden sunlight light up the immense antique columns of the nave. Outside, in the portico, are some of the oldest wooden doors in existence (5th century).

On the other side of the Aventine, in the shadow of the **Pirimide Cestio**, lies the **Cimitero Acattolico** (Protestant Cemetery), one of the most picturesque spots in Rome. Scores of unfortunate travellers who fell fatally ill on a wedding trip or Grand Tour are buried here. In the old part of the graveyard is Keats's tomb. Its sad epitaph reads "Here lies one whose name was writ in water".

Boy scouts on a cultural excursion.

The modern part of the cemetery contains Shelley's heart. His body was burned on the shore near Pisa. As his dear friend Lord Byron put it: "All of Shelley was consumed, except his heart, which could not take the flame and is now preserved in spirits of wine."

Outside the **Porta San Paolo** is the basilica of **San Paolo Fuori le Muri**, one of the major basilicas of Rome. It is believed to house the tomb of St Paul.

The beauty of baroque: Exuberant, awe-inspiring and outrageous, baroque architecture offers such an over-profusion of detail, painting, gilt and marble that it often overwhelms. But what pleasure there is in discovering a particularly winning *putto* winking at you from an architrave, in craning to see a fantastic ceiling by Pietro da Cartona or Andrea Pozzo, in calculating the time and expense spent on covering every inch of a building in marble, gilt and precious metals, and in seeing saints and biblical figures made flesh and blood by Caravaggio or Bernini.

The baroque style dominates in Rome and the best place to start appreciating it is the **Gesù**. The church was started in 1568 for the recently approved Jesuit order, champions of the Counter-Reformation. The Council of Trent (1545–63) laid down the rigorous principles for strengthening the Catholic Church against the Protestant heretics. Originally, the Gesù was meant to be austere; its baroque makeover was performed in the late 17th century. By this time the Counter-Reformers had discovered art's role as a means of making the intangible more accessible to the faithful. Baroque art also impressed upon the masses the immense power of the Church. Andrea Pozzo's altar to St Ignatius in the Gesù is particularly sumptuous.

But it is the Gesù's ceiling, with Baciccio's painting *The Triumph of the Name of Jesus*, that shows what baroque is all about. White statues cling to the gilt vault, some supporting the central painting which spills out of its frame. Here is the characteristic baroque blend of architecture, painting and sculpture, all working to reinforce the role of a

The Baths of Caracalla.

church as a place between this world and the next. The vault of the church seems almost to dissolve into the vault of heaven.

Another Jesuit church, **S Ignazio**, this time with a ceiling by Andrea Pozzo, is also an impressive example of baroque. To appreciate its fantastic perspective stand in the middle of the nave and look heavenwards: the vault seems to disappear as an ecstatic St Ignatius receives from Jesus the light he will disperse to the four corners of the earth. Pozzo also painted a fake dome, since the Jesuit fathers were unable to afford a real one.

The **Piazza S Ignazio** reveals the theatrical side of baroque. The perfectly balanced palaces were designed by Philippo Raguzzini to look like the wings of a set. Centre stage is the church.

Carnaval Corso: Via del Corso stretches from Piazza Venezia to **Piazza del Popolo**, a distance of almost a mile. Lined with elegant palaces and crowded with shoppers, this central artery has always been a good place in which to take the pulse of the city. In ancient times it was the main route north, known as the Via Lata (Wide Way), which gives an idea of how very narrow most ancient streets were. Its present name derives from races run down its length during the Middle Ages. More recently (between the 18th and 19th centuries) it was the scene of the Roman Carnival, when aristocrats and riff-raff alike used to pelt one another with flowers, bonbons and confetti. Masked revellers abandoned all discretion; to facilitate the ogling of ladies and the hurling of missiles, temporary balconies were attached to the palaces. This chaotic setting provided a dramatic background for the climax of Hawthorne's *Marble Faun*. Alas, Rome has sobered up since it became the nation's capital. So for Carnival, head for Venice.

First stop on a tour of the Corse is **Palazzo Doria**, home of the **Galleria Doria Pamphili**. The collection is superb (paintings by Titian, Caravaggio and Raphael), but nothing is labelled, so unless you're a connoisseur of 16th- and 17th-century art, buy a catalogue.

Left, baroque ceiling in the Jesuit church, **Gesù**. **Right**, Via del Corso.

The star of the collection is Velazquez's portrait of Pope Innocent X.

Via delle Muratte, to the right off the Corso, leads to the most grandiose and famous of Rome's baroque fountains: the **Fontana di Trevi** in whose waters the voluptuous Anita Ekberg frolicked in Fellini's *La Dolce Vita*.

But the ancient city rears its head even in the most up-to-date places. **Piazza Colonna**, on the left off the Corso, is home to the **Colonna di Marco Aurelio** (AD 180–93). Sixtus V (1585–90) crowned this column with a statue of St Paul and Trajan's column with one of St Peter. (Sixtus was always eager to appropriate Roman triumphal symbols to Christianity. He placed many fallen, forgotten obelisks in front of churches.)

Two particularly impressive relics of the Augustan era, cleaned up and reassembled during the fascist era, are the **Mausoleo di Augusto** and the **Ara Pacis Augustae** (left off Via del Corso). The emperor's funeral pyre burned in front of the mausoleum for five days. In the Middle Ages the ill-fated Cola di Rienzo

was cremated there. For centuries the Ara Pacis, built between 13 and 8 BC to celebrate peace throughout the Empire, was in pieces. Fragments were to be found as far away as the Louvre in Paris and the Uffizi in Florence. Finally, in 1983, the altar was reconstructed with fragments and copies of missing parts.

The gate of Rome: Nowadays most people enter the Piazza del Popolo from one of the three fingers that lead to its south side: Via del Corso, in the middle; Via Ripetta on the left (from the Mausoleo di Augustus); and Via del Babuino on the right, from Piazza di Spagna. But the Piazza was intended to be seen from the north. Everyone from emperors in triumph to pilgrims on foot used to enter Rome through the **Porta del Popolo** (Porta Flaminia). On the east rises the lush green of the Pincian where, in the Middle Ages, the Emperor Nero's ghost was believed to wander. According to legend, a walnut tree infested with crows sprang from Nero's final resting place. In the 11th century, however, Pope Paschall II dreamt that

The Trevi Fountain.

the crows were demons and that the Virgin Mary wanted him to cut down the tree and build her a sanctuary. The existing church of **S Maria del Popolo** dates from the late 15th century and contains splendidly decorated chapels of different periods, with works by Pintorrichio, Raphael (Chigi Chapel) and Caravaggio (*Conversion of St Paul* and *Crucifixion of St Peter*).

Take the Via del Babuino, on the left of the twin baroque churches, south to the **Piazza di Spagna**. The piazza is shaped like an hour glass. In the southern section is the **Palazzo di Spagna**, once the residence of the Spanish ambassador. But it is in the northern part that the famous **Scalinata della Trinità dei Monti** (otherwise known as the Spanish Steps) rise. Neither New York City's Times Square nor Paris's Champs-Elysées provides a better location for watching the world go by. Caricaturists sketch tourists; old women sell roasted chestnuts or coconuts; gypsy children solicit lire, often with the help of an accordion or an endearing kitten; tired

sightseers rinse their hands in Pietro Bernini's fountain; backpackers sunbathe on the steps; hippies play guitars; and shoppers crowd the windows of the elegant shops below. Off this piazza stretch the most fashionable shopping streets in Rome: **Via Condotti**, **Via Frattina**, **Via Borgognona**. Underneath the Pincian, the quiet **Via Margutta** is the place to buy art.

Years ago this area was inhabited by English and American expatriates. John Keats died in the house overlooking the steps, which contains a cluttered collection of memorabilia. The **Keats and Shelley Museum** is a must for all romantic ghost seekers.

Keep an eye out for plaques marking the past residences of famous foreigners. Henry James stayed in **Hotel Inghilterra**; Shelley in the Via Sistina and Via del Corso; George Eliot in the Via del Babuino; Goethe at 20 Via del Corso, where you can visit a museum devoted to the poet's travels in Italy. One of the most grandiose plaques marks James Joyce's residence at 50/52 Via

Left, one of many obelisks brought from Egypt, in Piazza del Popolo. Right, the church of Trinità dei Monti.

Frattina. The Irish novelist, it says, "made of his Dublin, our universe".

Climb La Scalinata to the church of **Trinità dei Monti**, where Mendelssohn listened to the famous choir of nuns who could be heard but not seen. Legend has it that in the 19th century one of the nuns would admit the public but make sure all handsome young men were excluded. The church, which was partially destroyed when French soldiers quartered here in 1816, contains paintings by Michelangelo's most talented pupil, Danielle di Volterra.

The bones and the bees: The street between Trinità dei Monti and S Maria Maggiore was cut by Sixtus V, a pope bent on improving Rome and glorifying his own name. The view down the length of the road is dramatic – culminating in the obelisk which Sixtus raised in front of S Maria Maggiore. Once called Strada Felice, the street now changes its name three times as it cuts through the tangled Roman streets.

The first leg, **Via Sistina**, leads down to **Piazza Barberini**, in the centre of which is Bernini's magnificently sensual **Fontana del Tritone**. The musclebound sea creature blows fiercely on a conch shell while a geyser of water shoots above him. In the base is the unmistakable coat of arms of the Barberini family: three bees. The family palace nearby is the work of, among others, Carlo Maderno, Bernini and Borromini. In the 19th century, William Wetmore Story, a second rate neoclassical sculptor from Boston, was able to rent a 50-room suite in the palace for a song, but today the **Palazzo Barberini** houses the **Galleria Nazionale**. Don't miss Pietro da Cortona's *The Triumph of Divine Providence*, a baroque celebration of the Barberini Pope Urban VIII – a pope who quarried the ruins of ancient Rome so extensively that he inspired the pasquinade: "What the Barbarians didn't do, the Barberini did".

Via Veneto swoops off the Piazza Barberini. Before strolling along its wide streets or retiring to one of its cafés, be sure to stop at the **Chiesa dei Cappuccini** to see its cemetery. According

The Spanish Steps.

to Catholic legend, a group of artistically and ghoulishly inclined friars decided to put the dead brothers' bones to a cautionary use. Four rooms of rococo sculptures contain a playful filigree of hip bones, a garland of spines and an array of skulls stacked as neatly as oranges and apples in a fruit vendor's stall. In case anyone should forget these are bones and begin to look on them as mere elements in an elegant design, there are also a few rotting corpses, still swathed in their humble brown robes.

La Dolce Vita: The Via Veneto became famous after World War II as the centre of Rome's "Dolce Vita", but today it seems more sleazy than glamorous. Yes, some of the best hotels are around here – the glitzy **Excelsior** and the ultra-comfortable **Jolly**, for example – but so are the prostitutes and fast-food restaurants. Buy a magazine, put on your dark glasses and adjourn to one of the streetside cafés for refreshment, then move onto the **Villa Borghese** where you can picnic or visit the **Giardino Zoologico**. Near the Via Veneto entrance to

the park is the **Galleria Borghese**, with many works by Bernini, Caravaggio and Raphael. If you're interested in Italy's more recent achievements in the arts, visit the **Galleria Nazionale d'Arte Moderna**.

To the north of the Villa Borghese is another aristocratic pleasure palace built for Julius III. The **Villa Giulia** has a beautiful Renaissance garden and, inside, the **Museo Nazionale di Villa Giulia**, full of pre-Roman art. Especially interesting are the Etruscan terracotta sculptures: a touching sarcophagus of a husband and wife and a magnificent statue of Apollo.

Bernini and Borromini: From the intersection of Via delle Quatro Fontane (the extension of Via Sistine) and **Via XX Settembre** you can admire the drama of Roman urban planning: in three directions obelisks scrape the sky. The Via XX Settembre contains a number of splendid baroque churches. First is **San Carlo alle Quattro Fontane**, also known as **San Carlino**. This tiny church, whose interior is the same size as one of the piers under the dome of St Peter's, was designed by Francesco Borromini (1599–1667). The undulating facade is characteristic of this eccentric architect's style. The all-white interior is a fantastic play of ovals. The financially pressed monks who commissioned the church were impressed by Borromini's ability to keep down the costs of the church – by using delicate stucco work rather than marble or gilt – without in any way lessening the beauty.

Up Via Quirinale, off the other side of Via delle Quattro Fontane, is another oval gem by Borromini's arch rival, Gianlorenzo Bernini (1598–1680). **San Andrea al Quirinale** offers quite a contrast to its neighbour. Every inch of this church is covered with gilt and marble. *Puttis* ascend the wall as if in a cloud of smoke. Yet the architect's masterful, classical handling of space creates a marvellous sense of simplicity.

For another Bernini masterpiece head in the other direction to **Santa Maria della Vittoria** in Largo Santa Susanna (off Via XX Septembre). Here in the Cornaro chapel is Bernini's sculpture of

Triton Fountain, Piazza Barberini.

the 17th-century Spanish mystic **S Theresa of Avila**. The artist captures her at the moment when she is being struck by the arrow of divine love.

To get a sense of how huge Roman baths were, visit **Santa Maria Degli Angeli** (near Piazza Repubblica), a church Michelangelo created from the tepidarium of the **Terme di Diocleziano**, the largest baths in Rome, constructed between AD 298 and 306. They also house the **Museo Nazionale Romano**, one of the greatest collections of ancient art in the world. Sculptures include the Venus of Cyrene, two copies of Myron's Discobolus and the Ludovisi throne. Roman wall painting is seen at its best in the delicate frescoes from the dining room of the Villa of Livia. They depict a refreshing garden scene with fruits, trees and birds, designed to sooth the digestion of the empress's guests.

Mary and Moses: The Italian reverence for mothers perhaps explains why Rome has more churches dedicated to the Virgin Mary than to any other saint. The largest and most splendid of these is **Santa Maria Maggiore**, one of the four patriarchal churches of Rome. Here the melange of architectural styles is surprisingly harmonious: early Christianity is represented in the basilican form and in the 5th-century mosaics above the architrave in the nave (binoculars are a must if you want to decipher them). Medieval input includes the Campanile (largest in Rome), the Cosmatesque pavement and the mosaic in the apse. But the overwhelming effect is baroque. The coffered gold ceiling seems miraculously suspended (it was supposedly gilded with the gold Columbus brought from America).

If your head is spinning with the excess of gilt and marble, head down the **Via Cavour** to **S Pietro in Vincoli**, where you will find Michelangelo's massive and dignified *Moses*. Originally the statue was to form part of an enormous freestanding tomb for Pope Julius II, but politics and constrained finances curtailed Michelangelo's imagination. Of this one statue Giorgio Vasari, artist and biographer of artists,

Borghese Park.

said: "No modern work will ever approach it in beauty, nor ancient either." Moses sits 3 metres (10 ft) high, every inch the powerful lawgiver. Today the tomb provides entrance, not to another world, but to a cluttered gift shop, where you can buy, among other things, replicas of the statue.

Medieval Rome: During the Middle Ages, most of Rome's population was crowded either into the region between Via Del Corso and the **Tiber (Campus Martius** to the ancients) or into **Trastevere** across the river. While wandering through the cobblestoned streets of these areas, especially late at night, it is easy to imagine the Rome of the medieval tyrant Cola di Rienzo, or Pope Julius II, or even Byron – at least until the spell is broken by the roar of a speeding motorcycle. An even better time to tour Trastevere or the Campus Martius is the early morning, when you will be able to admire the facades of buildings alone, enter churches with only the faithful as companions, and watch the Romans starting their day.

Windowless shops give directly onto crooked, narrow streets and workers leave their doors open for light and air. Look in and you will see bakers kneading loaves of *casareccio* bread, furniture restorers rubbing down wood with strong smelling ointments, and cobblers hammering heels onto worn boots. Children walk to school and women drag metal carts to market. Occasionally a door glides open in the side of a crumbling stucco facade to release a shiny black Fiat.

Have a *cornetto* (Italian croissant) and a cappuccino in the **Piazza della Rotondo** and admire the outside of the **Pantheon** – the best preserved of all ancient Roman buildings. For those who question the greatness of Roman architecture and dismiss it as inferior to Greek, the Pantheon is an eloquent answer. This perfectly proportioned round temple proves how adept the Romans were in shaping interior space. Rebuilt by the Emperor Hadrian, its architectural antecedents are not the Republican round temples such as the one in the Forum Boarum, but the round rooms used in baths. Western architecture owes the Romans a great debt for their skilful work with vaults and domes.

Near the Pantheon in front of **Santa Maria Sopra Minerva**, Bernini's much-loved elephant carries the smallest of Rome's obelisks. Inside the church (the only one in the Gothic style in Rome) are a chapel decorated by Fra Lippo Lippi and, to the left of the main altar, Michelangelo's statue of Christ bearing the Cross. Other ecclesiastical treasures are just a few blocks away. Caravaggio frescoes adorn both **San Luigi dei Francesi** (*Calling of St Matthew*) and **S Agostino** (*Madonna of the Pilgrims*). Borromini's **S Ivo** is tucked into the courtyard of **Palazzo Sapienza**. Like San Carlino's, this church's interior is dazzlingly white. Most startling, however, is its spiralling campanile.

Even the crowds of people milling around eating ice cream, the artists sitting on collapsible chairs hoping to sell their paintings, and Roman youths zooming through on their motorbikes cannot disguise the elegance of the Pi-

Michelangelo's *Moses* at the church of S Pietro in Vincoli.

azza Navona. This completely enclosed space was once the Stadium of Domitian, parts of which can still be seen outside the northern end. Hagiographers claim that when the youthful S Agnese was exposed naked in the vaulted areas of the circus beneath the church that bears her name, her hair grew to shield her.

Agnese had refused to marry because she had vowed to be a virgin bride of Christ. In another version of her martyrdom she was banished to a brothel where her chastity was miraculously preserved; a subsequent attempt to burn her was also unsuccessful; finally, she was beheaded.

The church **S Agnese in Agone** has another curvaceous facade by Borromini. His rival Bernini designed the **Fontana dei Fiumi** in the centre of the piazza. A popular tale claims that the statue of the Nile which faces S Agnese is covering its eyes for fear the church will collapse.

While in the piazza, you may wish to gorge on a *Tartuffo* from **Tre Scalini**.

Stony words: Close by, **Piazza di Pasquino** contains a battered statue that once functioned as the underground newspaper of Rome. The papal censors allowed so little criticism that irrepressible commentators attached their writings to statues in the city. The most famous satirist was Pasquino, hence the word pasquinade.

Near the piazza is the elegant little church of **S Maria della Pace**. The facade and piazza may be all you can see, since the church is rarely open. If you do make it inside there are frescoes by Raphael and a beautiful cloister. To the north, **Via dei Coronari** is lit with torches every night. The picturesque street is full of expensive antique stores.

At the end of Via dei Cornari, take a left and you will soon arrive at the **Chiesa Nuova**, dedicated to St Philip Neri, without question one of the most *simpatico* saints in the calendar. He arrived in Rome in 1533 and spent the rest of his life gently trying to reform the population of the sinful city. He invited young men off the streets and into his room for informal discussions of the

The Pantheon is the best preserved ancient building in Rome.

Gospel, prayers and song. From this simple beginning arose his oratory. St Philip refused to withdraw from the world or condemn it, preferring to work steadily and with great humour to save souls. He once advised an overly zealous penitent to wear his hairshirt on the outside of his clothes.

The baroque splendour of the Chiesa Nuova was never intended by this humble man, who had a weakness for practical jokes. But for fans of the style, Pietro da Cortona's interior is sumptuous. Behind the altar are three paintings by Rubens.

The last baroque church on this tour is perhaps the most ornate of all. Puccini chose **S Andrea della Valle** as a setting for the opening act of *Tosca*. Act II takes place at the nearby **Palazzo Farnese**, most splendid of Renaissance palaces and suitably intimidating as headquarters for the villainous Scarpia. The palace is now the French Embassy and, alas for the visitor who would like to pop in to see Annibale Carraci's frescoes, it is only open to the public for one hour on Sundays (11 am–12 noon). Other palaces in the neighbourhood include **Palazzo della Cancelleria**, and the **Palazzo Spada** which has a handsome gallery.

Act III of *Tosca* takes place across the river in the **Castel S Angelo**. The Mausoleum of Hadrian became in turn a fortress and then a prison; it is now a museum. The view from the parapet from which Tosca plunges to her death is splendid, enhanced by the presence of an enormous bronze angel.

The Vatican: From Castel S Angelo, via della Conciliazone leads to **St Peter's** and the **Vatican**. Church, museum, mausoleum, St Peter's is all three. No other temple surpasses it in terms of historical significance or architectural splendour. Some may feel that the immensity of the interior is more suited to moving commuters through a railway station than to inspiring the intimate act of prayer, but St Peter's many architects and patrons intended the building to symbolise worldly power as much as spiritual piety.

A tour of the Vatican should be divided into two parts: first, the piazza and church, then the museums.

Bernini's spectacular, colonnaded Piazza S Pietro is, according to one's viewpoint, either the welcoming embrace of the Mother Church or her grasping claws. The Via della Conciliazone, constructed in 1937 to commemorate the reconciliation between Mussolini and Pope Pius XI, changed the original impact of the space. Before this thoroughfare provided a monumental approach to St Peter's, the entrance was by way of a series of smaller streets, winding through the old Borgo and arriving, finally, in the enclosed open space, with the biggest church in the world at one end and an enormous, Egyptian obelisk in the centre.

Just about every important Renaissance and baroque architect from Bramante on had a hand in the design of St Peter's. The idea for rebuilding the original 4th-century basilica had been around since the mid-5th century, but not until Julius II became pope did a complete reconstruction get under way. Bramante was succeeded by Raphael, Baldassare Peruzzi, Michelangelo (usually credited with the dome), Giacomo della Porta and Bernini.

The vast size of the interior is offset by its proportions: thus the cherubic *putti* are actually 2 metres (6 ft) tall, as are the mosaic letters of the frieze that runs around the church. On the right as you walk in is Michelangelo's *Pietà*, an inspiration to beholders ever since the sculptor finished it in 1500 at the age of 25. At the end of the nave is the bronze statue of St Peter, its toe worn away by the kisses of pilgrims.

Over the high altar, which is directly above the tomb of St Peter, rises Bernini's garish bronze baldachin, thought by many to look like the canopy of an imperial bed. Pope Urban VIII stripped the bronze from the portico of the Pantheon. But Bernini outdid himself in the design for the Cathedra Petri (chair of St Peter) in the apse. Four gilt bronze figures of the church fathers hold up the chair. Above, light streams through the golden glass of a window crowned by a dove (symbol of the holy ghost). The chair bears a relief of Christ's command to Peter to "feed his sheep". Thus the position of the Pope is explained and bolstered by Christ's words and the teachings of the Church fathers, and blessed by the Holy Ghost.

Further confirmation of the Pope's sacred trust is found in the words of Christ inscribed in the dome: "You are Peter and on this rock I will build my Church and I will give to you the keys to the kingdom of heaven".

The **Musei e Gallerie del Vaticano** merits lifetime study. But for those who have only a few hours, some sights should not be missed. The **Museo Pio-Clementino** contains the pope's collection of antiquities. Be sure to visit the Belvedere Courtyard, home of the celebrated and cerebral Apollo Belvedere and the contrastingly writhing, muscle-bound sensual Laocoon. The Vatican Pinacoteca contains superb paintings including Raphael's *Madonna of Foligno* and *Transfiguration.*

Castel Sant' Angelo. There are also entire rooms covered in frescoes. The Stanze di Raffaello,

commissioned by Julius II, comprise three rooms painted by Raphael: **Stanza dell' Incendio di Borgo**; Stanza della Segnatura; Stanza di Eliodoro. Downstairs, delicate and colourful frescoes by Pintorricchio decorate the Appartamento Borgia.

But the triumph of fresco painting, not only of the Vatican Palace but of the entire world, is the **Cappella Sistina** (Sistine Chapel). The walls are covered in paintings by Botticelli, Pintoricchio and Ghirlandaio, but the breathtaking star of the show is Michelangelo's ceiling, begun in 1508 and completed by 1512. It is a shallow barrel vault divided into large and small panels tracing the history of the Creation.

No reproduction can ever do justice to the interplay of painting and architecture, to the drama of the whole chapel, alive with colour (considerably brighter since the controversial cleaning of the frescos in the 1980s) and human emotion. "All the world hastened to behold this marvel and was overwhelmed, speechless with astonishment," Vasari

wrote. The astonishment is no less to-day than it was in the Renaissance.

Trastevere: The heart of medieval **Trastevere**, literally "across the Tiber", is south of the Castello S Angelo. Here you can find many reasonably priced restaurants and, at **Porta Portese**, a popular flea market on Sunday. Traditionally Trastevere has been a working-class neighbourhood with strong communist leanings.

South of Viale di Trastevere are two churches worth visiting. **Santa Cecilia** was built on top of the house of a Christian martyr whom the Roman authorities attempted to scald to death in her own caldarium. When this failed, she was sentenced to decapitation, but three blows failed to sever her head and she lived for a further three days (enough time to consecrate her house as a church). Carlo Maderno's touching statue of the saint curled in a foetal position was inspired by his observations when her tomb was opened in 1599.

A contrastingly sublime statue of a woman in her death throes is Bernini's **Blessed Luisa Albertoni** in nearby **San Francesco a Ripa**. This late work of the master captures even more powerfully than his St Theresa the conflict between joy and sorrow felt by a woman who is between this world and the next.

Piazza S Maria in Trastevere contains one of the oldest churches in Rome. It boasts some beautiful mosaics illustrating the life of Mary. (This was the first of many Roman churches to be dedicated to the Virgin.)

After these sobering places of worship preoccupied by the horrors of this world and the glories of the next, it is a relief to come to the **Farnesina**, a jewel of the Renaissance, worldly and pagan. A ceiling fresco by Raphael details the love of Cupid and Psyche. The figures are robust, fleshy, almost Rubenesque. Breasts and buttocks are unabashedly displayed in a rollicking sea of banqueters. In the next room along, Raphael's *Galatea* captures the moment when the nymph, safe from the clutches of her pursuer, the cyclops Polyphemus, looks round.

Upstairs Baldassarre Peruzzi, who de-signed the entire villa, devised a fantastic *trompe l'oeil* . The room seems to open upon a restful village scene. In the bedroom is Sodoma's erotic painting *The Wedding of Alexander and Roxanne*.

To reach another important Renaissance monument, this time ecclesiastical, climb the steps up the Gianicolo to **S. Pietro in Montorio**. In the courtyard is Bramante's **Tempietto**, a circular church that marks what was once mistakenly believed to be the site of St Peter's martyrdom. Climb a little further to the **Fontana Paolo**, an impressive baroque monument that now serves as a busy car wash.

The shady **Passeggiata del Gianicolo** provides panoramic views over the city. You should be able to pick out some of your favourite monuments. Easiest to spot are the flat dome of the Pantheon, the twin domes of S Maria Maggiore and the Victor Emmanuel Monument.

Into the bowels of the earth: Visitors with more time in Rome should try to see remains from the early Christian era. The secretive beginnings of Christianity are recalled in **S Agnese Fuori le Mura**, about 2 km (1¼ miles) beyond Michelangelo's **Porta Pia** on the Via Nomentana. Beneath the church run extensive catacombs where the martyred Roman maiden St Agnes was buried. (*For her story, see page 155.*)

Also in the complex is the incomparable **Santa Costanza**, the mausoleum of Constantine's daughter. The ambulatory of this elegantly proportioned round building is encrusted with some of Rome's most beautiful mosaics.

And for those not averse to tortuous tunnels winding endlessly past burial niches dusty with disintegrated bones, there are countless catacombs outside the walls of Rome. The best way to see them is to spend a day on the picturesque **Via Appia Antica**. You can picnic amidst the remains of the **Villa Quintili** or an unnamed crumbling edifice overrun with wildflowers and lizards. Above ground sits the "stern round tower" (Byron) of the **Tomba di Cecilia Metella**. Below spread the **Catacombe di S Callisto** (most famous in Rome), **Santi Sebastiano** e **Domitilla**.

Right, inside St Peter's.

ROME ENVIRONS

The fascists' boast was that they represented the continuation of ancient Rome. Mussolini's claim to imperial inheritance was based on his aggressive foreign policy towards two East African countries – Ethiopia and Somaliland – which the other colonising nations, greedy for resources rather than for empty power, had left behind. In 1936 Mussolini proclaimed from the balcony of Palazzo Venezia that "the hour struck by destiny had finally arrived" and the imperial eagles, signs of the power in ancient Rome, had returned to its hills.

The official art of the regime appropriated forms of Roman grandeur. Mosaics in the style of ancient Roman floors pave the avenue and decorate the walls of the **Foro Italico**, the ambitious sports centre created in 1931 northeast of the capital. Bulky square columns support the **Palazzo della Civiltà del Lavoro** – commonly called the "Square Coliseum"

– at EUR (Esposizione Universale di Roma), an area south of Rome. Sixty colossal statues of athletes adorn the **Stadio Olimpico** in the Foro Italico. Stark lines and impressive bulk characterise the church of **SS Pietro e Paolo** at EUR. The aesthetic of the regime did succeed in creating some striking effects, but mostly the result was phony grandeur. In the city itself, urban planners ruthlessly drove roads through areas of historical importance, tearing down medieval quarters, which they considered an inheritance of dark times, and ripping through the very heart of Rome a triumphal way for the new eagles of the regime.

From this point of view EUR, an area undeveloped before the fascist era, is the least offensive of Il Duce's efforts in town planning. In 1938 Mussolini undertook to build, with the designs of Marcello Piacentini, a magnificent Third Rome which would be the natural successor to Imperial Rome and the Rome of the Renaissance. Plans for an exposition in 1942 to commemorate 20 years

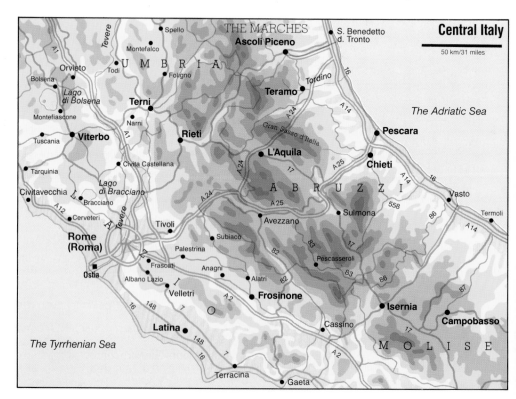

of fascism were overtaken by World War II, and the overall design was only partially completed. In the 1950s new buildings were added, government offices and museums moved here and EUR evolved into a residential quarter.

Apart from architectural interest, the EUR has a number of interesting museums, including the **Museo Preistorico ed Etnografico** (Prehistorical and Ethnographic Museum) and the **Museo della Civiltà Romano,** devoted to the history of Rome. The latter contains the famous **plastico di Roma**, a reconstruction of the city in the time of Constantine.

Ancient apartment dwellers: The town of **Ostia Antica** was founded around the end of the 4th century as a fortified city to guard the mouth of the Tiber. Later it developed into the commercial port of Rome as well as its naval base. Vital supplies of produce, mainly corn, arrived from Ostia to the capital through the **Via Ostiensis**. When Ostia became inadequate for the volume of trade, another port, Portus Augusti, originally planned by Augustus, was built by Nero,

northwest of the town. By the time of Constantine, Ostia had turned into a residential town for middle- and lower-class Romans. Ostia's ruins rival those of Pompeii for showing the layout of an ancient Italian city. Houses unearthed in Ostia offer valuable insights into the type of dwellings the same classes presumably had in Rome. The *insula* was usually a four-storey house with numerous rooms and built in brick, reaching a maximum height of 15 metres (49 ft). Each room had a window, covered in mica rather than glass. The *Domus*, the typical Pompeiian residence built for the very rich, usually on one floor only, was very rare in Ostia.

The Roman theatre, enlarged in the 2nd century by Septimius Severus to hold 2,700 people has perfect acoustics and houses the summer season of the **Teatro di Roma**.

The **Lido di Ostia** is an overcrowded seaside resort for Romans. Naturists can drive about 7 km (4½ miles) south (Tor Vaianica), where the beaches, served by very primitive facilities, offer a laid-back atmosphere for nudists.

Palestrina and Tivoli: The ancient **Praeneste** is one of the oldest towns of Latium. According to myth, it was founded by Telegono, son of Ulysses and Circe. The town was already flourishing in the 8th century BC and in the following centuries successfully resisted attack by the Romans. It wasn't until the 4th century, after the end of the Latin War against Rome, in which Praeneste had a leading role, that the town became a subject of Rome. Later, during the bloody civil war between Marius and Silla, Marius fled to Praeneste. The town was besieged by Silla's troops and eventually destroyed.

But Silla wanted to make amends and so ordered the reconstruction of the famous sanctuary of **Fortuna Primigenia,** containing an oracle. The temple, which occupied an area of about 32 hectares (79 acres), was one of the richest and grandest of antiquity. It comprised a series of terraces on the slopes of Mount Ginestro connected by vaulted ramps. Its cult lasted until the 4th century AD when the temple was aban-

doned. In the Middle Ages a new town rose on its ruins. Bombing in 1944, which destroyed the part of the town which stood on the third terrace, brought the temple to light and prompted excavations. The **Museo Nazionale Archeologico Prenestino** houses many of the local finds including the incomparable **Barberini Mosaic**.

At the height of the Roman empire the ancient site of **Tibur** (**Tivoli**) on the lower slopes of the Sabine hills, was a favourite retreat for poets and Rome's wealthier citizens. The lavish villas scattered around sacred woods and scenic waterfalls attracted such famous visitors as Horace, Catullus, Maecenas, Sallust and the Emperor Trajan. In the year AD 117 the Emperor Hadrian began building his luxurious retirement home on the gently sloping plain below the foothills on which Tivoli stands. The villa, which occupies 73 hectares (180 acres), was the largest and richest in the Roman Empire. Hadrian wanted to recreate the monuments and places which had impressed him most during his extensive travelling in the East (the peaceful **Canopus**, for example, was modelled on a sanctuary of Scrapis near Egyptian Alexandria), but Hadrian's overall conception goes beyond mere imitation. The endless succession of terraces, water basins and baths is a joyful reaction against functionality and common sense but the design doesn't resort to extravagant artifice and *trompe l'oeil*. Instead it is a rigorous, geometrical, classical controlling of nature.

The building standing at the heart of the complex, which a romantic archaeologist previously labelled **Teatro Marittimo**, is a good example of this. It is a circular building with a column portico and a moated island in the middle. The effect is metaphysical. It suggests escape from reality, retreat into the memory, even the lucid contemplation of death.

The spirit which pervades Tivoli's **Villa d'Este,** the sumptuous residence which Cardinal Ippolito d'Este had the skilful Pietro Ligurio transform into a Benedictine convent, is very different.

Villa Adriana at Tivoli.

The palace is light and gay, with its facade overlooking the park and rooms decorated with frescoes, it is a typical Renaissance mansion. Ippolito, one of the Dukes of Este, was more absorbed by mundane business than spiritual cares. But the real splendour here lies in the symmetrically terraced garden sloping down the hillside, covered with luxuriant vegetation, and the unrestrained play of water.

Water here is the prime element. Long pools of quiet water, escorted by rows of elegiac cypresses extending into the distance, suggest infinity. Water spouts from obelisks or gurgles from the mouths of mythological creatures and monsters, or gaily springs from the nipples of a sphinx or the multiple breasted Artemis of Ephesus. In this monument, dedicated to the ephemeral, in this superb triumph of theatricality, are the beginnings of the baroque.

The Etruscans: Before modern Rome, capital of unified Italy, or Renaissance Rome, capital of the popes, or Imperial Rome, capital of the world, Italy could claim a highly refined civilisation: the Etruscans. Their apparent zest for life and their emphasis on physical vitality fascinated the English novelist D. H. Lawrence, who saw them as a happy contrast to the puritanical Romans.

The "Etruscan Places" (as Lawrence named his travel book) were in the ancient region of Etruria northwest of the Tiber and encompassed parts of modern Tuscany (Etruscany), Umbria and Latium. Around 500 BC, at the height of their political domination, the Etruscans occupied a large part of ancient Latium and had established colonies in Corsica, Elba, Sardinia, the Balearic Islands and on the coast of Spain. They were not organised under a centralised government, but formed a loose confederation of city-states tied together for religious reasons. Etruscan wealth and power was partly based on knowledge of metal working and their exploitation of iron deposits in Etruria.

Cerveteri: The small medieval town of **Cerveteri**, north of Rome on the via Aurelia, was built on the site of the Etruscan town of Caere. In the 6th and 5th century BC Caere was one of the most populated towns of the Mediterranean. It had strong ties with Hellenic lands, the influence of whose merchants and artists made Caere the centre of a lively and sophisticated cultural life. Its decline began in AD 384, when Pyrgy harbour, its main port, was devastated by a Greek incursion. Eventually the rude, haughty, still barbaric strength of rising Rome blindly wiped away what had been a refined and joyous civilisation. Nothing remains today of the ancient town of Caere, bar a few walls.

Caere's necropolis occupies a hill outside the city proper. From here it could be seen from the ramparts of the city, gay with painted houses and temples. The oldest tombs (8th century BC) have a small circular well carved into the stone where the urns containing the ashes of the dead were placed. (Two modes of burial, cremation and inhumation, continued side by side for centuries.) The first chamber-tombs, also cut into the stone and covered with rocky blocks and mounds (tumuli), appeared

Renaissance Villa d'Este at Tivoli, with its fountains and gardens.

as early as the beginning of the 7th century. The noble Etruscans were either enclosed in great sarcophagi with their effigies on top, or laid out on stone beds in their chamber tombs.

Placed beside them in the tombs were treasures they would need in the next world: a miniature bronze ship in which to travel there, rich jewels for adornment, dishes for food, statuettes, tools, weapons, armour. Etruscan women, sometimes placed beside their husbands, were sumptuously attired for their journey: a mirror, comb, box of cosmetics, jewels, were all at hand, available for future use. A profound belief in life seems to have been the basic philosophy of the Etruscans. Life beyond the grave was seen as an extension of earthly pleasures.

Excavations of the tombs not already rifled – the Romans were the first collectors of Etruscan antiquities – revealed goods of gold, silver, ivory, bronze and ceramics. The vases show strong Greek influence as well as the excellent quality of the Etruscan craftmanship. Much

of this material is now on display in the **Museum of Cerveteri**, housed in the **Ruspoli Castle**, in the Museo di Villa Giulia and the Vatican Museum in Rome.

Tarquinia: The Etruscan town of Tarquinia stood on a hill northwest of the picturesque medieval town bearing the same name. The town existed as early as the 9th century BC and two centuries later was at its height. It is difficult to say whether the Roman dynasty of the Tarquini held the crown by virtue of military conquest of Rome or merely because of the political, economic and cultural influence they exerted on Rome.

Starting from the 4th century BC the status of the two cities switched and Tarquinia declined like all other Etruscan cities. It recovered in the Middle Ages when communities escaping the Barbarian invasions moved to the hill nearby and founded another town, Cornetum, which the fascist regime later renamed Tarquinia in their general attempts to recapture the glories of the **Monastery of St Benedict, Subiaco.**

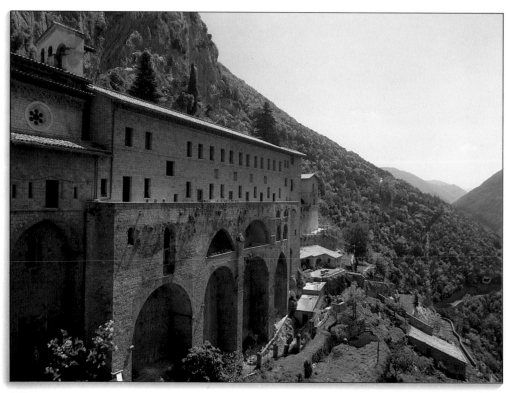

past. In 1924 the **Museo Nazionale Tarquinese** was founded. In it are many Etruscan treasures, including the famous terracotta winged horses.

The **Necropolis** of Tarquinia, together with that of Caere, is the most important Etruscan necropoli. It is located on a hill south of the old Etruscan Tarquinia and occupies an area which is 5 km (3 miles) long and 1 km (½ mile) wide. It was in use until the Roman age, so the whole area is covered with tombs of many different types and periods. There are well-tombs, hallway tombs and chamber tombs with or without tumuli.

The painted tombs with frescoes are not only the most important document of Etruscan painting but also a precious document of the life of the Etruscans, their costumes and beliefs. Horizontal ribbons of bright colours frame the animated scenes below: the banqueters and musicians in the **Tomba dei Leopardi**; the hunters in the **Tomba del Cacciatore**; the erotic scenes in the **Tomba dei Tori**; the prancing dancers, diving dolphins and soaring birds of the **Tomba della Leonessa**; the beautiful maiden from the Velcha family in the **Tomba di Polifemo o dell'Orco**. Ironically, visitors often leave these dusty, decayed houses of death feeling shored up by a renewed faith in life and its many joys and mysteries.

Subiaco already existed when the Emperor Nero began building his villas overlooking one of the three artificial lakes he had created by deviating the waters of the river Aniene. The slaves employed in the construction of the dam and villa founded the town. Five centuries later a rich young man from Norcia named Benedict came here in search of a place for meditation and prayer. He stayed for three years, living in a cavern, now known as the **Sacro Speco** (Holy Grotto). Subiaco, considered the birthplace of Western monasticism, now comprises a series of convents with their numerous cloisters and churches, bell towers, chapels decorated with frescoes and grottoes hewn out of the mountainside, all connected by picturesque stairs. The complex is one of the most interesting sights in the region.

Around 529 Benedict and his faithful monks left Subiaco and moved to **Monte Cassino** to continue their mystical experience. Here they established one of the most important religious and cultural institutions of the Middle Ages. Five centuries after Benedict's death in 543 the abbey he had founded was one of the richest in the world. The illuminated manuscripts, frescoes and mosaics were so skilfully executed that they became models for others throughout the rest of medieval Europe.

During World War II, Cassino rose to prominence once more. After the American forces entered Naples, Cassino became the German's front-line (the so-called Gustave line) designed to defend the environs of Rome. When repeated attacks by the Allies failed to penetrate the powerfully strengthened bulwark, a decision was made to bomb. It resulted in the total destruction of Cassino. The ancient abbey was swept away. What one sees today is a faithful, loving reconstruction of what existed before the catastrophe.

Allied bombs reduced the abbey at Monte Cassino to rubble in World War II.

ABRUZZO AND MOLISE

The Apennine Mountains, a geologically unruly region long ignored by mainstream travellers, unravel into three strands as they twist down between Rome and the Adriatic. It is characteristic of this area, formerly known by the single name Abruzzo, that it should have been the birthplace of the priest in Hemingway's *A Farewell To Arms* who recommended it for winter sport. That has been Abruzzo's traditional image among foreigners and Italians alike: a sort of Italian Montana popular among outdoor types.

The image, like all caricatures, leaves out many of the finer points of this old region, but it persists. Visitors flock to the Gran Sasso, the central mountain chain, to climb, ski, birdwatch and hunt, and to Pescara and other beach towns, where another form of sport discomforts bikini-clad girls. Yet the region has as indigenous history that may be the oldest in Italy, and its lovely towns, surrounded by snow-capped mountains even in June, contain first-rate monuments. Molise split off from Abruzzo to form an autonomous region in 1963, and has managed to retain its wild spirit more completely than its populous and faster-developing neighbour.

A dip into history: Human habitation of the region goes back more than 13,000 years to the so-called Fucino or Marsicano Man, whose fragmented bones have been discovered in caves in Ortucchio and Maritza. Archaeological evidence of a flourishing indigenous civilisation in the 6th century BC is gathering, hastened by the find of the famous Capestrano Warrior, now at the Museo Nazionale in Chieti. Signs of later Roman domination can be seen throughout the region, particularly at the interesting archaeological site of Alba Fucens, near **Avezzano**.

In the Middle Ages and later the region came under the sway of the various invading kingdoms from the south. The Spanish, for example, were responsible for most of the castles that pepper the region. Earthquakes, particularly one in 1703, have caused considerable damage, as did the two world wars. Massive migrations of farm workers into the cities after World War II resulted in economic imbalances between town and country, but recent efforts to encourage tourism and industry and the completion of the autostrada have started to reverse the post-war impoverishment.

Shy animals: Italy's voluptuous landscape is at its most magnificent in the **Parco Nazionale d'Abruzzo**, where over 400 sq. km (154 sq. miles) of high-altitude meadows, beech groves and snow-cappped peaks are protected from encroachment by Abruzzian housing developers. It is still possible to see the shy Apennine brown bear (*Ursus arctos marsicanus*), of which there are between 70 and 100. They feed on berries and insects in the remote upper pastures. The Abruzzo chamois (*Rupicapra ornata*), distinguished by the black-and-white pattern on its throat, also thrives here, as do the Apennine lynx and various foxes, wolves, otter, song birds, hawks and eagles. About 150 well-marked trails provide access to even the highest sections, most of which are within a day's walk from the main road.

Pescassèroli, the administrative headquarters for the park, was the birthplace of the philosopher Benedetto Croce. Today it is dedicated to physical pursuits such as hiking and skiing and you can pick up trail maps for the park here. If you are coming at Christmas, Easter or during August, book accommodation in advance – these are the peak seasons. Buses ply daily between Pescassèroli and **Avezzano**, a more convenient base if time is short.

The road and railway take one around the edge of the **Piana del Fucino**, a lake in Roman times which, after centuries of effort, was subsequently drained. In what was once the centre of the lake is the important *Telespazio* station, with its forest of satellite dishes. In the surrounding fields bright red poppies burst forth in May.

Fountain of 99 spouts: L'Aquila, chief town of Abruzzo, has a turbulent history belied by its fine architecture and the relaxing coolness of its arcaded streets. Founded in 1240 by Frederick II of Hohenstaufen as an outpost against the papacy, the city converted to papal rule shortly after Frederick's death in 1250. Nine years later, Frederick's son Manfred reclaimed the city after a siege that destroyed the city walls and led to its abandonment for seven years. Charles I of Anjou began rebuilding it after defeating Manfred at Benevento in 1266.

According to legend, the city of L'Aquila was formed from 99 palaces, 99 churches, 99 fountains and 99 squares, and in commemoration of this numerical coincidence, the city authorities commissioned a fountain of 99 spouts in 1272. The **Fontane delle Novantanove Cannelle** is one of the highlights of the city. The pleasant courtyard of red and white stone and the sound of water issuing from the 99 masks combine to convey a sense of peace.

L'Aquila's most well-known monument is the 13th-century church of **Santa Maria di Collemaggio**, located outside the city wall on the southeast corner of town. It is impossible to miss its red and white facade, whose three rose windows and corresponding doorways subtly combine the Gothic and the Romanesque. The church was begun in 1277 under the guidance of Pietro dal Murrone, a famous local hermit who was later crowned Pope Celestine V at the age of 85. He served only five months in office, claiming that his inexperience with the ways of the world made him unfit to sit on the throne of Saint Peter. His lovely Renaissance tomb can be seen to the right of the apse inside. The interior, relieved of baroque flourishes in 1973, has a long wooden ceiling and spartan walls made bright by afternoon sun streaming through its rose windows.

The newly-cleaned church of **San Bernardino** is considered by some to be the finest Renaissance monument in the Abruzzi. The interior, completely rebuilt after the earthquake of 1703, is actually dominated by its baroque ceiling and organ, both designed by Ferdinando Mosca of nearby **Pescocostanzo**. The Renaissance tomb of San

Turn of the century beach house in Pescara.

170

Bernardino (1488), in a chapel on the right, has a classical precision carried over in its delicate floral frieze. The tomb and, in the apse, the Monument of Maria Pereira (1496) are both the work of Silvestro dell'Aquila, a local artist. The floor repeats the theme of red and white marble.

Every weekday morning in the **Piazza del Duomo** there is a vibrant open-air market where local products of cane, wool, lace and copper are sold. The Duomo itself, completely destroyed by the 1703 earthquake, was rebuilt in the 19th century.

One of the best museums in Abruzzo is L'Aquila's **Museo Nazionale d'Abruzzo**, located in the castle at the north end of town. The **Castello** itself, built in 1532 by Pirro Luigi Escriba or Scriba, the architect of Castel Sant'Elmo in Naples, is known for its four protruding "ears" which enabled soldiers to cover every possible angle of approach. There's an amusing frieze of Medusa's head in the archaeological section on the ground floor. The first floor has a

collection of medieval religious art, most of it from local churches, while on the second floor are 16th–18th century works. The modern art on the third floor includes some interesting paintings by modern Abruzzians.

Unlike the Parco Nazionale, which is of interest for its wildlife and majestic beech groves, the **Gran Sasso d'Italia**, just outside L'Aquila, attracts mountaineers. The Gran Sasso itself, at 2,914 metres (9,560 ft), is the highest peak in the Apennines; the numerous trails, both for hiking and skiing, that radiate from the nearby *Campo Imperatore* are known throughout Europe. Trail maps are available at the Agenzia di Viaggi-Centro Turistico Gran Sasso in L'Aquila.

Sulmona: One of the most spectacular drives in Abruzzo takes Route 261 from L'Aquila to Sulmona, following the valley of the Aterno river past a number of medieval villages, each with its ruined castle and its church. **Sulmona**, the birthplace of Ovid, is considered by many Abruzzians to be the most beautiful town in the province. The evening

passeggiata is also worth seeing, when the streets, lined with shops selling *confetti* – sugared almonds that have been made here since the Middle Ages – become packed with people pouring arm in arm up the Corso. Others stroll through the vast **Piazza Garibaldi**, where shops sell traditional copper pots and pans and where the remains of a medieval aqueduct can be seen.

The **Palazzo della SS Annunziata** stands at the ancient centre of town. The harmony of its facade is constantly praised. Each of the three portals has a different size and shape corresponding to each of the three windows above. The left portal is Gothic, dating from 1415, the middle, Renaissance, dating from 1483, and the less interesting and less classifiable right portal from a still later date. A floral frieze running across the face links the three. Upstairs, on the first floor of the palazzo, is a museum of local archaeological finds and paintings by local artists. The church, originally more visibly connected to the palazzo, was rebuilt after an earthquake in 1706.

Italian towns take pride in their famous sons and daughters. **Pescara's** claim to fame is the writer Gabriele d'Annunzio (1863–1938), whose birthplace may be visited off **Piazza Unione**. But it is the 16 km (10 miles) of wide, sandy beach rather than d'Annunzio that draws so many tourists from Germany, France and the United States.

Just half an hour outside Pescara is the ancient hilltop town of **Chieti**, famous today for its archaeological museum, but known since antiquity for its views across mainland Abruzzo and the sea. Remains of three Roman temples can be seen off the main Corso Marrucino, just behind the modern-day post office. The recently modernised **Museo Archeologico di Antichità** is located at the far western edge of town in the **Villa Comunale**. Its extensive coin collection is one of the most interesting in Italy, with explanatory notes in both Italian and English. Visitors can trace the ancient trade routes along which coins were distributed. Particularly interesting is the case containing coins

Abruzzian native.

from Alba Fucens. A diagram charts the trenches in which the different coins were found. The rest of the museum contains local anthropological and archaeological finds including some from the Iron Age which date back as far as 9,000 BC and an interesting collection of Roman statues. The 6th-century BC Capestrano Warrior in his Huck Finn hat is the most famous exhibit here.

A festival in Molise: If you happen to take the train from Termoli to Campobasso between May 25 and May 27 of any year, stop at the medieval village of **Larino**. There you can take part in the *Sagra di San Pardo*, Larino's annual festival, when ox-carts are paraded through the streets in memory of Roman times. While there, visit the old cathedral, with its beautiful facade, and climb up the monumental staircase of the **Palazzo Reale**. Larino, like its province Molise, is one of the least known places in Italy, yet one of the most rewarding to visit.

Termoli, on the Adriatic, is a popular beach resort whose old town on the promontory offers fine views in all directions. Well garrisoned behind a small castle built by Frederick II are labyrinthine streets and a fine cathedral. Termoli is one of the starting points for boats to the **Isole Trèmiti**, a group of offshore islands celebrated for their mysterious grottoes and other marine phenomenon.

The town that most fully illustrates the difference between the old and the new in Molise is **Campobasso**, the region's capital. Presided over by the 15th-century **Castello Monforte**, from which tumble the steeply stepped streets of the old town, Campobasso has a very pleasant modern town spreading out to the train station below. It is in the new town that two of Campobasso's most well-known features are to be found: a top-security prison and a training school for the Carabinieri, the Italian police. You will find smartly uniformed young men strolling up the streets in twos and threes or quietly talking in the shade of the trees in the main square. Ask these cadets for directions to the old town, in particular to **San Giorgio**, the 12th-century Romanesque church.

Ninety minutes by train from Campobasso is **Isernia**, rich in regional lore, and a good starting point for explorations into the remote hill towns. The discovery, in 1979, of an ancient settlement on the outskirts of Isernia put the town in the archaeological spotlight. Although no human remains were discovered, the evidence proves that man lived here a million years before the birth of Christ – the oldest traces of humanity yet discovered in Europe. The unexpected discovery of a fireplace indicated that these prehistoric people used fire. Bones of elephants, rhinoceri, hippos, bison and bear were also discovered, indicating the presence of such animals at that distant time.

The town of Isernia, strung along a single street running downhill from the railway station, has an excellent archaeological museum. The old town (turn left out of the station) has been much damaged by earthquakes. Most of it is now held together with scaffolding. The dark lanes that criss-cross through the medieval buildings are shoulder-narrow.

Flower-filled corner.

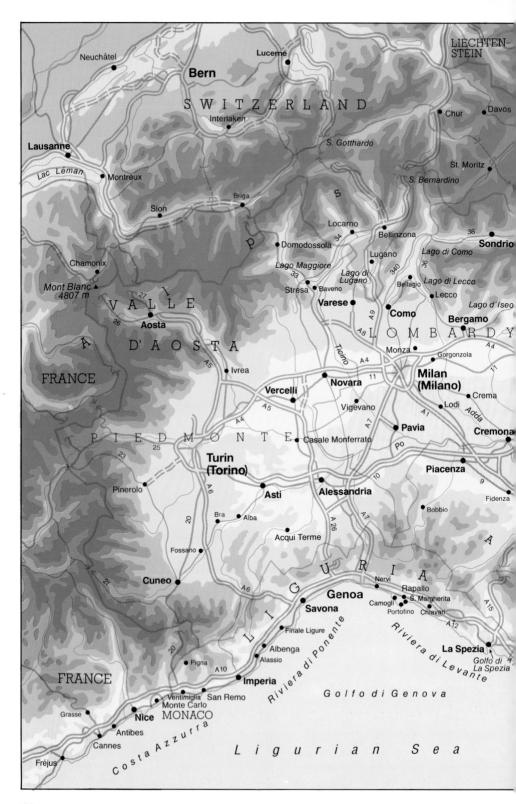

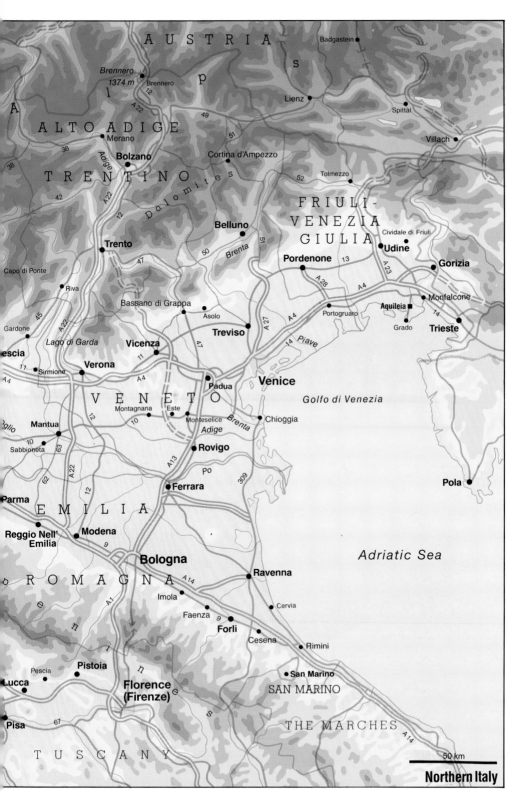

Northern Italy

179

THE NORTH

Above all the sense of going down into Italy – the delight of seeing the North melt slowly into the South – of seeing Italy gradually crop up in bits and vaguely latently betray itself – until finally at the little frontier Village of Isella where I spent the night, it lay before me warm and living and palpable...

—Henry James (from his *Letters*, vol. 1, ed. Leon Edel)

For centuries most travellers arrived in Italy from the north. They crossed the mountains from Switzerland or France and often, if physically fit and romantically minded, as was the young Henry James, they made part of the journey on foot. This way Italy came into focus gradually, as they left the cold north behind and made their way south from the lakes to Milan. From there, the cities of the Poe Valley beckoned.

If possible, this is still the best way to approach northern Italy. Rather than rush through, with your eyes on the train schedule and your mind checking off each town you have "done", see fewer cities, but see them well. Each one is so rich in history and art that it merits weeks. After all, this is the Italy of Shakespeare – *Romeo and Juliet* (Verona), *The Taming of the Shrew* (Padua) – and of medieval communes and Renaissance princes. The great families – the Visconti in Milan, the Gonzaga in Mantua, the della Scala in Verona, the d'Este in Ferrara – are still remembered for the artistic triumphs and political scandals of their courts.

In this section of the book we pass from Venice and Ravenna, the magnificent cities of Byzantium on Italy's east coast, to Padua and Bologna, magnets for university students since the Middle Ages; and then to Florence, birthplace of the Renaissance, for its paintings, sculptures and the spirit of Dante's *Divine Comedy*.

Northern Italians, though generally less intrusive than the more gregarious southerners, are always pleased to answer questions and make suggestions, always willing to spare a moment to give a stranger a little known fact or their personal opinion on a historical personage. Quite possibly that native will bear more than a slight resemblance to the figures in the 15th-century frescoes of the local *duomo* – in these regions, the past is always present.

Preceding pages: the Duomo of Milan; awaiting the start of the *palio* in Siena. **Left,** skiers near the resort of Marmolada in the Dolomites.

MILAN AND LOMBARDY

Beneath is spread like a green sea
The waveless plain of Lombardy,
Bounded by the vaporous air,
Islanded by cities fair
— Percy Bysshe Shelley

From the heights of the central Alps to the low-lying plains of the Po Valley, the province of Lombardy is remarkably diverse. Contrasts abound in this land named after the Lombards, one of the barbarian tribes that invaded Italy in the 6th century. Its cities, renowned for their elegance since Renaissance times, are complemented by dramatic scenery. The Italian Lakes jut into the heart of a steep mountain range, offset by fertile farmlands and fields of gently swaying poplars.

Above all the region includes one of Europe's great metropolises: **Milan** (Milano). It is one of the fashion capitals of the world, and home to both Leonardo da Vinci's *Last Supper* and the world's premier opera house, La Scala. Above all, Milan is the centre of business in Italy and it is here that the demand for federalism – embodied by the rightwing Northern League – is strongest. Despite having political scandals of its own, Milan looks upon southern Italy as listless, corrupt and a heavy financial burden.

The prosperous Milanese are courteous but reserved towards visitors and preoccupied with their own lives. Female tourists receive little of the unasked-for attention that is common further south (Milan is the centre of the Italian women's movement). The city's reserved northern European flavour made it, according to Henry James, more "the last of the prose capitals than the first of the poetic". But there is poetry in Milan in spite of its modernity.

A city tour: There is no better place to begin a tour of Milan than at its spiritual hub, the **Duomo**, described by Mark Twain as "a poem in marble". This gargantuan Gothic cathedral (the third largest church in Europe) was begun in 1386 but not given its finishing touches until 1813. Decorating the exterior are 135 pinnacles and over 2,245 marble statues from all periods. The "Madonnina", a beautiful 4-metre (13-ft) gilded statue graces the top of the Duomo's highest pinnacle.

TheEnglish novelist D. H. Lawrence called the Duomo "an imitation hedgehog of a cathedral", because of this pointy intricate exterior. But inside, the church is simple, majestic, and vast. Five great aisles stretch from the entrance to the altar. Enormous stone pillars dominate the nave, which is big enough to accommodate 40,000 worshippers. In the apse three large and intricate stained-glass windows attributed to Nicolas de Bonaventura shed a soft half-light over the area behind the altar. The central window features the shield of the Viscontis, Milan's ruling family during the 13th and 14th centuries. It was Duke Gian Galeazzo Visconti, the most powerful member of the family, who commissioned the Duomo.

A gruesome statue of the flayed St

Left, the Galleria, Milan. Right, the Sforza Castle, Milan.

Bartholomew, carrying his skin, stands in the left transept. In the right transept is an imposing 16th-century marble tomb made for Giacomo di Medici by Leone Leoni after the style of Michelangelo.

The crypt contains the tomb of the Counter-Reformation saint Charles Borromeo. This 16th-century Archbishop of Milan epitomised the Lombardian virtues of energy, efficiency and discipline. Ascetic and rigorously self-denying, he expected no less from his flock. His unbending character led to frequent battles with the lay authorities, especially when he tried to curtail dancing, drama and sports.

Outside, a lift will take you up to the roof of the Duomo, among the pinnacles and carved rosettes. The view from the top is spectacular; on a clear day it stretches as far as the Alps.

Come down into the **Piazza del Duomo** where Milan's many worlds converge. The large equestrian statue standing at one end of the square honours Italy's first king, Victor Emmanuel (after whom major boulevards in cities throughout Italy are named). On two sides the piazza is lined with porticoes, where Milanese of all ages and styles love to gather. To the north is the entrance to the **Galleria Vittorio Emanuele**, the world's oldest and most elegant shopping mall. Its four-storey arcade is full of boutiques, offices, bars and restaurants. But, before you sit down to watch the world go by, be forewarned: the cafés here are pricey.

At the other side of the Galleria is **Piazza della Scala**, site of the famed **La Scala** opera house, built between 1776 and 1778. The theatre suffered serious damage during Allied bombings in World War II, but has since been carefully restored. It was here that Verdi's *Otello* and Puccini's *Madama Butterfly*, were first performed.

The interior of the opera house is elegantly shabby. The walls are covered in red damask and trimmed with gilt. Crystal chandeliers provide light for a capacity audience of 3,000 people.

The **Museo Teatrale alla Scala** next door will appeal to opera buffs. Memo-

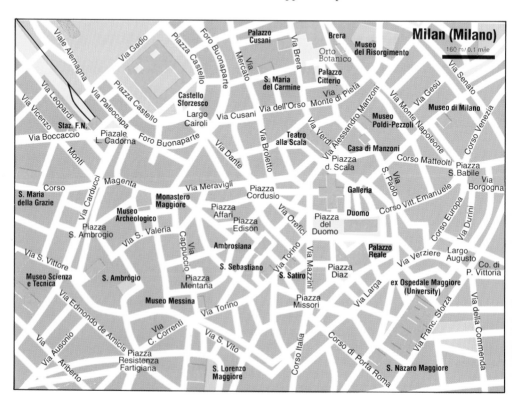

rabilia include original scores by Verdi, Liszt's piano and portraits of plump prima donnas and beefy tenors. There are even composers' death masks and casts of their hands.

Follow the via Verdi from La Scala to the **Palazzo di Brera**, home of one of Italy's finest art collections. Paintings of the 15th to 18th centuries are especially well represented in the **Pinacoteca di Brera**. Famous works included in the collection are Mantegna's *The Dead Christ* (viewed from the pierced soles of His feet), Caravaggio's *Supper at Emmaus*, the restored 15th-century *Madonna and Saints* by Piero della Francesca, and Raphael's beautiful *Betrothal of the Virgin* (*Lo Sposalizio*), a masterpiece of his Umbrian period which was his first painting to show powers of composition and draughtsmanship far in advance of his biggest influence, Perugino.

A despot's dwelling: Off the Piazza del Duomo is Via Mercanto. From there Via Dante leads to the **Castello Sforzesco**, stronghold and residence of the Sforza family, the despotic rulers of Milan in the 15th century (*sforza* means strong in Italian). The greatest of the Sforzas was Francesco, a mercenary general who became the fourth Duke of Milan. To design his stronghold, Francesco employed a local architect, Giovanni da Milano, but the decoration of the principal tower was undertaken by Filarete, a Florentine architect.

The residential part of the castle, the Corte Ducale, contains a magnificent collection of sculpture, including Michelangelo's *Rondanini Pietà*, an almost abstract work charged with emotional intensity. Michelangelo worked on this *Pietà* until within a few days of his death in 1564.

Three blocks west of the castle stands the church of **Santa Maria delle Grazie**, begun in 1466 but expanded in 1492 by Bramante, who also built the exquisite cloister. Next door, **Cenacolo Vinciano**, once a refectory for Dominican friars, is home to Leonardo's famous *Last Supper* (1495–97). Because Leonardo did not use the proper fresco technique – as

Piazza del Duomo.

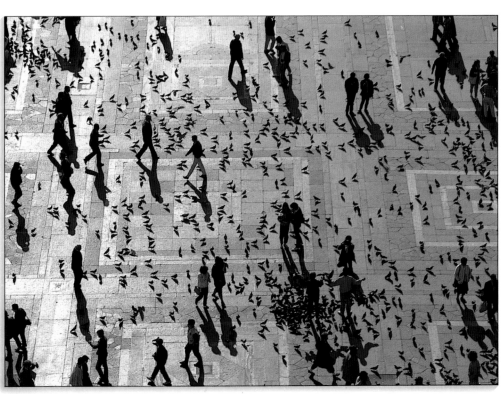

an experiment he worked on the plaster in oil instead of fresco – the painting is considerably damaged. The ongoing restoration cannot completely counteract the effects of time and damp.

Although the *Last Supper* is considerably faded, to visit it remains a powerful and moving experience. The work is far larger than expected, approximately 9 metres (30 ft) long and 4½ metres (15ft) wide. Not all of the expressions on the faces of the disciples can be discerned, but the careful composition of the work remains completely clear. On either side of Jesus sit two groups of three apostles, linked to each other through their individual gestures and glances. It vividly captures the moment when Jesus announces that one of them is to betray Him. This painting was seminal to the perception of the artist as a creative thinker rather than just an artisan.

From Santa Maria delle Grazie proceed to the **church of Sant' Ambrogio** on Via Carducci. This is the finest medieval building in Milan. To enter, you must step down from street level and cross an austere atrium. The church is dark and low, but strangely compelling in its antiquity. Originally founded between 379 and 386 by St Ambrose, then bishop and later patron saint of Milan – it was he who converted St Augustine – the basilica was enlarged first in the 9th century and later in the 11th. The brick-ribbed square vaults that support the galleries are typical of Lombard architecture. For a gruesome glimpse of the past, venture down into the crypt to see the skeletal remains of St Ambrose, Milan's patron saint, along with those of two early Christian martyrs.

Down Via San Vittore from the basilica is the **Museo Nazionale della Scienza e della Tecnica**. Although the large section devoted to applied physics will probably be of interest only to specialists, everyone will enjoy the huge room filled with wooden models of Leonardo's most ingenious inventions, some bearing more than a passing resemblance to modern machines. Included in the display is a reconstruction

The modern face of Milan.

of Leonardo's famous flying machine.

Return in the direction of the Duomo to find the **Biblioteca Ambrosiana**, a library founded by Cardinal Federico Borromeo and built by Lelio Buzzi between 1607 and 1609. It now houses a small but exquisite collection of paintings dating from the 15th to the 17th century. Most notable among the works are Leonardo's *Portrait of a Musician* in Room 8 and Caravaggio's *Basket of Fruit* in Room 11.

Fashion avenue: For a break from sightseeing and a glimpse of an important and more contemporary aspect of Milanese life, stroll down the **Via Monte Napoleone**, which extends off Corso Vittorio Emanuele between the Duomo and Piazza S Babila. This is the most elegant shopping street in Milan. You will find all the star names of Italian fashion here – Armani, Moschino, Valentino, Romeo Gigli, Krizia and Gianni Versace to name a few – as well as the latest in household design and contemporary art.

If you have time on your visit to Milan, there are two more churches which are worth seeking out. In the Via Torino, near the Piazza del Duomo, stands **San Satiro**, built by Bramante between 1478 and 1480. Inside, the architect cleverly used stucco to create a *trompe l'oeil* effect, giving the impression that the church is far larger than it actually is. **San Lorenzo Maggiore**, quite nearby on Corso di Porta Ticinese, attests to Milan's antiquity. The basilica was founded in the 4th century and rebuilt in 1103. Martino Bassi restored it between 1574 and 1588, but its octagonal shape and many beautiful 5th-century mosaics are original.

Certosa di Pavia: An easy day trip from Milan, or a stop-over on a longer journey south is the **Certosa di Pavia** (Charterhouse of Pavia). This world-famous church, mausoleum and monastery complex founded in 1396 is a masterpiece of the Lombard Renaissance complete with relief sculpture and inlaid marble. The interior of the church is Gothic in plan, but highly embellished with Renaissance and baroque details.

Certosa di Pavia.

Inside stand the tombs of Ludovico Visconti and his child-bride, Beatrice d'Este. Their bodies are not actually buried here, but life-sized effigies atop the tombs portray them in all their lifetime splendour.

Behind the Certosa is a magnificent Great Cloister where Carthusian monks, who had taken vows of silence, once lived in the individual cottages lining the sides of the elegant courtyard. Each cottage is two storeys high with two rooms on the ground floor and a bedroom and loggia above. The monk, in seclusion in his cottage, took delivery of his food through the small swing portal at the right of his doorway.

Nowadays Pavia is a country backwater, but between the 6th and 8th centuries it was the capital city of the Lombards. Pavia's fame was augmented in 1361 when the university was founded, and to this day it remains a prestigious centre of learning.

On the Via Diacono in the old centre of town is the church of **San Michele** consecrated in 1155. Here the great

medieval Lombard leader Frederick Barbarossa was crowned king of Italy. Look for the carefully sculpted scenes of the battle between good and evil above the three doorways. Inside, San Michele is plain and sombre; only the columns are highly decorated with fine, detailed sculpture.

Eclectic and electric: To reach the **Duomo** follow the Strada Nuova from S Michele. This cathedral is an eclectic mixture of four centuries of architectural styles. The basic design is Renaissance (Bramante and Leonardo worked on it), but the immense cupola is a late 19th-century touch and the facade was added in 1933. The rest of the exterior is unfinished.

If you continue on the Strada Nuova you will arrive at the **Università**, where 17,000 students currently attend classes. One of Pavia's most famous past graduates was Alessandro Volta, the physicist who discovered and gave his name to volts. His statue stands in the left-hand court of the university complex.

At the end of the Strada Nuova stands the **Castello Visconteo**, an imposing square fortress built between 1360 and 1365. Today, the castle is the home of the Museo Civico. Included in the museum's collection are many fine Lombard-Romanesque sculptures and remnants of Roman Pavia – inscriptions, glass and pottery.

Go west from the castle, to reach **San Pietro in Ciel d'Oro**, a fine Lombard-Romanesque church. San Pietro is smaller than S Michele, but otherwise quite similar. A richly decorated Gothic arch at the high altar is said to contain the relics of St Augustine.

Before leaving Pavia have a bowl of the town's speciality, the hearty *zuppa alla pavese,* a recipe said to have been concocted by a peasant woman for Francis I of France. The king was about to lose the Battle of Pavia (1525) to the Spanish when he stopped for a bite to eat at a nearby cottage. His hostess wanted her humble minestrone to be fit for a king, so she added toasted bread, cheese and eggs.

Cremona: About two hours' drive from Pavia lies the city of Cremona, a world-

Portrait of Isabella d'Este by Leonardo da Vinci.

famous centre of violin making and a pleasant market town on the banks of the Po River. The greatest of Cremonese violin makers was Antonio Stradivari (1644–1737) whose secret formula for varnish may account for the beautiful sound of a Stradivari violin. Some of these glorious instruments are on display at the 13th-century **Palazzo del Comune** on Corso Vittorio Emanuele and the modern International School of Violin Making nearby.

The **Duomo** at Cremona is a pink marble structure in the Lombard-Romanesque style. Although it was consecrated in 1190, it was not completed until much later. The fine rose window above the entrance dates from 1274. Inside the church, 17th-century tapestries of the life of Samson surround some of the heavy columns.

Mantua: Because **Mantua** (Mantova) lies on a peninsula in the Mincio River, surrounded by a languorous lagoon on three sides, it is sometimes called *Piccola Venezia* (Little Venice). But history, rather than geography, has given the city a more resonant name: "Ducal Mantua", because from 1328 to 1707 the enlightened, but nevertheless despotic, Gonzaga family ruled the town from its sombre fortress.

Mantua has always had a slightly musty medieval atmosphere about it. Wandering through the cobblestoned streets at night, the visitor might easily imagine being challenged by a couple of comic characters from a Shakespeare play, or happening upon one of the trysts between the unfortunate Gilda and the philandering Duke of Mantua from Verdi's *Rigoletto*. The city is loaded with legends, including one concerning the poet Virgil. Apparently, a simple peasant woman dreamed that she would give birth to a laurel bough, and soon produced the greatest of Roman poets, Virgil, who always looked on Mantua as his home town.

During the Renaissance, the Gonzaga court was one of the bright lights of Italian culture, especially under the influence of the Marchioness Isabella D'Este (1474–1539), who modelled her

Sheltering from the summer sun.

life on *Cortegione,* a textbook for courtiers and ladies written by Castiglione. She even gave Castiglione a palace in Mantua. Nor was her patronage limited to literary geniuses, since she also hired Raphael, Mantegna and Giulio Romano to decorate the **Reggia dei Gonzaga** (Palazzo Ducale), once the largest palace in Europe.

This royal blue-stocking left behind a correspondence of over 2,000 letters. But it is in the Palazzo Ducale that she left the strongest impression of herself. The public can visit a selection of the palace's 500 or more rooms by joining one of the guided tours.

Particularly worth seeing are the nine tapestries in the **Appartamento degli Arazzi** that were done in Flanders from drawings by Raphael. The **Camera degli Sposi** (the matrimonial suite) is decorated with frescoes by Mantegna depicting scenes from the lives of the Marquess Ludovico Gonzaga and his wife Barbara of Brandenburg.

Across town is **Palazzo del Tè**, the Gonzaga summer residence. Designed by Giulio Romano in 1525, this palace is delicate and charming. Many rooms are decorated with frescoes of summer scenes and there is a lovely garden, though the linden trees (*tigli*) that gave the palace its name are long gone.

The **Duomo** of Mantua, located near the Reggia, has a baroque facade added in 1756. Inside, the cathedral has a Renaissance design and stucco decoration by Giulio Romano, the architect of Palazzo del Tè.

Also worth a visit is the **Basilica di Sant' Andrea** in Piazza Mantegna. The Florentine L. B. Alberti designed most of Sant' Andrea, starting in 1472, but the dome was added in the 18th century. Inside, Sant' Andrea is at once simple and grand. The frescoes that adorn the walls were designed by Mantegna and executed by his pupils, among them Correggio.

Bergamo: If you want to escape from the hot stillness of "the waveless plain of Lombardy", there is no more restful or picturesque town than Bergamo, too often bypassed by tourists racing along

Rooftop view over Bergamo.

the autostrada between Milan and Venice. Bergamo is, in fact, two cities: Bergamo Bassa and Bergamo Alta. The modern **Bergamo Bassa**, where the railway station is, though pleasant and spacious, is less dramatic than its parent town which rises upon a rough-hewn crag. Beneath its shadow runs **Via Pignola** lined with elegant palaces built between the 16th and 18th centuries.

But the real treasure of Bergamo Bassa is the **Accademia Carrara**. Where else but in Italy can you find, in a small city, a collection of paintings that the grandest metropolis would be proud to have? In this case, it is thanks to the good taste of the 18th-century Count Giacomo Carrara. There is no need to queue to look at paintings by Pisanello, Lotto, Carpaccio, Bellini and Mantegna since the museum is deserted except for the cordial guards.

If you enjoy mountain climbing take the creaking funicular to **Bergamo Alta**, a fortified village built in a warm brown stone. The inhabitants keep their ancient town in beautiful condition. The best place in which to sit and admire it is the central **Piazza Vecchia** – a good place to find the local speciality *polenta con gli uccelli* (polenta with quail cooked in a pan). The piazza is flanked by the 17th-century **Palazzo Nuovo** and the 12th-century **Palazzo della Regione**. Beyond the medieval building's arcade is the small **Piazza del Duomo** packed with ecclesiastical treasures: the Romanesque **S Maria Maggiore** and the Renaissance **Colleoni Chapel** (designed by Amadeo who contributed to the Certosa di Pavia). The chapel was dedicated to the Bergamesque *condotierre* Bartolomeo Colleoni. The mercenary fought so well for the Venetians that he was rewarded with an estate in his native province, which, at that time, was under Venetian rule.

Music lovers will want to visit the **Istituto Musicale Donizetti**. The badly overworked composer was born in 1797 in Bergamo to a seamstress mother and pawnbroker father. He died here 51 years later, quite insane, having composed close to 70 operas.

The baroque interior of the Duomo, Bergamo.

THE LAKES

The Italian lakes have long been a retreat for romantics. Writers drawn to their shores include Pliny the Younger, Shelley, Stendhal and D. H. Lawrence. "What can one say of Lake Maggiore, of the Borromean Islands, of the Lake Como, except to pity people who do not go mad over them?" wrote Stendhal. Today, they are also a playground for the rich, as well as a popular destination for tourists and honeymooners from all over the world, drawn to their ravishing scenery. But despite the number of visitors, and the lakes' proximity to Milan's international airport (Lake Como, for instance, is a 90-minute drive away), the region has lost none of its allure.

The westernmost lake, **Lago Maggiore**, has a special attraction: the Borromean Islands, named after their owners, a prominent Milanese family whose members included a cardinal, a bishop and a saint.

Isola Bella, the most romantic of the three, was a desolate rock with just a few cottages until the 16th century when Count Charles Borromeo III decided to civilise the island in honour of his wife Isabella. With the help of the architect Angelo Crivelli, Charles designed the splendid palace and gardens.

Isola dei Pescatori is, as the name suggests, a fishing village. Another Borromeo palace and elaborate botanical gardens decorate **Isola Madre**. All three islands are serviced by ferries from the main lakeside towns.

The most famous and liveliest settlement on the shores of Lago Maggiore is **Stresa** (put on the literary map by Hemingway's *A Farewell To Arms*) with its many beautiful *belle époque* villas. Two famous villas adjoining the landing stage are the **Villa Ducale**, residence of the philosopher Antonio Rosmini (1797–1855), and the **Villa Pallavicino**, remarkable for its fine gardens. From Stresa, it's a short drive to the summit of **Monte Mottarone**, from where there is a stunning view of the Alps, the lake, and the town below.

Left, Limone, Lago di Garda. Right, Villa Carlotta, Lago di Como.

Baveno, northwest of Stresa, is a small, quiet town near the islands and the site of many villas, among them the **Castello Bianca** where Great Britain's Queen Victoria spent the spring of 1879. The drive south from Stresa to **Arona** along the Lungolago is especially pretty: the road is tree-lined, the views of the lakes and islands spectacular. Arona itself is a rather unremarkable resort town, but it does contain a number of attractive 15th-century buildings.

Lago di Como (Lake Como) is the most dramatic of the lakes. It is 19 km (31 miles) long and up to 5 km (3 miles) across. At many points the shore is a sheer cliff, and the Alps (providing year-round skiing on the glaciers) loom like a wall at the northern end of the lake. **Como** itself is a thriving industrial town. Silk weaving, which for many years was confined to homes and small workshops in Como, is now concentrated in several factories.

Como's **Giardini Pubblici** is a pleasant place to relax and look over the lake. In the midst of these gardens stands the

Tempio Voltiano, a classic rotunda dedicated to Alessandro Volta, who gave his name to the volt. Many of the instruments he used in his electrical experiments are on display.

It's an easy walk across the town to **Santa Maria Maggiore**, Como's 14th-century marble cathedral. The intricately carved portal is flanked by statues of the two Plinys, who were among the earliest admirers of Lake Como. "Are you given to studying, or do you prefer fishing or hunting or do you go in for all three?" the younger Pliny asked a friend and boasted that all three activities were possible at Lake Larius (the former name for Como). Some 2,000 years later, Como still offers sports to athletically inclined visitors, relaxation to harried city dwellers and inspiration to artists and poets.

The 11th-century **Sant' Abbondio** on the outskirts of Como will transport you back to Como's pre-resort days, when it was a pious and prosperous medieval village. Chances are you will have this solemn Lombard church to yourself. The 14th-century frescoes of the Life of Jesus, in the apse, make it worth the trip.

Although the distance between the two cities is not great, it takes an hour of driving on narrow, twisting roads to reach **Bellagio** from Como. Going by public boat from Como's pier is a more pleasant way of getting there. Bellagio sits on the point of land that divides Lago di Como into three parts. From here you can see the entire expanse of the lake and enjoy a spectacular view of the Alps. "Sublimity and grace here combine to a degree which is equalled but not surpassed by the most famous site in the world, the Bay of Naples," wrote Stendhal in *Chartreuse du Parme*. The Frenchman set the opening scenes of his novel in the **Villa Carlotta** (across the lake from Bellagio) after staying here as a guest. Today the villa, originally built by a Prussian princess for her daughter, is open to the public and its idyllic gardens provide the perfect setting for a picnic lunch.

Lecco, a pleasant city at the southeast

Bellagio, Lago di Como.

194

end of Lago di Como, is famous as the setting of Alessandro Manzoni's *I promessi sposi* (The Betrothed), a 19th-century novel which is a classic of Italian literature, and a revealing piece of social history. The author was a native of Lecco and a political activist instrumental in bringing about Italy's unification. Visitors can explore his childhood home, the **Villa Manzoni**.

Among the more antique attractions of the city is **Basilica** with its fine frescoes from the 14th century depicting the Annunciation, the Deposition and the Life of San Antonio. The oldest monument in the city is the bridge spanning the Adda river, the **Ponte Azzone Visconti**, built between 1336 and 1338.

Lago di Garda (Lake Garda) is the cleanest and largest of the Italian lakes. It is especially popular with Northern European tourists, who come to sail and water-ski. Its equable climate is responsible for soave and valpolicella wines.

On the shores of this lake is a garish remnant of the fascist era – **Il Vittoriale** – the home of the flamboyant Italian poet and patriot Gabriele d'Annunzio which was given to him by his greatest admirer, Benito Mussolini. Located in **Gardone Riviera**, at one time Lake Garda's most fashionable resort, Vittoriale is more than a house, it is a shrine to d'Annunzio's dreams of Italian imperialism. Included in the estate is the prow of the warship *Puglia,* built into the hillside. In the auditorium, the plane d'Annunzio flew during World War I is suspended from the ceiling. Mussolini subscribed to d'Annunzio's ideas wholeheartedly and accorded him a place of honour in fascist Italy.

From Salo and Gardone Riviera it takes no more than an hour to reach **Sirmione**, a medieval town built on a spit of land extending into the lake. The **Rocca Scaligera**, a fairytale castle, dominates the town's entrance. It was originally the fortress of the Scaliger family, rulers of Garda in the 13th century, and it is said that they entertained the poet Dante here. Across town, at the peninsula's end, are the ruins of a Roman spa, the **Grotte di Catullo**.

Fantail, Lago di Maggiore.

PIEDMONT, VAL D'AOSTA AND LIGURIA

If it is not so Italian as Italy it is at least more Italian than anything but Italy.
—Henry James

Piedmont (Piemonte) may strike today's visitor, as it did Henry James, as not very Italian. The bordering nations of France and Switzerland have contributed much to the cultural life of this northwestern region. Moreover, the Alpine landscapes of Piedmont, especially in the dramatic Valle d'Aosta, are very different from scenery elsewhere in Italy. But the particular Piedmontese twist on Italian life is not unappealing. It's as if the cool mountain breezes have bestowed a calming effect on the people. No wonder that it was a Piedmontese king, Victor Emmanuel, and his Piedmontese advisor, Camillo Cavour, who guided Italy to independence.

Turin (Torino), the capital of Piedmont, is a genuinely Italian city, but its proximity and century-old ties to France give it a strong Gallic flavour. During the Middle Ages, it was part of a Longobard duchy, but in the 16th century it became the capital of the French province of Savoy. Following the Risorgimento, it was the capital of United Italy from 1861 to 1865.

Today, Turin is headquarters for some of Italy's most successful industries, including the Fiat automobile company. It is also a centre for the chemical and confectionery industries, metal working and industrial design. But the factories of Turin are a long way from the city's gracious centre, with its wide streets and beautiful squares, gardens and parks where visitors can soak up the sun and sample the spirit of this most modern of Italian cities.

The centre of civic life in Turin is the fashionable **Via Roma**, an arcaded shopping street that connects the main railway station with **Piazza Castello**, a huge rectangular Renaissance square planned in 1584. In the centre stands **Palazzo Madama**, a 15th-century castle that now houses the **Museo Civico di Arte Antica** (Museum of Ancient Art). Included in this museum's collections are copies of the famous *Book of Hours* of the Duc de Berry, illustrated by Jan van Eyck.

Another fine building on the Piazza Castello is the baroque church of **San Lorenzo**, once the royal chapel. The royal residence was the 17th-century **Palazzo Reale**, in the nearby piazza of the same name. From the balcony of this palace, Prince Carlo Alberto declared war on Austria in March 1848. In the same square is the **Armeria Reale** (Royal Armoury).

Behind the Palazzo Reale, in **Piazza San Giovanni**, are the **Duomo** and **Campanile**. The former is a Renaissance construction designed by the Tuscan, Meo del Caprino; the campanile is the work of a baroque architect. Of far greater interest is the chapel behind the cathedral – **Cappella della Sacra Sindone** (Chapel of the Holy Shroud) – a work of Guarino Guarini. It contains the famous Turin Shroud, for centuries believed to be the shroud in which Christ

Left, view over Turin. **Right**, the city's Royal Garden.

was wrapped after the Crucifixion. The cloth is imprinted with the image of a bearded man crowned with thorns. However, carbon dating, conducted by three universities in 1989, revealed the shroud to be the work of clever medieval forgers. For four centuries the royal house of the Savoys owned the shroud, but on his death in 1983, the exiled king Umberto left the relic to the Vatican. It will, however, remain in Turin.

The Piedmontese capital may seem an unlikely centre for the study of Egyptian art, but there is a rich **Egyptian Museum** housed at the **Palazzo dell' Accademia delle Scienze**, off via Roma. The collection was assembled by Carlo Emanuele III. The same palazzo also contains a good picture collection on the second floor in the **Galleria Sabauda**. There are several beautiful Flemish and Dutch works, and many paintings by Piedmontese masters.

For a taste of France, visit the agreeable **Parco del Valentino**, on the bank of the Po, which contains miles of paths, a Botanic garden and the **Castello del Valentino**, a 17th-century palace built in the style of a French château. In 1884, Turin was the site of a great international exhibition for which the park's **Borgo Medioevale** (a pseudo-medieval town) was erected.

It is not surprising that the automobile capital of Italy should have a fine museum of cars. It can take hours to explore **Carlo Biscaretti di Ruffia Museo dell'Automobile**. Exhibits include the earliest Fiat, the Itala that won the world's longest automobile race (between Peking and Paris in 1907) and an elegant Rolls-Royce Silver Ghost.

Across the Po, a small hill, the **Monte dei Cappuccini**, is crowned by a Capuchin church and convent. After visiting here, take a bus or the rack railway to **Superga**, where you can visit the **Basilica di Superga**, a "great votive temple" (Henry James) by Juvarra which houses the tombs of the kings of Sardinia and the princes of Savoy. This basilica sits on a high hill commanding a splendid view of the natural amphitheatre of the Alps.

The Automobile Museum, Turin.

Val d'Aosta: For anyone who wishes to get away from the city, the beautiful Alpine valleys of Piedmont have much to offer in both winter and summer. During July and August the thrills of winter sports give way to the calmer delights of hiking and touring in an area with glaciers, hilltop castles, clear mountain lakes and streams, pine forests and green meadows.

The most striking part of this area is called Val d'Aosta. In 1947, this valley acquired political autonomy and became a region in its own right. Here rise Europe's highest mountains: Mont Blanc, Monte Rosa, and the Cervino (Matterhorn). The capital, **Aosta**, was an important city in Roman times and has many interesting Roman ruins. Roman walls surround the city, and the ruins of the **Roman Theatre**, in the northwest corner of Aosta, include the well-preserved backdrop of the stage. Emperor Augustus, nicknamed Aosta the "Rome of the Alps", and it is the Arch of Augustus that guards the main entrance to the city.

Dating from Aosta's medieval period are the cathedral and several smaller churches. Among the latter group, the **church of Sant' Orso** (outside the walls on Via Sant' Orso) is the most interesting. The architecture is a strange mix of Gothic and Romanesque. St Orso – he converted the first Christians in the Valle d'Aosta – is buried beneath the altar. Be sure to visit the cloister, which dates back to the 12th century and is known for its unusual carved pillars. Each carving represents a different scene from the history of Christendom.

The valley southeast of Aosta contains many fine castles, in particular those at **Fénis** and **Issogne**, which were used as both residences and fortresses. The lord of Verrès, Giorgio de Challant, commissioned the castle at Issogne in 1497. Today you can stroll through the former seigneurial apartments to see the collection of tapestries, jewellery and furniture.

Southeast of Turin Piedmont becomes rolling hills and long valleys, In some ways it is reminiscent of Tuscany, and

A cobbled street in Aosta.

like Tuscany it is an excellent wine-growing area. From Turin head towards Alba along the autostrada. If you have time, make a stop at **Bra** to see a fine baroque church, **Sant' Andrea**, and an attractive Gothic building called the **Casa Traversa**. The hills surounding the small town of **La Morra**, 10 km (6 miles) from Bra, are where one of Italy's greatest wines, Barolo, comes from. Between La Morra and Alba is the castle of **Grinzane Cavour**.

Alba has long been a favourite with gourmets. It sits at the centre of an area famous for white truffles. These treats are a principal attraction at the city's October fair. Alba also has a fine late 15th-century Gothic cathedral, with a 16th-century inlaid wooden choir.

For more taste treats, proceed to **Asti**, a city at the centre of a valley that produces Asti Spumante and other famous wines. The city's Gothic cathedral is a splendid edifice with three ornate portals and circular openings above. The nearby baptistry of San Pietro, dating from the 12th century, is the most interesting of the city's medieval monuments

The region of Liguria: A narrow strip of coastline sandwiched between sea and mountains, Liguria curves and twists in an east-west arch from the French border to Tuscany. Known as the Italian Riviera, the region is favoured by a year-round mild climate, excellent beaches, and the dramatic Maritime and Ligurian Apennines, which plunge in sheer cliffs or slope gradually to the sea. It is an area of sudden contrasts, not merely between rocky shores and deep green-blue water, but between cosmopolitan resorts and isolated villages, bustling ports and quiet inlets.

Genoa rises above the sea like a great theatre. Its tiers are elegant palazzi and its pit is a noisy, strong-smelling port, the most important in Italy. La Superba, as the city was known in its heyday, rose to prominence between the 11th and 15th centuries, growing rich on trade with the East, and economic and cultural control of Liguria and the island of Corsica.

Immediately behind the docks, the lower city begins. Here streets are ancient and narrow with twisting alleys called *carugi* – nowadays lined with exotic shops. The afternoon *passeggiata* in Genoa takes place on the elegant **Via Luccoli**, a *carugio* of slightly wider proportions than most. Strolling along with the prosperous Genoese, you can decide for yourself whether Mark Twain was right to consider the Genoese women the most beautiful in Italy.

Not far from the dock that serves large luxury liners is the **Stazione Principe**, an open and airy building facing a small square with a striking statue of Christopher Columbus, the most famous Genoese of all time. From the railway station follow the Via Balbi, an avenue lined on both sides with elegant Renaissance palazzi. Stop at No. 10, the 17th-century **Palazzo Reale**, famous for its mirror gallery and its art collection on the second floor.

Continue towards the centre on Via Balbi until it becomes **Via Garibaldi**. This street splits Genoa in two; to your right are the twisting alleys of the old **At the harbourside, Genoa.**

200

town, and to the left are the newer sections on the hillside. No. 11 Via Garibaldi is one of the most magnificent of Genoese palaces: **Palazzo Bianco**. This 16th-century structure was originally white, but the stone has darkened considerably with time. The facade is baroque, due to major remodelling in the early 18th century. Inside, an art collection features many extraordinary works by Flemish masters.

Across the street is the **Palazzo Rosso**; in this case time has wrought few changes in the colour. Enter this palace to see the beautiful courtyard. Most of the other Renaissance residences on Via Garibaldi are privately owned and can only be admired from the outside. The Romanesque-Gothic **Duomo** (12th–14th century) was, according to legend, founded by St Lawrence in the 3rd century. History, however, dates the building to 1118. One of the Cathedral's Gothic portals bears a relief sculpture of the Roman saint's gruesome martyrdom. While being burned alive, St Lawrence is supposed to have said to his tormen-

tors: "One side has been roasted, turn me over and eat it."

The doors open onto a severe interior, simply decorated with black and white marble in the central nave and galleries. At the end of the left nave is the entrance to the **Treasury**, a museum of the cathedral's artifacts. Among the sacred relics of the church is a basin of green Roman glass which, according to tradition, was used at the Last Supper. Some people believe it to be the true Holy Grail.

The Doria family who ruled Genoa in the Middle Ages built their houses and a private church around the **Piazza San Matteo**, lying two blocks behind the cathedral. Each of the buildings on this small, elegant piazza has a black and white facade.

To reach another fine Genoese church proceed from the cathedral down Via Chiabrera to Piazza Embriaci. Follow the precipitous Salita della Torre degli Embriaci up to **Santa Maria di Castello**, an elegant church with a complex of chapels, courtyards and gardens attached. This was once the site of a Roman camp, and several Roman columns have been incorporated into the Romanesque design of the central nave. The chapel to the left of the high altar contains a miraculous crucifix. Jesus's beard is said to grow longer each time there is a crisis in the city.

When you're tired of the churches and palaces, head down to the bustling waterfront for a plate of *trenette* with *pesto alla genovese* – a pungent sauce of basil, garlic and strong cheese.

The Italian Rivieras: Flanking Genoa on either side are two famous and beautiful coasts; each offers ample doses of sand, sun and sea, but they are quite different. The **Riviera di Ponente**, stretching from Genoa to the French border, is the longer of the two, and the one with more popular resorts. The **Riviera di Levante** is characterised by rocky cliffs and promontaries and has a large naval port at La Spezia.

Heading towards France from Genoa, the first city you will pass is **Savona**, a port and industrial centre. With the exception of a small Pinacoteca on Via Quatda Superiore, Savona offers little

The seafront, Portovenere.

of interest to the tourist. The town of **Finale Ligure**, a 30-minute drive further on, is a more inviting place. Visit the **Church of San Biagio**, which has an octagonal-shaped Gothic bell tower adjoining.

The most important town on the Riviera di Ponente, from the artistic and historic point of view, is **Albenga**. The Romans founded a port on this site in 181 BC, but over the centuries the topography has changed and today the old centre is about a mile from the beach. Surrounding the town is a well-preserved medieval wall and three large 17th-century gates. The cathedral of **San Michele** dates back to the 5th century. Even older are the Roman aqueduct and the ruins of a Roman amphitheatre. In addition to the historic monuments, are fine facilities for swimming and boating.

The nearby resort of **Alassio** has long been popular with celebrities and ordinary Italian tourists alike. The **Café Roma** in the centre of town has a wall – the **Muretto** – decorated with tiles bearing the signatures of, among others, Ernest Hemingway, Sophia Loren and Sir Winston Churchill.

Imperia was once two separate seaside towns: Oneglia and Porto Maurizio. It was Mussolini's idea to unite the two and name the city after a nearby river. The **Corso Matteotti**, a wide boulevard with magnificent views of the coast, links the two town centres. **Oneglia**, in the east, known for its olive oil and pasta production, is the more industrial and modern sector. A large church, **San Maurizio**, towers over the narrow streets of **Porto Maurizio**.

The Edwardian Age lives on at **San Remo**, a large, international resort that was once a gathering spot for the European aristocracy. Although there is a sense that San Remo's best days have passed, the city offers two enjoyable diversions: walking along the famous palm-lined promenade and gambling at the casino.

Near the tourist office at the city's centre is an authentic **Chiesa Russa**, recognisable by its dome and gilded

Far left, the Russian church of San Remo. **Left**, San Remo.

cross, which was built by a colony of exiled Russian nobles in the 1920s.

The gateway to France is at **Ventimiglia**, a centre of flower cultivation and a pleasant city with a fine medieval quarter. The major architectural attraction is the 11th-century **Duomo**. Of great natural beauty are the **Giardino Hanbury**, located in the village of Mortola, about 6 km (4 miles) from Ventimiglia, where you will find the living flora of five continents.

Riveria di Levante: Among the eastern suburbs of Genoa is **Quarto dei Mille**, famous as the starting point of Garibaldi's daring 1,000-man expedition that liberated Sicily and led to the unification of Italy. Nearby **Nervi** is the oldest winter resort on the eastern coast. Here you can take hot sea baths, or follow a 3-km (2-mile) cliff walk which is the city's pride.

After Camogli, take the branch off the main road that leads to **Portofino** via the way of **Santa Margherita** and **Paraggi**. Of these three resorts, Portofino is by far the most interesting. A tiny waterfront village of extraordinary, concentrated beauty, it was discovered by millionaires after World War II. Once, only fishing boats docked in the narrow, deep-green inlet, edged on three sides by high cliffs, but it is now a home for yachts. Part of Portofino's attraction is its small size. There are no beaches, and few large shops and restaurants. The pleasures of the port are visual – the reflection of brightly painted houses in the clear water, the ragged edges of stone heights set against the brilliant blue sky.

Rapallo is a family-style resort, with a large beach and many moderately priced hotels. Other attractions include the 17th-century **Collegiate Church** with its interesting bell-tower, and the 16th-century **church of San Francesco**, which houses several fine paintings by Borzone, a local artist. Nearby **Chiávari**, a wealthy shipbuilding city, once had close links with South America. The municipal museum contains a collection of Inca relics.

The Gulf of La Spezia has been praised so often by poets – Dante, Petrarch, Byron and Shelley, to name just a few of them – that it is simply called Golfo dei Poeti. On its western point the elongated orange and yellow houses of **Porto Venere** stretch up the precipitous mountain. The resort atmosphere here is friendly and relaxed as natives exchange gossip and tourists stroll alongside the pungent harbour, home to boats with names such as *Vergilia* and *Byron*.

Anglophiles and romantics should make a pilgrimage to the grotto – now littered with cigarette packets, drink containers and barely clad lovers – from where the virile Lord Byron began his famous swim across the Gulf to visit Shelley in **Casa Magni**. If you take the 20-minute boat ride to **Lerici** you will appreciate what a powerful swimmer the poet must have been to achieve such a feat. Shelley, alas, had less luck against the waves when his ship sank off the coast. The plaque, in Italian, on Casa Magni commemorates the tragedy: "Sailing on a fragile bark he was landed by an unforeseen chance to the silence of the Elysian Fields."

A street café, Portofino.

VENICE

I stood in Venice, on the 'Bridge of Sighs';
A Palace and a prison on each hand:
I saw from out the wave her structures rise
As from the stroke of the Enchanter's wand:
A thousand Years their cloudy wings expand
Around me, and a dying Glory smiles
O'er the far times, when many a subject land
Look'd to the winged Lion's marble piles,
Where Venice sat in state, throned on her hundred isles!

— Lord Byron: *Childe Harold's Pilgrimage*

When Lord Byron arrived in Venice in 1817, the "Queen of the Adriatic" had been in decline for many years. Though nonetheless enchanted by the beauty of the city, the poet describes her palaces as "crumbling to the shore".

The seeds of decline were sown at the turn of the 15th century when the Portuguese stripped Venice of its monopoly of the spice trade, and a decade later the League of Cambrai put an end to Venice's hold on crucial cities on the mainland. But if Venice has been on a downward trend for more than five centuries, it remains one of the most spectacular urban displays in the annals of tourism. It is not only tourists who are captivated by its charms. For centuries the city has lifted poets, painters and writers to new heights of inspired vision. Proust, James, Waugh and Hemingway are just a handful of the writers who have found her irresistible; few other cities in the world can boast a more prolific and talented school of painters, from Bellini and Giorgione through Titian and Tintoretto to Tiepolo and Guardi.

Built on over 100 islets, suppported by millions of wooden stakes and linked by 400 bridges, Venice is the only city in the world which is built entirely on water. The greatest advantage of this,

apart from the obvious aesthetic appeal, is the absence of cars. The biggest disadvantage is the fact that the city is prone to problems of flooding. The sense of precariousness, associated with the city for centuries, inevitably adds to the fascination for the visitor. There is always a feeling that once you turn your back on all this fragile but vibrant glory, the islands, once inhabited by refugees fleeing the hordes of Attila the Hun, will crumble and disappear like a mirage into the sea. It does indeed seem miraculous that Venice has stood for well over 1,000 years.

Most tourists have heard descriptions, seen pictures or read books about Venice before going there; but, however fervent the imagination, arriving is still a revelation.

The heart of Venice is the vast **Piazza San Marco.** Described by Napoleon as the most elegant drawing room in Europe, this is the great architectural showpiece of Venice. With its pigeons, café bands and exotic shops under the arcades, it is also the hub of tourist

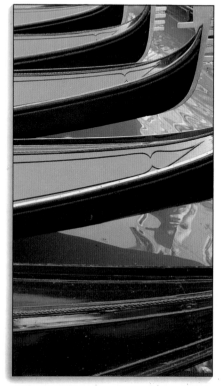

Preceding pages: the annual carnival of Venice with the Bridge of Sighs in the background. Left, the Palazzo Ducale. Right, gondolas, an essential part of the city.

Venice. At one end, crouching like an enormous, dark amphibious reptile, the great **Basilica di San Marco** (St Mark's Basilica) invites visitors to explore its mysterious depths.

The basilicia is named after the evangelist St Mark whose remains were recovered (or stolen, depending on your viewpoint) by the Venetians from Alexandria in the 9th century. The then ruler of Venice, Doge Giustiniano Participazio, built a church on this site to house the remains. The original church was destroyed by fire a hundred years later, and was replaced at the end of the 11th century by the huge ornate edifice we see today.

The sumptuous facade has five portals decorated with shimmering mosaics. The only original – in the doorway to the far left – gives a good idea of the basilica in the 13th century. Above the main portal are replicas of the famous bronze horses – the originals, looted from Constantinople in 1204, are now kept inside the basilica, protected from pigeons and pollution.

The basilica's interior, in the shape of a Greek cross, is thought to have been inspired by the Church of the Apostles in Constantinople. Above the columns of the minor naves, lining the arms of the cross, are the women's galleries or *matronei*, designed in accordance with Greek orthodox custom, which separates the sexes. The sumptuous atmosphere of the interior is enhanced by the decoration of the walls: marble slabs cover the lower part, while golden mosaics adorn the vaults, arches and domes. Following a complex iconographic plan, the mosaics cover 4,000 sq. metres (43,000 sq. ft), which is why St Mark's is sometimes called the Basilica d'Oro (Church of Gold). For a brief explanation of the mosaics join one of the groups that tour the basilica.

Among the many gems housed in the church are the Pala d'Oro, a jewel-studded gold and enamel altarpiece dating from the 10th century, and the Treasury, housing a priceless collection of gold and silver from Byzantium. The Marciano Museum, reached by steep

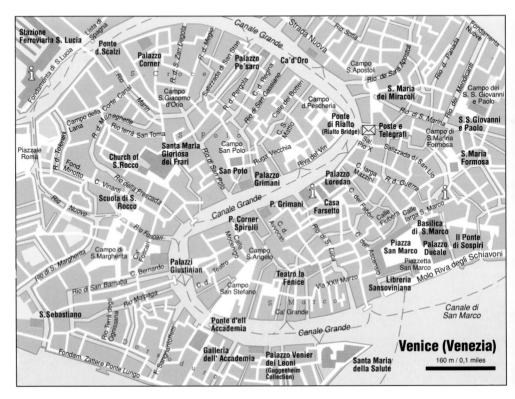

Venice (Venezia)

160 m / 0,1 miles

steps from the narthex, affords fine views of the interior as a whole, while the open-air terrace gives a bird's-eye view of Piazza San Marco. It was here that the doge and other dignitaries gathered to watch celebrations taking place below.

A striking feature of the square is the soaring **Campanile**, a faithful replica of the original tower that collapsed in 1902. Inside, a lift – or for the energetic a stairway – ascends 100 metres (327 ft) to the top for a sweeping panorama of the city and lagoon. The piazza's other tower is Coducci's intricate **Torre dell'Orologio** (Clock Tower), designed in 1496. On the top two mechanical bronze Moors strike the hour.

Adjoining the piazza and extending to the waterfront is the **Piazzetta San Marco**. On the right as you face the lagoon is the 16th-century **Libreria Sansoviniana**. Palladio, Italy's greatest 16th-century architect, considered this structure, with its finely sculpted arcades and detailed figures, one of the most beautiful buildings since ancient times. Today it houses the Archaeologi-

cal Museum, the National Library of St Mark and the Venetian Old Library – a collection of treasures from the city's golden years.

At the lagoon end of the Piazzetta stand two large 12th-century columns, one crowned with a winged lion, the symbol of Venice, the other with a statue of St Theodore, the original patron saint of the city. Public executions used to take place between the two columns.

Across the water lies one of Venice's great landmarks – the majestic **Church of San Giorgio Maggiore** on the little islet which takes its name. This classical masterpiece by Andrea Palladio has a huge white stone interior with works of art by Tintoretto and a campanile with views that, on a clear day, extend as far as the Alps.

The **Palazzo Ducale** (Doge's Palace) flanks the eastern side of the Piazzetta. This "vast and sumptuous pile", as Byron described it, is the grandest and most conspicuous example of Venetian Gothic in the city. The official residence of the Doge and the seat of government

San Marco.

during the republic, it stands today as eloquent evidence of the power and pomp of Venice in its heyday.

Inside, the three wings of the palace reveal a seemingly endless series of grandiose rooms and halls. The largest of these is the Sala del Consiglio Maggiore (the Great council Chamber) which could accommodate all 480 (and later 1700) of the Venetian patricians who sat on the council. The art collection here gives a foretaste of the countless artistic treasures scattered throughout the city, particularly the works by the two Venetian giants – Tintoretto and Veronese. One painting, *The Paradise* by Tintoretto, was for many years the largest painting in the world (7 metres x 22 metres/23ft x 72ft). Veronese's *Apotheosis of Venice*, in the same room, is another compelling masterpiece, though his finest work in the palace is *The Rape of Europa* in the Anticollegio.

Adjoining the palace is the former ducal prison. Once tried and convicted in the palace, prisoners were led across this slender covered bridge to their cell.

Since the windowed bridge offered him his last glimpse of freedom, it was called **Il Ponte dei Sospiri** (the Bridge of Sighs). Whatever its grim purpose, it has a romantic air, and is favoured today by young lovers who believe that if they kiss under the bridge, (presumably in a gondola) their love will last.

A completed tour of the ducal palace calls for a coffee break in the piazza. The most famous café is **Florian's**, for years a rendezvous of fashionable Venetian society. On the other side of the piazza, Quadri's was favoured by the Austrians during their occupation of Venice and hence cold-shouldered by the Venetians.

The Grand Canal: "The great street of Venice", as Henry James prosaically described the **Canal Grande** (Grand Canal), winds for some 3.5 km (2 miles) through the city. This splendid shimmering thoroughfare is flanked by pastel-coloured palaces in Byzantine, Gothic, Renaissance and baroque styles, built mostly between the 13th and the 18th century.

The Palazzo Ducale and the Piazzetta San Marco.

The best way to see the canal is from a boat. If you are feeling flush, hire a gondola from the San Marco waterfront. Thomas Mann, who commented that the gondolas of Venice were "black as nothing else on earth except a coffin", nonetheless found their seats "the softest, most luxurious, most relaxing in the world". Far cheaper, though less romantic and more noisy, is the No. 1 public waterbus which plies the length of the canal at frequent intervals.

Starting from San Marco, the entrance of the canal is marked on the left bank by the great baroque church of **Santa Maria della Salute**, designed by the great 17th-century baroque architect, Longhena Baldassare, and erected in thanks for the city's deliverance from the plague of 1630. To the enamoured James, the church was "like a great lady on the threshold of her salon… with her domes and scrolls, her scalloped buttresses and statues forming a pompous crown, and her wide steps disposed on the ground like the train of a robe."

On the same side further along is the one-storeyed **Palazzo Venier dei Leoni**, housing the Guggenheim Collection of modern art. The art works in the palace and gardens belonged to the late Peggy Guggenheim. When the American patron of the arts lived there the nude equestrian statue by Marino Marcini in the courtyard on the canal was rumoured to have a removable penis.

On the right bank opposite is the **Ca'Grande**, a three-storey Renaissance residence by Sansovino, now the office of the city magistrate.

The first bridge that spans the canal is the wooden **Ponte dell'Accademia**, built in 1932 as a temporary structure but retained through popular demand. It is named after the nearby **Galleria dell'Accademia** housed in the former Scuola della Cariá. This is the world's finest collection of Venetian paintings, with works by all the great exponents: Mantegna, the Bellinis, Giorgione (*The Tempest*), Carpaccio, Titian, Tintoretto, Veronese, Tiepolo, Guardi and Canaletto. Further down the canal on the same side stands the imposing baroque

Travelling by gondola.

palace of the **Ca'Rezzonico**, housing a museum of 18th-century Venice. The stately rooms are richly decorated with period paintings, furniture and frescoes. It was here that the poet Robert Browning died in 1889.

Wagner was staying at the second of the two Gothic **Palazzi Giustinian** on the left bank when he composed the second act of *Tristan and Isolde* during 1858–59. Next door the **Ca' Foscari** is a 15th-century palace in the Venetian Gothic style, named after the family of the great 15th-century doge who masterminded large Venetian conquests on the Italian mainland.

Beyond the S Angelo landing stage, on the right bank, the **Palazzo Corner Spinelli** was designed during the early Venetian Renaissance in the Lombardesque style by Coducci. Beyond the next side canal the **Palazzo Grimani,** now the Court of Appeal, is a late Renaissance masterpiece by Sanmicheli. In front of you Venice's most famous bridge, the **Ponte di Rialto**, arches over the canal. The former wooden draw-

bridges built across the canal at this point all collapsed, necessitating the erection of a more weighty stone struction. Antonio da Ponte, one of many eminent contenders for the commission, supervised its construction between 1588 and 1592. The single span, ballustraded bridge has two parallel rows of tightly packed shops, selling jewellery, leather, masks, silk and souvenirs.

The most beautiful Gothic palace in Venice, the **Ca d'Oro**, appears on the right at the first landing stage beyond the bridge. Originally it was covered in gold leaf, hence the name "House of Gold". Inside the Giorgio Franchetti art gallery comprises a varied collection of paintings, frescoes and sculpture. Further along on the left bank the enormous baroque **Palazzo Pe'saro** is another masterpiece by Longhena; this one houses the Galleria d'Arte Moderna and the Museo Orientale. The last building of note before the railway station is the **Palazzo Vendramin-Calergi**, one of the finest Renaissance palaces by Mauro Coducci (1440–1504). Wagner died here

Rialto Bridge.

in 1883. Today it is the winter quarters of the city's casino.

The sestieri of Venice: It is impossible to list all Venice's architectural and artistic treasures but perhaps the greatest experience the city can offer to the inquisitive visitor is the maze of tiny alleys, the narrow silent canals and the pretty squares and courtyards only minutes away from San Marco.

The city is divided into six *sestieri* or districts. The most central, **San Marco**, has the greatest concentration of sights, hotels, shops and restaurants. It also has some surprisingly quiet corners away from the piazza. Lovers of grand opera should visit **La Fenice**, Venice's jewel-box opera house. Two of Verdi's most popular works, *La Traviata and Rigoletto*, were first performed here. According to opera legend, Verdi kept the music of "La Donna è Mobile" a secret until just before the premier of *Rigoletto*, so convinced was he that if his catchy tune got out before the opening, every amateur tenor in Venice would be humming it and claiming it as his own. Verdi did not misjudge the song's popularity and to this day some gondoliers will sing it to paying passengers.

Leading north from the piazza and starting at the clock tower, is the **Merceria**. This ancient commercial thoroughfare is still one of Venice's busiest streets, flanked by small shops and boutiques.

The **Dorsoduro** is the most southerly section of historic Venice – an excellent area to stay if you are looking for a quiet *pensione* within easy access of central Venice. To the south the area is bounded by the **Zattere**, a long, broad quayside whose cafés and restaurants afford splendid views across the water to the island of Giudecca. East of the Accademia Gallery the Dorsoduro is quiet and intimate, characterised by pretty canals, small shops, galleries and chic residences of well-to-do Venetians and foreigners. Northwest of the Accademia the area around San Barnaba was traditionally the quarter for impoverished Venetian nobility. Today it is the scene of cafés, artisans and one of the

One of many quiet corners.

last surviving vegetables barges Further west the **church of San Sebastiano** was the parish church of Veronese and the interior is covered with many of his early works. The area becomes increasingly shabby towards San Nicolò dei Mendicoli, erstwhile home of sailors and fishermen. The charming Romanesque **church of San Nicolò dei Mendicoli** was expertly restored by the British Venice in Peril Fund in the 1970s.

The island of **Giudecca** across the Giudecca Canal is a quiet working-class area of narrow streets and tightly packed apartments. The main landmark on its waterfront is Palladio's **Redentore church**, built in gratitude for the city's deliverance from plague in 1576.

The *sestiere* of **San Polo** lies within the large bend of the Grand Canal, northwest of San Marco. The quarter around the **Rialto**, the oldest inhabited part of mainland Venice, became the gathering place of merchants from the east and thence the commercial hub of the city. It is still very much a bustling area, with shops, souvenirs and market stalls. Fruit and vegetables are laid out under the arcades of the Fabbriche Vecchie while the mock-Gothic stone loggia of the Pescheria marks the site of the morning fish market.

The major church of San Polo is the majestic brick Gothic **Santa Maria Gloriosa dei Frari**, usually referred to as The Frari. The interior houses some of Venice's finest masterpieces, including an exquisite *Madonna and Child* by Giovanni Bellini, Titian's celebrated and sublime *Assumption* (crowning the main altar) and – another masterpiece by Titian – the *Madonna di Ca' Pésaro*.

Close to the Frari, the **Scuola Grande di San Rocco** is celebrated for its series of religious paintings by Tintoretto. The dramatic scenes from the *Life of Christ* culminate in *The Crucifixion,* of which Henry James wrote: "Surely no single picture in the world contains more human life, there is everything in it including the most exquisite beauty. It is one of the greatest things of art."

Santa Croce, lying north and west of San Polo, is for the most part a relatively

Canal-side dining.

unexplored district. Its core is a maze of covered alleyways lined by peeling facades and criss-crossed by canals barely wide enough for the passage of a barge. Its squares are pleasingly shabby and homely, bustling with local life. The only real concession to tourism is the Piazzale Roma, the uninspiring arrival point for those coming to Venice by coach, bus or car.

Cannaregio is the quietest and most remote district in Venice, its name deriving from the word *canne* (reeds) recalling the time when all this area was marshland. The *sestiere* forms the northern arc of the city, stretching from the railway station to the Rio dei Mendicanti in the east.

At its heart lies the **Ghetto**: its name originated from an iron foundry (*getto*) which once stood here. This was Europe's first ghetto, an area for the exclusive but confined occupation of Jews. Built in the early 16th century, it gave its name to isolated Jewish communities throughout the world. It remained a ghetto until Napoleonic times. Though very few Jews still live here, the synagogues, tenements and kosher restaurants lend a distinctive Jewish air.

The northern part of Cannaregio is the most remote and the area around the lovely Gothic church of the **Madonna dell'Orto** the most appealing. Tintoretto was born here and lived at No. 3399, near the Campo dei Mori. Forming the northern border of Cannaregio, the Fondamenta Nuove is the main departure point for ferries to the northern islands. From here you can look across the water to the walled cemetery of the island of San Michele. Back from the main quayside, the baroque **church of the Gesuiti** has an outrageously extravagant green and white marble interior. The prize work of art is Titian's dramatic *Martyrdom of St Lawrence*.

To the east of Cannaregio, it is worth exploring the warren of alleys and canals. With luck you will stumble upon the **church of Santa Maria dei Miracoli.** Designed in the 1480s by Pietro Lombardo and members of his workshop, it is one of the loveliest Ren-

Venice is famous for its cats.

aissance churches in the city. Decorated inside and out with marble, it is often likened to a jewel-box,

Castello is the western section of the city, varied in character from the busy southern waterfront near San Marco to the humble cheek-by-jowl residences of the north. The area behind the Riva degli Schiavoni is worth discovering for its very pretty canals, quaysides and elegantly faded palaces. Essential viewing for art lovers is the frieze of paintings by Carpaccio in the **Scuola di San Giorgio degli Schiavoni** and the 16th-century **Church of San Zaccharia** by Coducci.

The **Campo Santa Maria della Formosa** is a pleasantly lived-in market square with a handsome Renaissance church. The spiritual heart of Castello is the **Campo Santi Giovanni e Paolo**, better known to Venetians as San Zanipolo. Standing prominently in this spacious square is Andrea del Verrochio's masterly bronze equestrian statue of the fierce *condottiere*, Bartolomeo Colleoni. Presiding over the square is the majestic Gothic **church of Santi Giovanni e Paolo**, where 46 doges are buried.

Part of eastern Castello is occupied by the **Arsenale**, the great shipyard of the republic where Venice's galleys were built and refurbished. It is now largely abandoned and inaccessible to the public, but you can see a small part from the No. 5 public waterbus. To the east of the public gardens is the venue of the **Biennale**, an international exhibition of modern art, held in even-numbered years.

Island excursions: There is plenty to see away from the historic centre of Venice. The lagoon was settled over a long period from the 5th century AD and you can still see the remains of the very first Venetian community on the tiny island of Torcello. Frequent ferry services link Venice to the main islands.

The **island of San Michele**, just north of Venice, is occupied by the cemetery and the early Renaissance church of San Michele in Isola, designed by Coducci. Napoleon, who forbade burials in the historic centre, established the cemetery

The island of Burano.

here. Ezra Pound and Igor Stravinsky are two of the eminent visitors to Venice who are buried here.

Further north the island of **Murano** is spread over five islets crossed with canals, which make it seem like a mini-Venice. In the late 13th century it became the centre of Venice's ancient glass-blowing industry, the factories being moved from the centre for fear of fire. The **Museo Vetrario** in the Fondamenta Giustinian has exquisite examples of glasswork of all periods. The island's main street, the **Fondamenta dei Vetrai**, is packed with glass-blowing shops that offer free demonstrations, followed by a tour of the show-rooms.

Venice's justly famous lace industry is based in **Burano**, northeast of Venice. This is a colourful island where canals are lined by brightly painted houses and stalls selling lace and linen. The prices tend to be cheaper than those of Venice, but beware of imitiation Venetian lace, made in the Far East.

Torcello, the most remote of these islands (an hour by ferry), is the least populated and, for many, the most interesting. This rural, marshy island was the site of the original settlement in the Venetian lagoon. In the 7th century its population exceeded 20,000. The island was effectively abandoned after the waters silted up, creating malarial marshes. Still standing is the magnificent Byzantine cathedral, dating from the 7th century but rebuilt in the 11th century. A large striking mosaic of *The Virgin*, standing above a frieze of apostles, decorates the chancel apse of the church; while the entire western wall is covered by a huge and elaborate mosaic depicting *The Last Judgement*.

To the south of Venice, on a different route, lies the **Lido**, where Thomas Mann's unhappy von Aschenbach loitered too long, feasting his tired eyes on Tadzio and died of cholera.

The Lido is no longer the fashionable resort depicted in *Death in Venice* but in the hot summer months, when the city and its sights overwhelm, the sands and sea air can provide a welcome break.

The symbol of Venice.

PAX EVAN
TIBI GELI
MAR STA
CE MEVS

VENICE ENVIRONS

"Fair Padua, nursery of Arts" was how Shakespeare described the city of Italy's second oldest university, where Renaissance Englishmen came to "suck the sweets of sweet philosophy". Dante and Galileo both lectured at **Padua** (Padova), and in the mid-17th century, a learned woman earned a doctorate here. (Padua's most famous daughter, however, is without a doubt Katherina, Shakespeare's tamable shrew.)

But long before the university was established in 1222, Padua was an important Roman town, believed by Virgil to have been founded by the brother of the Trojan King Priam after the fall of Troy, though in fact it had been a settlement of pre-Roman tribesmen. (The Roman historian Livy was born in the nearby hills and was always proud to call himself a Paduan.)

Padua is also a magnet for the faithful. Every June, pilgrims come from all over the world to honour St Anthony of Padua, a 13th-century itinerant preacher whose famously spell-binding sermons packed church pews throughout Italy. The **Basilica di S Antonio**, built over his remains between 1232 and 1307, celebrates his sanctity handsomely, with works by Donatello (who lived in Padua between 1443 and 1453), Sansovino and Menabuoi. Venetian influence is evident in the church's design. Byzantine domes, an ornate facade and two high, thin bell towers give the exterior an eastern appearance. The interior, despite its Gothic plan, also has many Byzantine decorative details. The chapel of St Anthony, where the revered tomb lies behind the altar, is a 16th-century design by Biosco.

In **Piazza del Santo**, to one side of the basilica, stands a famous equestrian statue of Erasmo da Narni, called *Gattamelata*, by Donatello. This sculpture of the great Venetian *condottiere* is believed to be the first great bronze cast in Italy during the Renaissance. Also in the piazza is the **Oratorio di San**

Donatello's *Gattamelata*.

Giorgio, originally a private mausoleum for the prominent Soranzo family. The oratory is completely decorated with beautiful frescoes depicting the lives of the saints by Altichiero and Avanzo. On the corner of the piazza is the entrance to the **Museo Civico** which houses paintings by Bellini, Titian and Giorgione, among others.

The Via Belludi leads to another notable square, the **Prato della Valle,** fronted by the **Basilica di Santa Giustina**. A small park at its centre is reached by crossing one of the four stone bridges over a circular moat. In the park a circle of statues represents the famous past citizens of Padua.

The city centres on the crowded **Piazza delle Erbe**, one of the three market squares. Here stands the **Palazzo della Ragione**, called locally **Il Salone**, a massive medieval structure. The interior is decorated with fine frescoes and houses a large wooden horse copied from Donatello's bronze masterpiece.

Behind Il Salone is a large coffeebar, **Caffè Pedrocchi**, famous throughout Italy as a gathering place for intellectuals. During the Risorgimento, liberals from the nearby university met here to discuss the founding of the new nation.

From here it is only a short walk through **Piazza dei Signori** to Padua's **Duomo**. Although the cathedral was designed by Michelangelo, many alterations were made to his plans and the result is rather disappointing. The most interesting corner of the church is the frescoed baptistry.

Miser's Madonna: To the north of the university lies the **Cappella degli Scrovegni**, also known as Madonna dell'Arena on account of the nearby ruins of a Roman amphitheatre. Enrico Scrovegni commissioned this richly decorated chapel in 1303 to atone for his father's sinful miserliness and usury. It contains a cycle of frescoes by Giotto depicting the history of Christian redemption from the Immaculate Conception of the Virgin Mary through to the Last Judgement. The panels rank among Giotto's masterpieces. The solidity and emotional depth of the figures

The Basilica di Santa Giustina from the Prato della Valle.

marked a turning point in Western painting. "In my opinion," wrote Giorgio Vasari in the 17th century, "painters owe to Giotto, the Florentine painter, exactly the same debt they owe to nature, which constantly serves them as a model and whose finest and most beautiful aspects they are always striving to imitate and reproduce… it was Giotto alone who, by God's favour, rescued and restored the art, even though he was born among incompetent artists."

It is lucky for art lovers that the Arena Chapel escaped the fate of the nearby **Degli Eremitani** whose apse, covered with precious Mantegna frescoes, was bombed during World War II – Italy's greatest art loss of the war.

Vicenza: Andrea di Pietro, nicknamed Palladio, the most prominent architect of the Italian High Renaissance, lived and worked for most of his life (1508–80) in Vicenza. Rich and eager to decorate their city with new buildings, the gentry gave Palladio many opportunities to use his talents. As a result there is hardly a street in central Vicenza not graced by a Palladian villa despite the destruction of 14 of Palladio's buidings during World War II.

In **Piazza dei Signori**, at the city's heart, stand two of Palladio's masterpieces. The **Basilica**, his first major work, is not a church but a remodelling of a Gothic courthouse (called basilica in the Roman sense – a place where justice is administered). Palladio's elegant design features two open galleries, the lower one with Tuscan Doric columns and the upper one with Ionic columns. Facing the Basilica is the **Loggia del Capitanio**, a later Palladian work with a far more ornate style. This building was commissioned in 1571 to honour the victory at Lepanto – a triumphant occasion which called for the garish details and the extravagant balustraded windows.

The city's Gothic-style **Duomo** stands two blocks behind the Basilica. It was badly bombed during World War II but has since been completely rebuilt. The interior is unremarkable. A Palladian cupola tops the roof.

A view over Vicenza.

North of the Duomo is **Corso Palladio**, the city's main street, lined with many fine villas. Number 163, the so-called **Casa del Palladio**, was built for one of the city's merchants and was never Palladio's home. With its classic lines and precise, geometric proportions, it is a typical example of Palladio's work. Another excellent example of the Palladian style is the **Palazzo Chiericati**, in the Piazza Matteotti, at the end of Corso Palladio. This beautiful building houses the city's art collection. Tintoretto's *Miracle of St Augustine* and several fine works by Flemish artists are on permanent exhibit.

Palladio was not the only famous architect to work in Vicenza. The younger Scamozzi, who learned much from Palladio, is famous in his own right. The **Palazzo del Comune** on the Corso Palladio is Scamozzi's work and reflects his strict interpretation of classical architecture. But, in general, he was less innovative than his master.

The finest example of Scamozzi's and Palladio's joint work is the **Teatro Olimpico**, said to have been the first covered theatre in Europe when it was built between 1580 and 1582. Palladio died before its completion and Scamozzi took over. The theatre is a wood and stucco structure with a permanent stage set of a piazza and streets in perfect perspective. In 1585, the first play performed here was Sophocles's *Oedipus Tyrannus*. The theatre is still in regular use today.

Monte Bérico, a forested hill visible from all parts of Vicenza, is well worth a visit. Take a bus from the Piazza Duomo, or walk for approximately one hour to reach the basilica that crowns the top of the hill. This is the **Madonna del Monte**, a 17th-century rebuilding of a chapel that commemorated the site of two apparitions of the Virgin. The final section of the approach is covered by a portico with 150 arches and 17 chapels. Inside, the basilica is spacious and airy. The works of art include a *Pietà* by Montagna to the right of the altar.

During World War I, the mountains beyond Vicenza were the scene of many

great battles. The **Piazza e della Vittoria**, a few yards from the church, is a memorial to all the Italians who died close to here. Further downhill is the **Villa Rotonda**, a famous belvedere built by Palladio, with a distinctive circle within a cube design.

Verona: Built in the distinctive local pink marble, Verona has a rosy hue, as if the sun were constantly setting. In actuality, there is nothing faded about this modern industrial centre, now at the peak of its glory. What was once a thriving Roman settlement is today one of the most prosperous and elegant cities in Italy.

The **Piazza Brà** is where the Veronese gather day and night to talk, shop and drink together. They sit or stroll in the shadow of the glorious 1st-century Roman **Arena**, the third largest structure of its kind in existence. It seems large today, but it was once even bigger. The highest fragment, called the Ala, reveals the arena's original height. The Veronese have taken an interest in the arena's preservation since the 16th century. It is often used for city fairs and, in summer, for opera.

The Roman Forum of Verona was located in what is now **Piazza delle Erbe**, off the **Via Mazzini**. This large open space has a quirky beauty due to the variety of palazzi and towers that line its sides. Among the most impressive is the baroque **Palazzo Maffei**, next to the **Torre del Gardello**, the tallest Gothic structure in the square. The palace, with the attractive double arched windows on the corner of **Via Palladio** is the medieval guild house – **Casa dei Mercanti**.

The adjoining **Piazza dei Signori** is more formal than its neighbour. The **Palazzo della Ragione** stands on the border between the two squares. It's a massive structure with heavy exterior decoration; but the interior courtyard has a delicate Gothic stairway. Opposite this palazzo rises the **Loggia del Consiglio**, considered the finest Renaissance building in the city. Nearby are the tombs of the Scaligeri, dedicated to the della Scala family, the one-time

Bridge over the Adige, Verona.

222

rulers of Verona. The high monuments have been elaborately sculpted in the 14th-century style.

Verona is, of course, the city of *Romeo and Juliet*. Though the Capulet and Montague families immortalised by Shakespeare did actually exist, the story of the star-crossed lovers was entirely fictional. However, what is now a rather seedy bar on the Via delle Arche Scaligeri was allegedly once the **Casa Romeo**. Rather better maintained is **Juliet's house** (No. 23 Via Cappello, near Piazza Erbe), a compact medieval townhouse complete with balcony. It is also possible to visit Juliet's purported final resting place. The "tomb" is several miles out of the centre on the Lungoadige Capuleti.

If your taste runs to the Gothic, head for **Sant' Anastasia**, which, behind its brick facade, houses a magnificent painting by Pisanello of St George, as well as frescoes by Altichiero and Turone. Verona's **Duomo** is nearby. Inside is Titian's *Assumption of the Virgin*.

The **Castelvecchio** on the Adige is a reminder of one of the grimmer chapters in the history of "fair Verona". The castle was first built in 1354 by the hated tyrant Can Grande II della Scala so that he might shut himself up safely if a rebellion occurred. As it turned out, he met his end not at the hands of the mob but through the treachery and ambition of his own brother, who stabbed him. As elsewhere in Italy, this fortress, whose closets are crammed with skeletons, is now a very pleasant museum with paintings by Veronese, Tiepolo, Bellini and other artists of the Veneto.

A saint: But in addition to a benevolent or malevolent ruling family, an Italian city must have a patron saint, and Verona is no exception. Little is known about S Zeno, a 4th-century holy man, though it seems he was a fisherman. His most famous miracle is depicted by Nicolas Pisano on the porch of the **Basilica di S Zeno**, Verona's most beautiful church. According to the story, the saint was out fishing when he saw a man being dragged into the Adige by crazed oxen. S Zeno made the sign of the Cross, exorcised the devils and the man continued safely on his journey.

The bronze doors of the church are of splendid workmanship though the artists who created the slightly crude, but emotionally powerful scenes are unknown. For an explanation of these panels and the rest of the art in the church, buy the explanatory booklet from the bookshop; it is well worth the price.

And a prophet: Although S Zeno and the Arena are Verona's most important monuments, there is no question that most people are drawn to Verona because of *Romeo and Juliet*. In recognition of the publicity that William Shakespeare has given their city, the Veronese frequently perform his plays during the summer months in their **Teatro Romano**, an ancient construction of perfect proportion and boasting superb acoustics. You may even be lucky enough to see *Romeo and Juliet*. The bereaved Montague's closing speech has certainly proved prophetic: "That while Verona by that name is known,/ There shall no figure at such rate be set/ As that of true and faithful Juliet."

Juliet's house.

TRENTINO-ALTO ADIGE

This mountainous region, which stretches north to the Italian-Austrian border, first came to the attention of tourists in the English-speaking world in 1837 when Murray, a London publisher, brought out a handbook for travellers. The book's description of the Dolomites sparked interest particularly among mountaineers who had conquered the Swiss Alps and were looking for new challenges: "They are unlike any other mountains, and are to be seen nowhere else among the Alps. They arrest the attention by the singularity and picturesqueness of their forms, by their sharp peaks or horns, sometimes rising up in pinnacles and obelisks, at others extending in serrated ridges, teethed like the jaw of an alligator."

Today, Trentino-Alto Adige (also known as South Tyrol) is a popular holiday retreat for hikers, skiers and water sports enthusiasts. It is marked by contrasts, in the landscape as well as in the culture. Here it is possible to hike around a secluded alpine lake in the morning, sample wine in an Italian vineyard at noon, stroll along the palm-lined promenade of a European spa in the afternoon and then slip into bed in a medieval castle at the end of the day.

Trentino-Alto Adige actually consists of two distinctly different provinces. Trentino, historically a part of Italy except for a period during the 19th and early 20th centuries when it was ruled by Austria, has a definite Italian flair. Alto Adige, on the other hand, was a part of the Austrian Tyrol for six centuries, first becoming an Italian domain in 1919 when the Austro-Hungarian empire was carved up and the European borders redrawn.

The Germanic traditions, culture and language have remained, despite post-World War I efforts by Mussolini to stamp them out. The dictator Italianised not only the names of the towns, mountains and rivers but even went so far as to force the South Tyrolean people to adopt Italian family names. Schools were forbidden to teach in German and huge numbers of Italians were sent into the region to run both the government and industries as well as to tip the ethnic balance within the population.

The South Tyroleans, however, insisted on clinging steadfastly to their cultural heritage, turning, in the 1960s, to acts of terrorism in an attempt to gain more autonomy for the province. Today, the atmosphere is once again peaceful as Italians and Germans live side by side, accepting and even appreciating each other's differences. The province is officially bilingual.

The mix of cultures is just one of the factors which makes Trentino-Alto Adige so diverse. The landscape in the east and north is marked by the awe-inspiring rocky Dolomite peaks while the rolling green hills of the south central region are blanketed with vineyards and orchards. The castles, of which there are more than 350, vary greatly, ranging from crumbling overgrown ruins reminiscent of the one described in *Sleeping*

Left, Castel Tirolo, one of the romantic castles that dot Trentino-Alto Adige. **Right**, German influences are clear.

Beauty to castles totally overhauled and now housing restaurants, hotels or well-appointed museums documenting the region's history.

The sleepy spa city of **Merano** (Meran), with its palm-lined promenades, exclusive shops, fine restaurants and grand old hotels offers the visitor a taste of old Europe. The largest and most renowned spa in the alps, Merano has played host to the great and the gracious for well over a century. Those who can afford it come to relax and take the cure in a Mediterranean-like climate. The city owes its famously mild climate to its position in a deep basin, protected to the north by the massive Alpine peaks and opening to the Etsch valley in the south. Merano flourished between the late 13th and early 15th centuries when it was the capital of the Tyrol. Thereafter, it passed into relative insignificance until its value as a spa was discovered.

Just a short distance north of Merano is the **Castel Tirolo**, one of the only castles in the world to have lent its name to an entire land. During the summer months concerts are performed in the castle. Just down the hill is the **Castel Brunnenburg**, where Ezra Pound (1885–1972) spent the last years of his life. From here the Passeier valley, birthplace of the Tyrolean freedom fighter Andreas Hofer, stretches north to the Austrian border.

To the west of Merano, the Venosta (Vinschgau) extends all the way to the Swiss/Austrian/Italian border. The route leading over the **Reschen Pass** was first constructed during Roman times as an important link between Augsburg and the Po valley. Vinschgauer bread, baked in small flat loaves and flavoured with aniseed, is worth sampling.

The **Val Senáles** (Schnals valley), which branches to the north just past Naturno, passes through the region of the Simulaun glacier. It was here that the 5,000-year-old "Simulaun Man" was found frozen in the glacier by hikers in the autumn of 1991. This well-preserved archaeological specimen, replete with tools, weapons and intact clothing, has

The place for winter snow.

provided valuable new insights into life in the early Bronze Age.

In the central part of Alto Adige is the **Valle Sarentina** (Sarn Valley), a region where time seems to have stood still. The simple lifestyle of the peasants in this valley presents a direct contrast to the wealth and splendour of Merano. Old farms perched precariously on the mountainsides, appearing to defy all natural laws of physics, wild rushing brooks carving deep gorges through the mountain walls; and the people themselves, celebrating traditional festivals dressed in colourful national costumes, all combine to give a feeling of yesteryear. The ancient craft of *Federkielstickerei*, or embroidering with peacock quills, is still practised here. The quill is split lengthways with a razor-sharp knife into thin threads. These are then used to embroider leather goods such as shoes, braces, handbags and book covers. In **Sarentino** (Sarntheim) you can watch the craftsmen at work.

The road leading out of the Sarn valley towards the provincial capital of Bolzano (Bozen) winds through numerous tunnels before emerging at **Castel Róncolo** (Schloss Runkelstein), built on a towering cliff in 1250 and today housing a museum with noteworthy Gothic frescoes.

Bolzano (Bozen) provides one of the most vivid examples of the coexistence of Italian and Germanic culture. The old part of the city, gathered around Piazza Walther and the arcades of the Via dei Portici, is marked by patrician houses and German Gothic architecture. Adjacent to Piazza Walther is the impressive Gothic Duomo, built in the 13th–14th centuries and reputedly the oldest hall church in Alto Adige. On the other side of the Talfer river, in "New Bolzano", the Italian influence is seen in the austere buildings constructed during the Mussolini era. As a part of the Italianisation effort after World War I, the city was industrialised, and today Bolzano, outside of the old town, is an unattractive mass of factories and fume-spewing smoke-stacks.

From Bolzano a cable car takes visi-

Bolzano.

tors on a scenic journey up to the **Renòn** (Ritten) **Plateau**, a popular resort area. On a clear day, the views of the Dolomite formations are spectacular. Here, too, are the unique earth pyramids, giant conical piles of sand with a slab of stone perched on the top of each. These impressive natural features are the result of centuries of erosion.

Just east of Bolzano is the **Sciliar** (Schlern) **massif**, towering like a great stone fortress above the surrounding area. At its base is the **Alpe di Siussi** (Seiser Alm), Europe's largest expanse of mountain pastureland comprising almost 50 sq. km (20 sq. miles) and offering an abundance of hiking and ski trails. The nearby town of **Fié** (Völs) is renowned for its hay baths, reputed to cure a wide variety of ailments.

Following the road from Scilia to **Castelrotto**, one emerges in the **Val Gardena** (Grödner valley) with the popular ski resorts of **Ortisei** (St Ulrich), **S Cristina** (St Christina) and **Selva** (Wolkenstein). This valley is also famous for its woodcarvers. From **Wolkenstein**, the Sella Joch Pass winds its way between the jagged peaks of Mt Langkofel and the majestic Sella massif. Travellers through this pass enjoy a panoramic view of Mt Marmolada, the region's highest mountain.

This route connects with the Great Dolomite Road which leads east to **Cortina d'Ampezzo**, the site of the 1956 Winter Olympics and today a popular winter resort, and west over the **Costalunga** (Karer Pass) to Bolzano. The road towards Bolzano passes the **Catinaccio** (Rosengarten) **massif**, steeped in the legend of the mythical mountain king Laurin. It is said that this dwarf turned his beloved rose garden into stone when enemies attacked his kingdom, decreeing that it would never bloom again, day or night. During the twilight hours, however, the rose-coloured rays of the setting sun bathe the cliffs in a sea of red, reminding visitors of the origin of the name.

Lana, located between Bolzano and Merano, is the centre of the apple-growing region. The parish church in **Nieder-**

Grazing under the Rosengarten Massif.

lana contains Alto Adige's largest late Gothic winged altar piece, measuring over 14 metres (46 ft) in height. Just across the valley from Lana is **Avelango** (Hafling), home of the famous Hafling breed of horses.

In central Alto Adige the **Isarco Valley** (Eisack valley) has, for the past 2,000 years, served as the major route connecting the German north to the Latin South via the Brenner Pass. The former commercial importance of **Vipiteno** (Sterzing), the northernmost town along this route, is still evident today in its patrician houses.

Bressanone (Brixen), the region's oldest settlement, was a bishop's see from 990 until 1964 when the bishop moved to Bolzano. Interesting sights include the prince-bishop's palace and the baroque duomo. The latter has impressive marble work on the walls as well as lovely ceiling frescoes. A stroll through the Gothic cloisters adjacent to the duomo is well worthwhile. The frescoes in the cloisters, dating from 1390 to 1509, are among the best examples of Gothic painting in all of Alto Adige. The late Romanesque chapel of St John, located at the southern end of the cloisters, was built as a baptismal church.

Just north of Bressanone, stretching to the east, is the **Pusteria Valley**. The valley's main town is **Brunico** (Bruneck) with its lovely main street lined with houses dating from the 15th–16th century. A bit west of Brunico the **Badia** (Gadera) **valley**, where the Rhaeto-Romanic language of Ladin is still spoken, branches to the south. From Brunico, the **Túres valley** leads north to **Campo Túres** (Sand in Taufers), site of **Castle Túres**. The castle has been restored with many of its original furnishings and is open to the public. The Pusteria valley is the gateway to the Sexten Dolomites where the majestic Three Pinnacles and the Sexten Sundial formations are located. The latter was used in early times by astronomers as a point of orientation.

In direct contrast to the rugged mountainous north, the **Adige** (Etsch) **valley** in south central Alto Adige is marked by

Making hay.

a more tranquil landscape. The fertile hills are blanketed with vineyards while orchards stretch across the plains. In the early spring, the entire region explodes in a sea of blossoms. Here the wine road leads south along the river through a series of quaint towns, all renowned for their wine. The tasting of the new wine accompanied by roasted chestnuts, ham and other specialties of the region, is an important autumn activity. In more recent years this has become quite a commercial operation, with buses disgorging swarms of tourists at the larger establishments. Visitors looking for traditional cellars, where the atmosphere is more genuine, are advised to seek them along hiking paths rather than along the main motor routes.

In addition to the wealth of castles, this region is also the site of numerous aristocratic residences dating from the late 16th and early 17th centuries when it was the fashion among the Tyrolean nobility to build country houses in the Italian Renaissance palazzi style. Many of these now serve as hotels and restaurants offering fine food and rooms fit for a king. **Lago di Caldaro** (Lake Kalterer), nestled between vineyards and a waterfowl preserve, is one of the warmest lakes in the Alps. A bit further south is **Termino** (Tramin), home of the world-famous traminer grape.

Trentino: The capital of the province of Trentino is **Trento**, site of the Council of Trent which was held intermittently between 1545 and 1563. It was during these sessions, called by the Catholic Church to discuss the rising threat of Lutheranism, that the seeds for the Counter-Reformation were sown. Noteworthy sights include the **Duomo**, built between the 13th and 14th centuries in an austere Romanesque-Gothic style, and the **Castello del Buonconsiglio** (Castle of Good Counsel), the residence of the prince-bishops who ruled the city for centuries. Located at the edge of the old part of town, the castle consists of several palazzi enclosed by a wall. Today it houses a museum of local art.

The province of Trentino is noted for **Roasting chestnuts.**

its landscape – beautiful valleys and plains, jagged mountains and more than 300 lakes, lending the area its nickname "the Finland of Italy". These characteristics have made Trentino a popular holiday resort. Recently, however, an effort has been made by the tourism office to lure more visitors through a variety of cultural events during the summer months. Theatre, concerts, dance performances and exhibitions are staged in castles throughout the province. Just as in Alto Adige, castles are abundant, ranging from cliff-top fortresses to lakeside palaces.

The region of **Lavarone** is located to the southeast of Trento. Here one finds dark green forests, mountain pastures, lakes and caves full of stalactite and stalagmite formations. The lakes invite meditative thought. It was on the shores of the small **Lago di Lavarone** that Sigmund Freud, the father of psychoanalysis, liked to stroll while letting his mind wander in its search for the relationship between the psyche and human behaviour.

The **Paganella mountains**, considered by many to be the most beautiful in Italy, range to the north of Trento. At the foot of this massif are the **lakes of Terlago**, **Lago Santo** and **Lamar**. Just a bit further south is **Lago Toblino** with a short hiking path leading to **Ranzo**, a small village with a breathtaking panorama over the valley of the lakes. More ambitious trekkers can follow the *translagorai* route through the wild **Catena dei Lagorai** in the eastern part of the province, passing by numerous serene alpine lakes.

History buffs might want to visit **Lago di Ledro** just west of **Lago di Garda** where the remains of a Bronze-Age stilt village can be seen as well as a museum with tools, canoes and other relics excavated from the former village. The northern tip of Lago di Garda is located within Trentino. Although many towns on the lake have, in the past, been obliged to close their beaches due to pollution, the northern waters remain uncontaminated and are well worth exploring (see *The Lakes, pages 193–195*).

Lakeside leisure in summer.

FRIULI-VENEZIA GIULIA

Since the 2nd century BC, when the Romans took over the northeast corner of what later became known as the Italian peninsula, Friuli-Venezia Giulia has been a victim of foreign invasions. The Visigoths poured into the area in 403 AD; Attila the Hun – who here earned his nickname "the Scourge of God" – took over in 452; and in 489 came Theodoric and the Ostrogoths. Many of the region's most gracious modern towns, including Cividale, started out as Barbarian outposts. Venice conquered most of Friuli in 1420, and though strong Trieste managed to hold out against the Venetians, she needed the help of the Dukes of Austria to do it. Once the Austrians had got a foot in the door, they stepped in the rest of the way, kicking out the Venetians and ruling from the 18th century until unification.

Of all Friuli's foreign invaders, however, perhaps the most well-known is James Joyce, who arrived in **Trieste** on March, 1905. He may not be Trieste's favourite son – he was constantly in debt, often drunk, and given to shouting in the theatre – but the city was his home for the following 10 years. Here Joyce's wife, Nora Barnacle, gave birth to their two children, and Joyce finished *Dubliners*, wrote the final draft of *A Portrait of the Artist as a Young Man*, and conceived the idea for *Ulysses*.

Today the city has an air of faded elegance. Once Venice's rival for trade on the Adriatic, later the gateway to the sea for the Austro-Hungarian empire, Trieste is now a port without a hinterland, a city that history left behind.

In the Città Nuova, long, straight avenues flank a Grand Canal where tall ships once anchored. Southwest of the canal is the **Piazza dell'Unità d'Italia**, said to be the largest piazza in Italy. Life in Trieste gravitates to the Piazza dell' Unità, where cafés provide pleasant roosting spots from which to eye the passing scene. At the head of the Piazza stands the ornate **Municipio**, of 19th-

Trieste on the Adriatic.

century Austrian inspiration. At the foot of the piazza, across the railroad tracks, stretches the long quay or *Riva*.

Behind the Municipio are the narrow, winding streets of the **Città Vecchia**. Stairs by the **Teatro Romano** (closed to visitors) ascend steeply to the 6th-century **Cattedrale di San Giusto**. The two basilicas that originally stood side by side here were combined into a single four-aisled structure in the 14th century.

At the top of the hill here – also named San Giusto after the city's patron saint – rises a 15th-century Venetian **Castello**, with a sweeping view of the city and the harbour. The **Museo Civico** inside the castle has exhibits of early weapons plus a small art collection.

On your way back down the hill, you may want to stop at the **Museo di Storia ed Arte**, which features relics from the various invaders and inhabitants of Friuli-Venezia Giulia: Roman sculpture and engravings, prehistoric vases, Lombard jewellery. Also worth a visit is the Basilica of **San Silvestro** on the hillside, dating from the 12th century.

For a last glimpse of Trieste, a city halfway between east and west, stop at **San Spiridione**, located near the canal. This Greek Orthodox church boasts more than 100 icons.

Seven km (4 miles) west of Trieste is the seaside town of **Barcola**. There, the **Castello Miramare**, once the home of Archduke Maximilian, brother of Emperor Franz Josef of Austria, sits on a promontory overlooking the waves. Built between 1856 and 1860, this residential fortress is a strange mix of a neoclassic linear style with mock medieval details. The interior is a museum honouring the ill-fated archduke, who later became Emperor of Mexico and died in front of a revolutionary firing squad.

The Romans based their Northern Adriatic fleet at **Aquileia**. The sea has receded in 2,000 years and today Aquileia lies several miles inland. The many Roman remains include ruins of the once-vast harbour, dating from the 1st century AD. Aquileia was also a grand city in the early Middle Ages. The best remnant of that time is the **Basilica**, with its beautiful mosaic floor.

Though off the beaten track for most tourists, **Udine** has an appealing style all its own. Echoes of Venetian rule are everywhere: the 16th-century **Castello** that towers over the city was built as the residence for Udine's Venetian governors. The area around it was the only part of Udine that was seriously damaged in the great earthquake of 1976. At the foot of the castle hill, lining the monumental Piazza della Libertà, are elegant buildings, Venetian in style.

Along the north end is the graceful **Porticato di San Giovanni**, built in 1523. Across the piazza is the **Loggia del Lionello**, the city hall constructed in the 15th century. The design of this colourful building shows a distinct Venetian influence. The masonry is layered pink and white, and the windows and arches have the pointed tops typical of the Venetian style.

Tiepolo, the greatest Venetian painter of the baroque, did some of his best work here. The city's **Duomo** on the Via Vittorio Veneto has three chapels decorated by him in golds and pinks.

The neo-classical church of Sant' Antonio by the Grand Canal, Trieste.

EMILIA-ROMAGNA

Emilia-Romagna's winters are cold, wet and foggy, and its summers long and hot. Together with the rich soil of the Po Valley, this climate makes it one of Italy's most prosperous farming regions.

Emilia-Romagna also has a rich cultural past. The Via Emilia, a road first built by the Romans, cuts through the centre of the region, linking Rimini, Bologna, Modena, Parma and Piacenza – all founded by the Romans as way stations along the road from the Adriatic to the interior. The other major cities of Emilia-Romagna, Ferrara and Ravenna, are off this main thoroughfare. In the Renaissance, Ferrara was home for the Este family whose court was a centre of culture and learning. Ravenna was a great international centre from the 4th to 8th centuries, originally as the last capital of the Western Empire then as the seat of the Byzantine emperors.

Bologna, the capital of Emilia-Romagna, is a city of half a million people and famous for its university, its sausage, its communist party and its beautifully preserved historic centre. The old buildings are of a soft orange-red brick and most have handsome marble or brick porticoes which shelter shoppers and pedestrians from inclement weather.

The old city revolves around two adjoining squares, the **Piazza Maggiore** and the **Piazza Nettuno**. On the east side of the Piazza Maggiore stands **San Petronio**, the largest church in Bologna. Originally the Bolognese had hoped to outdo St Peter's in Rome, but church authorities decreed that some funds be set aside for the construction of the **Archiginnasio** nearby. The design is by Antonio di Vincenzo, and although construction began in 1390, the facade is still unfinished. The completed sections are of red and white marble and decorated with reliefs of biblical scenes.

The interior of San Petronio is simple but elegant. Most of the bare brick walls remain unadorned. In the fifth chapel on the left is a spectacular 15th-century

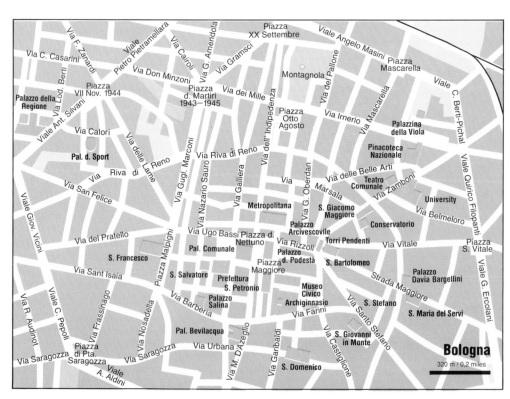

altarpiece of the Madonna and saints by Lorenzo Costa. At the east end of this aisle is a museum which includes plans for the completion of the facade and the enlargement of the church. Cross over to the south aisle to see, in the eighth chapel, intricately carved inlaid stalls by Raffelle da Brescia.

Behind San Petronio is the Archiginnasio, now home of the municipal library but once an important building of the university. The world's first lessons in human anatomy were given at Bologna University, and upstairs at the Archiginnasio is an actual 17th-century anatomical theatre.

The Piazza Nettuno has many attractions. At its centre is the **Fontana del Nettuno**, a 16th-century fountain with bronze sculptures of the muscle-bound god Neptune surrounded by cherubs and mermaids. On its west side is the majestic **Palazzo Comunale**, a medieval building remodelled in the Renaissance by Fieravante Fieravanti. The bronze statue above the gateway is of Pope Gregory XIII, a native of Bologna.

To the left is a beautiful terracotta Madonna by Nicolò dell'Arca.

From Piazza del Nettuno follow the **Via Rizzoli**, a picturesque street lined with cafés, down to the **Piazza di Porta Ravegnana** at the foot of the **Due Torri**, the "leaning towers" of Bologna. In medieval days 180 of these towers were built by the city's leading families; now only a dozen remain. Legend has it that the two richest families in Bologna – the Asinelli and the Garisenda – competed to build the tallest and most beautiful tower in the city. However, the Torre Garisenda was built on weak foundations and was never finished. For safety's sake it was shortened between 1351 and 1360, and is now only 48 metres (157 ft) high and leans more than 3 metres (10 ft) to one side. The Torre degli Asinelli is still standing at its original height of 97 metres (318 ft), but it too leans more than 1 metre (3 ft) out of the perpendicular.

The **Strada Maggiore** leads east from the two towers along the original line of the Via Emilia to the **Basilica di San**

News and gossip in Piazza Maggiore, Bologna.

Bartolomeo. Inside, look for an Annunciation by Albani in the fourth chapel of the south aisle, and a beautiful Madonna by Guido Reni in the north transept. Further down the Strada Maggiore is **Santa Maria dei Servi**, a well-preserved Gothic church that was built in the 14th century.

The **Basilica di Santo Stefano** – a complex of churches all dedicated to St Stephen the Martyr, is located off Via Santo Stefano. Of the several churches, the most interesting is the **San Sepolcro**, where San Petronio, patron saint of Bologna, is buried near the striking Romanesque pulpit. To the left is **Santi Vitale e Agricola**, the oldest church of the group, a 5th-century structure containing several Roman capitals and columns. In San Sepolcro is the entrance to the 12th-century **Cortile di Pilato**, "Pilate's courtyard", and beyond this open courtyard is the church of the **Trinità**, a dark, 13th-century building.

Bologna's **University**, the oldest in Italy, an institution founded in the 11th century and famous in its early days for reviving the study of Roman law, is located on **Via Zamboni**. Petrarch attended classes here, as did Copernicus. For many centuries the university had no permanent quarters. Today, although faculties are spread throughout the city, the official centre is the 16th-century **Palazzo Poggi**.

Past the university on the left is the **Pinacoteca Nazionale**, home of an interesting and varied collection of Italian painting. Although the emphasis of the Pinacoteca's collection is on the development of Bolognese artists from the Middle Ages through the 1700s, also included are a number of fine Renaissance works by artists who were not natives. Look out for works by Vitale da Bologna (especially the painting of St George and the Dragon), and Frederico del Cossa and Ercole de' Roberti of the Ferrarese school. On no account miss Raphael's great *Ecstasy of St Cecilia*.

South and west of the Piazza Maggiore, Bologna has more architectural treasures. Follow the Via Ugo Bassi west to **Piazza Malpighi**. On the west

Bologna is the sausage capital of the world.

side of this Piazza rises **San Francesco**, a church constructed between 1236 and 1263, with a design of French-Gothic inspiration. The larger of San Francesco's two towers and the surrounding decorative terracotta are the work of Antonio di Vincenzo. Though badly damaged in the war, the tower has been skillfully restored.

From San Francesco walk southeast to reach **Palazzo Bevilacqua**, a 15th-century building in the Tuscan style. Here, the Council of Trent met for two sessions after fleeing an epidemic in Trent. Nearby **San Domenico** is a church dedicated to the founder of the Dominican order. The tomb of St Dominic stands in a chapel off the south aisle.

Bologna has earned many epithets, "La Dotta" (the learned one), "La Turritta" (the turreted one), and finally "La Grassa" (the fat one), for here the rich cooking of Emilia-Romagna is at its best. Specialities are mortadella sausage, *tortellini*, and the *tagliatelle*, said to have been invented for the marriage feast of Lucrezia Borgia and the Duke of Ferrara. These long, light-coloured noodles were inspired by the bride's lovely locks. The Bolognese dress their *tagliatelle* with *ragù*, which in its home town is an incredibly thick blend of beef, ham, vegetables, cream and butter.

Modena and Parma: Since the Romans conquered Modena in the 2nd century BC, the city has thrived. In the past, the sources of Modena's wealth were the rich farmland of the Po plateau that surround it, and its position on the Via Emilia. This famous Roman road still runs through the centre of Modena, but the city has new riches; the auto factories where Maserati and Ferrari sports cars are manufactured.

Modena's massive and magnificent Romanesque **Duomo** sits right off the Via Emilia. The building dates from the end of the 11th century when Countess Matilda of Tuscany, ruler of Modena, commissioned a cathedral which would be worthy of receiving the remains of St Geminiano, the patron saint of the city. Matilda engaged Lanfranco, the greatest architect of the time, to mastermind the project.

The partly Gothic, partly Romanesque bell tower that stands to one side is the famous **Torre Ghirlandina**. It contains a bucket whose theft from Bologna in 1325 sparked off a war between the two cities. The poet Tassoni immortalised the incident in his celebrated poem *La Secchia Rapita* (The Stolen Bucket).

Frequently seen strolling around Modena are the smartly dressed students of the **Accademia Militare**, Italy's military academy, which is housed in a 17th-century palace at the centre of Modena. Another Modenese palace, **Palazzo dei Musei**, contains an interesting art collection and the **Biblioteca Estense**, the library of the Este family, dukes of Modena as well as Ferrara. On permanent display in the library is a collection of illuminated manuscripts, a 1481 copy of Dante's *Divine Comedy*, and the stunning Borso d'Este Bible which contains 1,200 miniatures of the Ferrara school of the 15th century.

If you think Parmesan cheese is just for sprinkling over pasta, you are miss-

University students sitting by the Neptune Fountain, Bologna.

ing a wonderful treat. True *Parmigiano* is best sliced and eaten just like any other cheese. There is no better place to become a connoisseur of this hard, sharp-flavoured cheese than **Parma**, a medium-sized city that enjoys a cooler, fresher climate than other towns in the muggy Po Valley.

The history of Parma is full of interesting personalities. Napoleon's widow Marie Louise (Maria Luigia to the Parmesans) was ceded this city after her husband's death. Despite her reputation for immodest behaviour, she did good things for Parma, building roads and bridges and founding orphanages and public institutions. She also founded the picture gallery in the 16th-century **Palazzo della Pilotta**, containing four great canvases by Emilia's master painter, Correggio.

However, the main aesthetic attraction of Parma is the **Duomo** and adjoining Baptistry. Its nave and cupola are decorated with splendid frescoes by Correggio. Contemporaries gushed over these masterpieces: Titian said that if the dome of the cathedral were turned upside down and filled with gold it would not be as valuable as Correggio's frescoes. Vasari wrote of the *Assumption*, "It seems impossible that a man could have conceived such a work as this is, and more impossible still, that he should have done it with human hands. It is extraordinary in its beauty, so graceful is the flow of the draperies, so exquisite the expression on the faces."

The Baptistry is the work of Benedetto Antelami, who built this octagonal building in the rich red Verona marble and then sculpted the reliefs that adorn both the interior and the exterior.

In the dome of **San Giovanni Evangelista**, another splendidly sensuous Correggio fresco can be seen. It depicts St John gazing up at heaven where the rest of the apostles are already sitting with Christ.

If you are driving northwest on the Via Emilia toward Piacenza, consider making a quick stop in **Fidenza** to see another glorious Romanesque cathedral. Just beyond Fidenza is the turn off for the little town of **Roncole**, where the humble cottage in which Giuseppe Verdi was born can be visited.

In the revolutionary year of 1848, when Prince Charles Albert of Savoy called for Italians to assemble under his leadership and form an independent nation, the citizens of **Piacenza** were the first to respond in a plebiscite. This vote of rebellion was a remarkable event in Piacenza's otherwise peaceful history. Situated at the point where the Via Emilia meets the Po, Piacenza has been a lively trading post and farmers' market since 218 BC. Although nothing remains of the Roman period, Piacenza is the site of many fine medieval and Renaissance buildings.

At the centre of the city is the massive **Palazzo del Comune**, called "Il Gotico". This town hall was built during Piacenza's "Communal Period" (approximately 1200–1400) when the city was an independent and important member of the Lombard League that defeated Emperor Frederick II of Hohenstaufen in his bid to conquer Italy completely. Il Gotico, begun in 1280, is a remarkably well-preserved building of brick, marble and terracotta. In front of it stand two massive baroque equestrian statues of Piacenza's 16th-century rulers, the Farnese dukes. On the left is Duke Alessandro Farnese, and on the right, Duke Ranuccio, his son.

At the end of the Via Venti Settembre stands Piacenza's Romanesque **Duomo**. Although gloomy on the inside, the cathedral is worth a visit for the frescoes on the columns near the entrance.

Ferrara: A prosperous modern market town on the banks of the Po River, Ferrara seems at first glance peaceful and provincial. But the city has a colourful history and splendid treasures. In the southern part of the city is a well-preserved medieval town, and to the north are long broad avenues lined with Renaissance *palazzi* and carefully groomed gardens.

The Este family ruled Ferrara from the late 13th century until 1598. It was a time of prosperity and their court attracted poets, scholars and artists. The Renaissance, the city's golden age, is reflected in all the major monuments.

Dominating Ferrara's skyline is the huge medieval **Castello Estense** complete with moats, drawbridges and towers. The interiors are disappointing, but it is possible to visit the dungeons.

Two blocks behind the castle is Ferrara's 12th-century cathedral. Among the noteworthy paintings in the Duomo and adjoining museum are Cosimo Tura's *San Giorgio* and his *Annunciation* and Jacopo della Quercia's *Madonna della Melagrana*.

Across from the Duomo is the **Palazzo del Comune**, a medieval building with a beautiful Renaissance staircase. The piazza in front of this town hall is the hub of life in modern Ferrara. The *passagiata* is a daily event. Not all Ferrarese are on foot, however – cycles are the rage in this town without hills.

The beautiful **Palazzo di Schifanoia**, one of the Este's summer residences, is on the other side of the medieval section. Many of these streets south of the cathedral are lined with fortified houses. And stretching across the **Via delle Volte**, a narrow street near the Po, are several elegant arches. At the Este palace, climb the steep stairs to the Salone dei Mesi, a large, high room decorated with colourful frescoes of the months. These were executed for the Duke of Borgo d'Este by masters of the Ferrarese school including Ercole de' Roberti.

Down Via Mellone from Schifanoia is another, smaller Este palace, **Palazzo di Ludovico il Moro**, designed by the famous Ferrarese Renaissance architect Biagio Rossetti. Although the plan of the building is actually simple and stark, the elaborate decoration gives the palazzo an ornate effect.

North of the Duomo, Ferrara is a city of broad avenues. Along one of the prettiest streets, Corso Ercole d'Este, is Rossetti's **Palazzo dei Diamanti**, a large Renaissance structure with a unique facade. The diamond, emblem of the Este family is repeated 12,600 times.

Rimini: Today Rimini is two cities: the old medieval and Renaissance town, and the ultra-modern beach resort a mile distant. In the skyscraper hotels that line Rimini's coast, you are more likely to

Este Castle, Ferrara.

hear German or English spoken than Italian, but the old centre retains its charm despite the influx of tourists.

The infamous ruler Sigismondo Malatesta has left his mark everywhere in Rimini. It was this anticlerical patron of art who presided over the transformation of a 13th-century Franciscan church into one of the most spectacular Renaissance buildings in Italy. The **Tempio Malatestiano** is considered more a personal tribute to Sigismondo's mistress Isotta degli Atti (who later became his third wife), than a church. But perhaps that is what Sigismondo intended since he and Church authorities were never the best of friends. Pope Pius II even went so far as to excommunicate the violent and sensual Sigismondo, and to condemn him publicly to hell.

Sigismondo had better luck with women and artists. He was patron of such great artists as Piero della Francesca and Leon Battista Alberti, among others. It was Alberti who designed the exterior of the Tempio. (He found inspiration in the Roman Arch of Augustus which still stands at the gates of Rimini.) Note the wide classical arches on each side of the entrance. The interior rebuilding was supervised by Matteo de Pasti, and although the simple, single-nave plan and wooden-trussed roof of the original Franciscan church remain, the side chapels (some added and others only redecorated) are opulent and intricate in design. Immediately on your right as you enter is Sigismondo's tomb, decorated with his initials intertwined with Isotta's.

To the left of the Tempio is the **Piazza Tre Martiri**, named in honour of three Italian partisans hung by the Nazis in this square in 1944. The piazza is also the site of the ancient Roman forum, whose columns now support the porticoes of the two eastern buildings.

Walk out of the piazza along **Corso di Augusto** for four blocks. At the end stands the **Arco di Augusto**, dating from 27 BC. With this archway the Romans marked the junction of the Via Emilia and the Via Flamina, the primary road north from Rome to the Adriatic Sea.

The beach at Rimini gets a little crowded.

Ravenna: When the unstoppable barbarians overran Rome in the 5th century AD, Ravenna benefited, gaining the honourable rank of capital of the Western Empire. This Adriatic port town continued as capital under the Ostrogoths, and the barbarian leaders Odoacer and Teodoric also ruled their vast dominions from here. Later, when the Byzantine emperor Justinian reconquered part of Italy, he too made Ravenna his seat of power, liking it for its imperial tradition under the Barbarians and – perhaps more importantly – for its direct sea links to Byzantium.

Under Justinian's rule the Ravenna we know today began to take shape. New buildings arose all over the city, including a handful of churches that are among the wonders of Italian art and architecture. There is no preparation in their simple brick exteriors for the brilliant mosaics within. It is these mosaics that make modern Ravenna, if no longer capital of the western world, at least a capital of the western art world.

Start with **San Vitale**, the city's great 6th-century octagonal basilica, famous for the mosaics in its choir and apse. These "monuments of unaging intellect", as the Irish poet W. B. Yeats called them, immediately draw the eye with their marvellous colours and intricate detail. Bright ducks, bulls, lions, dolphins and a phoenix intertwine with flowers and oddly angled corners of buildings to frame Old Testament scenes and portraits of Byzantine rulers with a humour and exactitude reminscent of the Nile scenes in mosaics from Pompeii. There is a sense of eternal colour and freshness here, an unalterable brightness of startled birdsong that, as Yeats wrote, might "keep a drowsy emperor awake".

Old Testament scenes in the lunettes of the choir include (left to right) Jeremiah and Moses on Mount Sinai; two scenes from the life of Abraham, including Abraham's hospitality to the angels (with Sarah in the background) and the Sacrifice of Isaac; Isaiah and the life of Moses; and the offerings of Abel and Melchisedech. In the dome of the

apse a purple-clad and beardless Christ sits on a blue globe flanked by archangels and, at the far sides, Saint Vitalis and Bishop Ecclesius. Christ hands the saint (Ravenna's patron) a triumphal crown, while the bishop (who founded the church in 521) carries a model of the structure as it finally appeared many years after his death. Below stretch imperial scenes of Justinian with his courtiers and Theodora, his beloved wife, with hers.

San Vitale is not the only place to see mosaics in Ravenna. Nearly every church contains a pristine example of the art. Just north, another set may be seen at the **Mausoleo di Galla Placidia**. This interesting lady was born a Roman princess, sister to Emperor Honorius, but after she was captured by the Goths, she married their leader, Athaulf and ruled with him. He, however, soon died, and she next married a Roman general to whom she bore a son. This son became Emperor Valentinian III. As Valentinian's regent, and a woman with connections in the highest barbarian circles, Galla Placidia played a powerful role in the world of "the decline". The building that houses her tomb has a simple exterior but inside the walls, floors, and ceiling are covered with decoration. Overhead, the Cross floats in a star-strewn sky. Above the doorway, Christ appears as the Good Shepherd, surrounded by lambs, and opposite is St Lawrence with his gridiron. Round about appear the apostles and the evangelists.

Through the gate that lies between San Vitale and Galla Placidia are two Renaissance cloisters that now house the **Museo Nazionale**. The museum includes, as one might expect, many mosaics as well as other relics from Ravenna's past. There's glass from San Vitale to see and also fabrics from the tomb of St Julien at Rimini.

A pleasant walk along Via Fanni, Via Barbiani and left onto Via d'Azeglio leads to Ravenna's **Duomo** – originally constructed in the 5th century but redone in the baroque style in the 1730s. Far more attractive than the cathedral itself is the adjoining **Battistero Neoniano**, a 5th-century octagonal baptistry that was once a Roman bath house. The interior combines spectacular Byzantine mosaics with marble inlay from the original bath house.

Across Piazza Cadutti from the cathedral complex is **San Francesco**, another 5th-century church almost completely redone in the baroque style. To the left stands **Tomba di Dante**, not a remarkable building architecturally, but of great historic interest. The author of *The Divine Comedy* was exiled from his home in Florence for his political outspokenness and found refuge in Ravenna in 1317. He spent the remaining four years of his life here, putting the finishing touches to his great work. His Latin epitaph, carved in 1327, may be roughly translated as follows: "The rights of monarchy, the heavens and infernal lakes of the Phlegethon that I visited I sang, as long as mortal destiny decreed. But my soul was taken to a better place and reached its creator among the stars. Here I lie buried, Dante, exile from my birth-place, a son of Florence, that loveless mother." The poignant epitaph was written by one of his comtemporaries.

After Dante's death, the repentant Florentines would dearly have loved to honour their famous son with a splendid tomb, but proud Ravenna refused to give up the poet's remains. The battle over the bones continued for hundreds of years. At one point in 1519, it looked as if Ravenna would lose. The powerful Medicis of Florence sent their representatives to Ravenna with a papal injunction demanding the relics. The sarcophagus was duly opened, but the bones were not inside. Someone had been warned of the Florentine scheme and had removed the bones to a secret hiding place. They were not found again until 1865, and now rest within the sarcophagus that is on display.

Down the Via di Roma from the troubled tomb is another church full of mosaics, **Sant' Apollinare Nuovo**. The scenes are of processions, one of virgins and the other of martyrs who appear to be moving towards the altar between rows of palms. Above, the decorations depict episodes from the Life of Christ.

San Vitale, Ravenna.

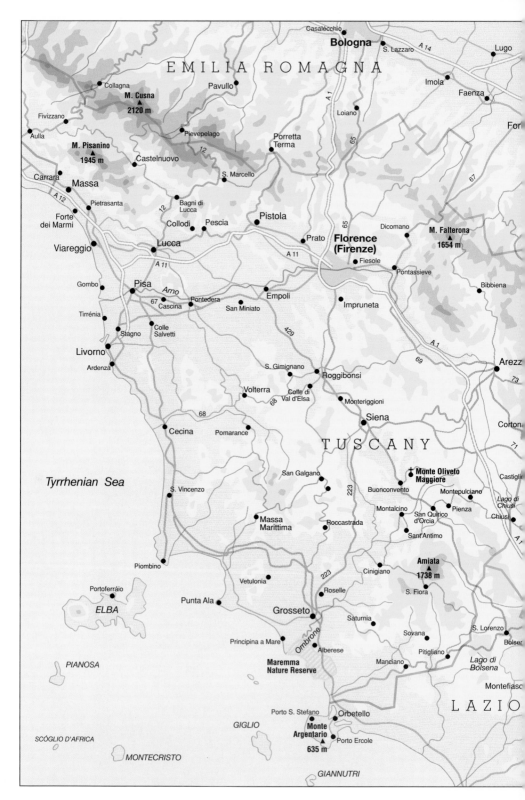

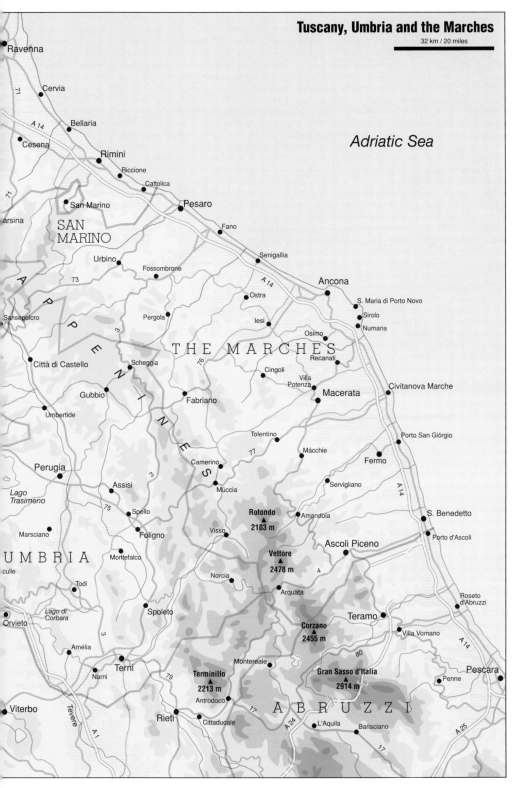

Adriatic Sea

Ravenna

71

Cervia

A 14

Bellaria

Cesena

71

Rimini

Riccione

Cattolica

arsina

San Marino

SAN MARINO

Pesaro

Fano

Urbino

Fossombrone

Senigallia

73

Ostra

Ancona

Sansepolcro

Pergola

Iesi

S. Maria di Porto Novo

Sirolo

Numana

Osimo

THE MARCHES

Città di Castello

Scheggia

76

Recanati

Cingoli

Villa Potenza

Macerata

Civitanova Marche

Gubbio

Umbertide

Fabriano

Tolentino

Mácchie

Porto San Giórgio

3

Fermo

Perugia

Camerino

77

Servigliano

A 14

Assisi

Múccia

Lago Trasimeno

75

Spello

Rotondo
2103 m

Amandola

S. Benedetto

Marsciano

Foligno

Visso

Porto d'Ascoli

UMBRIA

Montefalco

Vettore
2478 m

Ascoli Piceno

culle

Norcia

4

Todi

Arquata

Roseto d'Abruzzi

Lago di Corbara

Spoleto

Corzano
2455 m

Teramo

Orvieto

Villa Vomano

A 14

Amélia

3

Terminillo
2213 m

Montereale

Gran Sasso d'Italia
2914 m

Pescara

Terni

80

Penne

Narni

79

Antrodoco

Viterbo

Tevere

A1

Rieti

Cittaducale

17

ABRUZZI

A 24

L'Aquila

Bariciano

A 25

17

FLORENCE

Florence is the city that gave birth to the Renaissance and many visitors come here to trace the development of this extraordinary outpouring of artistic talent that took place in the 15th century. A huge number of Renaissance works have remained in the city where they were created; many paintings, statues and whole buildings, such as the Pitti Palace, were bequeathed to the people of Florence by Anna Maria Lodovica of the Medici family, whose death in 1743 brought an end to the dynasty that had ruled Florence since 1434.

Her far-sighted bequest has ensured that the great wealth of the Medici collections has remained intact and not been dispersed all over the globe. Napoleon stole a few choice pieces during his adventures in Italy (including the Medici Venus, now in the Louvre), and English collectors bought some splendid paintings very cheaply in the 19th century when the so-called "primitives" were out of fashion.

Despite this, you can still see in Florence many of the paintings and frescoes that Vasari, the first art historian, mentions in his entertaining and anecdotal *Lives of the Artists*, first published in 1550. Many of these works have been superbly restored since the great flood of November 1966, and the bulletproof glass installed to protect the most important paintings in the Uffizi proved effective when a terrorist bomb exploded in May 1993, reducing some minor masterpieces to shreds.

To see where the Renaissance began, it is traditional to begin with Piazza del Duomo. Approaching this massive square, now free of traffic thanks to a ban introduced in 1988, you file through sober streets lined with buildings presenting a stern and defensive face. Suddenly the 19th-century face of the **Duomo** (cathedral) is revealed, all festive in its polychrome marble – green from Prato, white from Carrara and red from the Maremma. The design echoes that of the tall Campanile alongside,

designed by Giotto in 1331. You can climb the 285 steps of the belltower for intimate views of the cathedral dome and roofline, or simply enjoy the flamboyant exterior of the cathedral from one of the open-air cafés on the south side of the square.

The little octagonal Battistero (baptistry), to the west of the cathedral, dates to the 7th century, though the interior was redesigned and given its ceiling mosaics of the Creation and Last Judgement in 1300. The baptistry has three sets of bronze doors and those to the north have an important place in art history. If it is possible to pin down the start of the Renaisance to a particular event, then it was the competition held in the winter of 1401 to choose an artist to design these doors. Of the six artists who entered the competition, Ghiberti and Brunelleschi were adjudged joint winners, but Brunelleschi, a fiery tempered genius, refused to work in partnership with Ghiberti and went off in a huff to Rome.

Ghiberti, left with sole responsibility

Left, postcards for sale outside the Duomo. Right, reading by the Arno.

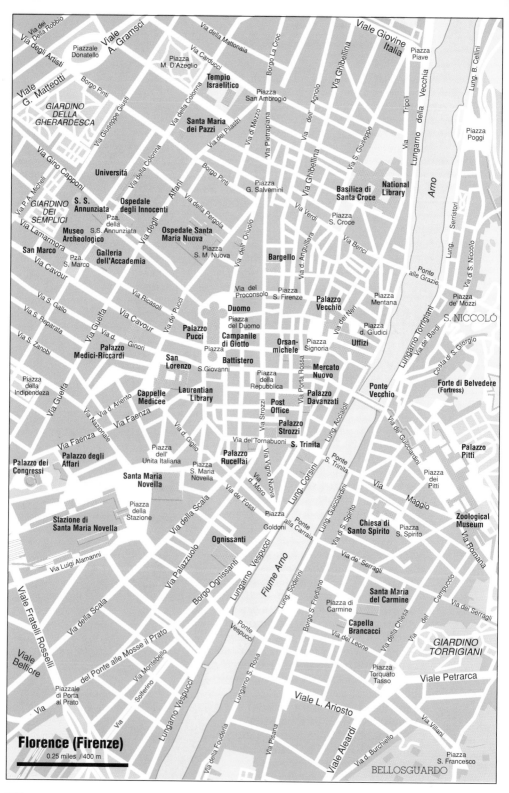

Florence (Firenze)

0.25 miles / 400 m

248

for the doors, did not complete them until 1424, but the resulting work shows many of the key features that define Renaissance art: realistic depiction of people, fully worked-out perspective and narrative clarity combined with dramatic tension. Ghiberti was immediately commissioned to design another set of doors, this time for the east portal, and these were unveiled in 1452 when Michelangelo hailed them as fit to serve as the "gates of Paradise", hence they are known to this day as the Paradise doors. The third set of doors, to the south, are the work of Andrea Pisano (1339) and they tell the story of John the Baptist, patron saint of the city.

Brunelleschi, meanwhile, spent his time in Rome studying ancient Roman architecture and he returned to Florence full of confidence that he could accomplish a task that had defeated other architects, namely to complete the cathedral by erecting the vast dome. In typically Florentine fashion, the city had decided to build the biggest dome in the world without actually knowing how to achieve it. If you enter the cathedral and climb the 436 steps to the top you can study how the problem was solved – by building a light inner shell of interlocking brick which serves as the support for the outer roof of the dome.

Brunelleschi was hailed as a new Icarus (the mythical hero who similarly defied gravity by inventing flight) and the city passed an ordinance forbidding the construction of any building taller than the dome out of respect for his achievement; to this day, the massive dome rises supreme above the red roofs of the city, rising almost higher than the surrounding hills. Brunelleschi was also buried in the cathedral – an honour granted to him alone – and his tomb can be seen in the crypt, among the excavated ruins of Santa Reperata, the city's first cathedral, built in the 4th century.

Much of the rest of the cathedral is bare. There is an interesting fresco on the north aisle wall, painted by Paolo Uccello in 1436, depicting Sir John Hawkwood, the English mercenary who served as Captain of the Florentine army from 1377 to 1394. Otherwise, to see the cathedral treasures you must visit the **Museo dell'Opera del Duomo** on the east side of Piazza del Duomo. This is full of outstanding sculptures, from Donatello's haggard Mary Magdalene carved in wood in the 1460s to the same artist's superb cantoria (choir gallery) decorated with angels and cherubs engaged in some frenzied ritual of music and song. The star exhibit here is Michelangelo's *Pietà*, begun around 1550. Michelangelo intended this for his own tomb, but left it unfinished (a pupil rather clumsily attempted to finish the work). Its magnetic hold over visitors derives from the fact that the tall hooded figure of Nicodemus, at the centre of the group, is a self-portrait.

From the cathedral square, **Via dei Calzaiuoli** leads south. This was the principal street of Roman and medieval Florence and, having been restored after World War II bombing, it is lined with good shops. Part way down, on the right, is the **church of Orsanmichele** (a contraction of Orti di San Michele – the garden of San Michele church, which

A niche of Orsanmichele.

once stood here). The niches around the exterior walls are filled with Renaissance statues sponsored by the guilds and depicting their respective patron saints. Of these, Donatello's *St George*, made for the Guild of Armourers, is the most important, and for that reason it has been removed to a place of honour in the Bargello museum (see below) and replaced by a copy.

The same fate befell Michelangelo's *David*, which once stood in the **Piazza della Signoria**, just to the south. The original was moved to the Galleria degli Accademia (see below) in 1873 but the copy that now stands in front of the Palazzo Vecchio is faithful to the original. David's companions are the rather constipated-looking figure of Hercules (1534 by Bandinelli), the mythical founder of Florence, and Ammanati's licentious Neptune Fountain (1575). Nearby, to the south of the square, the **Loggia dei Lanzi** shelters several ancient Roman statues and Giambologna's *Rape of the Sabine Women* (1583).

Most of the statues gathered here are symbolic, not least David himself, carved by Michelangelo to represent the aspirations of the Florentine people not long after the citizens had declared themselves independent of all rulers except for God. The fledgling Florentine Republic was threatened by a number of tyrannical Goliaths, including the Pope, the Holy Roman Emperor and the Medici. The combined forces of all three held the city to siege in 1530 and shortly afterwards Cosimo I was crowned Duke of Florence.

This Cosimo was a very different character from his earlier namesake, the humanist, classics scholar and patron of the arts, Cosimo il Vecchio, who ruled the city from 1434 to 1464 without ever holding office. Cosimo I was a no-nonsense military man who set about conquering all those cities in the region not already ruled by Florence. Cosimo I created the Tuscany of today by this means and he set up an efficient administration to rule his dukedom, which remained in place until Tuscany joined the United Kingdom of Italy in 1870.

The Duomo.

That administration was based in the **Palazzo Vecchio**, which remains the town hall of Florence to this day, and which was comprehensively redesigned during the reign of Cosimo I. Visiting the ancient town hall, you can see the delicately decorated entrance courtyard, or cortile, with its little fountain – Vasari's copy of the original Putto and Dolphin fountain made by Verrochio in 1470. By contrast, the vast Salone dei Cinquecento (Hall of the Five Hundred) was originally intended as the council chamber of the 500 citizens who governed the city during the Republic. Cosimo I set his stamp upon the chamber by commissioning a series of vast frescoes, painted by Vasari, glorifying his military triumphs.

The other rooms of the palace contain mementoes of various prominent Florentines: portraits of the Medici popes, Leo X and Clement VII, for example, and the room which Machiavelli used during his term of office as the Chancellor of Florence.

Under Cosimo I the size of the Tuscan bureaucracy grew to the point where new offices were required to house the burgeoning army of lawyers and notaries, the guilds and the judiciary. Thus it was that the **Uffizi** came to be built alongside the Palazzo Vecchio, now a famous art gallery but built to serve a more utilitarian purpose (the word *uffizi* simply means offices).

Vasari was the architect and he built a well-lit upper storey, using iron reinforcement to create an almost continuous wall of glass running round the long inner courtyard of the Uffizi. It was this glass wall that caused so much damage when a terrorist bomb exploded near the west wing of the Uffizi in May 1993, sending splinters of glass everywhere and destroying a number of paintings in the process. In the 16th century, such lavish use of glass was novel and Cosimo's heirs decided that the airy upper corridor of the Uffizi would make a perfect exhibition space for the family statues, carpets and paintings.

Thus began what has grown to be one of the richest and most illuminating art

Botticelli's newly cleaned *Primavera*.

collections in the world, arranged chronologically so that you can trace, almost in textbook fashion, the development of Florentine art from the formal style of the Gothic era (13th and 14th centuries), to the greater realism of the early Renaissance (15th century) and finally to the painterly use of exaggerated colours and the contorted poses designed to show off the artist's skill that is so characteristic of the High Renaissance and Mannerist periods (16th century).

The famous names and familiar works come thick and fast as you explore the collection; not to be missed are Botticelli's *Primavera* (1480) and the *Birth of Venus* (1485). You should also seek out the charming Medici family portraits gathered in the octagonal Tribunale, including Bronzino's, *Portrait of Bia*, illegitimate daughter of Cosimo I (1542). The corridors of the gallery are lined with ancient Roman and Greek statues, of which the most famous perhaps is the boy removing a thorn from his foot, in the south corridor. Look out too for Michelangelo's influential *Holy Family* (Doni Tondo) (1506–08), Raphael's tender *Madonna of the Goldfinch* (1506) and Titian's erotic *Venus of Urbino* (1538).

When Vasari planned the Uffizi, he incorporated an aerial corridor (the Corridoio Vasariano) into the design. This consists of a continuous covered walkway linking the Palazzo Vecchio to the Pitti Palace, passing through the Uffizi and along the top of the Ponte Vecchio. The Medici dukes used this corridor to walk between their various palaces without having to mix with their subjects in the streets below. We can follow the same route, but at street level, passing over the ancient **Ponte Vecchio**, with its jewellers, buskers and festive crowds. The bridge was built in 1345 and the workshops on the bridge were used by butchers and tanners until these noxious trades were banned by ducal ordinance in 1593. It is well worth browsing in the goldsmith's tiny shop windows to see the range of goods on display, from cheap trinkets to costume **The Ponte Vecchio.**

jewellery and from expensive antique pieces to modern creations.

Good shops line the route south of the bridge into the Oltrarno district where you will find the churches of Santo Spirito, an architectural masterpiece by Brunelleschi, and Santa Maria del Carmine, where the Brancacci Chapel contains Masaccio's fresco cycle on the *Life of St Peter*. The latter is one of the great works of the early Renaissance and the Brancacci chapel is tiny, so there are likely to be queues at the entrance. Visits are limited to 15 minutes.

Space is not a problem at the vast and and fortress-like **Pitti Palace**. This became the residence of the Medici Grand Dukes in 1550 and, like the Uffizi, it is stuffed with artistic treasures, housed in several museums, including the Palatine Gallery, the Modern Art Collection, the Argenti (Silver) Museum and the Costume Museum.

The most rewarding of these is the Palatine Gallery, especially the richly decorated rooms with ceiling frescoes by Pietro da Cortona. These illustrate, in allegorical form, the education of a prince under the tutorship of the gods. In Room 1, the prince is torn from the arms of Venus (love) by Minerva (knowledge) and in subsequent rooms learns about science from Apollo, war from Mars and leadership from Jupiter. Finally the prince takes his place alongside Saturn, who, in ancient mythology, presided over the Golden Age.

Among the paintings displayed in these rooms are some wonderful portraits by Titian who even manages to turn the reformed prostitute, Mary Magdalene, into a delectable study of the delights of the female form. More disturbing is Ruben's celebrated masterpiece, the *The Consequences of War* (1638), an allegory of the Thirty Years' War. The artist explained in a letter that the figure in black represents "unfortunate Europe who, for so many years now, has suffered plunder, outrage and misery." Next to her, Venus is trying to restrain the war god, Mars, who is trampling over books, symbolising his disregard for civilisation.

The **Boboli Gardens**, behind the Pitti Palace, were laid out in the 16th century and are a wonderful example of the Renaissance garden style. Here you will find box hedges clipped into formal geometric patterns set against wilder groves of ilex and cypress to create a contrast between artifice and nature. Dotted around the gardens are numerous grottoes, statues and fountains.

On one of those hills sits **San Miniato**, a jewel-like Romanesque church which features famously in E. M. Forster's novel (and the Merchant Ivory film) *A Room with a View*. If you walk up to the church you can descend via Piazzale Michelangelo, a terrace set high above the city and dotted with reproductions of Michelangelo's famous works.

Prominent in the view, to the east of the city, is the massive **church of Santa Croce** in which you will find frescoes by Giotto and his pupils and the tombs and monuments of famous Florentines, including Michelangelo, Machiavelli and Galileo (born in Pisa but protected by the Medici after his excommunication for holding the heretical view that

The church of San Miniato rises gracefully above Florence.

the earth goes round the sun, rather than the other way around).

Weaving your way back from the church through the alleys of the Santa Croce district you pass the **Casa Buonarroti,** a house owned by Michelangelo and now containing one of his earliest works, the *Madonna della Scala*. Call in at the **Bar Vivoli Gelateria**, in Via Isola delle Stinche, which, as everyone who samples it agrees, serves the best ice cream in the world.

From here it is a short step to the **Bargello**, once a prison and place of execution but now a museum devoted to sculpture and applied art where you can see works by Donatello, Michelangelo, Cellini and Giambologna. Dante was born in this district and opposite the Bargello you can see the abbey church, the **Badia Fiorentina**, where the poet used to watch his beloved Beatrice attending mass. Round the corner, in Via Dante Alighieri, is the **Casa di Dante**, the house in which the poet is supposed to have been born in 1265.

Continuing west, you will reach an-other important shopping street, Via Roma, which leads south into Via Calimala and the **Mercato Nuovo**. Despite its name, the "New Market" has been here since 1551 and was known as the Straw Market in the 19th century on account of it specialising in raffia goods. Today it sells leather and tourist souvenirs. The little bronze boar, Il Porcellino, in the south side of the market, has a shiny nose because of the number of visitors who have rubbed it for good luck.

From the north side of the market, Via Porta Rossa will take you to the **Palazzo Davanzati**, a delightful 13th-century townhouse complete with frescoed walls and contemporary furnishings, that will give you a good idea of domestic life in late medieval Florence. You are now close to the river **Arno** and the bridge called **Ponte Santa Trinità**, after the adjacent church, which features statues of the Four Seasons, blown up by the retreating Nazis in 1944 and dredged up from the river bed to be restored to their rightful place.

Il Porcellino, in the Mercato Nuovo.

254

The **church of Santa Trinità** contains frescoes by Ghirlandaio showing the Life of St Francis set not in Assisi, the saint's home town, but against the background of Florentine buildings. North from here, Via de' Tornabuoni is lined with the chic boutiques of high-class couturiers, such as Salvatore Ferragamo, Valentino and Gucci.

At the top of the street, the Palazzo Antinori contains an excellent wine bar and restaurant, but if the prices are too steep you can sample the cheap Chinese restaurants in **Piazza Santa Maria Novella**, with a view of the facade of the church of the same name. The latter features in the opening stanzas of Boccaccio's great work, the *Decameron*, and contains colourful frescoes by Ghirlandaio on the Life of the Virgin. In the adjoining cloister you can see what remains of Paolo Uccello's masterpiece, the *Universal Deluge* fresco, depicting the flood that drowned all but Noah and his entourage, a fresco that was, ironically, badly damaged by the Florentine floods of 1966. In the Spanish Chapel you can also see frescoes that depict the Dominican monks allegorically as hunting dogs (because the Dominicans were sometimes known as *Domine Cane*, Latin for Hounds of the Lord).

Heading back to the heart of Florence, it is easy to get lost in the streets surrounding **San Lorenzo church** because this is the venue of a crowded street market most days of the week. The popular market continues, despite official attempts to ban it, and is a good place in which to buy almost anything – from picnic food to souvenirs.

At the back of San Lorenzo is the entrance to the **Cappelle Medicee**, the mausoleum of the Medici family, for which Michelangelo carved two splendid tombs featuring the allegorical figures of Night and Day, Dusk and Dawn. The church itself, entered through the rough unfinished facade, is an example of Renaisaance rationalism in architecture, all cool whites and greys and restrained classical decoration. By contrast, the two huge pulpits carved by Donatello with scenes from the Life of Christ are full of impassioned emotion, and Michelangelo's staircase leading to the Biblioteca Laurenziana (Laurentian Library), off the cloister, is considerably more exuberant.

Michelangelo's most famous work, *David*, almost the trademark of Florence, is in the **Galleria dell' Accademia**, two blocks away in Via Ricasoli. When you see the length of the queues for this museum you may prefer to give it a miss, especially as the entry price is steep for a museum that contains little else of great interest, apart from Michelangelo's unfinished works, the *Four Slaves*.

Instead, the nearby convent of **San Marco**, which contains nearly every painting and fresco ever produced by the saintly artist, Fra Angelico, may prove more rewarding. On your return to the city centre you can also take in the **Piazza della Santissima Annunziata**, with its delicate Renaissance colonnade fronting the Innocenti orphanage, the work of Brunelleschi, and the **Archaeological Museum**, with its ancient Etruscan and Egyptian treasures.

Outside San Lorenzo church.

TUSCANY

For those not fascinated by frescoes, the delights of Florence can quickly fade and the desire to escape the cauldron-like atmosphere of this hot dry city can prove overwhelming, as it did in the case of the English writer Laurie Lee: "I'd had my fill of Florence, lovely but indigestible city. My eyes were choked with pictures and frescoes... I began to long for the cool uplands, the country air, the dateless wild olive and the uncatalogued cuckoo."

Lee escaped by walking south along the Chiantigiana, the Chianti Way, shown on maps as the N222 road, which takes you to Siena via several pretty towns in the Chianti Classico wine-growing region. If you are driving, the journey will take little more than an hour, unless you are tempted to stop along the route at the scores of *fattorie* (wine estates) offering free tastings and wine sales direct to the public (*vendita diretta*). This is one way to learn about the region's famous red wines; another is to leave the N222 road at Castellina in Chianti and drive east, stopping for a walk round the pretty town of Radda in Chianti before heading south on the N408 and N484 to Castello di Brolio.

The **Castello di Brolio** is the birthplace of the modern Chianti industry and offers well-organised guided tours of the vineyards, castle and winery. It was here that Barone Bettino Ricasoli established the formula for making Chianti wines in 1870 that has been used ever since, requiring a precise blend of white and red grape juice and the addition of dried grapes to the vat to give the wine its characteristic flavour.

Knowledgeable about the region's wines, you can tackle the traffic headaches that await in **Siena**. Finding space to park may prove difficult, but the medieval core of the city is largely traffic free, simply because the narrow medieval alleys that thread between high *palazzi* of rose pink brick are too narrow for vehicles. All roads in Siena eventually lead to the **Campo**, the huge main square at the heart of the city, which is shaped like an amphitheatre – the Sienese like to think that it is shaped like the protecting cloak of the Virgin, the city's patron saint.

From the comfort of a pavement café on the curved side of the Campo you can note the division of the paved surface into nine fields, commemorating the beneficent rule of the Council of Nine Good Men which governed Siena from the mid-13th century to the early 14th, a period of exceptional stability and prosperity when most of the city's main public monuments were built.

Twice a year, on 2 July and 16 August, the Sienese faithfully recreate their medieval heritage in the Palio, a sumptuous pageant-cum-horserace around the Campo. This is no mere tourist event; the residents of the city's *contrade*, or districts, pack the square as their representative horses and riders career around the Campo, and the rider who wins the race and the Palio, a heraldic banner, becomes an instant local hero.

At the square's base is the Palazzo

Pubblico, with its crenellated facade and waving heraldic banners. Erected in the early 14th century, it housed the offices of the city government. At its left corner is the slender tower fondly called the Mangia, or wastrel, after an early bellringer. Climb its more than 500 steps for a panorama of the city.

The modern functions of the Palazzo Pubblico reflect perfectly Siena's links to – and respect for – its past. Although bureaucrats still toil in parts of the Palazzo as they have for nearly seven centuries, much of the complex has been given over to the **Museo Civico**, which houses some of the city's greatest treasures. Siena's city council once met in the vast **Sala del Mappamondo**, although the huge globe that then graced the walls has disappeared. What remains are two frescoes attributed to the medieval master Simone Martini: the majestic mounted figure of Guido Riccio da Fogliano and, opposite, the *Maestà*. The *Maestà* is signed in Simone Martini's own hand, but in recent years a squabble has broken out among art historians about the authenticity of the Guido Riccio. Some now believe that a smaller fresco recently uncovered below the huge panel may be Simone Martini's original, and that the Guido Riccio was, in fact, executed long after the artist's death.

In the Sala della Pace is Ambrogio Lorenzetti's *Allegory of Good and Bad Government*. Intended as a constant reminder to the city fathers of their responsibilities, it depicts the entire sweep of medieval society, from the king and his court down to the peasants working the terraced hillsides outside the city walls.

Exiting again to the Campo, turn left and head up the hill via one of the winding streets to **Piazza del Duomo**. The facade of the vast striped cathedral is a festival of green, pink and white marble, which will help prepare you for the stunning black-and-white geometric patterns of the interior. Take special care to study the 15th- and 16th-century marble inlaid paving of the Duomo, which depicts allegories and scenes from **Siena overview**.

the New Testament (unfortunately, many are covered most of the year to protect from heavy traffic). Off the north aisle is the decorative Libreria Piccolomini, built in 1495 to house the personal papers and books of Pope Pius II. The frescoes by Pinturicchio show scenes from the life of the pope, and in the centre of the room is the famous *Three Graces*, a Roman copy of a sculpture by the Greek artist, Praxiteles.

For those with more time, Siena boasts two other important museums: the **Museo dell'Opera del Duomo** or Cathedral Museum, to the right (south) of the cathedral, and the **Pinacoteca Nazionale** (Picture Gallery), in the Palazzo Buonsignori on the Via San Pietro, about two blocks south of the Campo. The Cathedral Museum's main attraction is the entire room devoted to the works of Duccio, including his moving *Maestà*.

Siena sits at the geographical centre of Tuscany and whichever way you drive you will be spoilt for choice in terms of attractive historic towns and beautiful countryside. Drive southwest along the N438 to **Asciano** and you will pass through the dramatic Crete region, the Tuscany that appears on countless postcards and posters. Here the bare, rounded clay hills have no trees except for the occasional stately avenue of cypresses, winding across the landscape and marking the way to an isolated farm, a simple Romanesque church or a *borgo*, a small defended village.

Asciano's main street, Corso Giacomo Matteoti, is lined with smart shops and classical *palazzi*, some with pretty balconies. At the top end is the simple Romanesque **collegiate church** and the **Museo di Arte Sacra** (Religious Art) which houses an unusually good collection of Siena school masterpieces. By contrast, the **Museo Amos Cassiolo**, on Via Mameli, has a good collection of 19th- and early 20th-century paintings by local artists.

A short drive on is the **Abbazia di Monte Oliveto Maggiore**, a 15th-century Benedictine monastery with an air of aloof dignity, set among groves of

The Duomo, Siena.

statuesque cypress trees. The Great Cloister is covered in frescoes on the Life of St Benedict, begun by Luca Signorelli in 1495 and completed by Il Sodoma from 1505. The excellent monastery guidebook gives a detailed description. In one scene Il Sodoma portrays himself with his pet badgers (one wearing a scarlet collar) looking like a pair of well-trained dogs.

Buonconventi is worth a brief stop, if only to admire the massive medieval city gates of iron-bound wood, before driving through fertile countryside, scattered with vineyards, to the hilltop town of **Montalcino**, a wine-producing town where every other shop seems to sell the local Brunello wines. It is also a town of timeless character with several old-fashioned wood-panelled bars where vineyard workers shelter from the midday sun. The streets are narrow and steep and from the airy heights of the walls there are entrancing views over sunlit countryside. The highest point is the **Fortezza** (Fortress), housing yet another bar where various Montalcinese

wines can be sampled and purchased.

South again is another sight that features on countless postcards, but which is far more beautiful in the flesh. The ancient **abbey church of Sant'Antimo**, built of creamy travertine and set against a background of tree-clad hills, has inspired numerous poets and painters. The main part of the church was built in 1118 in a style that owes much to the influence of French Romanesque. The simple interior has capitals carved with biblical scenes, and recorded plainsong echoes around the walls as you explore. The small community of Augustinian monks who tend the church sing the Gregorian chant at Mass every Sunday afternoon throughout the year.

A tortuous mountain route will take you through **Castiglione d'Orcia** and **Rocca d'Orcia**, both with medieval castles built to watch over the valley of the River Orcia, and down to the tiny spa town of **Bagno Vignone**. This has, at its heart, where the main square ought to be, a large stone-lined pool where sulphurous vapours rise above the hot, **Romanesque abbey of Sant'Antimo.**

bubbling waters which well up from volcanic rocks deep under the earth. Some famous bodies have bathed in this pool in times past, including St Catherine of Siena. Bathing is now forbidden but there is a spa hotel nearby, the Posta-Marucci, with modern hydrotherapy facilities and a swimming pool.

Just north of Bagno Vignone, a minor road takes you east along the wide vale of the Orcia river and then up to **Castellucico** and **La Foce**, from where there are spectacular views of an ancient Etruscan road zig-zagging up the hill and lined with cypresses. The next town is **Chianciano Terme**, a post-war spa town and one of the biggest in Italy, but with few attractions for anyone not booked in for a week of water therapy.

More interesting is **Chiusi**, one of the most powerful cities in the ancient Etruscan league. The **Museo Nazionale Etrusco** is packed with funerary urns excavated from various tombs around the town. Arrangements can be made at the museum to visit one of the tombs in the vicinity, but many are now closed to protect their fragile wall paintings from further deterioration, including the famous Tomba della Scimmia (Tomb of the Monkey).

The town's Romanesque church is a delight, built from recycled Roman pillars and capitals and with "mosaics" on the nave walls that were painted by Arturo Viligiardi in 1887. The **Museo della Cattedrale** displays a fascinating collection of Roman, Lombardic and medieval sculpture and you can arrange to visit one of the underground galleries that run beneath the city, dug by the ancient Etruscans and reused as catacombs by early Christians in the 3rd to 5th centuries.

Chiusi stands almost on the border with Umbria, but our Tuscany tour continues north, up the fertile Val di Chiana, where cattle are bred to supply the restaurants of Florence with the raw ingredients of *bistecca alla Fiorentina* (steak Florentine), then west to **Montepulciano**. This splendid hilltop town, with its long, winding main street, deserves long and leisurely exploration,

Rape field in full bloom.

with frequent stops to sample the local Vino Nobile wines, either in the city's rock-cut cellars, or in the Café Poliziano (Via di Voltaia nel Corso 27), a characterful Art Deco bar with an art gallery in the basement.

The spacious main square, the **Piazza Grande**, sits at the town's highest point. On one side is the 15th-century **Palazzo Comunale** (Town Hall), a miniature version of the Palazzo Vecchio in Florence. Nearby is the **Duomo**, which contains one of the greatest masterpieces of the Siena school, the huge Assumption triptych (1401) over the high altar by Taddeo di Bartolo.

As the road to Pienza leaves Montepulciano, it is worth diverting right for the **church of the Madonna di San Biagio**, perched on a platform below the walls of the city. This domed church of honey and cream-coloured stone, is the masterpiece of Antonio di Sangallo, a Renaissance gem begun in 1518.

Pienza is a tiny town that would be famous for nothing but its sweet sheep's milk cheeses, had not the future Pope

Pius II been born here in 1405. The Pope decided to rebuild the village of his birth as a model Renaissance city, but was thoroughly swindled by his architect, Rossellino, who embezzled most of the funds. Only the papal palace and the cathedral were completed and both are now suffering from serious subsidence – see them before they collapse.

Despite the great cracks and buckled pillars, the cathedral is uplifting, and flooded with light from the great windows that the pope specifically requested – he wanted a *domus vitrea*, a house of glass, to symbolise the enlightenment of the Humanist age. The **Palazzo Piccolomini** alongside is filled with the pope's personal posesssions and the loggia at the rear was designed to frame views of Monte Amiata, the distant, cone-shaped peak of an extinct volcano.

The next stop after Pienza is **San Quirico d'Orcia**. This stands beside the N2 road, once the main highway linking Florence and Siena to Rome, until the A1 Autoroute was built further to the east. Grand Tourists travelled this way in the 18th and 19th centuries, and medieval pilgrims came too, which is why San Quirico d'Orcia has such a splendid collegiate church, featuring no less than three ornately carved Romanesque portals. The west portal is particularly splendid with its dragons and mermaids. The N2 will carry you swiftly back to Siena.

From Siena southwards, the N73 will take you on a winding and often empty road through the green and sparsely populated foothills of the Colline Metallifere, the Metalliferous Hills, so-called because they have been a rich source of iron, copper, silver and lead ores since ancient Etruscan times.

Some 20 km (12 miles) out of Siena, be sure to stop off at the ruined Cistercian abbey of **San Galgano**, with its huge and roofless abbey church, where swallows skim in and out of the glassless Gothic windows and sunlight plays on the richly carved capitals of the nave. On a hill above the church is the beehive-shaped oratory built in 1182 on the site of San Galgano's hermitage. Look out for the sword in the stone, thrust there by San Galgano when he renounced his **Detail in Pienza.**

military career to become a hermit. The excellent shop alongside sells local herbs, wines, toiletries and books on the history and sights of the region.

Massa Marittima is the ancient mining capital of the region, but there are no ugly industrial scars to remind us of this fact, just two museums devoted to the history of mining in the region (which flourished in the 13th century) and one of Tuscany's finest Romanesque churches, decorated with humorous sculptures illustrating the adventures of St Cerbone, the town's patron saint. Massa Marittima is the gateway to Tuscany's south, a holiday land with many fine and unspoilt beaches and a Mediterranean climate, notably different from that only a short way north.

From **Piombino** ferries take visitors to the island of **Elba**, either on day trips to see the villa where Napoleon spent a short period in exile, or for a relaxing week in one of the island's many luxury hotels. Further south along the busy coastal road, the Via Aurelia, the city of **Grosseto** is worth a stop only if you want to visit the excellent archaeology museum. This has displays and finds that will help you understand the excavated remains of nearby Etruscan cities, such as Vetulonia (22 km/13 miles northwest of Grosseto) and Vetulonia (7 km/ 4 miles north).

Just south of Grossetto is the **Parco Naturale della Maremma**, a protected nature reserve officially open only on Wednesdays and weekends. The park office in Alberese sells tickets and information on the unspoiled beaches within the park and the rich wildlife. Another wildlife haven is the lagoon north of Orbetello, managed by the Worldwide Fund for Nature and an important wintering spot for birds. **Orbetello** was, in the 16th century, a Spanish garrison town and the baroque architecture reflects this fact. The sea laps right up to the stout city walls and visitors come from afar for the excellent restaurants specialising in fish that are found here and on the island of Monte Argentario.

Inland, tiny villages like **Capalbio**

Resort of Port' Ercole.

specialise in more robust Tuscan dishes, such as wild boar and even baked porcupine (both are hunted locally). For a totally sybaritic experience, you can swim beneath the stars in the hot falls just south of Saturnia before heading into the town for a leisurely meal.

The other villages of this beautiful region, known as the forgotten corner of Tuscany, are situated above dramatic cliffs of soft tufa. These are especially spectacular at **Pitigliano**, where local people have excavated caves in the rock for storing wine and olive oil, and at **Sovana**, where the ancient Etruscans excavated a series of tombs in the soft rock below the town. Sovana itself was the birthplace of Hildebrand, who became Pope Gregory VII in 1073, and the tiny one-street village has two outstanding proto-Romanesque churches of the same period.

West of Siena: It may prove difficult to drag yourself back to Siena from the delights of southern Tuscany, but more spectacular sights await to the west of the city. Taking the N2, you will first pass **Monteriggioni**, a hilltop town built in 1213 to guard the northern borders of Sienese territory, completely encircled by walls and 14 bristling towers.

Next, drive through the lower, modern town of **Colle di Val d'Elsa** and, taking the Volterra road, look for the more ancient upper town. Here the main street is lined with 16th-century *palazzi* of unusual refinement and, at one point, the stately procession of buildings is interrupted by a viaduct from which there are splendid views of the surrounding landscape. Your nose will help you find the old-fashioned bakers (Via del Castello 28) in the oldest part of the town that lies beyond, along with several antique shops and museums.

Perhaps the most spectacular sight anywhere in Tuscany is the town of **San Gimignano**, bristling with medieval towers, scarcely changed in appearance since the Middle Ages and richly rewarding – despite the huge number of visitors it gets. (It is best to stay overnight here, in one of the characterful hotels, to savour the peaceful beauty of the town in the evening and early morning, after the coach trippers have gone.) The main street is lined with shops, many of them selling good quality crafts as well as locally produced Vernaccia wines and wild-boar ham.

The tall defensive towers lining the two squares at the highest point of the town were built as status symbols rather than for genuinely defensive purposes. They alone make a visit here worthwhile, but the town also possesses such an embarrassment of artistic riches that few visitors get to see everything. The highlights are the Wedding Scene frescoes in the **Museo Civico**, showing the newly married couple taking a bath together and climbing into bed, plus the frescoes that cover every inch of wall space in the collegiate church, depicting the Last Judgement and stories from the Old and New Testaments.

Volterra is another rewarding place, sited high on a plateau with distant views to the sea. The entrance to the city is dominated by a Medicean castle, now used as a prison, and if you wander through the park that lies beneath its

San Gimignano's medieval skyline.

walls you will come to the **Museo Guarnacci** in Via Don Minzoni. This is packed with ancient Etruscan urns excavated from cemeteries uncovered by landslides in the 19th century. The urns are arranged according to the subjects carved upon them and give an intriguing glimpse into everyday Etruscan life and beliefs. The Married Couple urn is a masterpiece of realistic portraiture and even more stunning is the bronze statuette known as L'Ombra della Sera (The Shadow of the Night), which resembles a Giacometti sculpture, but was cast in the 5th century BC.

The attractive main square of Volterra has some of the oldest civic buildings in Tuscany, dating from the 13th century, and a showroom for the local alabaster carving industry; galleries selling alabaster are located all over the town. The cathedral has a wealth of carvings from an earlier age, including a balletic Deposition, sculpted in wood in the 13th century.

As one drives west or north from Volterra, the landscape changes rapidly from hilly terrain to flat marshy coastline. You could be forgiven for missing out **Livorno**, for, although it has an interesting harbour area and a famous Renaissance statue (the Four Moors Monument), World War II bombing and modern industry have stripped the city of its character.

Pisa, by contrast, is a must. All the main attractions lie in the northwestern angle of the city walls, around the well-named **Campo dei Miracoli** (the Field of Miracles). The bizarre appearance of the cathedral and baptistry owes much to the influence of Islamic architecture which Pisan merchants and scholars experienced through their extensive trade contacts with Moorish Spain and North Africa. The marble surfaces of these buildings are covered in arabesques and other ornamentation, as densely patterned as an oriental carpet.

The famous **Torre Pendente**, the Leaning Tower, is still standing but is closed to the public while experiments are conducted to try and resolve the imminent threat of collapse. It is esti-

Romanesque cathedral of Pisa with the celebrated tower.

mated that the tower will fall by the year 2200 if nothing is done to arrest the continuing subsidence, caused by building on too shallow foundations in unstable, silty soil.

Lucca, a short way north, is a city of many seductive charms, not least the fact that the ramparts encircling the city were transformed into a tree-lined promenade in the 19th century. You can do a complete circuit of the city by following the walls. The city has more than its fair share of splendid churches in the Pisan Romanesque style, with ornately patterned facades of green, grey and white marble. Many are locked, because the interest is on the outside, but there are exceptions: the church of **San Michele**, with its tiers of arcading and hunting scenes, the church of San Frediano, with its massive Romanesque font, and the splendid cathedral.

The cathedral contains one of the most famous relics of medieval Europe, the *Volto Santo* (Holy Face), said to have ben carved by Nicodemus, who witnessed the Crucifixion – hence it was believed to be a true portrait of Christ (in fact, the highly stylised figure is probably a 13th-century copy of an 11th-century copy of an 8th-century original).

Lucca is the gateway to several regions of Tuscany which all have their own special character. To the west is the Tuscan Riviera, known as the **Versilia**, a string of coastal towns developed in the late 19th century. The beaches here are regimented (you pay for access but get facilities such as sun loungers, showers, beach cabins and a bar or restaurant). **Viareggio** is the most interesting for its Liberty-style (art nouveau) architecture, its plentiful fish restaurants specialising in *cacciucco* (a hearty fish soup) and its atmospheric harbour area.

To the north is the **Garfagnana**, a wild area of high mountains, seemingly covered in snow all year round because the peaks are made of marble. Recently designated as a huge nature reserve, this is a paradise for those who like pony trekking and walking. Information on waymarked trails is available from the

Once Lucca's Roman amphitheatre, now a piazza assuming the same shape.

region's main town, **Castelnuovo di Garfagnana**. On the fringe of the region is the marble town of **Carrara** with several quarries offering guided tours and workshops where you can see marble being turned into just about anything.

Just outside Carrara is **Luni**, once a Roman town and now a place of well-preserved ruins. It gave its name to the Lunigiana, the northernmost part of Tuscany, dotted with castles built by the Malaspina overlords from the 11th century on.

Nearer to Lucca, there are several ornate villas and gardens open to the public, notably the Villa Reale, at **Marlia**, whose *teatro verde* (green theatre) surrounded by clipped yew hedges, is the setting for concerts during Lucca's summer music festival. Another splendid villa, with theatrical gardens spilling down the steep hillside, is the Villa Garzoni, at **Collodi**. Collodi was also the pen name of Carlo Lenzini, the author of the *Adventures of Pinocchio* (1881), who spent his childhood here. The Pinocchio theme park in the village is a wonderful distraction for children and is dotted with sculptures based on episodes from the book.

Montecatini Terme is the most elegant spa town in Tuscany, if not in all Italy, with ornate buildings surrounded by flowerbeds and manicured green lawns. You can buy day tickets which will allow you to sample the waters and admire the marble-lined pools, splashing fountains and art nouveau tile pictures of languorous water nymphs at the **Terme Tettuccio** (built 1928).

Nothing like so attractive is **Pistoia** and its neighbour **Prato**, both hugely successful industrial towns specialising in textiles and metal working, but with surprisingly attractive historic centres awaiting those prepared to drive to them through the dreary suburbs. Pistoia's churches together contain a remarkable number of carved fonts and pulpits dating to the period just before the Renaissance; they include Giovanni Pisano's pulpit of 1301 in **Sant'Andrea church**, which art historians consider to be his masterpiece, more accomplished even

than the pulpit he made for Pisa's cathedral in 1302. You can also see the work of one of Italy's best-known modern sculptors, Marino Marini (1901–66) in a new museum, the **Centro Marino Marini**, on Corso Silvano Fredi.

Prato was the birthplace of Francesco di Marco Datini (1330–1410), better known as The Merchant of Prato, the title and subject of Iris Origo's historical biography. Datini died one of the richest men in Europe and left his money to city charities so, as you might expect, the town has several statues of the great man, as well as a museum located in his former home, the **Palazzo Datini**.

Another local merchant, one Michele Dagomari, married a Palestinian woman in 1180 and discovered that her dowry included a girdle. According to legend, this had been given to Doubting Thomas, the Apostle, by the Virgin. The precious relic was brought to Prato, and it is exhibited to the faithful four times a year from the external pulpit on the facade of the cathedral in the city's main square. Inside the cathedral there are

Statue at Collodi.

frescoes by Fra Lippo Lippi, the reprobate monk who seduced the nun Lucrezia Buti and often incorporated her strikingly beautiful features into his paintings. Here she plays the role of Salome dancing at Herod's feast and demanding the head of John the Baptist as a favour.

Despite the industrial sprawl that mars this part of Tuscany, rural delights are not far away. South of Pistoia is the tiny hilltop village of **Vinci**, birthplace of Leonardo da Vinci, where the castle has been turned into an entertaining museum dedicated to the great polymath and his numerous inventions. The displays consist of wooden models, beautifully crafted and based on Leonardo's notebooks, of a bicycle, submarine, tank, and helicopter, to name just a few.

From Vinci, you can take a winding rural road into Florence, stopping at **Poggio a Caiano**, the villa built for Lorenzo de'Medici which became the archetype for many another Renaissance villa, and greatly influenced the architect Palladio.

Skirting Florence, you can speed south to Arezzo on the A1 autoroute, or you can break the journey by coming off at the Incisa intersection and following the signs for **Vallombrosa**. The reward is not so much the monastery, whose 18th-century buildings are not very attractive, but more the splendid beech woodland that surrounds it; the poet John Milton visited in 1638 and was so impressed that he wrote a description of the autumnal leaves that strew the brooks in Vallombrosa in *Paradise Lost*.

Similarly leafy delights await if you continue north to Consuma and the N70 to **Stia**. From here, you can visit two sacred sights set high up in spectacular woodland, cut by mountain streams and waterfalls, where mushroom hunters come in autumn and pilgrims at all times of the year. One is the hermitage at **Camaldoli**, 17 km (10 miles) east of Stia, and the other is the monastery at **La Verna** further south (best reached by driving east from Bibbiena). It was at La Verna that St Francis received the stigmata (the wounds of Christ) to his hands and feet in 1224, and the monas- **Arezzo.**

tery built upon the site commands panoramic views.

On the way south from here to Arezzo, it is also worth seeking out little **Caprese Michelangelo**, the birthplace of the great artist after whom it is named. There is little to see, except for a sculpture park in the grounds of the castle where Michelangelo was born, but the views over alpine countryside explain why Michelangelo always attributed his good brains to the mountain air he breathed as a child.

Arezzo contains many interesting sights, including a good archaeological museum full of Arretine tableware, fashionable for a time during the Roman period. For most visitors, though, the highlight will be Piero della Francesca's fresco cycle in the **church of San Francesco**. The frescoes illustrate the Legend of the True Cross, a complex story whereby the wood of the Tree of Knowledge, which bore the fruit that Adam and Eve ate, becomes the Cross on which Christ died and then is instrumental in converting Constantine the Great, who made Christianity the state religion of the Roman world.

The artist's style, compelling and mysterious, attracts superlatives from art historians and you can easily become hooked on his work, following the Piero della Francesca trail, like the heroine of *A Summer's Lease*, a novel by the English writer John Mortimer. If so, the trail leads from here to **Monterchi**, 25 km (15 miles) west along the N73, where the cemetery chapel contains his striking *Madonna del Parto*, the Pregnant Madonna. From there, you should continue 12 km (7 miles) north to **Sansepolcro**, the town where Buitoni pasta is produced. Here the **Museo Civico** has della Francesca's 1463 masterpiece, the *Resurrection*, hailed by Aldous Huxley as "the best picture in the world".

To complete the trail, you should ideally visit **Urbino**, in the Marches, to see *The Flagellation of Christ* and other works in the Ducal Palace, but you are likely to be detained along the route by the many attractions of the neighbouring region of Umbria.

Tuscan landscape.

UMBRIA AND THE MARCHES

Perugia is the sun around which the other towns of Umbria all orbit. One of the 12 members of the ancient Etruscan defensive league in the 6th century BC, it fell into Roman hands 300 years later. During the Middle Ages, it spent most of its time fighting neighbouring free communes, finally challenging papal forces around the turn of the 16th century during the infamous salt wars when the Perugians refused to pay Pope Paul III's tax on salt. To this day, Perugians bake saltless bread – crisp, no butter – to dip in a glass of Torgiano.

The **Piazza IV Novembre** is the epicentre of the city, freshened and serenaded by the 13th-century **Fontana Maggiore**. This splendid fountain is one of the great works of the Pisa-born sculptors, Niccolo Pizano and his son Giovanni, carved in 1277 and covered in elegant figures representing sundry subjects: the Labours of the Months, Adam and Eve, scenes from Aesop's *Fables*. Such accomplished art, used to decorate a fountain, says just how important a reliable water supply was to the survival of any medieval city.

Just to the north of the fountain, the steps of the Gothic cathedral are where people and pigeons gather to preen and flirt. Inside, the mystic *Deposition*, painted by Barocci whilst under the influence of poison fed to him by a rival, inspired the famous painting by Rubens known as the *Antwerp Descent*.

Sweeping down from the piazza is the **Corso Vannucci**, choked with pedestrians day and night. On the right hand is the **Palazzo dei Priori** or **Town Hall** (13th to 15th century). Up its steps is the **Sala dei Notari**, painted at the end of the 13th century and since restored.

In the same building is the **Galleria Nazionale dell' Umbria** containing an extensive collection of Romanesque and Gothic church masterpieces and a comprehensive collection of the most important of the many artists who lived in Umbria. Francesco da Rimini, Fra Angelico, Piero della Francesca, and Pinturicchio, painted the hills that can be seen from the gallery's windows.

Across the Corso Vannucci is the **Collegio del Cambio** (15th century), distinguished by frescoes of Perugino and his school, and by 17th-century inlay woodwork.

The rest of the Corso Vannucci is best appreciated at night. Relax in one of the cafés on the street and watch the students watching you. Stop at the end of the Corso in the **Giardini Carducci** to enjoy the second best view in Perugia: the hills twinkling under the stars.

Near the **Arco Etrusco**, through whose ancient masonry run cars and bicycles, is a long staircase atop which is the best view in Perugia. From this vantage you can map out your strategy for visiting Perugia's various churches. The choice is wide. South of the town is **San Pietro** with its 16th-century choir stalls, carved with a whole medieval bestiary – ducks, crocodiles and elephants included. Nearer in is the barnlike **San Domenico** with a little-visited tomb that ranks as one of the finest of its

age in Italy – that of Pope Benedict XI, who died in Perugia in 1304 having eaten poisoned figs.

The adjacent cloister contains Umbria's **Museo Archeologico**, the gathering place for vast quantities of ancient Etruscan pottery and metalwork. West of the city centre is the church of **San Bernardino**, its facade decorated with angels and musicians with diaphanous robes, looking just like the stone version of the figures in Mucha 's art nouveau posters, except that these date to 1451 rather than the 1890s.

To the north of the city is another rarity, the 5th-century round church of **Sant'Agostino**, with its operatic baroque plasterwork, created by French artists in the early 17th century.

Assisi and Gubbio: There is no place quite like **Assisi**. Yes, it is one of the few places in Umbria full of foreign holidaymakers, and all that means in terms of commercialisation. However, the sight, as you approach Assisi, of the mighty arches supporting the **Basilica di San Francesco**, rising above the perpetual Umbrian haze, and of **Monte Subasio**, the great peak towering behind, is sufficient to make the rest of the world seem blissfully far away. Inside the town itself, a nun might open an automatic garage door set in a 13th-century stone wall, while a monk passes in berry-brown robes, hardly making a sound in his soft sandals.

The streets are almost too postcard perfect: cascades of flowers fall from wall sconces, alleyway gardens hoard every scrap of sunlight, the smell of roses and wood smoke permeates the air. The Basilica di San Francesco is perfectly situated for sunsets. The facade of the basilica, designed by a military architect, is like the saint it commemorates, beautiful in its poverty. The basilica is entered throught the lower of its two naves, one stacked on top of the other. The walls of the Basilica Inferiore (Lower Basilica) are a jigsaw puzzle of frescoes by many hands, all of them inspired by the example and life of St Francis. They vary between the sweetly cheerful frescoes of Simone

Perugia under a rainbow.

Martini, where even the horses seem to smile, to the sternly didactic vault frescoes depicting the monastic virtues of Chastity, Poverty and Obedience. Equally stern is the crypt where St Francis is buried, but the face of the little monk, with his jutting out ears, painted in the transept by Cimabue and said to be a faithful portrait, tells a different story.

Upstairs in the Upper Basilica, you can see Giotto's famous fresco cycle on the Life of St Francis, completed in 1300. Almost singlehandedly, Giotto revived the art of fresco painting in Italy (he learned by watching and copying artists from Greece) and this is his most accomplished work, admired by all the great artists of the Renaissance for the degree to which it introduced realism into Western art.

Chronologically, a tour of the rest of Assisi begins with the **Roman Forum** beneath the **Piazza del Comune**. The forum's above-ground vestige is the **Tempio di Minerva**, whose interior has been revamped in an unfortunately gaudy manner. In the northeast sector of town, the **Anfiteatro Romano**, where live naval battles were staged, has been topped by homes that follow its original oval structure.

The **Rocca Maggiore**, grim and immobile above the town, destroyed and rebuilt, was part of a string of towers guarding Assisi. The **Duomo** (12th-century, dedicated to San Rufino) is best appreciated for the imagination of its Romanesque exterior details; its interior was revamped in 1571.

Chiesa Santa Chiara's pink and white exterior is supported by wing-like buttresses that are decidedly feminine in their generous curves, their airiness and strength. The chapel houses the 12th-century crucifix supposed to have spoken to St Francis. In an adjoining chapel hang the tunics of saints Francis and Clare.

To experience something of the solitude and spirituality that matched the lives of both these saints, it is well worth visiting a couple of churches on the outskirts of Assisi. **San Damiano,** nearly

Assisi.

2 km (1 mile) south of the town, is the convent where St Clare spent most of her reclusive life, and it retains the air of a simple religious retreat. More rural still is the favourite hermitage of St Francis, the **Eremo delle Carceri**, a tranquil spot nestling into the tree-covered slope of Monte Subasio, 3 km (2 miles) east of the town.

Assisi sits on the rim of a dried-up lake bed, finally drained of water in the 16th century, called the Vale of Spoleto. Several other towns of great character line the eastern shore, including **Spello**, which boasts renowned frescoes by Pinturicchio, one of the main artists of the Umbrian school. **Spoleto** sits at the southernmost point of the former lake, a city of great cosmopolitan sophistication, renowned for its summer arts jamboree, the Festival dei Due Mondi (of the Two Worlds, meaning Europe and the Americas). The emphasis in this festival, also one of the high points in the Italian social calendar, is on the avant garde, and the legacy is a number of modern sculptures dotted about the town, plus numerous art galleries selling work of dubious merit.

The town's dominant building, the **Rocca del Albornoz**, was built as a papal stronghold, became the home of Lucrezia Borgia, served as a prison where members of the Red Brigades were held and has now reopened as a cultural complex – see it if you can. Alongside is the striking **Ponte delle Torri** spanning the gorge that yawns between the castle and the opposite hill. The Bridge of the Towers, as the name translates, was actually built as an aqueduct in the 13th century and you can walk across the top of the (now dry) water channel.

Spoleto's outstanding treasure is the **Duomo** (12th-century). Its medieval porch is surmounted by a rose window. The cathedral floor has an intricate herringbone and spiral Romanesque design. The chapel to the right was decorated by Pinturicchio. The apse is ablaze with Filippo Lippi's final work, the coronation of an exquisite Madonna surrounded by a rainbow and an arc of angels.

Madonna by Filippo Lippi in the cathedral, Spoleto.

On the north side of the stairs leading to the Piazza del Duomo is the jewel-like 12th-century **Chiesa Sant'Eufemia** whose chaste perfection contrasts with the cathedral's perfect grandeur. Note Sant' Euphemia's massive stone throne behind the altar.

Visitors to Spoleto with time and a taste for the wild can use the town as a base for exploring the moutainous area to the east of Umbria, where winding narrow roads carry you up to the snowy peaks of the Monti Sibillini range, part of the Appenines.

You can drive, via Triponzo, to **Norcia**, the birthplace of St Benedict and a major centre of the truffle and salami industries. From here, roads climb ever higher to the spectacular **Piano Grande**, a vast open plain that is covered in wild flowers and rare alpine species in summer. On the return journey you can take in the charming 8th-century monastery at **San Pietro in Valle** with its Lombardic sculpture and 12th-century frescoes.

Hill-top Todi: West of Spoleto is the hill-top town of **Todi**. Here the lovely view from the **Piazza Garibaldi** is enhanced by the fragrance of a garden beneath. Nearby is the grand **Piazza Vittorio Emanuele** or **Piazza del Popolo**. Facing the **Duomo** is the **Palazzo dei Priori** (13th-century). To the right, up the stair, are the **Palazzi del Capitano** (14th-century) and **del Popolo** (13th-century), the former in the Gothic style with a bay of triform windows, the latter in the Lombard style resting on an impressive network of pillars.

At the head of the square stands the Duomo which was begun in the early 12th century. The Gothic campanile, built 100 years later, strays from the church's fine Romanesque style.

The Duomo's entrance wall is decorated by a Faenzone fresco. To the right is a 16th-century Giannicola di Paolo painting of the Madonna enthroned. The interior is softly lit by some of the finest stained glass in the region.

A constitutional around the hill brings you to the **Chiesa di San Fortunato**. The structure was built in stages during

Exterior of the cathedral at Spoleto.

200 years of architectural revolution beginning in 1292. The exterior shows its seams in a not unattractive way. On the facade of San Fortunato, the central portal's sculptures deserve close examination of their tiny, whimsical depictions of humans and beasts.

The interior is light and airy; the eggshell whiteness of the stone enhanced by the deep sable colour of the carved choir and the formidable pillar-mounted lectern. In the crypt, Jacopone, the Franciscan poet who wrote the *Stabat Mater*, is buried.

Through the **Parco della Rocca**, replete with good views, and on down the mountain the **Tempio di Santa Maria della Consolazione** is perched on a little shelf of green. The 16th-century structure was long thought to be the work of Bramante because of the similarities with St Peter's in Rome, but it is now attributed to one Cola di Capsorala. The altar may seem to some a bit too much, but the space is light and airy, the intricate sunburst of stones on the floor, a marvel of geometrics.

Vine-growing Orvieto: The hill which supports **Orvieto** is volcanic in origin, therefore porous, therefore in danger of bringing the city down as it crumbles. The volcanic slopes are covered in the vineyards that produce Orvieto's famously crisp white wines.

After climbing up serpentine curves and through narrow streets, you will burst into the unexpected and exquisite expanse of the **Piazza del Duomo**. With any luck, the hour will be late afternoon as the sun is glittering off the tesserae of the 14th-century cathedral's astonishing facade. The cathedral's steps are generally crowded with a mixture of Orvietans, soldiers garrisoned down the street, and visitors.

The cathedral was begun on 15 November 1290 to house relics of the miracles of Bolsena (1263): principally a chalice-cloth onto which blood flowed from the host during a celebration of the Mass. Although the identity of the original architect is a matter of some debate, by its completion in the late 14th century the Duomo's construction required

Todi, classic Umbrian hilltown.

the input of legions of architects, sculptors, painters and mosaicists. The result is amazing. The facade, designed by Lorenzo Maitani, is bolstered by zebra horizontals of basalt and travertine.

Inside the cathedral, the black and white stripes point up the curvilinear arches. The wall of the apse is decorated with scenes from the life of the Virgin. These were begun by Ugolino di Prete Ilario and completed by Pinturicchio and Antonio Viterbo during the late 14th century. On the left-hand side of the altar is the **Cappella del Corporale** painted by Ugolino and his assistants, depicting the miracles of Bolsena. To the right side of the altar is the **Cappella Nuova** whose decoration was begun by Fra Angelico in 1447 and completed finally by Luca Signorelli at the turn of the next century. The frescoes feature lurid scenes of hellfire with a deep contextual nod to Dante.

The **Via Duomo** and the **Corso Cavour** are both generously equipped with examples of Orvietan ceramics – whose simple, medieval designs are some of the prettiest in the region – elegant restaurants, chic clothiers, and purveyors of unique Orvietan wood sculptures. To the right off the Corso Cavour is the **Palazzo** and **Piazza del Popolo** (the latter now a parking lot).

Straight ahead are the **Palazzo Comunale** and the **Chiesa di S Andrea** in the **Piazza della Repubblica**. To the left is the **Old** or **Medieval Quarter**, which is easily the most charming part of the town with its antique walls hung with pots of tumbling geraniums, high-walled gardens and the songbirds they attract, and tiny cave-like workrooms of Orvietan artisans.

Lakeside pursuits: The road north from Orvieto will take you to **Città della Pieve**, birthplace of Perugino, father of the Umbrian school of painting and best-known for his ability to capture the limpid blues and greens of the Umbrian sky. The town has several of his works, including the *Adoration of the Maji*, which features Lake Trasimeno in the background. Today that lake is Umbria's summer holiday playground, ringed by campsites offering tennis, swimming and trekking on horseback. Castiglione del Lago is the lake's capital, and there are splendid views from the ramparts of the castle which gave the town its name. Here, and at the restaurants around the lake, you can sample the locally caught fish: eel, pike and trout.

North of the lake, the road through Umbertide takes you to the atmospheric city of **Gubbio**, once known as the city of silence because of its desolate loneliness in the Umbrian backwoods, but now, thanks to modern roadbuilding, a town within easy reach of those who love good food and architecture. Gubbio literally clings to the side of Monte Ingino, and its major buildings just fit onto the narrow terraces that step up the mountainside.

At the top of Monte Ingino (it is best to take the funicular railway up and then walk down) rises the jewel of the **Basilica di Sant' Ubaldo** wherein lie the remains of the saint in stately, if somewhat grisly splendour. Legend has it that Sant' Ubaldo intervened in a battle against Perugia, gaining a decisive vic-

Umbrians are among the most reserved of Italians.

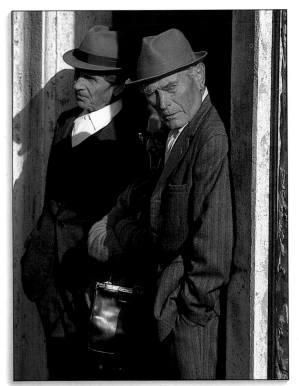

tory for the badly outnumbered Gubbians. The basilica also displays the three immense *ceri* (candles) with which the sturdy men of Gubbio race up the hill in an orgiastic celebration of the saint's day every 15 May.

Returning to the town, your path should take you to the fine cathedral to see the great Gothic ribs of the vault and the 13th-century stained glass.

Across a small passage from the cathedral is the **Palazzo Ducale** begun in 1476 by Federico da Montefeltro, Duke of Urbino, inspired by the palace in that town. The Ducal Palace's rooms sport frescoes and various interesting architectural features.

The outstanding element of Gubbio's skyline is the belltower of the **Palazzo dei Consoli** (14th-century). The Palace's Great Hall houses a quixotic collection of medieval paraphernalia and is sided by a high staircase that affords some remarkable acoustic effects. Up the staircase are the famous **Tavole Eugubine**: seven bronze plates upon which a purposeful and precise hand has translated the ancient Umbrian language into Latin.

The Marches: After the stunning hilltowns of Umbria, the neighbouring region of the Marches holds very few sights that can compete, with the singular exception of **Urbino** with its stronghold of the wise old warrior Duke Federico da Montefeltro. Here he constructed one of the great treasures of cinquecento architecture. Urbino is an eyrie of a town whose golden buildings are set high amid spectacular mountains. Urbino remains one of the few hill towns left in Italy not ringed by the unsavoury intrusions of modernity. The original old city remains almost completely "unimproved", perched at the top of its two peaks.

The **Piazza del Popolo** is a tourist centre by day. By night some of the University of Urbino's 16,000 students recline here on the steps or in the cafés, or stand in the street and discuss politics, the latest foreign film, last night's poetry reading. The facades are old; the faces are generally young. The contrast ex-

View over Urbino in the Marches.

emplifies the relaxed symbiosis that exists between Urbino's walls and the lives they enclose.

The duke and his humanist contemporaries felt man was the centre of the universe – a significant break with previous Christian philosophy. The courtyard of his **Palazzo Ducale** is paved with a hub, with radiating spokes of marble to symbolise man's central position. The building itself is part palace and part fortress: a graceful, secure nest in the rarefied mountain air for the duke to feather with marvellous works of art.

The **Galleria Nazionale delle Marche**, now housed in the palace, has several fine works by Piero della Francesca and by the town's most famous artist, Raphael. Also remarkable is the *trompe l'oeil* inlay work in the duke's study.

Down the street from the ducal palace is the house where Raphael spent the first 14 years of his life. The middle-class house contrasts with the ducal splendour. There is a beamed kitchen with arcane fittings. Outside in the court-yard is the stone upon which Raphael and his father, Giovanni, also an artist, ground their pigments.

Pocket-sized republic: Urbino stands a little inland from the Adriatic, a sunny coastline lined with hectare after hectare of orchards growing peaches and nectarines for export, and of regimented beaches and seaside hotels. You will see something of this if you visit the Republic of **San Marino**, a self-governing state within Italy that has remained independent for 1,600 years. Stamp collectors will know it as a republic that issues big pictorial postage stamps in a variety of shapes other than square – the philatelic ouput is there to see in specialist museums.

The republic stands on the peak of Monte Titano, with sweeping views out over Rimini to the Adriatic. You can do a complete circuit of the town's historic walls, visiting the several museums that are housed in the bastions, and visit the diminutive building that serves as the parliament of this pocket-sized republic. All cars are banned.

Left and **right**, cobbled streets and narrow alleys in Urbino.

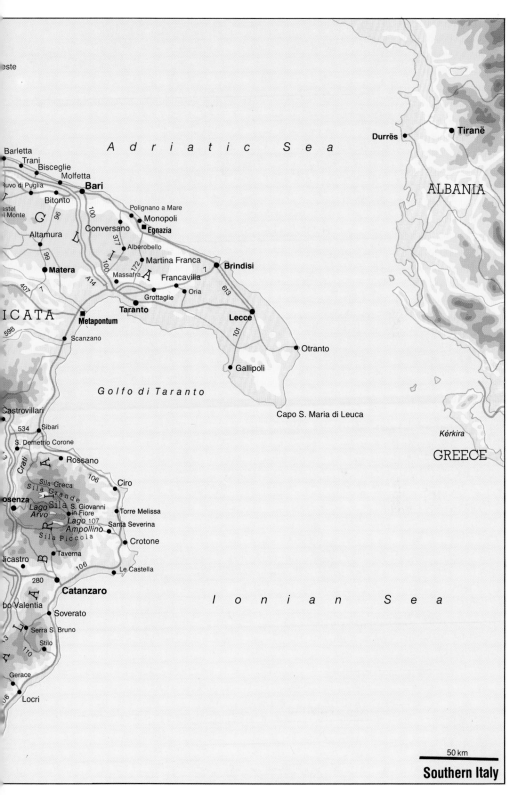

Southern Italy

THE SOUTH

When foreign travellers visit Apulia, Basilicata and Calabria, they are usually greeted by stares. The stares are not hostile. Nor are they necessarily suspicious. They're just surprised. So few foreigners – so few northern Italians, even – visit these remote and sunbaked regions that anybody who does is looked upon as a bit of an oddball.

This was the case when the English writer Norman Douglas visited in 1911; it was the case when the anti-fascist Carlo Levi was banished here in 1935. So few people have come to this area for pleasure or insight that nobody knows of the pleasures and insights to be found. Those who do come, follow in the footsteps of the Greeks and Romans to Naples, Pompeii, Cumae and Capri. They flock to Sicily and its temples. But Apulia? Basilicata? Calabria? Italy's heel? Her instep? Her toe?

Then there is northern prejudice. Northerners are industrial, pragmatic, fair-skinned. The southerners are agricultural, superstitous, dark. The northerners are rich. The southerners are poor, and emigrate if they get the chance. Nobody moves south to take their place. This is *Le Problema del Mezzogiorno*.

The truth is that southern Italy is one of the most interesting places to visit in Europe. It is a romantic land of castles and churches; vast, wheat-covered plains; and misty mountains where shepherds roam. Apulia is a place for novel architectural forms: the Apulian Romanesque; Leccian baroque; castles by Frederick II – and odd, conical, peasant dwellings known as the *Trulli*. In Basilicata are the *Sassi*, cave-dwellings carved into the side of a ravine, many adorned with frescoes, and La Trinità, an unfinished 11th-century Benedictine monastery covered with Roman inscriptions. In Calabria visitors rediscover the Greeks – in particular, two made of bronze, recently dredged up by fishermen off Riace. There are Norman castles, Byzantine churches, rich red wine and landscapes which were first described by Homer.

Naples, the Bay of Naples and Sicily are the richest regions historically, and this is reflected in this guide. Apart from Naples, which it is best to explore on foot, the descriptions are geared towards travelling by car. A car is especially important in the *Mezzogiorno*, where sights are too scattered to justify spending long hours waiting for infrequent trains.

Preceding pages: Trulli houses at Alberobello; Albanian villager in Calabria. Left, an ancient fresco of spring in Naples Archaeological Museum.

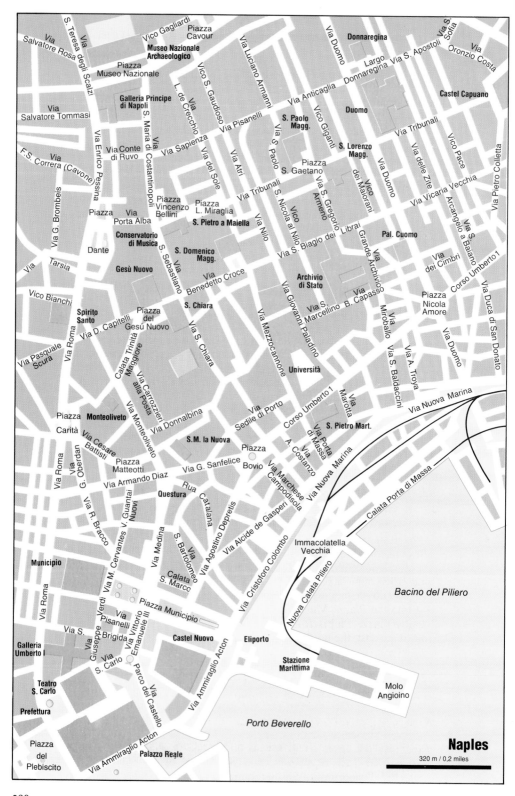

Via S. Teresa degli Scalzi
Via Salvatore Rosa
S. Teresa degli Scalzi
Vico Gagliardi
Piazza Cavour
Via S. Sofia
Via Oronzio Costa
Via

Museo Nazionale Archaeologico
Piazza Museo Nazionale
Donnaregina
Largo Donnaregina
Via S. Apostoli
Castel Capuano

Via Salvatore Tommasi
Galleria Principe di Napoli
L. de Crecchio
Vico S. Gaudioso
Via Luciano Armanni
Via Anticaglia
Vico Giganti
Duomo
Via Tribunali

Via Enrico Pessina
Via Conte di Ruvo
Via Santa Maria di Costantinopoli
Via Sapienza
Via Pisanelli
Via S. Paolo
S. Paolo Magg.
Via Duomo
S. Lorenzo Magg.
Via delle Zite
Vico Pace

Via F.S. Correra (Cavone)
Via G. Brombeis
Piazza Porta Alba
Via del Sole
Via Atri
Via Tribunali
Piazza S. Gaetano
S. Nicola al Nilo
Via S. Gregorio Armeno
Vico dei Maiorani
Via Duomo
Via Vicaria Vecchia
Arcangelo a Baiano
Via S. Arcangelo a Baiano
Via Pietro Colletta

Piazza Vincenzo Bellini
Piazza L. Miraglia
S. Pietro a Maiella
Via Nilo
Vico S. Nicola al Nilo
Via S. Biagio dei Librai
Grande Archivio
Pal. Cuomo
Via dei Cimbri
Corso Umberto 1

Via Tarsia
Piazza Dante
Via Porta Alba
Conservatorio di Musica
S. Domenico Magg.
Gesù Nuovo
Via S. Sebastiano
Via Benedetto Croce
Archivio di Stato
Via Mirobalo
B. Capasso
Piazza Nicola Amore
Via Duca di San Donato

Vico Bianchi
Spirito Santo
Piazza del Gesù Nuovo
Via D. Capitelli
S. Chiara
Via S. Chiara
Calata Trinità Maggiore
Via Giovanni Paladino
Via S. Marcellino
Via S. Baldaccini
Via A. Troya
Via Duomo

Via Pasquale Scura
Via Roma
Calata Carrozzieri alla Posta
Via Mezzocannone
Università
Via Marotta
Via Nuova Marina

Piazza Carità
Monteoliveto
Via Donnalbina
Via Monteoliveto
S.M. la Nuova
Via Sedile di Porto
Corso Umberto 1
S. Pietro Mart.
Via Porta di Massa
Calata Porta di Massa

Via Roma
Via Cesare Battisti
G. Oberdan
Piazza Matteotti
Via G. Sanfelice
Piazza Bovio
Via Marchese Campodisola
Via Nuova Marina

Via R. Bracco
V. Guantai Nuovi
Questura
Rua Catalana
Via Agostino Depretis
A. Costanzo
Immacolatella Vecchia

Municipio
Via M. Cervantes
Via Medina
S. Bartolomeo
Via Alcide de Gasperi
Via Cristoforo Colombo
Nuova Calata Piliero
Bacino del Piliero

Via Roma
Verdi
Via Pisanelli
Via Giuseppe Brigida
Via Vittorio Emanuele III
Piazza Municipio
Calata S. Marco

Galleria Umberto I
Via S.
S. Carlo
Castel Nuovo
Eliporto
Molo Angioino

Teatro S. Carlo
Parco del Castello
Stazione Marittima

Prefettura
Via Ammiraglio Acton

Piazza del Plebiscito
Via Ammiraglio Acton
Palazzo Reale
Porto Beverello

Naples
320 m / 0,2 miles

NAPLES

Naples (Napoli) has always been the black sheep of Italian cities, the misfit, the outcast, the messy brother that nobody knew quite what to do with. It is burdened by the densest population of any city in Europe, intense poverty, unemployment, bureaucratic inefficiency and organised crime, and has come to be seen as an Italian Calcutta. That Naples is, in fact, one of the most beautiful Italian cities, with a friendly population and a long cultural heritage evidenced in art, churches, castles and pizza, does not deny its less appealing side. In the end, like all black sheep, troubled Naples is the most interesting member of its family.

Orientation: The city has its own special shape, defined partly by landscape, partly by chance and partly by governmental edict. The only way to get a feel for the place is to walk its different quarters. To orientate yourself, find **Piazza Garibaldi**. From here, the long **Corso Umberto** I juts down to the southwest to the Piazza Bovio, where, changing its name to Via Agostino Depretis, it continues on to the **Piazza Municipio**. By day, the corso, one of the main traffic routes in Naples, is jammed with buses, taxis, cars and motorbikes. At night, it is lined with prostitutes. The thoroughfare was forced through the narrow, crowded streets that surround it in 1888 in an effort to improve air circulation following a cholera epidemic. The rather drab **Università** looms halfway down, on the right-hand side.

From the Piazza Municipio and the nearby **Piazza Plebiscito** the city fans out to the east, the north and the west. Directly north, up the Via Toledo, also known as the Via Roma, is the red palazzo housing the **Museo Archeologico Nazionale**. East of the Museo, in the triangle it forms with the Piazza Plebiscito and the Piazza Garibaldi, lies most of Old Naples, with its medieval streets and its churches. North of the museum, on a hilltop, stands the art gallery of **Capodimonte**. Farther south, on a spur of land out in the bay, rises the egg-shaped **Castel dell'Ovo** and, along the waterfront, the Via Partenope, where the city's most expensive hotels overlook the water. The shoreline then curves away west, passing the **Villa Comunale** with its famous aquarium, to the Marina at **Mergellina**, near Virgil's tomb. From Mergellina views stretch back over the entire city, with Mount Vesuvius looming in the background haze.

The city's roots: The name Naples derives from Neapolis, the New City founded by settlers from Cumae in the 6th century BC. Nearby stood Paleopolis, the Old City, founded in the 9th century BC, also by Greeks from Cumae. The two cities grew side by side like brother and sister until their violent overthrow by Samnites in 400 BC. Rome wrested them away after a three-year siege in 326 BC, at which point they began to grow into a single entity called Neapolis.

From the beginning Romans flocked here, drawn by the mild climate, the sparkling bay and the political freedom which retention of the Greek constitution allowed. Virgil wrote the *Aeneid* here; emperors built gardens and bathed.

The Dark Ages were indeed dark in Naples – nobody knows quite what happened – and until shortly after the first millennium the city was ruled by dukes loosely allied to Byzantium. Then, in 1139, Roger the Norman took Naples under the wing of his Kingdom of Sicily. The seven dynasties that followed produced most of the architectural landmarks that can be seen today. Their statues, together with one of Roger, peer out from niches in the facade of the Palazzo Reale at the centre of town: Frederick II of Hohenstaufen, who founded the university but never lived here, preferring the plains of Apulia; Charles I of Anjou, who lived here and made his stamp; Alphonso I of Aragon, Charles I of Austria, Charles I of Bourbon, Joachim Murat and Victor Emmanuel II. They line up like wrinkles in the broad face of the building, testimonies to the city's past.

Castles and music: When Charles I of Anjou built the **Castel Nuovo** in 1272, he could not have known that seven centuries later it would still serve as the political hub of the city. The Municipal Council of Naples meets in the huge **Sala dei Baroni**, where the cruel Charles is said to have performed some of his bloodiest executions. Perhaps the finest architectural element in this imposing fortress is the Triumphal Arch, built between 1454 and 1467 to commemorate Alphonso I's defeat of the French. It is the only Renaissance arch ever to have been built at the entrance to a castle.

A short walk up the Via San Carlo leads to the **Teatro San Carlo**, the largest opera house in Italy and one of the finest in the world. It is all red velvet and gold trim, with six tiers of boxes rising from the stage. Built in 1737, under the direction of Charles III of Bourbon, the theatre retains its perfect acoustics, helped by the insertion, after a fire in 1816, of hundreds of clay pitchers between the walls. The monthly tourist magazine *Qui Napoli*, available at tourist offices, gives detailed listings of concerts, operas and recitals. Even on the sixth tier, you can sit in a red velvet seat in your own private box, inches beneath the ceiling.

Across the street is the **Galleria Umberto I**, erected in 1887 on a neo-classical design similar to that of its older brother in Milan. Its glass ceiling, 56 metres (184 ft) high, and its mosaic-covered floor were reconstructed after bomb damage in World War II. Pleasant cafés permit a moment's rest.

The wide **Piazza Plebiscito** around the corner is embraced by the twin arcades of the **Chiesa di San Francesco di Paola** (1817–32), modelled after the Pantheon in Rome. The interior of this imposing church has little to offer tourists other than the pungent shade of its dingy arcades.

The sprawling red facade of the **Palazzo Reale** (1600) looms across the street with its eight statues illustrating the eight Neapolitan dynasties (*see page 291*). At the foot of its monumental marble staircase stand the original bronze doors from the Castel Nuovo.

Castel dell'Ovo guards Naples harbour.

The cannonball lodged in the left door is a reminder of an early siege. Upstairs are a throne room and a small but lavish theatre. Further rooms stretch off in a seemingly endless series of period furniture and Dresden china.

Another famous castle, the **Castel dell'Ovo**, on the waterfront, is also still in use, this time for scientific conventions. Its oval shape (hence the name) was commissioned by the Spanish viceroy Don Pedro de Toledo in1532, but the original castle was built by William I in 1154, finished by Frederick II and enlarged by the not-to-be-outdone Charles I of Anjou. Pleasant restaurants line the shore, children bellyflop from the causeway, and the speedboats of the Guardia di Finanza lurk just along the quay.

House of history: The **Museo Archeologico Nazionale di Napoli** is one of the great museums of the world, housing the most spectacular finds from Pompeii and Herculaneum and fine examples of Greek sculpture. A trip to the museum will take an entire morning.

The ground floor is devoted to classical sculpture and Egyptian art. In the main entrance hall, a monolithic sarcophagus depicts a famous and important scene: Prometheus creating man out of clay. Another awesome sarcophagus presents a raucous Bacchanalian celebration. Through a doorway to the right, a pair of statues of Harmodius and Aristogeiton, who killed the tyrant Hipparchus, fairly leaps out at you as you enter the room. These are actually Roman copies of originals once installed in the Agora in Athens.

In a further room stands a Roman copy of the famous statue of Doryphorus by Polycleitus (440 BC), considered the "canon of perfection" of manly proportions. This statue, found at Pompeii, and others of its period are evidence of the refined tastes of early Greek settlers.

The rich collection of mosaics on the mezzanine floor come from the floors, walls and courtyards of houses unearthed at Pompeii. The freshness and colour of these works after centuries buried in lava are an amazing tribute to the crafts-

<u>Left</u>,
vulnerable
wallet in a
moment of
passion.
<u>Right</u>, priests
relax in a
Neapolitan
bar.

manship of their ancient makers. Room LIX contains two of the most famous of the mosaics, both signed by a master of the craft named Dioscorides from the island of Samos. The one labelled 9987 depicts, according to some, two women consulting a sorceress, or, according to others, three women gossiping. This mosaic and 9985, which depicts a dwarf, two women and a man with musical instruments, are thought to represent scenes from a Greek comedy.

The Nile scenes in room LX, from a later period, feature ducks, crocodiles, hippopotami and snakes. These mosaics originally framed the *Battle of Issus*, now in Room LXI. In this huge scene Alexander the Great is presented in his victorious battle against the Persian emperor Darius in 333 BC. The thicket of spears creates the illusion of an army far larger than the one actually shown.

Through the large Salone dell'Atlante at the top of the stairs is a series of rooms containing wall-paintings from various Campanian cities. Especially startling is the 6th-century BC *Sacrifice of Iphigenia*, the Greek equivalent of the biblical sacrifice of Isaac. The deer borne by Artemis in the top of the picture replaced Iphigenia at the last minute, just as Isaac was replaced by a ram. Far happier is *The Rustic Concert*, in which Pan and nymphs tune up for a Roman celebration.

Neapolitan churches: The churches of Naples, like the churches of any Italian city, offer glimpses into Italian life. In Italy a visit to a church, a quick confession, a curtsy in front of an altar are still a daily ritual for large sections of the population.

The church of **Monteoliveto**, about halfway up the Via Roma, contains a wealth of Renaissance monuments hidden away in surprising corners. Far in the back of this aisleless basilica, begun in 1411, stands a bizarre group of terracotta figures by the artist Guido Mazzoni. The eight statues, looking almost alive in the dim light that filters into the chapel, represent the *Pietà*, and are said to be portraits of Mazzoni's 15th-century friends. Further back, down

Neapolitans shop in the Galleria Umberto I.

a side passage, is the Old Sacristy, containing frescoes by Vasari and wooden stalls, inlaid with biblical scenes. In the very front of the church, to the left of the entrance, another passage leads to the Piccolomini Chapel where a relief of a Nativity scene by the Florentine Antonio Rossellino (1475) is a delight to behold.

Unlike in Rome, which is heavily baroque, no single architectural style dominates Naples. The Gothic, the Renaissance and the baroque are all represented. The church of **Gesù Nuovo**, at the top of the street called **Trinità Maggiore**, presents perhaps the most harmonious example of the Neapolitan baroque. The embossed stone facade originally formed the wall of a Renaissance palace. At noon on Saturdays, when marriages take place here, the massive front doors are thrown open to give a splendid view of fully-lit baroque at its best. The interior has a unique design, being almost as wide as it is deep. The coloured marble and bright frescoes seem to spiral up into the dome. Directly above the main portal, just inside the church, stretches a wide fresco by Francesco Solimena (1725) depicting Heliodorus driven from the temple. The ubiquitous Solimena dominated Neapolitan painting in the first half of the 18th century.

A more austere, and older architectural approach is demonstrated by the Gothic church of **Santa Chiara**, just across the street. Founded between 1310 and 1328 by Robert the Wise for his queen, Sancia, the huge church – the biggest in Naples – became the favourite place of worship of the Neapolitan nobility. Extensive bomb damage during World War II destroyed many of its most important works of art, but worth seeking out in its vast, now relatively empty interior is the Tomb of Robert the Wise (1343) behind the main altar, by the brothers Giovanni and Pacio Bertini of Florence. Through a courtyard to the left of the church is the entrance to its immense and peaceful cloister, where majolica-tiled pathways meander through a wild and beautiful garden of roses and fruit trees.

The steep **Via Santa Maria di Costantinopoli** leads up to the **Conservatorio di Musica**, founded in 1537, the oldest musical conservatory in Europe. Its important library and museum are open from 9am until 1pm, but best of all is to wander through its courtyard listening to the music of violins, organs, harps and pianos spilling down from upper storeys. Just down the block, the church of **San Pietro a Maiella**, built between 1313 and 1316, has one of the most famous ceilings in Italy. The Calabrian Mattia Preti began painting it in 1656, at the age of 43, a few months after leaving his native Taverna for the more rigorous artistic challenges of Naples. Five years later he completed his work, establishing himself as one of the most talented painters of his generation. The panels in the nave tell the story of Saint Celestine V, while the panels in the transept present the life of Saint Catherine of Alexandria, the virgin martyr who was beheaded for out-arguing pagan scholars.

The Naples **Duomo** is a magnificent Gothic warehouse of relics from every

Grand Opera House, San Carlo.

period of the city's history. Kept in a chapel off the right aisle are the head of Saint Januarius, the patron saint of the city, and two phials of his blood. The mysterious powers of the crusted blood are the subject of what Mark Twain called "one of the wretchedest of all the religious impostures in Italy – the miraculous liquefaction of the blood." The miracle has been taking place every year on the first Saturday in May, 19 September and 16 December since the saint's body was brought to Naples from Pozzuoli, the place of his martyrdom, by Bishop Severus in the time of Constantine. It is said that if the blood fails to liquefy, a disaster is in store for the city.

Other notable churches, all in the historical centre of the city, include **San Lorenzo Maggiore**, where archaeological excavations have revealed the old Decumano running through its cloister, the Gothic **San Domenico Maggiore**, **San Giovanni a Carbonara**, **Girolomini** and **Santa Patrizia** with its **monastery of San Gregorio Armeno**. The street in which the monastery is situated is famous for its workshops producing *presepe* (cribs), an important Christmas tradition.

The **Capella San Severo**, a small unconsecrated church near the church of San Domenico Maggiore, should not be missed. It contains the famous *Cristo Velato* (Veiled Christ) by the sculptor Sammartino. The remarkable realism of this statue, carved out of a single piece of marble, combined with the setting of the chapel conjures up an eerie atmosphere, which is sacred and superstitious at the same time. The chapel was once the workshop of Prince Raimondo, a well-known 18th-century alchemist who was excommunicated by the pope for dubious activities.

Museums in the clouds: Two of the greatest museums in Naples stand high on bluffs overlooking the city. The National Gallery of Naples, formerly in the **Museo Nazionale**, has been relocated to the **Palazzo Reale di Capodimonte**, situated in a shady park directly north of the museum. It contains the best paintings in southern Italy.

Among the high points are Masolino da Panicale's *Foundation of Santa Maria Maggiore in Rome*, in which Christ and Mary ride a cloud as if it were a magic carpet; Bellini's *Transfiguration*; various works of Titian; two startling allegorical paintings by Peter Breughel the Elder (*The Blind Leading the Blind* and *The Misanthrope*); and, most famous of all, Caravaggio's *Flagellation*.

A trip up the Montesanto funicular brings the visitor to the top of the Vomero hill, home of the **Museo Nazionale di San Martino**, located in the Carthusian monastery of the same name. Here are 90 rooms of paintings, furniture, ceramics and costumes illustrating the life and history of Naples. Some of the top painters of the Neapolitan baroque are represented here, including Francesco Solimena and the prolific Luca Giordano. Belvederes give access to the best views in town.

Good views can also be had from the **Castel Sant' Elmo** next door, a 14th-century fortress long used as a prison for political troublemakers. The stately gar-

Mosaic of battle in Naples' Archaeological Museum.

dens of the **Villa Floridiana**, also on the Vomero, are favoured among young mothers as a place to teach infants to walk. The gardens house the **Museo Nazionale della Ceramica**, which contains one of the most extensive collections of European and Chinese porcelain in Italy.

A secret known to sailors in navies around the world is that the Bay of Naples is one of the most beautiful ports in Europe. To appreciate the splendour of the bay walk through the **Villa Nazionale** to the far-western district of **Mergellina**. The Villa Nazionale itself is a mile-long public garden containing, in the centre, a small aquarium where 200 species of fish, including eels and sting-rays, cavort in murky tanks.

The **Piazza Sannazzaro**, at the heart of the Mergellina district, repays walkers with some of the best pizza in Naples. Pizza was born in Naples and genuine Neapolitan pizza is unbeatable. Its secret, aside from the fact that it is made with fresh mozzarella – another speciality of the Naples region – lies in the baking. It is baked in an oven shaped like a mound, over a wood fire. Generally the chef, usually an old man, works only in the evening, so it is often difficult to order pizza for lunch. But local specialities invariably available include octopus (*polpo*), mussel soup (*zuppa di cozze*), numerous varieties of fish, various spaghettis made with a fish-sauce, such as the Neapolitan catch-all *spaghetti alla pescatora* (fisherman's wife's spaghetti); and various kind of *mozzarella e prosciutto*, swordfish, baked mozzarella, fried mozzarella and *spaghetti alla mozzarella*.

After dinner, you can take a stroll down to the marina, where half a dozen cafés with swinging chairs and views of Vesuvius siphon off the wealthy yachting crowd.

Naples is a big, brawling city that exists for nobody, ultimately, but itself. It neither actively discourages visitors nor makes any real attempt to draw them in. It just continues on its crowded, noisy, irremediable way, a gypsy caravan of all that is best and worst in Italy.

Bay of Naples at dusk seen from Mergellina.

ENVIRONS OF NAPLES

Campania has been a magnet for generations of tourists. "Whether we turn towards the Miseno shore of the splendid watery amphitheatre, and go by the Grotto of Posillipo to the Grotto del Cane and away to Baiae: or take the other way, towards Vesuvius and Sorrento, it is one succession of delights," declared Charles Dickens. At least a week should be devoted to exploring the area, preferably tied to a visit to the Museo Archaeologico in Naples, where the region's most important works of art are displayed.

The entrance to Hell: In Greek times, Naples was a mere stripling overshadowed by its powerful parent **Cumae**, 30 km (19 miles) to the west. Founded by Aeolians from Asia Minor around 750 BC, Cumae had become by the 6th century BC the political, religious and cultural beacon of the coast, controlling the Bay of Naples and its islands.

Here Aeneas came to consult the Sybil before his descent into the underworld. The famous **Antro della Sibilla Cumana** (Cave of the Cumaean Sybil), recently uncovered by archaeologists, consists of a trapezoidal *dromos* (corridor), 44 metres (144 ft) long, punctuated by six airshafts. At the far end is a rectangular chamber cut with niches where the Sybil apparently sat and uttered her prophecies. The eerie echo of footsteps in the corridor recalls Virgil's description of "a cavern perforated a hundred times,/ having a hundred mouths with rushing voices/ carrying the responses of the Sybil." From the cave's mouth it is possible to climb up the acropolis, whose ruined, lizard-haunted temples offer fine views of the coastline and the sea.

The region between Cumae and Naples, known traditionally as the **Campi Flegrèi** (Burning Fields), has been a centre of volcanic activity for the whole of recorded history. Unexpected rumblings and gaseous exhalations from below have linked the area to the mythi-

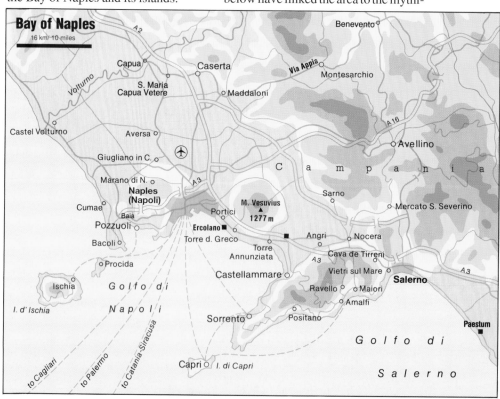

cal Greek underworld, Hades. The **Lago di Averno**, a once gloomy lake in the crater of a now extinct volcano, is the legendary "dark pool" from which Aeneas began his descent into the underworld. No bird was said to be able to fly across this lake and live, due to the poisonous gases. For many years this theory was cruelly tested at the **Grotta del Cane** on the nearby Lago d'Agnano. Dogs were subjected to the carbon dioxide that issued from the floor of the cave until knocked out or killed. "The dog dies in a minute and a half – a chicken instantly," reported Mark Twain. The experiment was repeated nine or ten times a day for the benefit of tourists.

Pozzuoli, a wealthy trading centre in Greek and Roman times but later devastated by wars and malaria, is now famous for its **Solfatara**, a volcanic crater releasing jets of sulphurous gases. The Solfatara is thought to have inspired Milton's description of Hell in *Paradise Lost*. Pozzuoli also boasts a magnificent amphitheatre. On the waterfront, enclosed in a small park, lies a rectangular

structure formerly known as the **Serapeo** (Temple of Serapis), but now thought to have been a *macellum* (marketplace). Shellfish encrustation around the bases of its four Corinthian columns has led to speculation that the ground once sank 5 metres (16 ft) below sea level before rising again to its present height.

Baia apparently derives its name from Baios, Odysseus's navigator. Here Roman society came to swim. The modern town, with its view across the Gulf of Pozzuoli, contains extensive ruins of Roman palaces enclosed in a picturesque **Parco Archeologico** on the hillside. At the lowest level of the park is a rectangular *piscina* from which an arched pathway, hidden in foliage, leads to a domed building believed to have been a bath. Archaeologists have pinpointed this perfect circular structure as the model for the Pantheon in Rome. The hall, partially filled with brackish water, is a natural echo chamber. The slightest scuff of a shoe is picked up and broadcast throughout the dome.

Pompeii and Herculaneum: These two

Roman cities, buried by the eruption of Mount Vesuvius in AD 79, have solved what the archaeologist Amedeo Maiuri has called "the essential problem in the history of civilisation: the origin and development of the house". Pompeii, originally settled by indigenous Oscans some time before the 8th century BC and later ruled by Etruscans, Greeks and the warlike Samnites, was a thriving commercial centre at the time of its sudden immersion in pumice stone and ash. It was a city of shops, markets and comfortable townhouses, with paved streets, wide pavements, a stadium, two theatres, temples, baths and brothels. Its rediscovery during land reclamation operations in the 16th century, and subsequent years of excavation (sometimes piratical but increasingly respectful) have revealed an intimate picture of life in a 1st-century Roman city.

The Pompeiian house is thought to have evolved from the relatively simple design of the Etruscan farmhouse. The structure was built around a central courtyard (atrium) whose roof sloped inwards on all four sides to a rectangular opening in the centre known as the compluvium. Through the compluvium rainwater fell into a corresponding rectangular tank called the impluvium. Around the atrium itself were the various family quarters, including the bedrooms (cubicula), the dining rooms (triclinia), and directly opposite the narrow entranceway (vestibule), the living room (tablinum), the most important room in the house.

As the plan developed, a further peristyle courtyard was added, often containing a fountain. Shops were built into the front of the house; sections of the house were blocked off and rented out, with separate entranceways, to strangers (for example, **Villa di Julia Felix**); another storey was added up top, until the Etruscan prototype had metamorphosed into the comfortable and palatial townhouses typified by **Casa dei Vettii** and the **Casa del Fauno**.

Wedding whips: A striking feature of the Pompeiian house was the colourful and often highly refined artwork covering its walls. Many of the most beautiful frescoes have been taken to the Museo Nazionale in Naples, but at the **Villa dei Misteri**, just outside the Porto Ercolano, a series of 10 scenes apparently depicting the initiation of brides into the Dionysiac mysteries has been left *in situ*.

The meaning of these paintings, which depict, among other things, the whipping of a young bride, is still far from clear, although it is generally agreed that the mantled woman in the final scene is probably a portrait of the mistress of the house, who may have been a Dionysiac priestess.

The most remarkable thing about Pompeii is the mass of detail. Carved into the polygonal paving stones of the streets, for instance, are small phalluses pointing to the centre of the city. These are thought by some to have warded off evil spirits, by others to have pointed to the brothel district. And walls and monuments throughout the city are covered with inscriptions of every kind, from lists of upcoming plays to the scribbled accounts of shopkeepers, from election notices to *billets-doux*. "It is a wonder, O Wall," wrote one cynic on the wall of the basilica, "that thou hast not yet crumbled under the weight of so much written nonsense."

Unlike Pompeii, **Herculaneum** was a bedroom community built for the enjoyment of sea breezes and views across the Bay of Naples. Instead of the compact townhouses of Pompeiian businessmen, there are sprawling villas of wealthy patricians. There is a freer, more spontaneous form of architecture, and the houses, finally freed of the mud in which they were encased for so long, are generally in a better state of preservation than those at Pompeii.

One of the pleasures of Herculaneum (aside from the fact that it is less crowded with tour groups than Pompeii) is the carbonised pieces of wooden furniture, door mouldings and screens still inside the houses. Fine frescoes, such as the *Rape of Europa* in the **Casa Sannitica**, adorn the walls, and carpet-like mosaics cover the floors. Particularly striking are the black-and-white mosaics on the floor of the **Casa dell'Atrio a Mosaico**. The city derives its name from Hercules, and was originally called *Herakleia* by its Greek founders.

Herculaneum is the best starting point for an afternoon ascent of **Mount Vesuvius**, which looms directly over the modern city of **Ercolano**. No longer is it necessary, as in Dickens's time, to be carried up the mountain on a litter borne by 15 attendants. Buses leave regularly from the Ercolano train station and drop passengers at the roadhead, from which there is a 20-minute climb up a well-beaten track (sneakers may be rented).

Since the volcano's first eruption about 10,000 years ago, periods of violent activity have alternated with periods of calm. Just before the infamous eruption of AD 79, trees and olive groves covered Vesuvius up to its very peak. In this century, a constant plume of smoke billowed from a cone inside the crater until 1944, when, during the volcano's last eruption to date, the cone was destroyed. Now only a few scattered *fumarole* (whisps of smoke) around the brim of the crater indicate that the volcano is still active and could erupt again.

Islands of pleasure: Of the three islands just outside the Gulf of Naples, **Capri**, on the Sorrento side, has traditionally been the most popular. Its mild climate, luxuriant vegetation and seemingly inaccessible coast have drawn visitors for centuries. Emperor Tiberius retired here in AD 27, either to pursue his lifelong love of privacy or to indulge in the secret orgies which the historians Tacitus and Svetonius claim characterised the closing years of his reign. While on Capri, writes Suetonius, the emperor "devised little nooks of lechery in the woods and glades… and had boys and girls dressed up as pans and nymphs posted in front of caverns or grottoes; so that the island was now openly and generally called 'Caprineum' because of his goatish antics." The writer Norman Douglas, who also lived on Capri, attributed such legends to the idle exaggerations of resentful peasants.

The modern traveller, arriving by ferry or hydrofoil from Naples or Sorrento, can reach the remains of **Tiberius's Villa** by bus from the town of Capri.

A road in the ruined city of Pompeii.

The most famous sight on the island, however, is the **Grotta Azzurra** (Blue Grotto), a cave on the water's edge. Its strange light has made it the most visited attraction in Campania after Pompeii.

From **Anacapri**, located on the far side of the island, you can take a chairlift up **Monte Solaro**. Its 360° view encompasses the Southern Apeninnes, Naples, Vesuvius, Sorrento and Ischia. In Anacapri itself the church of **San Michele** is worth a visit for its majolica-tiled pavement depicting the *Story of Eden* by Francesco Solimena.

On Capri, as on the fellow islands of Ischia and Procida, the pleasures of the body take precedence. **Ischia**, the largest island off Naples, is famous among Germans for its hot mineral springs. The island is of volcanic origin. Some say the Giant Typhoeus, struck by Zeus's thunderbolt, was buried under Ischia, causing the occasional groanings and shakings that have marked its long history. Visitors generally stay in a comfortable hotels in **Porto d' Ischia**. One of the most pleasant, with a luxurious spa, is the modern **Jolly Hotel**.

The town of **Lacco Ameno**, on the coastal road, is known for its mud baths, which contain the most radioactive waters in Italy. **Sant' Angelo** has some of the best beaches on the island. At **Ischia Ponte**, a causeway crosses to the **Castello Aragonese**, built by Alphonso I of Naples in 1450. The crypt of the ruined cathedral is adorned with frescoes in the style of Giotto. The nearby convent has an interesting cemetery where the dead sisters were placed upright in chairs. **Procida**, the smallest of the islands, has good beaches and a thriving fishing industry. It is quiet and serene and generally free of tourists.

Old Campania: Inland from Naples, at **Santa Maria Capua Vetere**, are the remains of the second largest amphitheatre in Italy. Few tourists are aware of this magnificent crumbling structure, yet it may be the one amphitheatre in Italy were visitors can actually climb down into the subterranean passages where wild beasts roamed.

<u>Left</u>, a fisherman at Ischia harbour. <u>Right</u>, a well-dressed horse waiting to ferry tourists around.

The basilica of **Sant' Angelo in Formis**, 6 km (4 miles) north of Capua, is an ancient, musty structure containing bright Byzantine frescoes illustrating the Life of Christ. **Caserta**, often called the Versailles of Naples for its lavish **Palazzo Reale**, is of little interest, but **Caserta Vecchia**, on a mountaintop 10 km (6 miles) to the northeast, is one of the most beautiful towns in Campania. Founded in the 8th century, it still looks much as it did then, with stone streets, stone houses and good views. Its Romanesque cathedral has a wonderful facade with a cow over the central portal. Inside are a pair of holy water stoups supported by lions and a monolithic 4th-century baptismal font in which baptism by total immersion was practised. There are some excellent restaurants scattered around the town where you can eat wild boar, the local speciality.

One of the most important cities in Campanian history is **Benevento**, where the noble king Manfred voluntarily died in battle after the defection of his allies in 1266. The city was named Beneventum upon becoming a Roman colony in 268 BC. Before that it was called Maleventum, apparently on account of its bad air. Its original settlers, the fierce Samnites, called it Malies.

In the centre of town, on the route of the ancient **Via Appia** from Rome to Brindisi, stands the **Arch of Trajan**, one of the best-preserved triumphal arches in Italy. Of the splendid reliefs depicting scenes from Trajan's life, those on the side facing Rome celebrate the emperor's domestic policies while those on the side facing Brindisi record his foreign policies. The **Museo del Sannio** is worth visiting not only for its collection of local antiquities but also for the hunting scenes on the column capitals that surround its 12th-century cloister.

Paradise regained: The visitor to **Sorrento**, whether arriving from the noisy streets of Naples or from the scorched ruins of Pompeii, will find a cool and peaceful town of lemon groves, with a small beach and plentiful cafés. There's not much more to Sorrento,

The cliffside town of Positano.

save for a 15th-century **Loggia** with fine column capitals on the Via San Cesareo, and the fact that the poet Tasso was born here in 1544, but that is exactly why the town is such a popular resort among Italians and foreigners alike. It's a good place in which to relax, and an excellent starting point for excursions to Capri and the **Amalfi Coast**.

This dramatic coast stretches from **Positano** to **Salerno** and boasts some of the most spectacular scenery in Italy. The **Amalfi Drive** faithfully follows its length, keeping a respectful distance above the waves but doggedly following each frightening twist of the shoreline. Bright houses cling to the slopes and gardens descend in steps to the sea. Its climate, views and picturesque gorges draw artists and honeymooners.

Positano consists of a semi-circle of houses set back in a cove, with numerous hotels, good swimming and wonderful views. The road then passes through several tunnels before reaching the **Grotta di Smeraldo**, famous for its greenish light. Through yet more tun-nels (watch out for cyclists) lies **Amalfi**, a major trading centre in Byzantine times and now a major tourist centre. From the main piazza, with its fountain, a flight of steps ascends to the 11th-century bronze door of Amalfi's **Duomo**. Here, in the crypt, lies the body of Saint Andrew the Apostle, delivered from Constantinople in 1208. On either side of the main altar are ambones (pulpits) with fine mosaics.

Ravello: The most beautiful town on the Amalfi coast is **Ravello**, famous for its architecture, its gardens and admirers. Here Richard Wagner found inspiration for the Magic Garden of Klingsor in *Parsifal*. Ravello's **cathedral** is celebrated for its bronze doors by the Apulian Barisano da Trani. Cast in Trani in 1179, the doors were transported to Ravello by ship. Inside, the floor slopes upwards towards God and a fine marble pulpit supported by pillars resting on the backs of six hungry lions. The pulpit was presented to the church in 1272 by Nicola Rufolo and his wife Sigilgaida, who built the splendid **Villa Rufolo** across the street. The villa's lush gar-

Left, off the Amalfi coast. **Right**, a street café in Positano.

dens and Moorish cloister overlook the sea several miles away. The best view, however, is from the more extensive gardens at the **Villa Cimbrone**, built at the end of the 19th century by a wealthy Englishman, Ernest William Beckett. Beckett's ashes are buried beneath the **Temple of Bacchus**, which he built on the edge of the cliff.

Salerno and Paestum: It was just south of Salerno that the Allies began their assault on Italy on 9 September 1943. The city, strung out along the shore, has a good beach and one of the loveliest cathedrals in southern Italy. The **cathedral** is reached through an atrium incorporating 28 columns from Paestum. Inside, as the removal of 18th-century plaster continues, more medieval frescoes are coming to light. Particularly beautiful is a fresco of the Virgin (behind the fourth pier in the right aisle). As at Ravello, this cathedral contains a pair of exquisite ambones, dating from the 12th century. The great Hildebrand is buried in a tomb in the right apse. The crypt contains the body of Saint Matthew.

The English writer George Eliot regarded the **Temple of Neptune** at Paestum as "the finest thing, I verily believe, we have seen in Italy". Her words echo the sentiments of many 19th-century travellers for whom this Greek city, founded in the 6th century BC, was the final stop on the Grand Tour.

There are few sights so arresting as Paestum's three well-preserved Doric temples standing empty on the grassy plain that surrounds them. The Temple of Neptune, the most majestic of these, was built in the 5th century BC of a reddish travertine whose warmth, as Eliot wrote, "seems to glow and deepen under one's eyes".

The so-called **basilica,** of a greyer tinge, beside the Temple of Neptune, dates from the 6th century BC. The third temple, the **Temple of Ceres**, is separated from the other two by the **Roman forum** and **baths**, and a **Greek theatre**. Across the street, in the **museum** are famous mural paintings from the **Tomb of the Diver** (480 BC), rare and beautiful examples of Greek painting.

Spectacular remains of Greek temples at Paestum.

APULIA

Some visit Apulia (known in Italian as Puglia) for its architecture, some for its landscape, some for its archaeology and some for its food, but all go away haunted by memories of a single man: Frederick II of Hohenstaufen. Known to Dante as "the father of Italian poetry" and to his 13th-century contemporaries as *stupor mundi et immutator mirabilis* – the wonder of the world and the extraordinary innovator – Frederick built most of the castles that are still the dominant architectural feature of the region.

He also founded many of Apulia's most splendid churches, carrying on the tradition of the Apulian Romanesque begun by his Norman predecessors a century before. An enlightened ruler who waged a bitter and ultimately unsuccessful feud with the popes in Rome, he was also an avid sportsman whose brilliant treatise on falconry still ranks among the most accurate descriptions of the subject. His just laws and tolerance of the Islamic beliefs of the Saracens are legendary. Frederick's death in 1250 and the tragic defeat of his illegitimate son Manfred at the Battle of Benevento in 1266 ushered in a period of economic and spiritual decline that is only now being reversed.

If Frederick II is the dominant figure in Apulia's long and varied history, the Apulian Romanesque is its most important architectural legacy. The style, fusing Byzantine, Saracenic and Italian decorative techniques with the French architectural forms introduced by the Normans, first appeared in the church of San Nicola at Bari in 1087. The plans of most other Apulian churches of the period derived from this elegant cathedral; short transepts; three semicircular apses corresponding to three naves and three portals; a tall, plain facade; richly decorated doorways carved with animals, flowers and biblical scenes.

The food of Apulia is fresh and simple, making good use of the abundant tomatoes, wine and olive oil. The most famous pasta here is *orecchiette*, an ear-shaped variety sometimes made with whole-wheat flour.

The visiting Archangel: The landscape of northern Apulia is dominated by vast inland plains planted with wheat. The only real mountains are clustered on the Gargano Promontory, a thickly forested peninsula that juts out into the Adriatic to form the "spur" of the boot of Italy. Here, in the medieval town of **Monte S Angelo**, is the **Santuario di San Michele**, a cave where the Archangel Michael is said to have revealed himself to local bishops in AD 490, 492 and 493. The cave is entered through a pair of bronze doors manufactured in Constantinople in 1076. Brass rings in the doors were supposed to be knocked loudly to wake the Archangel within. This pleasant town also has a fine municipal museum devoted to the popular arts of the Gargano. Particularly interesting are the presses once used for creating wine and olive oil, and a stone flour mill originally turned by mules.

Monte S. Angelo is a good place to buy components for a lunch in the **Foresta Umbra**, a parkland in the centre of the peninsula where 100-year-old beech trees, oaks and chestnuts shade winding trails and pleasant picnic spots. From here, you can drive along the coastline to **Vieste**, a bright town on the tip of the promontory containing a castle built by Frederick II. The road continues west along a serpentine coastline studded with beaches and grottoes, passing en route an odd, phallic rock formation known as *Pizzomunno*. Signs indicate turnings for the grottoes.

Manfredonia, back on the mainland, is a port and beach resort with a pretty historic centre including a Castello, begun by Manfred in 1256 and later enlarged by Manfred's enemy, Charles I of Anjou. Near Manfredonia are the beautiful medieval churches of **Santa Maria di Siponto**, with a 5th-century crypt, and **San Leonardo**, with a facade guarded by two stone lions.

South to Bari: The coastal route to Bari is lined with seaport towns, all carrying on a brisk trade in vegetables, fruit and wine. The oldest, most important and, today, least attractive of these is **Barletta**

where Manfred established his court in 1259. Here, at the intersection of the Corso Garibaldi and the Corso Vittorio Emanuele, stands the intriguing **Colosso**, a 4th-century Byzantine statue thought to represent the emperor Valentinian I (364–75). Only the head and torso are original, the rest having been recast in the 15th century. Behind rises the **Basilica di San Sepolcro**, with a nice Gothic portal and an octagonal cupola reminiscent of Byzantine designs. Barletta's **Duomo** (newly restored) is a confusing edifice built on a Romanesque plan, with five radiating apses in the French Gothic style and a Renaissance main portal. By the sea rises Manfred's castle.

A far more picturesque town, 13 km (8 miles) south of Barletta, is **Trani**, whose Romanesque cathedral, founded in 1097 but not completed until the middle of the 13th century, is perhaps the most beautiful church in Apulia. Beneath its richly carved rose window is a small monofora window flanked by pillars resting on the backs of elephants.

The wonderful bronze doors are the work of the local artist Barisano da Trani, who is also responsible for the celebrated doors on the cathedral at Ravello. The interior of the church, bright and austere, has the usual three apses and three naves, with triforium arcades above the side-aisles supported, here, by six pairs of columns on either side. Steps descend to the underground church of **Santa Maria della Scala** and the crypt. Even further down is the underground **Ipogeo di San Leucio**, 1.5 metres (5 ft) below sea level, containing two crude and delightful frescoes.

Windy Bari: The ancient Barium, founded by Greeks, developed by the Romans, as an important trading centre, destroyed by William the Bad in 1156 and restored by William the Good in 1169, is today the largest and most important commercial centre in Apulia. The city is divided into two distinct parts, the *Città Vecchia*, with its tight tangle of medieval streets and dazzling white houses, and the *Città Nuova*, the modern city, with wide boulevards laid

A limestone grotto on the Apulian coast.

out at perfect right angles to each other. The tortuous alleyways of the old city protected the inhabitants from the wind and from invaders.

The church of **San Nicola** was founded in 1087 to contain the relics of St Nicholas stolen from Myra in Asia Minor by 47 sailors from Bari. Its facade bears many resemblances to the facade of the cathedral at Trani, though it is even plainer. A small round window (oculus), crowns three bifora windows, a monofora window, and a richly carved portal flanked by columns borne by a pair of time-worn bulls.

The interior of the church is best visited in the evening, when sun shoots through the windows of the facade, creating unusual light effects on the three great transverse arches (structural additions of 1451). Among the many noteworthy objects in this church are the beautiful column capitals of the choir screen separating the nave from the apse and the ciborium (freestanding canopy) over the high altar, dating from the early 1100s. Behind the ciborium is the church's most well-known work of art, an 11th-century episcopal throne supported by three grotesque telemones. To the left is a Renaissance altarpiece, *Madonna and Four Saints*, by the Venetian Bartolomeo Vivarini.

The crypt contains the precious relics of St Nicholas, said to exude a wonder-working oil and visited by pilgrims for centuries. The Byzantine icon of St Nicholas in the central apse of the crypt was presented to the church by the King of Serbia in 1319.

Bari's **cathedral**, a short walk west of S Nicola, was erected between 1170 and 1178 over the remains of a Byzantine church destroyed by William the Bad during his rampage through the city in 1156. Basilican in plan, the church follows San Nicola in most details of its design, with deep arcades along both flanks and a false wall at the rear that masks the protrusions of the three semicircular apses. A particularly fine window adorns the rear facade. Nearby, off the Piazza Federico II di Svevia, is the **Castello**, built in Norman times, refur-

Vieste, on the Gargano coast.

bished by Frederick II, and considerably enlarged by Isabella of Aragon in the 16th century.

Bari's **Pinacoteca Provinciale**, containing paintings from the 11th century to the present, is located in the Città Nuova, along the Lungomare Nazario Sauro. The best painting in the museum is undoubtedly Bartolomeo Vivarini's *Annunciation* in Room II. Further rooms contain Giambellino's startling *S Pietro Martire* and a number of works by Neapolitan baroque painters including Antonio Vaccaro and the prolific Luca Giordano. Francesco Netti, the Italian impressionist, a native son of Bari, is also represented and there is a new collection of contemporary art.

Bari's small but worthwhile **Museo Archaeologico**, in the Piazzo Umberto I, has a rich collection of attic black- and red-figure vases.

Around Bari: An interesting one-day excursion into Apulia's architectural past begins 18 km (11 miles) west of Bari in the town of **Bitonto**, whose famous cathedral, built between 1175 and 1200, represents perhaps the most complete expression of the Apulian Romanesque. The beautiful facade has a rose window and an elegantly carved portal, flanked by the usual lions. The pelican above the doorway is a symbol of Christ.

The town of **Ruvo di Puglia** 18 km (11 miles) farther west, was known as Rubi in Roman times, when it was famous for its ceramics. The 12th-century **cathedral** was widened in the 17th century to provide room for baroque side-chapels, and though restorations have shrunk the interior's width back to its original Romanesque proportions the wide facade retains its baroque girth, giving the church a somewhat squat appearance. The seated figure at the top of the facade is thought to represent the ubiquitous Frederick II. Beneath the nearby Chiesa del Purgatorio lie some Roman remains. Ruvo's excellent **Museo Jatta** is devoted to Rubian ceramics excavated from nearby necropoli and dating from the 5th to the 3rd century BC.

On a hilltop 30 km (19 miles) west of Ruvo stands the **Castel del Monte**, often cited, as is the Colosseum in Rome, as a supreme example of the architectural aims of an age. Historians differ on whether Frederick II erected the small fortress as a hunting lodge or as a military outpost, but all agree that he married his daughter, Violanta, to Riccardo, Count of Caserta, here in 1249. In 1266 the implacable Charles I of Anjou imprisoned the hapless sons of Manfred after their father's tragic defeat – and voluntary death – at Benevento. The castle served as a refuge for the noble families of Andrea, a nearby town, during the plague of 1665, and was later abandoned, becoming a hideout for brigands and political exiles. Restoration began in 1876. The eerie emptiness of the building is reinforced by its isolation in the middle of wheat-covered plains.

An entirely different kind of architectural unit – the odd, conical peasant dwellings known as the *trulli* – can be seen in the town of **Alberobello**, 50 km (31 miles) southeast of Bari. Nobody knows the exact origins of these houses, but they did allow for easy home-exten-

In the old city of Bari.

sions by the addition of another unit, and modern building in the area is often based on the *trulli* shape. Now many of them have been turned into gift shops. The **Grotte Castellane**, another of the region's great tourist attractions, are also surrounded by gift shops, but the caves themselves (20 km/12 miles back towards Bari from Alberobello) are really quite interesting, containing pools, grottoes and ceilings that literally drip with stalactites.

Spartan Taranto: Taranto, the ancient Taras founded by Spartan navigators in 706 BC, was in the 4th century BC the largest city in Magna Graecia, boasting a population of 300,000 and a city wall 15 km (9 miles) in circumference. It was, like many towns on this coast, a centre of Pythagorean philosophy and visited by such luminaries as Plato and Aristoxenes. Today the city, with its ancient and modern quarters separated by a canal on the waterfront, is the home of Italsider, one of Europe's most important iron works.

Taranto's **Museo Nazionale** is the second most important museum in southern Italy, rivalled only by the Museo Archaeologico in Naples for the splendour of its antiquities. The collection includes Greek and Roman sculpture and a series of wonderful Roman floor mosaics, including a fragment depicting a lion and a boar fighting. Rooms on the first floor house one of the most complete collections of ancient ceramics in Italy. Of particular interest are the many proto-Corinthian ointment boxes decorated with geometric and human figures; the Corinthian vases; a rare Laconian cup dating from the 6th century BC with a design of radiating fishes; and numerous attic black- and red-figure vases.

Of interest in Taranto's old city is the church of **S Domenico Maggiore**, founded by Frederick II in 1223, rebuilt in 1302 by Giovanni Taurisano, and much altered in baroque times. Taranto's **Duomo** contains fine mosaic floors and antique columns from pagan temples.

For those with the time, a fascinating side trip (21 km/13 miles) can be made

Castel del Monte.

from Taranto to the nearby town of **Massafra**, known for its early Christian cave churches hewn into the sides of a deep ravine that snakes through the centre of the town. The Santuario della Madonna della Scalla contains a 12th-century Madonna and child fresco. It can be reached via a baroque staircase from the town centre. At the bottom of the ravine is the Farmacia del Mago Gregorio – a maze of caves and tunnels once used by monks as a herb store. Ask in the town about access to these and other cave churches but avoid coming in the middle of the day when there will be very few people around.

From Massafra by back roads (37 km/ 23 miles) or from Taranto by *superstrada* (22 km/14 miles) you can reach **Grottaglie**, a hilltop town where you can watch Apulian potters make the ceramic pitchers, plates, bowl and cups available in gift shops across the region. The decorative spaghetti plates produced in the town are known throughout Italy.

Baroque Lecce: Lecce is known for its profusion of baroque houses and churches. The city owes its appearance to the malleable characteristics of the local sandstone, which is easy to carve when it comes out of the ground but hardens with time. Intensive building in the 17th and 18th centuries created an architectural uniformity unique in Southern Italy. Churches drip with ornate altars and swirling columns. Outside, shadeless streets meander past curving yellow palaces bright with bursts of bougainvillea.

At the centre of town, in the cobble-stoned **Piazza S Oronzo**, stands a single Roman column stolen from its twin in Brindisi. The pair originally marked the southern terminus of the Via Appia from Rome. A bronze statue of Saint Orontius, patron saint of the city, stands on top of the column. The southern half of the square is dominated by excavations of part of a well-preserved Roman amphitheatre, while the strange Renaissance pavilion, which has been glazed, used to be the town hall but now houses the tourist information office.

Lecce's harmonious **Piazza del**

A fine example of Leccian baroque: Palazzo del Governo.

Duomo, just off the **Corso Vittorio Emanuele**, is framed by the facades of the Duomo, the **Palazzo Vescovile** and the **Seminario**, all built or reworked in the 17th century. The Duomo actually has two facades: the lavish one facing the Corso, with its statue of Saint Orontius, and the more austere (and older) one facing the Palazzo Vescovile. The altars inside the Duomo, carved with flowers, fruit and human figures, are typical of the ornate local style.

Bright basilica: The most complete expression of Leccian baroque is the **Basilica di Santa Croce**, whose exuberant facade sports a balcony supported by eight grotesque caryatids. The bright interior has an overall restraint that unifies the different designs of its chapels. A chapel in the left transept contains a series of 12 bas-reliefs by the local artist Francesco Antonio Zimbalo showing the life of San Francesco di Paola.

Lecce's modern and informative **Museo Provinciale**, just outside the old city, is built around a spiral ramp reminiscent of the Guggenheim Museum in New York. In the archaeological section, attic black- and red-figure vases are nicely arranged around a central core containing bronze tools and suits of armour. The picture gallery, on the third floor, contains paintings by various southern Italian artists including the great Calabrian Mattia Preti.

The rewards of travelling in Apulia, as in its neighbours Basilicata and Calabria, include the pleasure of ending a day on the beach. Apulia has the longest coastline of any region in Italy, a fact which has made it peculiarly attractive to foreign invaders, from the ancient worshippers of Zeus to the sun-worshipping visitors of today. Lecce is within easy reach of beaches at **Gallipoli** on the Ionian and **Otranto** on the Adriatic seas.

In the peace and the wave-song of the pristine Apulian sands you could lie dreaming for many months, lost in reveries on the passage of so many heroes through these parts, from wily Odysseus to the broad-minded, gallant, brooding Frederick II.

Piazza del Duomo, Lecce.

CALABRIA AND BASILICATA

Calabria is closer in spirit than any other region in Italy to the Italy of Byron and Shelley – the land of mouldering ruins that inspired the romantic thoughts of 19th-century travellers. But the region is fast changing. The completion of the *autostrada* from Salerno to Reggio Calabria, governmental support of housing and industry, and vast improvements in the quality of hotels have begun to lure both northern entrepreneurs and foreign tourists to this long isolated part of Italy. No major city is now without its *Zona Industriale*, no village without its roar of motorcycle engines. But the tourist industry is still in its infancy here. Much of Calabria's heritage still lies buried among the roots of the many olive trees.

The landscape of the region is dominated by its backbone of mountains that descend in fantastic foothills to the sea. Only 9 percent of the territory consists of flat land. It was from the sea that Calabria's first invaders, the Greeks, came in the 8th century BC, crossing the Straits of Messina from Sicily.

Also from the sea have come the **Bronze Warriors**, Calabria's most celebrated reminder of those early settlers. Discovered by fishermen off Riace in 1972, these two colossal Greek statues, thought to have been lost overboard from a ship sailing between Calabria and Greece 2,000 years ago, have been undergoing a special treatment to prevent corrosion but are expected to be back on view shortly in the **Museo Nazionale della Magna Graecia** in **Reggio di Calabria**.

The coastline just north of Reggio was first described by Homer in Book XII of the *Odyssey*, the earliest navigational guide to the Tyrrhenian sea. Here lurked the infamous monster Scylla, whose "six heads like nightmares of ferocity, /with triple serried rows of fangs and deep/gullets of black death" did away with six of Odysseus's best men. Nowadays the Rock of Scilla provides the foundation for a youth hostel. Modern **Scilla** has an excellent view across the Straits of Messina.

Farther north, **Palmi** is worth visiting for its ethnographic museum, containing an extensive collection of ceramic masks designed to ward off the evil eye. The museum is housed, along with other collections, in a newly-built complex just outside the town. **Tropea**, suspended from a cliff over one of the many fine beaches that line the shore, is perhaps the most picturesque town on the coast. The old town has a beautiful Norman **cathedral** containing, behind the high altar, the *Madonna di Romania*, a portrait said to have been painted by Saint Luke.

Saints and brigands: Highway 111 is the loneliest road in Calabria. It twists across the central mountain chain following what is believed to be an ancient trade route connecting **Gioia Tauro** on the Tyrrhenian with **Locri** on the Ionian sea. Fierce brigands once ruled the woods through which it passes. From the **Passo del Mercante**, the road's highest and loneliest point, both seas are

Left, woman from the Albanian community of San Demetrio Corone. **Right**, a Greek bronze (in the Archaeological Museum of Reggio Calabria) dragged up from the sea.

visible. From here the road descends to the beautiful town of **Gerace**, situated on the hump of a nearly inaccessible crag. It is best to visit Gerace in the evening, and on foot, to appreciate the romantic sunset views from the grassy ruins of its castle. It is said that in the 10th century the city's inhabitants survived an Arab siege by subsisting on ricotta cheese made from mothers' milk.

In still earlier times, a miracle-working saint, San Antonio del Castello, is said to have conjured up a spring of pure water in a cave in the cliff that surrounds the castle. The imprint of the saint's knees, they say, can still be seen in the floor of the cave.

Gerace is a city of many layers, justifying the phrase, "If you know Gerace, you know Calabria". Its cathedral is the largest in Calabria. It was begun in 1045 on top of an older church – now in the crypt. Both cathedral and crypt contain columns from the Greek settlement at Locri. Some parts of this 7th-century BC town, including walls and temples, can still be seen.

The famous **Cattolica** at **Stilo**, one of the best-preserved Byzantine churches in existence, is a reminder that in medieval times Calabria's rugged interior was a vibrant religious centre. The tiny church, built on a square floor plan with five cylindrical cupolas, clings to the flank of Monte Consolino, just above Stilo, like a miniature castle overlooking its town. Its bright interior is adorned with fragments of frescoes. The ornate capitals on the marble columns are turned upside down to symbolise the triumph of Christianity over paganism.

Another important religious centre further inland is the Carthusian monastery at **Serra San Bruno** (visiting hours 11 am–12 noon and 4–5 pm, men only). In this peaceful sanctuary – reconstructed around the ruins of an earlier abbey destroyed by earthquake in 1783 – 16 bearded, white-robed monks live according to vows of silence, solitude and poverty prescribed by the founder of their order, Bruno of Cologne, in the 11th century. The monks eat no meat, a discovery that pained the writer Nor-

Scilla, where Odysseus is reputed to have sailed.

man Douglas, who said he'd be inclined to "pray more cheerfully with a prospect of *Déjeuner à la Fourchette* looming ahead". The monks make an excellent cheese, sold in the town's grocer's.

Where shepherds wander: Of Calabria's four great mountain clusters – the Aspromonte, the Sila Piccola, the Sila Grande and the Sila Greca – the **Sila Piccola**, in the middle, has most to offer. Among its dense pine groves and cool meadows shepherd boys still wander with their flocks. The climate up here is refreshing after the dry heat of the coast. The twisty road up from **Catanzaro** climbs first to **Taverna**, a serene town whose name suggests that it was once a way-station. In 1613, the baroque painter Mattia Preti was born here. He left Calabria at the age of 43 to become one of the most influential painters in Naples. The church of **San Domenico**, just off the main square, contains the best of Preti's local work; paintings of his may also be seen in the churches of **Santa Barbara** and **San Martino**.

A few "tourist villages" have been developed in the vast pine-covered area of the inner Sila as skiing or fishing centres but they have not altered its sense of isolation. The roads are empty and winding and barred when the snow gets too deep in winter. Even the **Lago Ampollino**, a man-made lake created earlier this century to encourage tourism and produce electricity, lacks the noisy crowds found at even the most remote Italian vacation spots. Here, nature still rules the day.

San Giovanni in Fiore, the biggest town in the Sila, is noted for the black and purple costumes of its women. More compelling is the lovely hilltop town of **Santa Severina**, famed for its medieval scholastic tradition. Attached to the cathedral is an 8th/9th-century Byzantine baptistry of circular design, built originally as a martyrium (shrine for the sacred relics of martyrs) when it stood alone. One of its four "arms", or entrances, was removed in the 16th century to accommodate the abutting cathedral sacristy. At the entrance to the town, the Byzantine church of **San Filomena** has a cylindrical cupola of Armenian inspiration, and three tiny apses that seem to anticipate Romanesque designs. The long central Piazza Vittorio Emanuele, leads to the 10th-century Castello which is now a school.

A city worth visiting for its memories of former inhabitants is the seacoast town of **Crotone**, corresponding to the ancient Croton, founded by Greeks in 710 BC. Here the mystical mathematician Pythagoras came up with his theorem about right-angled triangles and taught the doctrine of *metempsychosis*, in which the soul is conceived as a free agent which, as John Donne later imagined, can as easily attach itself to an elephant as to a mouse before briefly inhabiting the head of a man. The English novelist George Gissing composed some of the most amusing passages of *By the Ionian Sea* in Crotone before his death here in 1901, and the inimitable Norman Douglas, during his lengthy sojourn in the "flesh-pots of Crotone", speculated that the cows he encountered wandering along the beach might very well be "descendants of the sacred cat-

The Byzantine Catolica at Stilo.

tle of Hera". The modern town, on its crowded promontory, has little to offer the tourist other than an excellent wine from the nearby village of **Melissa**, an interesting archaeological museum and indifferent hotels.

Northern Calabria and Basilicata: Steamy **Cosenza** is a flat, modern and very large city surrounding an old town on a hill. Its beautiful Gothic cathedral, in the old town, was consecrated in the presence of Frederick II in 1222. In the **Tesoro dell'Archivescovado** behind the cathedral (apply to the marriage office) is a Byzantine reliquary cross that Frederick II donated to the church at the time of its consecration. The partially ruined **Castello** at the top of the old town has excellent views over the town. Its interior is being slowly restored.

When Douglas visited the Albanian village of **San Demetrio Corone** in 1911, he was told by the amazed inhabitants that he was the first Englishman ever to have set foot in the town. The modern visitor may feel equally unique as he confronts the curious stares of barbers, policemen, shopkeepers and women in bright Albanian dresses.

The Albanians first fled to Calabria in 1448 to escape persecution by the Arabs. Today they form the largest ethnic minority in the region. They possess their own language, literature and dress, and their own Greek Orthodox bishop. As isolated as San Demetrio is in the back hills of the Sila Greca, it was once one of the most important centres of learning in Calabria, the site of the famous Albanian College where the revolutionary poet Girolamo de Rada taught for many years. The little church of Sant' Adriano stands just inside the college. Inside it contains a Norman font and a wonderful mosaic pavement.

On the Ionian coast overlooking the sea stands lonely **Rossano**, which was the most important city in the south between the 8th and 11th centuries. Today Rossano is home of the famous **Codex Purpureus**, a rare 6th-century Greek manuscript adorned with 16 colourful miniatures drawn from the Gospels and the Old Testament. This ex-

The *sassi* (dwellings dug into the hillside) at Matera.

traordinary book can be seen in the **Museo Diocesano** beside the cathedral. At the top of the grey, stone town stands the Byzantine church of **San Marco**, with five domes and a breathtaking view across the valley. Below the old town lies the bustling resort of Rossano Scalo.

Basilicata is the poorest and most underdeveloped region in southern Italy, yet it is a land of considerable historical and sociological interest with a remarkably varied landscape. Its beaches on both the Tyrrhenian and Ionian coasts are among the finest in the south.

Matera, the second largest city after **Potenza**, presents perhaps the most unsettling example of the clash between the ancient and modern in Southern Italy. Until quite recently, people in Matera literally lived in caves. Their rock-cut dwellings, called *sassi* by local inhabitants, date back to Byzantine times when they were originally built as churches. In later years, overcrowding caused many of the churches to be converted into homes where humans and livestock crowded together in unsanitary

Frecoes from a rock chapel dating from the 13th century, Matera.

dankness, watched over by Byzantine frescoes painted on the rock.

Recently Matera has developed the *sassi* area as a tourist attraction and you can pick up maps and itineraries from the tourist office at Via de Viti de Marco, 9. The church of **Santa Lucia**, in the main part of town, contains the two most famous frescoes in Matera, the *Madonna del Latte* and *San Michele Arcangelo*, both dating from the second half of the 13th century. Nearby, the Apulian Romanesque Duomo has a striking rose window. Across the valley, built into a hillside, is the church of the **Madonna delle Tre Porte**, with an exquisite fresco of the Virgin.

Venosa, in northern Basilicata, was the birthplace of both Horace and Manfred. Here lie the remains of **La Trinità**, a Benedictine abbey begun in the 11th century and never completed. The structure, built of stones from an earlier Roman temple on the site, is a topless treasure trove of inscriptions, portals, sarcophagi and frescoes romantically situated in a grassy park surrounded by olive trees and close to some Roman remains. **Melfi**, just to the west, has a fine Norman castle containing the **Museo Nazionale del Melfese**, with interesting archaeological finds. It was here that Frederick II promulgated his *Constitutiones Augustales*, the just code of laws for which his regime is still remembered by local inhabitants.

Of the many beautiful coastal towns in Basilicata, **Metaponto** on the Ionian sea is best known, mainly on account of its **Tavole Palatine**, a Doric temple dating from the 6th century BC, with 15 standing columns. The Greek city of Metapontum was founded in the 7th century BC and is today an active archaeological centre with an excellent antiquarium. **Maratea**, over on the Tyrrhenian coast, rivals Ravello in Campania for its pleasant streets and its breathtaking views over the sea. Above the abandoned medieval town (Maratea Superiore) rises *The Redeemer*, a monumental statue sculpted in 1963 by Bruno Innocenti. The nearby resort of **Acquafredda** has a charming hotel, the Villa Chieta, just above a beach.

SICILY

Nature and history have made Sicily a land of considerable and striking contrasts. The greatest island in the Mediterranean Sea, Sicily was for centuries the centre of the known world. Its peculiar geographic position – smack in the middle of the Mediterranean Sea – made the island vulnerable to attacks by foreigners, but at the same time a meeting-place of Mediterranean civilisations, a bridge between East and West. Witness the Greek colonisation (8th–3rd century BC), the Arab invasions (9th–10th century) and the Norman domination (11th–12th century). These were Sicily's great epochs, when commercial towns were founded and developed along the coast.

Invaders generally confined themselves to the coast, because of the difficult, mountainous terrain inland. Sicily's volcanic features, represented by Mt Etna and the Aeoliean Islands, testify to relatively recent geological origins. The island still suffers violent earthquakes occasionally, and intermittent lava flows have made the plain below immensely fertile.

The reasons for the island's relative state of underdevelopment are rooted in its feudal past. Land in the interior is still organised along semi-feudal lines while industry suffers from mis-management and Mafia involvement (though oil refining and chemicals are growth areas). Sicilians have been forced to emigrate en masse both to northern Italy (Milan and Turin) and to foreign countries (Germany, Belgium, Switzerland), where they are often hired to do the worst jobs.

The Ionian coastline: A ferry plies between Villa San Giovanni in Calabria and **Messina** in half an hour. Travellers arriving at Messina are invariably surprised to find themselves in a modern city with low-rise buildings and wide avenues; the surprise turns to astonishment when they see the wonderful scenery which is offered by the **Peloritani Mountains** that cradle the city.

Although founded in the classical age by Greek settlers and developed mostly between the 15th and 17th centuries, Messina has little to show for its ancient origins. A fateful morning in the year 1908, terrifying earthquake jolts, followed by a violent seaquake, shook the city and razed it to the ground. After the disaster, discussions were held as to whether the city should be rebuilt, but at last, in 1911, the people opted for building a new Messina.

But even if it is difficult to find any traces of the ancient Messina which Cicero described as *civitas maxima et locupletissima* (a great and wealthy city), an unhurried traveller can take a walk along Via Garibaldi to see the church of **SS Annunziata dei Catalani** (12th century) and, near it, the **Duomo**. In spite of reconstruction, this cathedral preserves its medieval structure, dating to the period of Norman splendour, when Messina was enriched with a wealth of beautiful monuments and fortifications on account of its strategic importance.

The **Museo Regionale**, too, on the

coastal road leading to the **lighthouse**, is worth visiting for the Polyptych of S Gregorio, a masterpiece by Antonello of Messina, the city's most famous Renaissance artist. After a stop at **Billè** in **Piazza Cairoli** to taste a Sicilian sweet, keep driving along the Ionian coast through luxuriant vegetation in the direction of Taormina.

In the shadow of Etna: After 45 km (28 miles), the road winds up to a town that is the essence of Sicily. "It is the greatest work of art and nature!" exclaimed Goethe in his *Italian Journey*. **Taormina** has no middle tones, knows no greys. Its beauty is made up of light, colour and sea. Lying on a short terrace of the coast against a mountain, it slopes down a cliff "as if," wrote Guy de Maupassant, "it had rolled down there from the peak." Its shoulders are embraced by the enormous, sometimes puffing, Etna.

Climb the hillock to the **Greek Theatre**, Taormina's most famous monument, celebrated by many writers for its magnificent position. Built in the 3rd century BC but completely remodelled by the Romans, it illustrates the Greeks' knack of choosing settings where nature enhances art. The jagged coastline of Taormina is dramatic: outcrops of rocks are intercut by narrow creeks, ravines and inlets.

In town, **Corso Umberto,** which cuts through the old centre, is the place for shopping and people-watching. The bars here are usually packed with an international crowd, but the atmosphere somehow remains that of a village. You can see this village in its churches (for example, the harmonious and massive **Duomo**) or in the grand palazzi (**Palazzo Corvaia, Palazzo Ciampoli, Palazzo Duca di S Stefano**), with their mullioned windows, marble tracery, scrolls and billowing balconies.

Sicily's smokestack: The landscape south of Taormina is dominated by **Mt Etna**, the majestic volcano (3,323 metres/10,959 ft) with its snowcapped peak. It is one of only a few volcanoes in the world which are active; it occupies an area of 1,337 sq. km (516 sq. miles) and its perimeter is 165 km (103 miles). Its

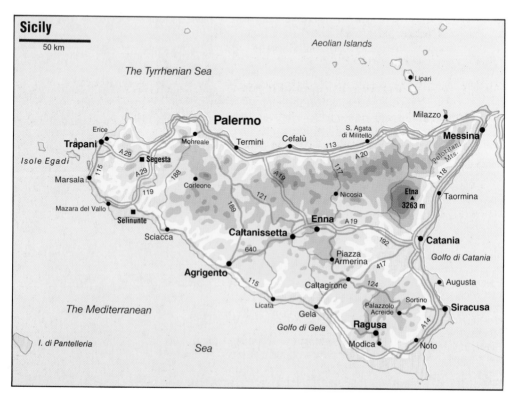

Sicily

50 km

The Tyrrhenian Sea

Aeolian Islands

Lipari

Milazzo

Palermo

Erice

S. Agata di Militello

Messina

Trapani

Monreale

Termini

Cefalù

113

A20

Peloritani Mts.

Isole Egadi

A29

Segesta

A29

115

188

A19

117

A18

Marsala

Corleone

119

121

Nicosia

Etna 3263 m

Taormina

Mazara del Vallo

189

Selinunte

Enna

A19

Sciacca

Caltanissetta

192

Catania

640

Piazza Armerina

Golfo di Catania

Agrigento

115

Caltagirone

417

124

Augusta

The Mediterranean

Licata

Gela

Palazzolo Acreide

Sortino

A14

Siracusa

Golfo di Gela

Ragusa

I. di Pantelleria

Sea

Modica

Noto

surface is punctuated by about 200 cones, smaller craters, accumulated layers of lava, gashes and valleys. Etna's history is a series of more or less ruinous eruptions, from the one in 396 BC, which halted the Carthaginians, to one in 1981, which destroyed part of the cableway. Even a smaller eruption in 1992 required help from the American marines to staunch the lava flow.

In the fertile plain stretching from the southern foot of Mt Etna rises the city of **Catania**. It was an important Greek and Roman colony and suffered from the various powers that succeeded in dominating the island. Destroyed twice by violent earthquakes (in 1169 and 1693), the city was covered in 1669 by lava which even advanced into the sea for about 700 metres (2,300 ft).

Catania is the economic centre of the richest area of Sicily: its continuing development is based mainly on citrus fruits, vineyards and market gardening, but commercial and industrial enterprises also flourish and have earned it the title Milan of the South, a double-edged compliment given recent corruption scandals in both cities.

The city feels modern, with an urban plan characterised by wide streets designed in the 18th century by G. B. Vaccarini, an architect influenced by grand Roman baroque. Catania's main axis is **Via Etna**, where people gather for the *passeggiata* and window shopping. At the beginning of this street is **Piazza dell' Università**, surrounded by baroque buildings (to the right, the **Palazzo S Giuliano,** to the left the noble **Palazzo dell' Università** and a few steps further the **Chiesa Collegiata** with its elegant facade). But Catania's baroque soul is better tasted in the smaller **Via dei Crociferi** in which churches and monastic buildings open like wings of a theatre. The street is covered by a wonderful arch, also baroque, leading to **San Benedetto**, a vast yet unfinished Benedictine monastery.

Another landmark in the history of the baroque style is the church of **S Niccolò**, which can be reached from Via dei Crociferi. This striking church makes

Etna
smoulders.

an impression on the visitor with its unfinished facade looking like a portent of decay. Be sure to go up to the cupola from where there are wide views of Mt Etna and Catania. Any visit would be incomplete without seeing **Castello Ursino**, erected by Emperor Frederick II (1239–50) and since restored. Rest in the landscaped gardens of **Villa Bellini**.

Town of tyrants: From the wide plain of Catania head for **Syracuse** (Siracusa) through landscapes of classical beauty, counterpointed by archaeological remains. Built in 734 BC by a group of Corinthian farmers who settled on the small isle of **Ortigia**, Syracuse developed so rapidly that in a short time it was establishing new colonies along the Sicilian coast. In 485 BC, when it had developed into a prosperous town, it was conquered by the tyrant Gelon. From this moment Syracuse enjoyed its greatest political, economic and artistic magnificence, becoming one of the most important centres of the Mediterranean. It defeated the Carthaginians, Etruscans and even Athenians until it ruled over almost the whole of Sicily. After a dalliance with democracy, Syracuse flourished under despotism. Dionysius, the city's most enlightened tyrant, presided over Syracuse's golden age.

Great monuments and public works testify to the epoch's glory and wealth; at **Ortigia**, the ancient, but still lively heart of town, you can admire some exceptional temples: **Tempio di Apollo** (7th–6th centuries BC), and the grandiose **Tempio di Athena** (5th century BC), which, in a later epoch, was transformed into the **Duomo**.

Leave Ortigia across the **Ponte Nuovo** and head north to Neapolis, the sprawling archaeological zone and the **Teatro Greco**, one of the greatest theatres in the Greek world (138 metres/452 ft in diameter). Here, during the months of May and June, a series of high-quality classical performances are held.

Nearby lie the **Latomie**, which are ancient honeycombed quarries. Later, the *latomie* were used as prisons for Athenians sentenced to hard labour. In the **Latomia del Paradiso**, there is a

Harbour at Syracuse.

man-made cave known as Dionysius's Ear, which has an amazing echo. A whisper becomes a scream which the walls send back and amplify. This phenomenon permitted the tyrant Dionysius to eavesdrop on prisoners.

If you relish ancient legends, stop at the **Aretusa Fountain** (back in Ortigia). According to local lore, the beautiful nymph jumped into the sea in order to escape from the river god Alfeo and was transformed into this spring.

An interesting destination close to Syracuse is the small town of **Noto**. It stands on a ridge of the **Iblei Mountains**, furrowed by a long and straight road which widens out into wonderful scenes of inclined squares. Here the Spanish baroque architecture triumphs in churches, palaces, monasteries and squares, all in a golden-coloured stone. Noto's most interesting monument is the **church of SS Salvatore**, a triumph of pilasters, adorned windows, loggias, terraces and bell-towers. The highlight is **Palazzo Villadorata**: a facade incorporating Ionic columns and baroque

balconies awash with lions, cherubs, medusae and monsters.

Sicily's harsh and imposing heart: From the coast, an excursion leads through the bare interior, with its reddish sulphur mines, vivid vegetation and little villages clustered on hills. One hilltop town is **Piazza Armerina**, famous for its Villa Romana, an imperial mansion or grand hunting lodge. This is a complex construction, built between the 3rd and 4th centuries when the great noble families of the Roman Empire relaxed in the country. The villa has a series of extraordinary mosaics, the work of African and Sicilian artists, representing hunting scenes, imaginary creatures, and natural landscapes; an entire ancient world – one which, curiously, included bikinis – comes to life before your eyes.

Also of interest is the baroque **Duomo** crowning a terraced hill. Theatrical staircases also accentuate the spacious belvedere and the Duomo's baroque facade. A Catalan-Gothic campanile with blind arcading remains from the original church and sets the tone for the

Mosaics in Piazza Armerina.

lavish interior. Decorated like blue and white porcelain, the church boasts a Byzantine icon of a Madonna, a baroque tabernacle and a luminous *provençal* painted Crucifix.

Land of the gods: The neglected landscapes of the mining area lead to the solar beauty of **Agrigento**, described by the Greek poet Pindar as "the most beautiful city of mortals". The symbol of the city is a group of magnificent temples occupying a valley. The origins of Agrigento (Akragas to the Greeks) date from 581 BC. The 5th century marked the apogee of the town, and it was then that the main temples were erected.

The town was later conquered by the Carthaginians and the Romans. Its importance diminished under the successive Byzantine and Arab domination, but grew again with the arrival of the Normans. The classical city comprises magnificent temples and tombs. The finest are: Tempio di Giove (Olympian Zeus), the largest Doric temple ever known; Tempio di Giunone (Juno/Hera), which commands a view of the valley; and Tempio della Concordia, one of the best preserved temples in the world.

Compared with the classical splendour, the medieval town is insignificant. The only points of interest are the hybrid **Duomo** and the Gothic church of **S Maria dei Greci**.

The temples of **Selinunte** can be seen from afar, on a promontory between a river and a plain in the middle of a gulf with no name. The massive and slender columns lift up to the skies from a sea of rocks that crush the dark red earth. Selinunte looks like a puzzle made of stone pieces: columns divided into many trunks, chipped capitals, and white and grey cubes are all heaped together, as if a giant hand had mixed the pieces to make the reassembling of the original image more difficult. However, the stones speak volumes, revealing libraries, warehouses, courthouses, temples – all testifying to a prosperous ancient town in the middle of fertile lands.

Amid the stones *selinon* grows, the wild parsley which gave its name to the powerful Greek colony. Selinunte was

Greek Temple, Selinunte.

destroyed in its attempt to expand at the expense of Segesta: in 409 BC, 16,000 citizens of Selinunte were slain by their Carthaginian rivals.

To complete the plunge into the past, go to **Segesta**, Selinunte's rival in the 5th century. In spite of the frequent devastations resulting from wars between the Greeks and the Carthaginians, an imposing Doric **Temple** has survived. It stands on the side of an arid and wind-beaten hill and is propped up by 36 columns. A few hundred feet further up is the **Theatre**, constructed in the 3rd century over the top of Mount Barbaro and from which stretches a splendid view over the **Gulf of Castellammare**.

The Conca d' Oro: Enclosed by a chain of mountains, the Conca d'Oro, an evergreen valley that widens as it approaches the sea, is still irrigated and cultivated according to old custom. The valley is dominated by **Monreale**, which was founded in the 11th century around the famous Benedictine abbey bearing the same name.

Next to the monastery is the cathedral, a masterpiece of Norman architecture. The church owes its fame to the mosaics, made by Byzantine and Venetian artists and craftsmen. The mosaics illustrate Biblical scenes, from the Creation to the Apostles, in a golden splendour which fades away into grey, giving a tone of "sad brightness" summed up by the gesture and glance of the huge Pantocrator. To pass from the cathedral to the cloister is to move from the East to the West. Here, the beauty lies in the 109 groups of capitals whose sculptures show an unusual freedom in execution, typical of the Romanesque style.

After admiring the view of the Conca d'Oro from the church's terraces (180 steps), proceed to **Palermo**, chief town and port of Sicily, at the bottom of a wide bay enclosed to the south by Capo Zafferano and to the north by Mount Pellegrino, which Goethe described as "the most beautiful promontory in the world". When you first arrive, it is difficult to understand why Palermo has been celebrated as an extraordinary cultural crossroads. Miserable shacks and desolate old buildings greet the eye. But be patient and set out to discover the city without preconceived ideas.

The best place to start an itinerary is from the **Palazzo dei Normanni**, the splendid Norman royal palace. Inside are the **Cappella Palatina**, and **La Sala di Re Ruggiero**, glittering chambers encrusted with mosaics of eastern influence. From there, follow the former **Cassaro** (nowadays **Corso Vittorio Emanuele**), the city's oldest thoroughfare, where it is easy to imagine the picturesque commercial life of Arab and Norman times.

Corso Vittorio Emanuele goes down to the **Quattro Canti**, in the centre of the old town, a busy crossroads cut by **Via Maqueda**, the other axis of Palermo. Here Sicily's baroque soul dominates in the four monuments decorated with fountains and statues. Another beautiful fountain is in nearby **Piazza Pretoria**. A few steps further leads to the Norman period, when Palermo was defined by the geographer Idrisi as the "town which turns the head of those who look at it". Here are two churches:

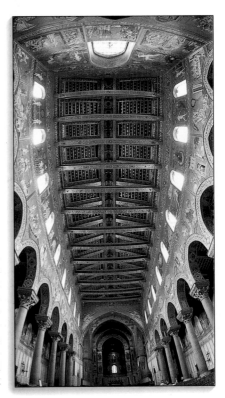

Duomo, Monreale.

the **Martorana**, decorated with Byzantine mosaics, and **San Cataldo**, which preserves three red, Moorish domes. The nuns of the church of Martorana are famous for inventing *pasta reale*, the popular marzipan fruit-shaped sweets.

Between Via Maqueda and the Palazzo dei Normanni extends the **Albergheria Quarter**. In spite of the desolate facades of new buildings, it is still possible to discover old Palermo near an open market in the quarter's centre. Isolated by an oasis of green is the small church of **S Giovanni degli Eremiti**, a masterpiece of medieval architecture. Its five Moorish domes recall the 500 mosques that once dotted the town, as described by the traveller Ibn Hawqal in the 10th century. The southeastern quarter of the old town, called the **Kalsa**, is largely reduced to crumbling houses. But a witness to its turbulent history is the massive **Palazzo Chiaramonte**, also called the Steri. This Catalan-Gothic fortress was a feudal stronghold before becoming the seat of the Inquisition in 1598. Not far from here, the church of **S Maria della Catena** is a synthesis of Gothic and Renaissance art. Along **Via Alloro** is the **Palazzo Abatellis**, built in the 15th century and now home to the **Galleria Regionale della Sicilia**, an intimate art collection.

Rest in the park of **Villa Giulia**, a typical Italian garden, planted in 1777 with rigorous symmetry. Close by is the **Orto Botanico** which offers exotic plants and rare trees among which Goethe loved to rest.

You can then continue along the **Foro Italico**, an esplanade leading to the **Cala**, the old port. Although it no longer functions as a port, the Cala remains a picturesque shelter for its gaily-coloured fishing boats. Today's city centre is situated in **Via Ruggero Settimo** and in the first part of **Viale della Libertà**. Here are the best shops, several bookstores and cinemas, but few bars.

Palermo's picturesque side is still visible in the food market of the **Vucciria**, a triumph of colour, light and sound, and in the **Zisa** palace, built in 1160 by

Piazza Pretoria in Palermo.

William the Bad, which recalls the time when Palermo was virtually the centre of the known world.

Along the Tyrrhenian coast: Along the intense blue Tyrrhenian sea the road is full of flowers and bordered by luxuriant citrus and olive groves. The winding road offers glimpses of **Cefalù**. A panoramic view of the town, possible only from the sea, is extraordinary: a little town clinging to a promontory at the foot of an enormous rock and, to the west, a beautiful sandy beach crowded with bathers and flanked by hotels. Cefalù's fame lies in its medieval charm and great Norman cathedral.

Aeolian Islands: The Sicilian experience should end with a taste of adventure. The best place for this is an archipelago of seven little isles emerging in the **Golfo di Patti** off the north coast of Sicily: the **Aeolian Islands**, a name alluding to Aeolus who, in Greek mythology, is the god of the winds.

Vulcano, the first stop for the ferry, offers yellow sulphurous baths and volcanic craters. **Lipari**, the largest and most populated island, is the most complex geologically and the richest historically. Its pumice beach has the only white sand in the whole archipelago. **Salina**, the highest and the greenest, is topped by two symmetrical volcanos.

Panarea, with its little white houses framed by luxurious vegetation, is the most exclusive island, a refuge for rich tourists and luxury yachts. **Stromboli**, on the other hand, is the "black giant". Like Etna, it is constantly active and rumblings can be heard 5, 15 and even 25 minutes apart. Stromboli is nothing more than lava, ash and slag. It is the youngest of the seven "sisters", born only 40,000 years ago.

The visitor to **Filicudi** and **Alicudi**, has to forget modern comforts, for there is neither electricity nor running-water on these islands. Despite such inconvenience, Filicudi and Alicudi are a paradise not only for divers and fishermen (the offshore contours are very rocky and irregular so destructive trawling is impossible), but also for people who love peace and solitude.

<u>Left</u>, dancers at a church in Palermo. <u>Right</u>, mosaic in the Palace of the Normans in Palermo.

SARDINIA

The island of **Sardinia** (Sardegna) is the relic of a land that emerged from the sea more than 600 million years ago, before the Italian peninsula was formed and when a larger sea covered much of Europe and Africa.

No other Italian region of this size has such a rich geological history. A trip through the island's interior is especially rewarding from an environmental point of view. The island is more attractive and less spoiled than almost any other Italian region. While the landscape of continental Italy is typical of the gentle landscapes depicted in the paintings of 19th-century landscape artists, Sardinia's scenery is extraordinarily dramatic and bewitching. It's a strange, moving landscape that soothes and disturbs in turn.

Olbia is the usual arrival point in Sardinia. It has a modern airport and a flourishing port and is considered to be the gateway of the Costa Smeralda. North of Olbia lies the region of **Gallura** with its tormented granite profile, its continuous alternation of hills and sloping mountains rounded and chiselled in the most varied forms; picturesque rocks towering like inaccessible castles on a background of pastures and bleeding cork-trees.

The east coast of Gallura, the **Costa Smeralda** (Emerald Coast), is a rocky shore of granite covered with fragrant maquis and punctuated by fine white beaches. Developed by the Aga Khan in the 1960s, it is one of the most exclusive coastlines in Europe. A road offering panoramic views winds along the coast from Golfo Aranci up to the wide bay of **Cala di Volpe**, where there stands a fabulously decorated luxury hotel, the setting for the film *Return to Oz*.

Further north along the Costa Smeralda is the Capriccioli and the famous beach of **Romazzino**, a springboard for excursions to the nearby islands of **Mortorio** and **Soffio** with their enchanting coves. On the way to **Porto Cervo** – the most elegant resort of the coast and a meeting place for the international jetset – the road skirts **Golfo Pero**, a large bay with wide, empty beaches. After Porto Cervo you come to **Liscia di Vacca**, **Baia Sardinia** and **Porto Quato**, all pleasant beach resorts.

Palau, a small town with a resident population of NATO officers, is also the terminus for a ferry boat that services the **Isole della Maddalena**. Among these islands is **Caprera**, where Garibaldi spent his last years. His house is now a museum, the second most popular museum in Italy after the Uffizi in Florence. Another worthwhile excursion from Palau is to **Porto Raphael** with its villas, beautiful gardens and famous *piazzetta* protruding on to the beach. Nearby is the promontory of **Capo d'Orso**, topped by a granite bear carved by the wind.

The most stunning of the granite rocks on Sardinia are found west of **Santa Teresa di Gallura**, near lonely **Capo Testa**, at the beach of **Calla Spinosa**.

Rugged heart: Barbagia, the most rugged part of Sardinia, is the heart of the

Woman wearing a traditional costume in Sardinia.

island, historically, culturally and geographically. The highest of the regions of Sardinia, it offers a unique spectacle of imposing tablelands, green pine woods stretching high into the mountains, massive walls and granite amphitheatres. Its name is thought to stem from the Latin *Barbaria*. The region was the last place in Sardinia to succumb to Roman rule.

In this inaccessible region, easy to defend but difficult to conquer, the Carthaginians, the Romans and later rulers of the island left few traces of their presence. It was here, safely sheltered from foreign raiders, that a population of shepherds developed a fierce and isolated society, which even recent history has done little to transform. Here there are no urban centres of interest (**Nuoro** is the biggest town, with a population of between 35,000 and 40,000) nor artistic achievement of great merit. But the most genuine aspects of Sardinia are here: ethnic arts and crafts (look out for horn-handled shepherds' knives), rustic cuisine, traditional festivals, and the splendid costumes still worn on a daily basis in some places.

South of **Dorgali** up to the **Sopramonte**, an immense uninhabited mass of rock with caves, canyons, woods and wild animals, lies one of the most important natural environments in Europe. This is the place to head for mountain walks. The rare mouflon – a wild, short-fleeced mountain sheep – can still be seen here. Apiculture is also important, thanks to the increasing number of uninhabited areas reserved for protected flowering plants.

Besides the harsh peaks and secluded villages, the Barbagia also includes a vast eastern seafront. The most interesting segments of this coast are the **Golfo d'Orosei** and the shore of the **Ogliastra** region. The former winds through 40 km (25 miles) of white limestone walls that reach as high as 500 metres (1,640 ft). Rarely does the Mediterranean offer a shore that is so wild, harsh and constantly surprising. To see the wonders of this coast, start at **Cala Gonone**.

A trip further south will lead to **Santa Maria Navarrese**, from which you can enjoy a stupendous view of the island of Ogliastra. Next stop should be the famous cliffs of **Arbatax**. To reach the coast, take exits off State road 125.

The Campidano: Typical of the south coast of Sardinia is the wide, picturesque, shallow bay called the **Golfo degli Angeli**, at the head of which looms the lofty, golden-coloured town of **Cagliari**, the island's capital, whose ancient history is recorded in a wealth of museums and a fascinating old quarter crammed with churches and palaces.

Beyond the white pyramids of the local salt factories begins the fertile **Piano di Campidano**, flourishing with trees and crops. It's a long hallway – once a sea channel – bordered by ancient masses of rocks, that extends to the bay of Oristano. It's the only plain in Sardinia. The landscapes are almost African, the colours strong and clear.

In the extreme southwest of the island is the wild region of **Sulcis** with its black rocks fringing into a restless sea, sparkling with foam. It is the most ancient chunk of Italy.

Map of Sardinia showing: I. Asinara, Golfo dell'Asinara, La Maddalena, I. Maddalena, Palau, I. Caprera, Costa Smeralda, I. Mortorio, I. Soffi, Castelsardo, Porto Torres, Olbia, Golfo Aranci, Tempio Pausania, Sassari, 127, 199, 125, Alghero, Ozieri, Siniscola, 131, Bosa, 129, Macomer, Nuoro, Dorgali, Cala Gonone, Golfo di Orosei, 128, Oristano, 125, Santa Maria Navarrese, Aritzo, Arbatax, Barumini, 131, 128, 125, Samassi, S. Priamo, I. di S. Pietro, Iglesias, Cagliari, S. Antico, I. di S. Antioco, Teulada, Golfo di Cagliari, 50 km, Sardinia

INSIGHT GUIDES
Travel Tips

FOR THOSE
WITH MORE THAN
A PASSING INTEREST
IN TIME...

Before you put your name down for a Patek Philippe watch *fig. 1,* there are a few basic things you might like to know, without knowing exactly whom to ask. In addressing such issues as accuracy, reliability and value for money, we would like to demonstrate why the watch we will make for you will be quite unlike any other watch currently produced.

"Punctuality", Louis XVIII was fond of saying, "is the politeness of kings."

We believe that in the matter of punctuality, we can rise to the occasion by making you a mechanical timepiece that will keep its rendezvous with the Gregorian calendar at the end of every century, omitting the leap-years in 2100, 2200 and 2300 and recording them in 2000 and 2400 *fig. 2.* Nevertheless, such a watch does need the occasional adjustment. Every 3333 years and 122 days you should remember to set it forward one day to the true time of the celestial clock. We suspect, however, that you are simply content to observe the politeness of kings. Be assured, therefore, that when you order your watch, we will be exploring for you the physical—if not the metaphysical— limits of precision.

Does everything have to depend on how much?

Consider, if you will, the motives of collectors who set record prices at auction to acquire a Patek Philippe. They may be paying for rarity, for looks or for micromechanical ingenuity. But we believe that behind each $500,000-plus

bid is the conviction that a Patek Philippe, even if 50 years old or older, can be expected to work perfectly for future generations.

In case your ambitions to own a Patek Philippe are somewhat discouraged by the scale of the sacrifice involved, may we hasten to point out that the watch we will make for you today will certainly be a technical improvement on the Pateks bought at auction? In keeping with our tradition of inventing new mechanical solutions for greater reliability and better time-keeping, we will bring to your watch innovations *fig. 3* inconceivable to our watchmakers who created the supreme wristwatches of 50 years ago *fig. 4.* At the same time, we will of course do our utmost to avoid placing undue strain on your financial resources.

Can it really be mine?

May we turn your thoughts to the day you take delivery of your watch? Sealed within its case is your watchmaker's tribute to the mysterious process of time. He has decorated each wheel with a chamfer carved into its hub and polished into a shining circle. Delicate ribbing flows over the plates and bridges of gold and rare alloys. Millimetric surfaces are bevelled and burnished to exactitudes measured in microns. Rubies are transformed into jewels that triumph over friction. And after many months—or even years—of work, your watchmaker stamps a small badge into the mainbridge of your watch. The Geneva Seal—the highest possible attestation of fine watchmaking *fig. 5.*

Looks that speak of inner grace *fig. 6.*

When you order your watch, you will no doubt like its outward appearance to reflect the harmony and elegance of the movement within. You may therefore find it helpful to know that we are uniquely able to cater for any special decorative needs you might like to express. For example, our engravers will delight in conjuring a subtle play of light and shadow on the gold case-back of one of our rare pocket-watches *fig. 7.* If you bring us your favourite picture, our enamellers will reproduce it in a brilliant miniature of hair-breadth detail *fig. 8.* The perfect execution of a double hobnail pattern on the bezel of a wristwatch is the pride of our casemakers and the satisfaction of our designers, while our chainsmiths will weave for you a rich brocade in gold *figs. 9 & 10.* May we also recommend the artistry of our goldsmiths and the experience of our lapidaries in the selection and setting of the finest gemstones? *figs. 11 & 12.*

How to enjoy your watch before you own it.

As you will appreciate, the very nature of our watches imposes a limit on the number we can make available. (The four Calibre 89 time-pieces we are now making will take up to nine years to complete). We cannot therefore promise instant gratification, but while you look forward to the day on which you take delivery of your Patek Philippe *fig. 13,* you will have the pleasure of reflecting that time is a universal and everlasting commodity, freely available to be enjoyed by all.

Should you require information on any particular Patek Philippe watch, or even on watchmaking in general, we would be delighted to reply to your letter of enquiry. And if you send us

fig. 1: *The classic face of Patek Philippe.*

fig. 4: *Complicated wristwatches circa 1930 (left) and 1990. The golden age of watchmaking will always be with us.*

fig. 6: *Your pleasure in owning a Patek Philippe is the purpose of those who made it for you.*

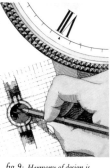

fig. 9: *Harmony of design is executed in a work of simplicity and perfection in a lady's Calatrava wristwatch.*

fig. 2: *One of the 33 complications of the Calibre 89 astronomical clock-watch is a satellite wheel that completes one revolution every 400 years.*

fig. 5: *The Geneva Seal is awarded only to watches which achieve the standards of horological purity laid down in the laws of Geneva. These rules define the supreme quality of watchmaking.*

fig. 7: *Arabesques come to life on a gold case-back.*

fig. 10: *The chainsmith's hands impart strength and delicacy to a tracery of gold.*

fig. 11: *Circles in gold: symbols of perfection in the making.*

fig. 3: *Recognized as the most advanced mechanical regulating device to date, Patek Philippe's Gyromax balance wheel demonstrates the equivalence of simplicity and precision.*

fig. 8: *An artist working six hours a day takes about four months to complete a miniature in enamel on the case of a pocket-watch.*

fig. 12: *The test of a master lapidary is his ability to express the splendour of precious gemstones.*

PATEK PHILIPPE
GENEVE
fig. 13: *The discreet sign of those who value their time.*

your card marked "book catalogue" we shall post you a catalogue of our publications. Patek Philippe, 41 rue du Rhône, 1204 Geneva, Switzerland, Tel. +41 22/310 03 66.

THOMAS COOK MASTERCARD TRAVELLERS CHEQUES...

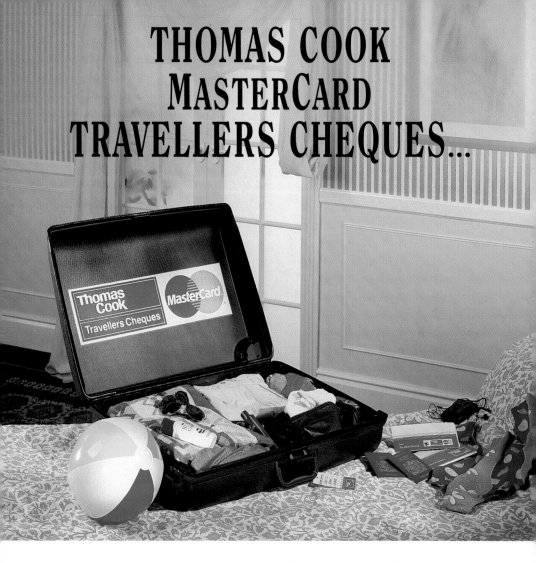

...HOLIDAY ESSENTIALS

Travel money from the travel experts

THOMAS COOK MASTERCARD TRAVELLERS CHEQUES ARE
WIDELY AVAILABLE THROUGHOUT THE WORLD.

Getting There

By Air 338
By Road 338
By Rail 338

Travel Essentials

Visas & Passports 339
Money Matters 339
Tipping 339
Customs Regulations 339
Animal Quarantine 340
What to Wear 340

Getting Acquainted

Government & Population .. 340
Weights & Measures 340
Time Zones 340
Climate 340
Electricity 340
Business Hours 340
Holidays 341
Festivals & Seasonal
Events 341

Communications

Postal Services 341
Telephone & Telegram 341

Emergencies

Security & Crime 342
Medical Services 342

Getting Around

Domestic Travel 343
City Transport 344
The Metro 344
Taxis 345
Water Taxis & Gondolas 345
Private Transport 345

Where to Stay

Hotels 346

Food Digest

What to Eat 351
Where to Eat 351

Things to Do

National Parks 358

Culture Plus

Museums 359
Theatres 360
Concerts 360

Nightlife

Where to Go 360

Shopping

Shopping Areas 361

Sports

Spectator 362

Useful Addresses

Tourist Information 363

Further Reading

Bibliography 363
Other Insight Guides 364

Art/Photo Credits 365

Index 366

GETTING THERE

In addition to the national airline, Alitalia, most airlines run direct flights to Italy, including many charter flights offering bargain tickets. Alitalia itself offers a variety of cut-price tickets, including Eurobudget (return within one year), Pex fares (return within three months) and Apex (valid for three months but booking must be made at least seven days prior to departure). All these incur a penalty (20 percent in the case of Eurobudget and 50 percent in all other cases) if changes are made to reservations.

Italy has 29 main airports, but only two of them are Intercontinental airports: Roma Leonardo da Vinci (known as Fiumicino) and Milano Malpensa. Roma Ciampino serves some charter flights.

For information and reservations, look under "Linee Aeree" in the *Yellow Pages* of any telephone directory.

Leonardo da Vinci Airport (Fiumicino) is 35½ km (22½ miles) southeast of downtown Rome. It is the fourth busiest airport in Europe. It was built in 1961 in expectation of 6 million passengers a year, but these days about 14 million arrive annually.

Transportation to and from Fiumicino is provided by the ACOTRAL bus every hour from 6am–midnight. Fare for the 45-minute ride is L3,300. A night service is also available every 1½ hours from 1.30am and costs L6,000. This bus will stop at Stazione Ostiene, which is linked by the metro stop Piramide line B, which takes you to the central terminal or Stazione Termini. Taxi fares to the central terminal average L60,000 to and from the city centre by yellow taxi. Do not take unofficial taxis which can ask for about L150,000 or more.

Roma Ciampino is a dowdy military airport where charters usually land. From here, the ACOTRAL bus will take you to the Anagnina stop on subway Line A, which will take you to Termini, the Spanish Steps, or the Vatican (the end of the line). Taxis charge about L55,000.

Marco Polo Airport is located at Tessera on the mainland 9 km (5½ miles) north of Venice. Facilities are inadequate, but the construction of a new terminal is underway. From the airport to Venice there is a choice of public bus to Piazzale Roma, the Cooperativa San Marco water launch which crosses the lagoon to Piazza San Marco via the Lido or –

if you are prepared to fork out over L100,000 – a water taxi direct to Venice.

Milano Malpensa Airport is 46 km (28½ miles) from the centre of Milan. Buses to Malpensa leave from the bus terminal at Stazione Garibaldi (Viale Sturzo) or at Stazione Centrale 2½ hours before flights.

When calculating the cost of travelling to Italy by car, allow for motorway tolls as well as accommodation en route and petrol. If you want to travel by toll-free roads in Italy, get hold of the Italian State Tourist Office's *Traveller's Handbook*, which lists them.

The usual route from France to Italy is via the Mont Blanc Tunnel (between Chamonix and Courmayer) and from Switzerland through the Gran San Bernardo Tunnel (between Bourg St Pierre and Aosta). Some of the many alpine passes are seasonal, so it is best to check the viability of your route with the tourist board or a motoring organisation before setting off.

To take your car into Italy, you will need your current driving licence (with an Italian translation unless it is the standard EC licence), your vehicle registration document (which must be in the driver's name or supported by the owner's written permission for the driver to use the vehicle) and Green Card insurance. You are also required to carry a warning triangle in case of breakdown.

The cost of travelling to Italy from Great Britain by scheduled coach is not much cheaper than travelling by air. National Express Eurolines run from London Victoria, via Paris and Mont Blanc, to Aosta, Turin, Genoa, Milan, Venice, Bologna, Florence and Rome. To book, contact: National Express, Eurolines, Victoria Coach Station, Buckingham Palace Road, London SW1. Tel: 071-730 0202.

This is not a particularly cheap option unless you are travelling as part of the Inter-Rail scheme (providing a month's unlimited train travel in Europe for anyone under the age of 26 at a very reasonable price). However, it can be an attractive option, especially if you are planning to stop off en route.

When travelling from Great Britain via Paris (the usual route when travelling to Rome, for example), it is necessary to change in Paris (from Gare du Nord to Gare de Lyon).

EC (Eurocity) and TEE (Trans Europe Express) trains are luxury first-class only trains running between the main European cities. A special supplement is charged and seat reservation is obligatory.

The following rail services to Italy transport cars: Paris–Milan; Boulogne–Lille–Milan; Schaerbbeek (Brussels)–Milan; 's Hertogenbosch (The Netherlands)–Domodossola–Genoa–Milan; 's Hertogenbosch–Chiasso–Milan; Düsseldorf–Cologne–Milan–Genoa; Hamburg–Hanover–Verona; Munich–Rimini; Düsseldorf–Cologne–Bolzano; Vienna–Venice; Boulogne–Bologna; Boulogne–Rome; Boulogne–Alessandria; Boulogne–Leghorn.

Travel Essentials

VISAS & PASSPORTS

Visitors arriving from EC countries do not need a visa or a passport to enter Italy, an identification card valid for foreign travel is sufficient.

Visitors from the following countries need a passport but are exempt from needing a visa providing they do not stay for more than three months: Australia, Austria, Barbados, Belgium, Canada, Finland, Iceland, Jamaica, Japan, Kenya, South Korea, Kuwait, Malaysia, Maldives, Malta, Mexico, Monaco, New Zealand, Niger, Norway Paraguay, Poland (for a stay up to 30 days), Singapore, Sweden, Switzerland, Trinidad and Tobago, United States, Uruguay, Venezuela (up to 60 days).

Other nationalities should contact their nearest Italian consulate.

You are supposed to register with the police within three days of arriving in Italy. In fact, this procedure will be taken care of by your hotel, whatever the level of accommodation. If you are not staying in a hotel, contact the local police station.

MONEY MATTERS

The monetary unit is the *lira* (plural *lire*). Travellers' cheques are recommended as they can be replaced if stolen or lost. However, commission will be charged for changing them. Most shopkeepers and restaurateurs will not change money, so it is best to change a limited amount at the airport when you arrive, especially if it is the weekend when banks are closed. Try to avoid changing money in hotels, where the commission tends to be higher than in banks.

Banks are generally open 8.30am–1.20pm and for one hour in the afternoon (usually between 3 and 4pm). You can also change money at airports and main railway stations and, in the big cities, there are an increasing number of automatic exchange machines (they take major European currencies and US dollars) with multilingual instructions.

Current exchange rates are published in the press and posted in banks. The rate fluctuates considerably. The official exchange rate at the time of going to press was approximately US$1 to L1,613 and UK£1 to L2,416.

CREDIT CARDS & CASH MACHINES

In cities, many restaurants, hotels, shops and stores will take major credit cards (Visa, American Express, Mastercard, Diner's Club and Carte Blanche), but some petrol stations require cash. Don't bank on being able to use credit cards in country areas. Establishments which take credit cards normally have a *Carta Si* (Card Yes) notice in the window.

If your credit card has a blue and red EC sign, you can use it to obtain cash from cash machines showing a similar sign – providing you know your card's PIN number. However, remember that interest will be charged from the moment you obtain the cash, and a handling charge will be added to the final bill.

TIPPING

In nearly every restaurant, a service charge is included in the bill and may be indicated as *servizio e coperto* or only as *coperto*. Tipping above this is discretionary, but much appreciated, especially when service has been good.

Taxi drivers should be tipped 10 percent. In hotels it is customary to tip the maids and the head waiter at the end of your stay. Custodians of sights and museums also expect a tip (L1–2,000), particularly if they have opened something specially for your benefit.

CUSTOMS REGULATIONS

Used personal effects may be imported and exported without formality.

The import of narcotics, weapons and pirated materials is forbidden. Alcoholic drinks, tobacco and perfume can be imported in limited quantities, depending on your nationality. EC citizens are free to import up to 800 cigarettes/400 cigarillos/200 cigars or 1 kg tobacco; 10 litres of spirits; 20 litres of fortified wines (sherry, port); 90 litres of wine (no more than 60 litres of which should be sparkling); and 110 litres of beer.

For US citizens, the duty free allowance is: 200 cigarettes, 50 cigars or 3 lb of tobacco; 1 US quart of alcoholic beverages and duty-free gifts worth up to $100.

The following airports have duty-free shops: Genoa, Milan, Pisa, Turin, Venice, Rome Fiumicino, Rome Ciampino, Naples, Rimini, and Bologna.

ANIMAL QUARANTINE

Pets must be vaccinated against rabies and you should obtain an officially stamped document stating that your animal is healthy. This should be done no more than one month before you arrive in Italy.

WHAT TO WEAR

The Italians are known for their sense of style. However, this does not mean that one has to dress formally – for example, only top restaurants require men to wear jackets and ties. Remember that neither women nor men can enter churches or Catholic museums dressed in shorts (or short skirts in the case of women) or with uncovered shoulders.

Unless you are going to visit mountain areas, the moderate climate makes heavy clothing unnecessary in summer. A light jacket will be adequate for summer evenings. In winter (November–March), the climate can be cold and wet throughout Italy.

GETTING ACQUAINTED

GOVERNMENT & POPULATION

About 58 million people live in this democratic republic with a Western-style economy. Parliament and government are based in Rome, the capital and largest city (around 3 million). The second largest city is Milan (just over 1½ million), the third largest Naples (1.2 million) and the fourth largest Turin (about 1 million people). Almost 100 percent of the population is Roman Catholic.

Italy's president is elected for a term of seven years by Parliament, which is composed of two houses: the Senate (with 315 elective members) and the Chamber of Deputies (comprising 630 elective members). The president nominates the prime minister and, on the prime minister's recommendations, the Cabinet.

WEIGHTS & MEASURES

The metric system is used for weights and measures.

To convert	Multiply by
Centimetres to inches	0.393701
Metres to feet	3.2808
Metres to yards	1.09361
Kilometres to miles	0.621371
Gallons to litres	4.546
Kilograms to pounds	2.20462

TIME ZONES

There is one time zone through the country – Central European Time (one hour ahead of Greenwich Mean Time). From the last weekend of March until the last weekend in September, time is advanced one hour (Italian Summer Time) to give extended daytime through the summer.

During Standard Time periods, when it is noon in Rome, it is:
1pm in Athens and Cairo
2pm in Moscow and Istanbul
4.30pm in Mumbei (Bombay)
6pm in Bangkok
6.30pm in Singapore
7pm in Hong Kong
8pm in Tokyo
9pm in Sydney
1am in Honolulu
3am in San Francisco and Los Angeles
5am in Chicago
6am in New York and Montreal
8am in Rio de Janeiro
11am in London
Noon in Bonn, Paris and Madrid

CLIMATE

The climate is generally temperate but the weather changes according to latitude and altitude. There are three main kinds of climate:

1) In the mountainous areas (Alps and Apennines), the winter is long and cold and the summer is short and cool. Even for summer visits, you are advised to bring sweaters and light boots.

2) In the Pianura Padana (region around Milan), the climate is characterised by harsh winters and sultry summers.

3) In the rest of Italy, the winters are fairly mild and the hot, dry summers are tempered by sea-breezes (more along the Tyrrhenian coastline than along the Adriatic). Summers can be torrid in the south, on the islands, along Sicily's African seaside and in the interior lands.

ELECTRICITY

The supply is 220 volts and the plugs are of the standard European variety. You will need an adaptor to operate British three-pin appliances and a transformer to use 100–120 volt appliances (generally from the US and Canada).

BUSINESS HOURS

Shops are open for business from 9am–12.30pm and 3.30 or 4pm until 7.30 or 8pm in the evening. In areas serving tourists, hours are generally longer than these. Shops often close on Monday (or Monday morning only). Some close on Saturday. Everything closes on Sunday.

INSIGHT *Pocket* GUIDES

North America	Corsica	Middle East and Africa
Atlanta	Costa Blanca	Istanbul
Boston	Costa Brava	Kenya
British Coumbia	Cote d'Azur	Maldives
Florida	Crete	Morocco
Florida Keys	Denmark	Seychelles
Hawaii	Florence	Tunisia
Miami	Gran Canaria	Turkish Coast
Montreal	Hungary	Asia/Pacific
New York City	Ibiza	Bali
North California	Ireland	Bali Birdwalks
Quebec	Lisbon	Bangkok
San Francisco	Loire Valley	Beijing
South California	London	Bhutan
Toronto	Madrid	Canton
Latin America and The Caribbean	Mallorca	Chiang Mai
	Malta	Fiji
Bahamas	Marbella	Hong Kong
Baja	Milan	Jakarta
Belize	Moscow	Kathmandu,
Bermuda	Munich	Bikes & Hikes
Jamaica	Oslo/Bergen	Kuala Lumpur
Mexico City	Paris	Macau
Puerto Rico	Prague	Malacca
US Virgin Islands	Provence	Nepal
Yucatan Peninsula	Rhodes	New Delhi
Europe	Rome	New Zealand
Aegean Islands	Sardinia	Penang
Algarve	Scotland	Phuket
Alsace	Seville	Sabah
Athens	Sicily	Sikkim
Barcelona	Southeast England	Singapore
Bavaria	St Petersburg	Sri Lanka
Berlin	Tenerife	Sydney
Brittany	Tuscany	Thailand
Brussels	Venice	Tibet
Budapest	Vienna	Yogyakarta

United States: Houghton Mifflin Company, Boston MA 02108
Tel: (800) 2253362 Fax: (800) 4589501

Canada: Thomas Allen & Son, 390 Steelcase Road East
Markham, Ontario L3R 1G2
Tel: (416) 4759126 Fax: (416) 4756747

Great Britain: GeoCenter UK, Hampshire RG22 4BJ
Tel: (256) 817987 Fax: (256) 817988

Worldwide: Höfer Communications Singapore 2262
Tel: (65) 8612755 Fax: (65) 8616438

" I was first drawn to the Insight Guides by the excellent "Nepal" volume. I can think of no book which so effectively captures the essence of a country. Out of these pages leaped the Nepal I know – the captivating charm of a people and their culture. I've since discovered and enjoyed the entire Insight Guide Series. Each volume deals with a country or city in the same sensitive depth, which is nowhere more evident than in the superb photography. "

Sir Edmund Hillary

Don't be overcharged for overseas calls.

Save up to 70% on calls back to the U.S. with WorldPhone.®*

While traveling abroad, the last thing you need to worry about is being overcharged for international phone calls. Plan ahead and look into WorldPhone – the easy and affordable way for you to call the U.S. and country to country from a growing list of international locations.

Just dial 1-800-955-0925 to receive your free, handy, wallet-size WorldPhone Access Guide – your guide to saving as much as 70% on phone calls home.

When calling internationally, your WorldPhone Access Guide will allow you to:

- Avoid hotel surcharges and currency confusion
- Choose from four convenient billing options
- Talk with operators who speak your language
- Call from more than 90 countries
- Just dial and save – regardless of your long distance carrier back home

WorldPhone is easy. And there's nothing to join. So avoid overcharges when you're traveling overseas. Call for your free WorldPhone Access Guide today – before you travel.

Call 1-800-955-0925.

THE TOP 25 WORLDPHONE COUNTRY CODES.			
COUNTRY	**WORLDPHONE TOLL-FREE ACCESS #**	**COUNTRY**	**WORLDPHONE TOLL-FREE ACCESS #**
Australia (CC)◆		**Japan (cont'd.)**	
To call using		To call anywhere other	
OPTUS ■	008-5511-11	than the U.S.	0055
To call using		**Korea** (CC)	
TELSTRA ■	1-800-881-100	To call using KT ■	009-14
Belgium (CC)◆	0800-10012	To call using DACOM ■	0039-12
China (CC)	108-12	Phone Booths+	Red button 03,
(Available from most major cities)			then press*
For a Mandarin-speaking		Military Bases	550-2255
Operator	108-17	**Mexico** ▲	95-800-674-7000
Dominican Republic	1-800-	**Netherlands** (CC)◆	06-022-
	751-6624		91-22
El Salvador◆	195	**Panama**	108
France (CC)◆	19▼-00-19	Military Bases	2810-108
Germany (CC)	0130-0012	**Philippines** (CC)◆	
(Limited availability in eastern		To call using PLDT ■	105-14
Germany.)		To call PHILCOM ■	1026-12
Greece (CC)◆	00-800-1211	For a Tagalog-speaking	
Guatemala◆	189	Operator	108-15
Haiti (CC)+	001-800-444-1234	**Saudi Arabia** (CC)+	1-800-11
Hong Kong (CC)	800-1121	**Singapore**	8000-112-112
India (CC)	000-127	**Spain** (CC)	900-99-0014
(Available from most major cities)		**Switzerland** (CC)◆	155-0222
Israel (CC)◆	177-150-2727	**United Kingdom** (CC)	
Italy (CC)◆	172-1022	To call using BT ■	0800-89-0222
Japan◆		To call using	
To call to the U.S.		MERCURY ■	0500-89-0222
using KDD ■	0039-121		
To call to the U.S.			
using IDC ■	0066-55-121		

(CC) Country-to-country calling available. May not be available to/from all international locations. Certain restrictions apply.	+ Limited availability. ▼ Wait for second dial tone. ▲ Rate depends on call origin in Mexico.	■ International communications carrier. ◆ Public phones may require deposit of coin or phone card for dial tone.

* Savings are based on typical hotel charges for calls back to the U.S. Your savings may vary depending upon originating country and hotel, time of day and length of call. All rates effective 7/94.

WORLDPHONE ℠
From MCI

Let it take you around the world.

Banking hours are Monday–Friday 8.30am–1.20pm. Some banks are open in the afternoon from 3–4pm but do not exchange foreign currency during these hours.

Shops and banks close during holidays.

HOLIDAYS

New Year's Day: 1 January
Easter Monday: the day after Easter
Liberation Day
(Anniversario della Liberazione): 25 April
Labour Day (Festa del Lavoro): 1 May
Assumption of the Blessed Virgin Mary
(Assunzione S. Vergine): 15 August
All Saints (Ognissanti): 1 November
Immaculate Conception of the Blessed Virgin Mary
(Immacolate Concezione): 8 December
Christmas Day: 25 December
St Stephen's Day: 26 December

In addition to these national holidays, some cities have a holiday to celebrate their own patron saint, for example St John the Baptist, 24 June (Turin, Genoa and Florence); St Ambrose, 7 September (Milan); St Mark, 25 April (Venice); St Petronius, 4 October (Bologna); St Gennaro, 19 September (Naples); St Nicholas, 6 September (Bari); St Rosilia 15 July (Palermo); St Peter, 29 June (Rome).

FESTIVALS & SEASONAL EVENTS

The year is packed with special events, some linked to festivities of the Catholic church, others to cultural activities or commercial fairs. Here are some of the highlights in the festival calendar:

Festival dei Due Mondi di Spoleto, from late June–early July, offers opera, theatre, concerts, ballet and exhibitions each year. At Spoleto, near Rome.

Biennale. A large exhibition in Venice of international modern art, held every June to September in even-numbered years. An exception will be made in 1995, the centenary of the Biennale.

International Film Festival also in Venice, at the Lido, each year at the end of August.

Carnevale. This period of festivities preceding Lent (February and March) is celebrated in unrivalled style in Venice.

Fair of Rome. This national industrial exhibition takes place in late May or June.

Festa di Noiantri. During the latter half of July, this great pagan feast, involving music, fireworks and food, is celebrated in Trastevere, one of the oldest quarters of Rome.

Gioco del Calcio is held in Florence on 19, 24 and 28 June. The Gioco del Calcio ("football in costume") is football played by men wearing 16th-century costumes.

Fiera Internazionale di Milano, held in late April, is one of the most important fairs in the world.

Festa del Redentore is held on the evening of 18 July. A bridge of boats is built across the Giudecca Canal to the Redentore – the church which was built in gratitude for deliverance from plague in 1567. People row out to picnic on the river. The event ends with firework displays on Euodeccca Island and at St Mark's Church at midnight.

Palio Horse Race is held on 2 July and 16 August (dates vary each year) in Siena's Piazza del Campo. The bare-back riders taking part in a two-hour procession before the race wear 15th-century costumes.

COMMUNICATIONS

POSTAL SERVICES

Post office hours are usually 8am–1.30pm, but every town has a main post office open throughout the day.

Stamps may also be purchased from tobacco shops, which can supply information about Italian postal codes.

The post office can provide such services as *raccomandata* (registered), *espresso* (express) and *via aerea* (air mail) to speed up delivery of letters.

You can receive mail addressed to Poste Restante, held at the Fermo Posta window of the main post office in every town, picking it up personally with identification.

A very fast delivery service, CAI-post, is also provided by the post office to send documents almost anywhere in the world in 24 to 48 hours.

Remember that you do not have to line up to post your mail: you can simply post it in the red letter-boxes near the tobacconists or at the station.

TELEPHONE & TELEGRAM

Public telephones are found almost everywhere in Italy, but especially in bars, which practically double as telephone offices. From some bars, but mostly from post offices, you can call *scatti* (ring first, pay later). Most public telephones now take phonecards (*carta telefonica*) and these are available from tobacconists or newsstands for either L5,000 or L10,000. Alternatively, you can buy a *gettone* token which costs L200 (these are sometimes given as change when buying goods) or use coins (L100, L200 or L500), depending on the type of phone. Some public telephones only accept cards.

If you have no small change, phone card or tokens, it is best to make international and collect calls from the public telephone offices (PTP). PTP (Posto Telefonico Pubblico) offices in the major cities are:

Rome: ASST Piazza San Silvestro or at Termini
Milan: ASST Piazza Edison, in the post office; ASST Stazione Centrale; SIP, Galleria Vittorio Emanuele
Florence: ASST Palazzo delle Poste, Via Pellicceria; SIP, Stazione S. Maria Novella
Venice: at the main post office, Fontego dei Tedeschi, near the Rialto Bridge.
Naples: at the train station and in the Galleria across from San Carlo.

The cost of long distance calls depends on the distance and the time of day. Within Italy the cheapest time to call is between 10pm and 8am, though reduced charges also operate between 6.30pm and 10pm. If you are telephoning outside Italy, off-peak rates are affected by whether it is the peak or off-peak period in the country you are calling.

For numbers outside your area, dialling must be preceded by "0" and then the area code, which you can obtain from Information (no fee for calling this service). The area codes of main cities are: Rome (06), Milan (02), Florence (055), Pisa (050), Venice (041), Turin (011), Naples (081), Como (031), Palermo (091). If you are dialling from outside Italy, you drop these initial zeros.

EMERGENCIES

SECURITY & CRIME

Terrorism has recently resurfaced in the form of bomb blasts in Milan, Florence and Rome, but the main problem for tourists is pick-pocketing, bag-snatching and robbery. It is advisable to have insurance coverage against these.

Observe these simple rules: don't linger in non-commercial areas after dark and don't carry all your cash with you, use travellers' cheques or Eurocheques rather than large quantities of cash; never leave your luggage unattended; keep valuables in the hotel safe (most hotels provide a storage service). Always deposit your room key at the desk before going out. If you are the victim of a crime (or suffer a loss) and wish to claim against your insurance, it is essential to make a report at the nearest police station and get documentation to support your claim.

When you need the assistance of a policeman, dial 113 (or 112 for the *Carabinieri*, an armed police force, which is technically an arm of the army).

One final note: if driving, lock your car and never leave luggage, cameras or other valuables inside.

WOMEN TRAVELLING ALONE

The difficulties encountered by women travelling in Italy are often overstated. However, women – especially, as the cliché goes, if they are young and blonde – usually have to put up with much male attention, especially in the south. Though this is often annoying, it is rarely dangerous.

MEDICAL SERVICES

In cases of real need, such as medical aid or ambulances, you can dial 116, or the Public Emergency Assistance number, 113. These numbers and their services operate on a 24-hour basis, and the number 113, in the principal cities, will answer in the main foreign languages. You can also call the number 112 for the Carabinieri Immediate Action Service.

The Italian National Health Service operates through the Local Health Units (USL). So, if you need medical assistance, you have to go to the Health Unit in the city or place where you are. The addresses and telephone numbers of the Local Health Units are found in the directory under "Unità Sanitaria Locale". Information about the nearest hospitals and the name of a physician can be obtained by dialling 116.

To receive free treatment in cases of illness, accident or even child-birth, EC citizens (and of countries with other ties to Italy, such as Brazil, Monaco, and the former Yugoslavia), must obtain (in their country of residence before arriving in Italy) the E-111 form. This form is to state that the bearers are registered with their national health service and therefore have the right to the same assistance offered to Italian citizens (it won't provide repatriation, which you may require in the case of serious illness). Citizens of non-EC countries must pay for medical assistance and medicine. Health insurance is recommended while travelling in Italy – you must keep receipts for all medical expenses if you want to claim.

Most hospitals have a 24-hour emergency department called *Pronto Soccorso*.

For more minor complaints, seek out a *farmacia*, identified by a sign displaying a red cross within a white circle. Trained pharmacists give advice and prescribe drugs, including antibiotics. Normal opening hours are 9am–1pm and 4–7pm, but outside these hours the address of the nearest *farmacia* on emergency duty will be posted in the window.

GETTING AROUND

BY AIR

The major centres – Rome, Milan, Florence, Venice, Naples – and towns of touristic interest are connected by flights provided mostly by Alitalia Airlines. Smaller airlines are ATI, Alisarda (to and from Sardinia) and Aligiulia. Flying in Italy is expensive compared to taking the train, but it can be useful for long distances. Discount flights are often available if you are prepared to arrive and return on certain days, but such fares must be booked in Italy. For detailed information, contact your nearest travel agent or Alitalia office.

Remember that infants under two years accompanied by an adult have a 90 percent discount; children over two years and under 12 have a 50 percent discount, and young travellers of 12–21 years have a 25 percent discount.

BY RAIL

The cheapest and fastest way to travel in northern and central Italy is by train. Sometimes it can be complicated to get from one medium-sized city to another but you can always ask at the Uffici Informazione FS in the main railway stations. Check their number in the directory under "Ferroive dello Stato".

Italian trains are divided into six categories: 1) *Locale* is the slowest and stops almost everywhere; 2) *Diretto* is faster than locale, but pretty slow; 3) *Espresso* are long-distance express trains with first and second-class carriages; 4) Inter City (IC) trains include first and second-class carriages and run between the main Italian cities; they are faster than *Espresso*, require a reservation and entail a special supplement; 5) Eurocity (EC) are fast international trains connecting the main European cities; a supplement is payable and reservations are obligatory; 6) ETR 450 *Pendolino* are luxury first-class only trains, reservations are obligatory and the ticket includes a meal, newspapers and service.

You can buy a ticket at the station or at any FS Travel Agency without paying tax. In addition to standard tickets and the much-publicised Inter Rail scheme (a month's unlimited travel in Europe and Morocco for travellers under the age of 26), there is usually a range of special tickets (group fares) and budget schemes (for multiple journeys) available and it is worth making enquiries about these when you arrive in Italy. They tend to change fairly regularly, so it is not worth explaining current schemes here. Suffice to say, savings are considerable.

Buffet facilities are attached to most services, and restaurant cars (including some which are self-service) are provided on long-distance services. Sleepers are available on long-distance trains; as a rule, first-class passengers have a choice between single or double compartments, while second-class passengers travel in compartments with three berths (though a few trains offer double sleepers in second class). Couchettes (in which the seats convert to beds at night) accommodate four people in first class compartments and six people in second-class.

COACHES & BUSES

Each province in Italy has its own inter-city bus companies and each company has its own fares and lines. It is worthwhile taking buses, especially when you are going to the mountainous interior, they are generally cheaper and faster than the train. Some of the principal coach companies operating long-distance travel are:

GENOA
AMT, Via Lagaccio, 21. Tel: 010-252 241. Services from Genoa to Alassio, Rapallo, Milan; **Pesci**, Corso Perrone, 50/2, Corniglianno. Tel: 010-420619. Services from Genoa to many parts of Italy.

FLORENCE
Lazzi, Via Mercadante, 2. Tel: 055-363041. Services all over Italy; **Sita**, Viale dei Cadorna, 105. Tel: 055-278611. Services to most parts of Italy.

MILAN
Autostradale, Piazzale Castello, 1. Services throughout Lombardy and the Lakes.

ROME
Appian Line, Via Barberini, 109. Tel: 06-464151. Services from Rome to Florence, Assisi, Naples, Capri, Sorrento, Pompeii, Venice; **Lazzi**, Via Tagliamento, 27. Tel: 06-8840840.

SICILY
Etna Transporti, Via San Giuseppe la Rena, 25. Tel: 095-340076. Services throughout Sicily; **Saistours Travel and Tourist Office**, Via Libertà, 169. Tel: 091-343698. Runs special tours and regular coach services throughout Sicily.

TRENTINO-ALTO ADIGE
Sad, Via Conciapelli 60, Bolzano. Tel: 047-1971259. Services throughout the Dolomites area.

FERRIES & HYDROFOILS

There are a great many ferryboat and hydrofoil speedboat lines that offer connections between the mainland and Italy's many large and small islands. The services run by the State Railways, the Tirrenia, Grandi Traghetti, Trans Tirreno Express and

Nav.Ar.Ma. provide all connections with Sicily and Sardinia.

Many other lines connect the peninsula with the smaller islands. Here is some basic information regarding some ship lines:

State Railways: Civitavecchia–Golfo Aranci (Sardinia): departures many times a day for passengers with cars. The crossing takes nine hours.

Tirrenia Lines: Civitavecchia–Olbia; Civitavecchia–Cagliari: both direct and via Arbatax. These connections with Sardinia are daily for passengers and cars, with both day and night runs. Tirrenia Line also runs Genoa–Porto Torres, Genoa–Cagliari, Naples–Cagliari, all to Sardinia, with an average crossing time of 12–15 hours.

Trans Tirreno Express: Leghorn–Olbia, particularly during the high season.

Grandi Traghetti: This line offers connections from Genoa–Porto Torres (about 11 hours) and from Genoa to Palermo (22 hours) both for passengers and cars.

Nav.Ar.Ma: This line offers a ferry service from Piombino (Tuscany) to the island of Elba and to Bastia (Corsica).

Toremar-Siremar-Caremar: Toremar offers connections with the Tuscan island (Elba, Giglio) while Siremar runs to the Aeolian islands and Caremar has runs from Naples to the Naples Gulf islands (Capri, Ischia).

Alimar-Aliscafi SVAV: This is a hydrofoil speedboat line which connects Naples and Palermo, via Ustica, in only five hours.

Adriatic: Carries passengers and cars from Venice, Trieste, Ancona, Pescara, Bari and Brindisi both to Adriatic and foreign ports.

To obtain further information about fares and schedules, call in at any of the many travel agencies or the EPT offices.

CITY TRANSPORT

BUSES

ROME

The bus system (ATAC) is still cheap, but not as fast and efficient as it used to be. Buses are slowed down by the traffic and are sometimes extremely crowded. There is a flat rate fare in all the major cities and tickets (valid for 1 hour) are sold at special kiosks, bars, tobacco shops and some newsstands.

Maps of bus routes are sold at the ATAC Information Office on Piazza Cinquecento in front of Termini Station; check also Tutto Città for detailed maps of each zone of Rome.

MILAN

Bus and tram service (ATM) is fast and efficient. Tickets must be purchased in advance at tobacconists or newsstands and are good for 70 minutes of travel.

FLORENCE

ATAF is the city bus company. Tickets are sold at bars, tobacconists and newsstands displaying the ATF sticker and are dispensed by special machines near bus-stops. Each ticket is valid for 60-minutes of travel, during which you can change from one bus to another as often as you need. The ATAF Office at Piazza del Duomo 57r will give you a free bus map, but the best transportation in Florence remains, simply, your feet.

VENICE

The city is small enough to be covered by foot and a good map is essential for exploring the maze of small streets and squares. The main form of public transport is the *vaporetto* or waterbus. Passengers who have not bought a ticket before boarding will be surcharged. The most scenic line is the No.1 which takes you slowly down the Grand Canal and costs L2,500. The circle line No.5 provides an enjoyable ride around the periphery of Venice. Twenty-four-hour or three-day passes are available for L15,000 or L20,000 respectively. A private and more costly water-taxi service can be hired from most hotels.

NAPLES

Buses run everywhere and are the only public transportation available along the waterfront. They are generally packed during rush-hour. Due to the traffic's intensity, taxis are not much faster than buses and are much more expensive.

THE METRO

ROME

The Metropolitana (subway) is good for longer hauls. There are two lines: line A covers an 18-km (11 miles) route through the centre of the city, from Ottaviano near the Vatican to the eastern edge of the city, just past Cinecittà (Anagnina), and line B which runs north of the city suburbs (Rebbibia) to EUR the modern industrial zone of the south. The lines intersect at the Termini. There is a special ticket, called Big, which permits travel by both bus and subway for one day on every line (fare is L2,800).

MILAN

The Metropolitana Milanese (MM) is the best subway in Italy. MM has two lines (1 and 2) which serve almost all the city and the hinterland. Usually tourists get on line 1, which runs south from near the Stazione Centrale through the Piazza del Duomo and west beyond Piazza Santa Maria della Grazie. Tickets are sold at coin-operated machines in each station and allow 70 minutes of transportation. A day ticket provides travel on all forms of transport.

NAPLES

The fast, clean and frequent Metropolitana connects the Stazione Centrale at one end of the city with Mergellina on the other, with only three stops in between. Funiculars (Funicolare Centrale, Funicolare di Chiaia, Funicolare di Montesanto) run up the steep Vomero hill. The Circumvesuviana commuter line runs from the Stazione Centrale around the Bay of Naples, via Ercolano (Herculaneum), Pompeii and Castellemmare di Stabia, to Sorrento. There are two lines, so check that you are on the right one. For complete information, check the monthly tourist publication *Qui Napoli*, available at the tourist office in the train station and at major hotels.

TAXIS

Taxis are expensive, but are sometimes necessary. You can call for a taxi by dialling the following telephone numbers:
Rome: Radio Taxi 3570, 3875, 4994 and 8433.
Milan: 6767
Florence: 4390 and 4798
Naples: 364-444, 364-340
Venice: *see Water Transport*

For other towns check the *Tutto Città* (First Page) or the *Yellow Pages*. Fares are clocked up on meters. There is a fixed starting charge and then a charge for every kilometre (and standing charge for traffic jams). Taxi drivers are obliged to show, if asked, the current list of additional charges. Extra charges are added for night rides (10pm–7am), luggage, journeys outside town and journeys on Sunday and public holidays. It is a general rule to leave a small tip rounding off the fare to the nearest L1,000.

Always use official taxis, which do not tout for customers.

WATER TAXIS & GONDOLAS

In Venice, in addition to taking water buses (*see Buses*), you can take water-taxis and, of course, gondolas. The former take up to four people and, like regular taxis, display meters. You can find taxi "ranks" at main points in the city.

The flat rate for hiring a gondola is about L80,000 for 50 minutes during the day and L110,000 at night, though it is advisable to haggle. Rather cheaper, for those who want a quick taste, is the *traghetto* gondola, which crosses the Grand Canal in six different places; one-way ticket L500.

PRIVATE TRANSPORT

BY CAR

The speed limit in the cities is 50 kph (about 30 mph), while on Italian highways (*autostrade*) it is posted along the road. Autostrades are fast and uncrowded (except in summer), but Italians some-

times drive faster than the speed limit. It is compulsory to wear seat-belts at all times and infants up to nine months must occupy a baby seat. Children between nine months and four years must sit on the back seat.

Pay attention to street signs advising no-parking because police are strict on illegal parking and will remove vehicles found in no-parking areas. You'll need plenty of cash to reclaim your car. Try to park in a garage for the night: it will be a little expensive, but much safer.

In the south, especially in Naples where parking is a nightmare, it is best to leave your car with official car parking attendants, who wear white caps. Never leave a car under the guardianship of somebody who is not wearing a white cap; he may be guarding his right to steal. Never leave valuables in a car.

Hitchhiking is forbidden on the autostrade and is not advised for women travelling alone, especially in the south.

When travelling into the mountain areas during the winter months, it is advisable to call 194 for road conditions. When there is ice and snow, chains will be required.

CAR RENTALS

Hiring a car is expensive in Italy, as is petrol. Major car rental firms such as Avis, Hertz and Europcar are represented in most cities and at all airports, though local firms often offer better rates. Agencies are listed in the *Yellow Pages* under *Autonoleggio*. Collision damage waiver and recovery in case of breakdown are usually included in the price of hiring a vehicle, but be sure to check exclusions carefully. Additional insurance cover is usually available at fixed rates. Also make sure that the price you are quoted includes VAT (which is 18 percent).

The renter must be over 21 and must be in possession of a valid driver's licence (an EC licence, an international driving licence or a national driving licence with Italian translation). A deposit equal to the cost of hiring the vehicle is usually required.

WHERE TO STAY

HOTELS

Italy offers many elegant and luxurious hotels together with inexpensive hotels often called *Albergo* or *Pensioni-Soggiorno*.

The grand hotels are expensive, but well-suited to the international traveller. Hotels in the luxury category have every comfort and are often attractive landmarks in themselves.

Hotels are classified according to a star system, ranging from 1-star to 5-star. The rates of the best hotels range from approximately L250,000 to L500,000 per night, for a single room, depending on season. Be sure to call or write beforehand to verify and make reservations. Smaller hotels are not necessarily cheaper – some of the more exclusive small hotels match the grand hotels in style and expense. Even inexpensive hotels usually offer basic comfort and good service.

The listing below offers a small selection of hotels at all levels. Your travel agent or the EPT offices in Italy can give more complete information.

ROME

GRAND HOTELS

Le Grand Hotel, Via Vittorio Emanuele Orlando, 3. Tel: 4709. Located between the railway station and Via Veneto area. This formal, dignified hotel belongs to the CIGA chain and, like all the others, is very well run and stylish. Expensive.

Hassler-Villa Medici, Piazza Trinità dei Monti, 6. Tel: 6782651. Ideally located at the top of the Spanish Steps, this hotel is one of the best hotels in Rome. Provides excellent food and service and free bicycles for exploring the city. Particularly beautiful is the roof garden restaurant, with its view of the city (good for Sunday brunch, if you can't afford to stay here). Expensive.

Cavalieri Hilton, Via Cadlolo, 101. Tel: 31511. At the top of the hill of Monte Mario. Another resort hotel in Rome, offering a beautiful swimming pool, tennis-courts and more. Expensive.

Excelsior, Via Vittorio Veneto, 125. Tel: 4708. Preferred by Americans, this grand hotel has been a meeting-place for actors, actresses and society people for almost half a century. Expensive.

Lord Byron, Via Giuseppe de Notaris, 5. Tel:

3220404. Close to Villa Borghese, this first-class small hotel looks like a private club. Only 47 rooms, but a good restaurant (Le Jardin). Expensive.

Jolly Hotel Vittorio Veneto, Corso d'Italia, 1. Tel: 8495. High-quality Jolly service, as in the other hotels of the chain. Expensive.

D'Inghilterra, Via Bocca di Leone, 14. Tel: 562161. Very traditional and old-fashioned, Ernest Hemingway, Anatole France and Alec Guinness have all stayed here. Very good location in the centre of the shopping area. Moderate to expensive.

Parco dei Principi, Via G. Mercadante, 15. Tel: 8845104. Modern, with a swimming pool, on edge of Villa Borghese. Moderate.

The Cardinal, Via Giulia. Tel: 6542719. In the medieval part of the city and close to the Vatican. Atmospheric. Moderate.

Forum, Via Tor dè Conti, 25. Tel: 6792446. Charming hotel in the Roman Forum area, with a view of the ancient city from its roof garden. 82 rooms. Moderate.

Raphael, Largo Febo, 2. Tel: 650881. Close to Piazza Navona and near the Senate and the Chamber of Deputies, this hotel attracts many Italian politicians. The service is good, but not excellent. Moderate.

Nazionale, Piazza Montecitorio, 131. Tel: 6789251. Near the Chamber of Deputies, it is another central hotel famous for former guests, including Simone de Beauvoir and Sartre. 78 rooms. Moderate.

SMALL HOTELS

Gregoriana, Via Gregoriana, 18. Tel: 6794269 or 6797988. The attraction here is the Art Deco interior, with room letters by the 1930s fashion illustrator Erte. Only 19 rooms and no restaurant. Moderate to inexpensive.

Columbus, Via della Conciliazione, 33. Tel: 6865435. A 3-star hotel near St Peter's, with ancient furniture. 107 rooms. Moderate.

La Residenza, Via Emilia, 22.. Tel: 4880789. Just off the busy Via Veneto, this is a small, quiet hotel with only 27 rooms. Moderate.

Margutta, Via Laurina, 34. Tel: 6798440. Near Piazza del Popolo, this hotel has no restaurant and only 21 rooms, but it is still pleasant. Moderate.

Hotel Doria, Via Merulana, 4. Tel: 44465889. Simple, recently refurbished hotel just five minutes' walk from the station. Small and clean, offering TV and mini-bar in some rooms. Good sightseeing base. Inexpensive.

Fontana, Piazza di Trevi, 96. Tel: 6786133 or 6790024. In a restored 13th-century monastery next to the Trevi Fountain, with a beautiful rooftop bar. Inexpensive.

GRAND HOTELS

Hotel Principe di Savoia, Piazza della Republica, 17. Tel: 6230. Located north of the cathedral, this is a classic luxury hotel, with superb service. 298 rooms. Expensive.

Palace Hotel, Piazza della Republica, 20. Tel: 6336. Close to the railway station, in front of the Principe di Savoia, this very comfortable hotel has been renovated in an ultra-modern style. Expensive.

Duca di Milano, Piazza della Republica, 13. Tel: 6284. In the same league as the two hotels above.

Diana Majestic, Viale Piave, 42. Tel: 202112. Luxury hotel. Expensive.

Excelsior Gallia, Piazza Duca d'Aosta, 9. Tel: 6785. Luxury category, an historic hotel located close to Stazione Centrale, near the air terminal and business centre. Expensive.

Milano Hilton, Via Galvani, 12. Tel: 69831. Contemporary. Decorated in a provincial/modern style. Located in the new commercial centre of the city. Expensive.

Executive Hotel, Via Don Luigi Sturzo, 45. Tel: 6294. American-style, with first-rate service and a good restaurant. Expensive.

The Jolly Hotel chain has two hotels in Milan:

Jolly Touring, Via Ugo Tarchetti, 2. Tel: 6335. Top class comfort. Expensive.

Jolly President, Largo Augusto, 10. Tel: 7746. Excellent. Expensive.

SMALL HOTELS

Antica Locanda Solferino, Via Castelfidardo, 2. Tel: 6570129. This is a delightful hotel, with old-fashioned furniture and atmosphere. From the windows, you can look out on the Brera quarter. Inexpensive.

Pensione Kennedy, Via Tunisia, 6. Tel: 29400934. A clean and small *pensione* in a convenient location. Inexpensive.

GRAND HOTELS

Excelsior, Piazza Ognissanti, 3. Tel: 264201. In the luxury category, overlooking the Arno, which you can admire from the terrace restaurant. Expensive.

Villa Medici, Via il Prato, 42. Tel: 2381331. With its huge bedrooms, roof garden restaurant and swimming pool, the hotel offers everything your heart could desire, including a good location near the railway station. Expensive.

Villa Cora, Viale Machiavelli, 18. Tel: 2298541. Luxury category. Located on the hills of Florence. Built by the Baron Oppenheim in a neoclassical style, this hotel hosted Eugenia di Montijo, the widow of Napoleon III, and the rich Baroness Von Meck, patroness of Tchaikovsky and Debussy. The hotel offers a quiet atmosphere, a huge park and a pool. Expensive.

Savoy, Piazza della Repubblica, 7. Tel: 283313. In the heart of Florence, the hotel is classic in style and service. Many rooms are decorated in Venetian style. Expensive.

Hotel de la Ville, Piazza Antinori, 1. Tel: 2381805. Quiet and elegant, located in the centre of Florence, next to Via Tornabuoni. Good service and comfort. Expensive.

SMALL HOTELS

Hotel Regency, Piazza d'Azeglio, 3. Tel: 245247. This is the right place for people who like quiet and comfort. The hotel offers a charming garden, beautiful furniture, a gourmet restaurant and a central position. Expensive.

Lungarno, Borgo San Jacopo, 14. Tel: 264211. This modern hotel overlooks the Arno between Ponte Vecchio and Ponte Santa Trinita. Moderate.

Beacci Tornabuoni, Via Tornabuoni, 3. Tel: 212645. This small and attractive *pensione* is built on the most elegant street in Florence. Inexpensive.

Pensione Bencistà, Fiesole. Tel: 59163. Situated outside the city, between Fiesole and San Domenico, this small hotel in a 15th-century villa is small and simple, with no phones in the rooms, but it is quiet and rates are inexpensive. Closed: November to mid-March.

Pensione Annalena, Via Romana, 34. Tel: 222402. Located across the Ponte Vecchio, just beyond the Pitti Palace, this elegant little place offers a lovely Florentine experience at reasonable prices.

Castello di Gargonza, Monte San Savino, 52048, Arezzo. Tel: 847021. A restored country hamlet in the Tuscan hills between Arezzo and Siena. Visitors stay in modernised 13th-century cottages. The place has been meticulously restored. Excellent restaurant. Moderate.

Hotel rates in Venice are about 30 percent higher than those on the mainland.

GRAND HOTELS

Gritti Palace Hotel, Campo Santa Maria del Giglio, 2467. Tel: 794611. The most elegant hotel in Venice, renowned for formal luxury, charming setting (right on the Grand Canal) and discreet, attentive service. Doge Andrea Gritti lived here and the hotel still has the air of a private *palazzo*. Hemingway, Winston Churchill, Herbert von Karajan and Greta Garbo all stayed here. The cuisine, which you enjoy on the canalside terrace, is very refined. Very expensive.

Danieli Royal Excelsior, Riva degli Schiavoni, 4196 Castello. Tel: 52264880. Part of the CIGA chain of hotels, the Danieli is rich with memories of eminent guests: George Sand, Alfred de Musset, Dickens, Balzac, Wagner, kings, princes, stars. The splendid Gothic foyer, built around a courtyard is an attraction in itself, and the rooms are exceptionally comfortable. The roof garden restaurant has a splendid view over the lagoon. Very expensive.

Cipriani, Isola della Giudecca, 10. Tel: 5207744. A small oasis hidden on the tip of the island of Giudecca, the Cipriani feels far removed from the city centre. Among its comforts and facilities are lavish bedrooms furnished with Fortuny fabrics, a swimming pool (the only private pool in Venice), gardens and tennis courts, a yacht harbour, piano bar and a launch service which whisks you, in a couple of minutes, to San Marco. Very expensive.

Excelsior Hotel, Lungomare Marconi, 41, Lido di Venezia. Tel: 5260201. A member of the CIGA chain, this is a huge luxury beach hotel with a facade reminiscent of a Moorish castle. Attractions include numerous sports facilities and a free launch service to Venice. Very expensive.

Europa & Regina Hotel, San Marco, 2159. Tel: 5200477. In front of the Church of the Salute, with rooms overlooking the Grand Canal, this old hotel has been tastefully redecorated. The service is first-class. Expensive.

Grand Hotel des Bains, Lungomare Marconi, 17. Tel: 5265921. CIGA run, this grand old hotel is remembered for its role in Thomas Mann's *Death in Venice*. It is located across the road from its private beach. Facilities similar to those at the Excelsior (above). Expensive.

SMALL HOTELS

Locanda Cipriani, Piazza Santa Fosca. Tel: 730150. Tiny and exclusive, far from the madding crowds of San Marco. Half-board terms only. Reserve well in advance – there are only six rooms. Expensive.

Monaco & Grand Canal, San Marco, 1325. Tel: 5200211. First category. Located where the Grand Canal flows into the Laguna. Very intimate and comfortable, though the rooms are perhaps a little small and sometimes noisy. Good service. Moderate.

Saturnia & International, Via Larga XXII Marzo, 2398. Tel: 5208377. A very romantic hotel, near Piazza San Marco, in a 16th-century palace. Intimate and comfortable. Moderate.

Flora, Calle Larga XXII Marzo, 2283/A. Tel: 5205844. Charming friendly hotel within five-minutes' walk from Piazza San Marco. The garden with fountains and flower beds is particularly appealing. Bedrooms vary enormously and can be quite basic. Moderate.

Accademia, Fondamenta Maravegie, 1058 Dorsododuro. Tel: 52100188. Reservations should be made months in advance for this sought-after *pensione*. Close to the Accademia gallery, it is a 17th-century villa with delightful gardens front and back. Moderate.

La Fenice et des Artistes, Campiello de la Fenice, 1936 San Marco. Tel: 5232333. Within a stone's throw of the Fenice Opera House, the hotel is popular with actors musicians and artists – as well as some tourists. Moderate.

San Cassiano, Calle della Rosa, 2232 Santa Croce. Tel: 5241768. One of the few hotels actually on the Grand Canal, the San Cassiano is converted from a 14th-century *palazzo*. About half the rooms have canalside views looking across to the Ca' d'Oro. Moderate.

Bucintoro, Riva San Biagio, 2135 Castello. Tel: 5223240. Simply furnished, friendly *pensione* on the waterfront with splendid views over the Basin of San Marco and the island of San Giorgio Maggiore. Inexpensive.

Metropole Riva Schiavoni 4149. Tel: 5205044. In front of St George's Island. Beautifully furnished with excellent service. Moderate.

TURIN

Villa Sassi, Strada Traforo del Pino, 47. Tel: 890556. Located on the hill of Torino, the hotel is an 18th-century villa, in the middle of a great park, with only 12 bedrooms, excellent service and great comfort. Very exclusive and expensive.

Jolly Hotel Principe di Piemonte, Via Piero Gobetti, 15. Tel: 532153. The most central hotel in Turin. Very comfortable, with excellent service. Expensive.

Jolly Hotel Ambasciatori, Corso Vittorio Emanuele, 104. Tel: 5752. Favoured by businesspeople. A good position and excellent service. Expensive.

City, Via F. Juvarra, 25. Tel; 540546. A small, comfortable hotel close to the station of Porta Susa. 40 bedrooms. Moderate.

TRIESTE

Duchi d'Aosta, Piazza Unita D'Italia, 2. Tel :7351. This hotel is small but very charming, with big, well-furnished rooms, an excellent restaurant (Harry's Grill), efficient service and a central position. Expensive.

Savoia Excelsior Palace, Riva del Mandrachio, 4. Tel: 7690. Every comfort. Expensive.

Jolly, Corso Cavour, 7. Tel: 7694. Jolly-style, the usual great service and comfort. Expensive.

GENOA

Colombia Excelsior, Via Balbi, 40. Tel: 261841. CIGA-style: luxury category, close to the railway station, in an Art Nouveau-style palace, with big, comfortable rooms and excellent service. Expensive.

Bristol Palace, Via XX Settembre, 35. Tel: 592541. First category. Despite its modest entrance, this is a well-furnished hotel – particularly the dining-room – which is decorated in the Louis XVI style. Good service. Moderate.

Savoia Majestic, Piazza Acquaverde. Tel: 261641. First category, comfortable, good service, in a central position. Expensive.

Plaza, Via M. Piaggio, 11. Tel: 893642. This hotel was a small villa before being transformed into comfortable lodgings in an ideal location close to Piazza Corvetto.

BOLOGNA

Royal Carlton, Via Montebello, 8. Tel: 249361. This big hotel, close to the railway station, is extremely comfortable but a little anonymous. Excellent service. Expensive.

Jolly, Piazza XX Settembre, 2. Tel: 248921. Close to the station and the Alitalia terminal. Large and comfortable. Moderate.

Grand Hotel Elite, Via Aurelio Saffi, 36. Tel: 437417. Very modern and comfortable, with one of the best restaurants in Bologna. Expensive.

RAVENNA

Jolly, Piazza Mameli, 1. Tel: 35762. Excellent standards. Restaurant. Expensive.

Bisanzio, Via Salara, 30. Tel: 217111. Close to the most important monuments in Ravenna, modern and comfortable, with simple rooms and a good service. Moderate.

Villa Bolis, Via Corriera 5-Barbiano, località Cotignola (Ravenna). Tel: 0545-79347. A quarter of an hour away from Ravenna, in the middle of the Romagna countryside, lies this perfect countryclub hotel, with swimming pool, tennis courts and excellent cuisine. Moderate.

UMBRIA & THE MARCHES

La Rosetta, Piazza Italia, 19, Perugia. Tel: 20841. A good hotel of the second category, with a new and an old part. Eat in the courtyard under pergolas and palms in the summer. Fine service. Moderate.

Subasio, Via Frate Elia, 2, Assisi. Tel: 812206. The columns of this hotel link to the church of San Francesco, the terraces command a wonderful view of the town and countryside. Many famous people have stayed here, including the king and queen of Belgium, Charlie Chaplin, James Stewart and Marlene Dietrich. Good rooms and service. Moderate.

Umbra, Vicolo degli Archi, 6, Assisi. Tel: 812240. Close to the Piazza del Comune, it is the most central hotel in Assisi. Though small, rooms are comfortable and the restaurant is very good. Moderate.

Piero della Francesca, Viale Comandino, 53, Urbino. Tel: 4570. Fine hotel. Moderate.

Le tre Vaselle, Torgiano Perugia. Tel: 982447. A few kilometres from Perugia. This is a wonderful small hotel in an ancient villa owned by Giorgio Lungarotti, one of the most famous wine-collectors in Italy. This hotel has a pleasant atmosphere and great cooking. Expensive.

ABRUZZO

Duca degli Abruzzi, Via duca degli Abruzzi, 10, L'Aquila. Tel: 28341. A second category hotel that is very well run. From the restaurant there is a wide panorama. Moderate.

Esplanade, Piazza 1 Maggio, 46, Pescara. Tel: 292141. Old-style hotel with modernised interior, right across from the beach. Excellent views. Moderate.

MOLISE

Skanderbeg, Via Novelli, Campobasso. Tel: 93341. The best in town, comfortable. Moderate.

LIGURIA (THE RIVIERA)

Grand Hotel Diana, Via Garibaldi, 110, Alassio. Tel: 42701. First category, open from April till October, with good service, a swimming pool and a terrace-garden at moderate prices.

Royal, Corso Imperatrice, 74, San Remo. Tel: 79991. Luxury category. Gardens filled with flowers, palms and terraces surround this classic hotel with big comfortable rooms which overlook the sea or the hills. Expensive.

Grand Hotel Londra, Corso Matuzia, 2, San Remo. Tel: 79961. First category. Old, quiet and pleasant. Close to the Casino. Moderate.

Grand Hotel Cap Ampelio, Via Virgilio, 5, Bordighera. Tel: 264333. Ideally located on the hill of Bordighera, this refined hotel has a splendid view over the sea and coastline. Expensive.

Grand Hotel del Mare, Via Aurelia a capo Migliarese, Bordighera. Tel: 262201. First category, overlooking the sea, preferred by adults for its quietness, its comfort and its beautiful rooms. Expensive.

La Riserva, A Castel d'Appio, Ventimiglia. Tel: 39533. This is a small place with a wonderful view of the Riviera dei Fiori and the Costa Azzurra. The rooms are comfortable and the service is homely, but courteous. Moderate.

Cenobio dei Dogi, Via Cuneo, 34, Camogli. Tel: 770041. First category. This hotel, in a wonderful spot overlooking the sea, is surrounded by a splendid park. It is known for its beautiful rooms, fine restaurant, salt-water swimming pool and solarium, its private beach and its nightclub during the summer. Expensive.

Imperial Palace, Via Pagana, 19, Santa Margherita Ligure. Tel: 88991. Luxury category. This is a big hotel in the classic tradition, surrounded by a tropical garden. Old-fashioned decor, big rooms and excellent service. Expensive.

Splendido, Portofino. Tel: 69551. Luxury category. This hotel is a peaceful oasis along a street lined with olive-trees, with a splendid view of the Portofino promontory. Every comfort. Expensive.

Grand Hotel dei Castelli, Via alla Penisola, 26, Sestri Levante. Tel: 41044. In front of the church of S. Niccolò, very quiet and pleasant, surrounded by a big park overlooking the sea. An elevator descends to the private beach. Excellent service. Expensive.

NAPLES

Excelsior, Via Partenope, 48. Tel: 760111 or 769272. A CIGA hotel. Just across the street from the Castel dell'Ovo, with a wonderful view of the Gulf of Naples. Expensive.

Vesuvio, Via Partenope, 45. Tel: 7640044 or 7640606. Another top hotel just down the street from the Excelsior, with more moderate prices.

Jolly, Via Medina, 70. Tel: 416000. This modern high-rise has a roof-garden restaurant with great views of the city. Moderate.

Parker's, Corso Vittorio Emanuele, 135. Tel: 7612474 or 7615081. First category hotel, located in a 19th-century palace with casual decor. Good service. Moderate.

Britannique, Corso Vittorio Emanuele, 133. Tel: 7614145. Attached to Parker's. In the first category with good service. Moderate.

Royal, Via Partenope, 38. Tel: 7644800 or 5518888. Elegant hotel in the centre of town on the sea front. Good service, large conference hall, popular with businesspeople.

Paradiso, Via Catullo, 11. Tel: 7614161 or 7612397. Located in a quiet, residential area on the hill of Posillipo with views of the sea and the Mergellina port. Moderate.

BAY OF NAPLES

La Palma, Corso Vittorio Emanuele, 39, Capri. Tel: 8379133. Located in the shopping area. Sauna available.

Punta Tragara, Via Tragara, 57, Capri. Tel: 8370844. Comfortable and quiet with a beautiful view of the Faraglioni.

Grand Hotel Quisisana, Via Camerelle, 2, Capri. Tel: 837088. The most famous and the most expensive hotel in Capri. Expensive.

Ambasciatori, Via Califano, 18, Sorrento. Tel: 8782025. Quiet, with a swimming pool and large garden.

Excelsior Vittoria, Piazza Tasso, 34, Sorrento. Tel: 8071044. A very old, elegant hotel with a views across the port.

Regina Isabella, Piazza Santa Restituta, Lacco Ameno Ischia. Tel: 994322. Located in a small port. Thermal bath available.

Il Moresco, Via Emanuele Gianturco, 16, Ischia. Tel: 981355. Sited on the beach with good service and comfortable rooms.

Grand Hotel Punta Molino, Lungomare, C. Colombo, 14. Tel: 991544. Located near a pine wood. Good service.

APULIA

Palace Hotel, Via Lombardi, 13, Bari. Tel: 5216551. Modern, big, comfortable. Moderate to expensive.

Jolly, Via Giulio Pietroni, 15, Bari. Tel: 5364366. A new, comfortable and quiet hotel in the Jolly style. Expensive.

President, Via Salandra, 6, Lecce. Tel: 311881. A top-class hotel with good service. Expensive.

CALABRIA

Grand Hotel Excelsior, Via V. Veneto, Reggio di Calabria. Tel: 812211. First category. Very comfortable rooms and good service. Moderate.

Grand Hotel San Michele, on the SS (Strada Statale) 18 at Cetraro (Cosenza). Tel: 91012. It is a sheer drop from this hotel to the sea, and the place is located in a wonderful park. The hotel offers all the comforts (tennis courts, swimming pool and lift to the beach).

SICILY

Grand Hotel Villa Igea, Salita Belmonte, 43, Palermo. Tel: 543744. Located near the Lido di Modello, under the Monte Pellegrino, this hotel was built by the architect Basile in the Liberty style for don Ignazio Florio, a famous Sicilian shipowner. The outside looks like a Norman palace, but the interior is richly decorated with flowers. It has terraces and a big park with a swimming pool overlooking the sea. Very expensive.

Jolly, Foro Italico, 22, Palermo. Tel: 6165090. Big and modern, this hotel offers the top-class comfort and service of all Jolly hotels. Moderate to expensive.

Jolly Hotel dello Stretto, Corso Garibaldi, 126, Messina. Tel: 43401. Every comfort, as usual, and at moderate prices. First category.

Hotel San Domenico Palace, Piazza San Domenico, 5, Taormina (Messina). Tel: 23701. This hotel is quite famous for its location, its park and its rooms which have extraordinary views. Expensive.

Jolly dei Templi, Villaggio Mosé, SS 115, Agrigento. Tel: 606144. This is a modern hotel in a central location, and though the surroundings are a little bit noisy, the rooms are comfortable and the service is good. Moderate.

Villa Politi, Via Politi, 2, Siracusa. Tel: 412121. This hotel has an atmosphere similar to that of the hotel in Giuseppe di Lampedusa's *The Leopard*. Quiet rooms and good service. Moderate.

Jolly, Corso Gelone, 45 Siracusa. Tel: 461111. Close to the archaeological sites, comfortable, elegant. Expensive.

FOOD DIGEST

WHAT TO EAT

The gentle lifestyle of Italy is partly a product of its civilised eating habits: eating and drinking in tranquillity at least twice a day are the norm here.

Italian breakfast is usually light and consists of *cappuccino* (coffee and milk) and a *briosche* (pastry), or simply *caffè* (black and strong *espresso*).

Except in the industrialised cities, *pranzo* (lunch) is the big meal of the day. It consists of *antipasto* (hors-d'oeuvre), a *primo* (pasta, rice or soup) and a *secondo*, meat or fish with a vegetable (*contorno*) or salad. To follow, comes cheese and/or fruit. Italians usually drink coffee (*espresso*) after lunch and/or a liqueur, such as *grappa, amaro* or *sambuca*.

Traditionally dinner is similar to lunch, but lighter. However, in the cities people are tending to eat less at lunchtime and making dinner the major meal of the day.

Every region in Italy has its own typical dishes: Piedmont specialises in pheasant, hare and truffles and *zabaglione* (a hot dessert made with whipped eggs and Marsala wine); Lombardy is known for *risotto alla Milanese*, minestrone, veal and *panettone* (a sweet, celebration bread with sultanas and candied fruits); Trentino-Alto Adige is the place for dumplings and thick soups to keep out the cold; Umbria is best for roast pork and black truffles; Tuscany is good for wild boar, chestnuts, steak and game; Naples is the home of Mozzarella cheese and pizza and is good for seafood; and Sicily is the place for delectable sweets.

Italy still claims the best ice cream in the world, as well as *granite* (crushed ice with syrup flavoured with different fruits). According to many Italians, the best ice-cream in Italy is found at Vivoli's, Via Isola delle Stinche 7, in Florence; *granita* is a speciality of Sicily.

Remember the further south you travel, the spicier and heavier the food and the stronger the wine.

WHERE TO EAT

Italy has thousands of restaurants, *trattorie* and *osterie* (in roughly descending order, from the more expensive and fancy to the inexpensive).

If you do not want to have a complete meal, you can have a snack at the bar or at *tavole calde* and *rosticcerie* (grills).

If you go to a restaurant, don't order just a salad: the waiters may look down on you and treat you with disdain. If you think a complete meal is too big, forego the *antipasto*, but take a *primo* and a *secondo* at least.

The restaurants listed below have been recommended by Italian food writers and/or the authors of this guide. We categorise our restaurants as follows:

I = inexpensive (about L30,000 per head)
M = moderate (from L30,000–50,000 per head)
E = expensive (over L50,000 per head).

We even list some very high quality restaurants, indicating them by L = luxurious (from L70,000–100,000 or more).

ROME

El Toulà, Via della Lupa, 29/B. Tel: 68773498. Very elegant decor. The cuisine is refined and international, but the regional dishes are the best. An impressive wine list. Reservations necessary. Major credit cards accepted. Closed: Saturday midday, Sunday and some of August. L

Hosteria dell'Orso, Via dei Soldati, 25. Tel: 6864250 or 6864221. In a Renaissance building, between Piazza Navona and the Tiber river, with a beautiful terrace and a nightclub. The cuisine is international too. Wine list mostly national. Closed: Sunday and some of August. Reservations. L

Le jardin dell'Hotel Byron, Via de Notaris, 5. Tel: 3609541. Exquisite, elegant, in a lovely garden. L

Passetto, Via Zanardelli, 14. Tel: 6540569. Classic Italian cuisine. Traditional atmosphere and good service. Closed: Sunday, Christmas and August. E

Ranieri, Via Mario Dè Fiori, 26. Tel: 6791592. Founded in 1849, the restaurant is just right for *tête-à-tête* dinners. *Fin de siècle* furniture, historic motif. Closed: Sunday. E

Girarrosto toscano, Via Campania, 29. Tel: 4821899. Modern tavern with traditional Tuscan cuisine. Closed: Wednesday. E

Piperno, Via Monte de' Cenci, 9. Tel: 6540629. Traditional Roman *trattoria*, with romantic outside dining during the summer on a little piazza in old Rome. Roman cuisine: *ravioli ricotta e spinaci*, *saltimbocca*. Closed: Sunday, Monday, Christmas and part of August. E

La Tavernetta, Via Sistina, 143. Tel: 47441939. Centrally located in the chic Via Sistina, close to the Spanish Steps. A wide variety of both meat and fish dishes combined with a fun, comfortable atmosphere. Closed: Sunday and some of August. E

Il Tinello, Via Di Porta Pinciana, 16B. Tel: 486847. Hidden off the Dolce Vita beaten track, offers traditional cuisine and excellent service. Serves great pizza at lunchtime. Closed: Sunday. E–M

Eau Vive, Via Monterone, 85. Tel: 6541095. In a 15th-century palace managed by nuns. International cuisine, especially French. Closed: Sunday and August. M

Taverna Giulia, Vicolo dell'Oro, 23. Tel: 6869768. A classic restaurant which serves food outside during the summer. Great national and Genoese cuisine. Try *trenette al pesto* (thin noodles in a sauce of fresh basil, pine nuts, garlic and olive oil), and *stinco al forno* (roast shoulder of veal). Closed: Sunday and some of August. M

Chianti, Via Ancona, 17. Tel: 8551083. Rustic *trattoria* with tavern. Great Tuscan cuisine. Closed: Sunday and August. M

Checchino dal 1887, Via Monte Testaccio, 30. Tel: 5743816. Authentic old-time family atmosphere, typical Roman cuisine. Closed: Sunday dinner, Monday, Christmas and from 15 July–15 August. Reserve. M

Ciceruacchio, Via del Porto, 1. Tel: 5806046. At Trastevere. Very touristy place on the lines of an old-fashioned tavern. Roman cuisine, list of local wines. Closed: Monday and some of August. M

Romolo, Via di Porta Settiminiana, 8. Tel: 5818284. Trastevere ambience with a summer court. Good Roman cuisine. Closed: Monday and part of August. Reserve. M

Il Falchetto, Via Dei Montecatine, 12. Tel: 6791160. Small, family-run restaurant, just off the lively Via Del Corso. Positioned in a narrow, quiet road which makes eating outside a pleasure. Closed: Friday and some of July.

Colline Emiliane, Via degli Avignonesi, 22. Tel: 4817538. Classic ambience, rich Emilian cuisine. Closed: Friday and August. Reserve. I

Al Ceppo, Via Panama, 2. Tel: 8551379. Typical restaurant with Roman cuisine. Closed: Monday and August. I

Pierdonati, Via della Conciliazione, 39, in front of St. Peter's. Tel: 6543557. Medium-comfort tavern. Traditional Italian cuisine, local wines. Closed: Tuesday and some of August. I

Elettra, Via Principe Amedeo, 72. Tel: 4745397. Crowded with regular diners, it has a pleasant homely atmosphere and traditional but varied cuisine. Closed: Saturday and some of August. I

Cannavota, Piazza S. Giovanni in Laterano. Tel: 775007. Crowded with tourists and locals alike very informal, Roman cuisine. Closed: Wednesday and some of August. I

La Vigna dei Cardinali, Piazzale Ponte Milvio, 34. Tel: 3965846. A nice restaurant with a beautiful summer garden. Traditional cuisine, with variations. Closed: Saturday and 15 August. I

NEAR ROME

Allo sbarco di Enea, Via dei Romagnoli, 657, Ostia. Tel: 5650034. Crowded with tourists. During the summer, meat and fish are cooked under a bower. M

Cinque Statue, Largo S. Angelo, 1, Tivoli. Tel: 20366. Great ambience, plain cooking, modern furniture and, in summer, tables outside. Closed: Friday and Sunday night.

Antico Ristorante Giudizi, Piazza Cavour, 20,

Tarquinia. Tel: 855061. In front of the Museum. Regional seafood cuisine. Closed: Monday. I

Trattoria del Gobbo, Lungoporto Gramsci, 29/35. Tel: 23163. Traditional seafood. *Civitavecchia*. Closed: Wednesday. Reserve. I

Stella, Piazza della Liberazione, 3, Palestrina. Tel: 9558172. Modern ambience, local cuisine. I

La Taverna, Via Nemorese, 13, Nemi (Colli Albani area). Tel: 9378135. Nice and simple with a great fire-place. Traditional cooking. Closed: Monday. Reserve. I

Belvedere, Via dei Monasteri, 33, Subiaco. Tel: 85531. Wonderful restaurant in a small hotel. Closed: Tuesday. I

MILAN

Gualtiero Marchesi, Via Bonvesin della Riva, 9. Tel: 741246. The temple of Italian cuisine, the best in Italy, modern ambience. For the élite. Closed: Sunday and from 15 July–30 August. Reservations necessary. L

Savini, Galleria Vittorio Emanuele, 11. Close to Piazza Duomo. Tel: 8058343. Exquisite decor, ultra-professional service and classic Italian cuisine. Closed: Sunday and August. Reserve. L

Scaletta, Piazza Stazione Genova, 3. Tel: 8350290. A modern ambience, with a library. International level cuisine. Very fashionable. Closed: Sunday, Monday, Easter and Christmas. Reserve. L

Gran San Bernardo, Via Borghese, 14. Tel: 389000. A large and friendly restaurant where some of the best regional cooking is served. Try *casseoeula* (a stew of pork, sausages, carrots served with cornbread) and *polenta*. Closed: Sunday and August. Reservations necessary. E

Al Mercante, Piazza Mercanti, 17. Tel: 8052198. Friendly, overlooking the piazza. In summer you can eat outdoors under a very old loggia. Closed: Sunday and August. Reserve. M

Trattoria della Pesa, Via Pasubio 10. Tel: 665741. Traditional Milanese cuisine is served. Closed: Sunday and August. Reserve. M

Osteria al Pontell, Via Mameli, 1. Tel: 733818. Typical Milanese *osteria*, with friendly service. Closed: Monday and August. Reserve. M

Brasera Meneghina, Via Circo, 10. Tel: 808108. Genuine *osteria* of old Milan, dating back to the 17th century; it boasts a fireplace and small porch painted with frescoes, and offers outdoor dining in summer. Closed: Friday, Saturday lunch and August. M

La Bella Pisana, Via Sottocorno, 17. Tel: 708376. Pleasant ambience, with a garden for summer. Padana plain cooking and fresh fish. Closed: Sunday, Monday lunch and August. Reserve. M

Taverna Gran Sasso, Via Principessa Clotilde, 10. Tel: 6597578. Kitsch restaurant, with Abruzzese cooking. Closed: Sunday and August. Reserve. I

Trattoria Aurora, Via Savona, 23. Tel: 8354978. This typical family-run *trattoria* offers Piedmontese cooking. Closed: Monday and August. I

LOMBARDY

La Pergola, Via Borgo Canale, 62, Bergamo. Tel: 256353. Located on a hill with a wonderful terrace. Known for traditional high-level cooking. Closed: Sunday, Monday lunch and August. Reserve. E

Cigno, Piazza Carlo d'Arco, 1, Mantova. Tel: 327101. In a wonderful piazza, in an ancient building, the service is as excellent as the regional cooking. Closed: Monday, Tuesday night and August. Reserve. E

Bixio, Piazza Castello, 1, Pavia. Tel: 25343. Nineteenth-century ambience and traditional cuisine. Closed: Sunday dinner and Monday. M

Ceresole, Via Ceresole, 4, Cremona. Tel: 23322. Classic national cuisine. Closed: Sunday night, Monday and August. Reserve. M

Agnello d'Oro, Via Gombito, 22, Bergamo. Tel: 249883. Good regional food in an old hotel in the upper part of town. Closed: Monday and January. Reserve. M

Ai Garibaldini, Via S. Longini, 7. Tel: 329237. Old bourgeois style ambience, 16th-century furniture and summer terrace. Regional cuisine. Closed: Wednesday dinner, Friday and July. M

Trattoria del Teatro, Piazza Mascheroni, Bergamo. Tel: 238862. 19th-century furniture; the food is simple, traditional and delicious. Closed: Monday. I

Ferrari da Tino, Via dei Mille, 111, Pavia. Tel: 31033. Old-fashioned homely *trattoria*, regional cooking. Closed: Monday and 15 July–15 August. I

TURIN

Del Cambio, Piazzo Carignano, 2. Tel: 546690. Opened in 1757, one of the most beautiful restaurants in Italy, 19th-century furniture and atmosphere. International and national cuisine. Closed: Sunday and August. Reservations necessary. L

Villa Sassi, Strada Traforo del Pino, 47. Tel: 890556. In a cardinal's villa, this is a restaurant for VIPs, with an attached hotel (only 24 beds). Exclusive and fancy, with superb cuisine. Closed: Sunday. Reserve. L

Ostu Bacu, Corso Vercelli, 226. Tel: 264579. Modern ambience. Come here to taste plain old-fashioned Piemontese cooking. Closed: Sunday and August. Reserve.

La Capannina, Via Donati, 1. Tel: 545405. The ambience is rustic, as in the twin restaurant at Alba, and the food is strictly cooked in the Langarola-style (The Langhe are a part of Piemonte). The *fritto misto* is superb. Closed: Sunday and August. Reserve. M

Spada Reale, Via Principe Amedeo, 53. Tel: 832835. Modern-style, Tuscan and Piemontese cuisine. Closed: Sunday, Christmas and Easter. Reserve. I

Tre Galline, Via Bellezia, 7. Tel: 546833. A typical old-fashioned *piola* (a meeting-place to drink wine and eat snacks); regional cooking. Closed: Monday and August. Reserve. I

AOSTA & THE ALPS

Cavallo Bianco, Via E. Aubert, 15. Tel: 2214. 19th-century atmosphere, overlooking an 18th-century court. Good regional cuisine. Closed: Sunday night and Monday, 16 June–15 July and 12–24 December. Reserve. E

Batezar, Via Marconi, 1, St Vinceny. tel: 3164. Close to the Casino, with an elegant atmosphere, this restaurant offers personalised cooking and efficient service. Closed: Wednesday, Thursday lunch, 20 June–10 July and 10–24 December. E

AGIP, Corso Ivrea, 138. Tel: 44565. On the highway. Modern ambience, large windows overlook a green panorama. The food is both national and regional. Closed: Monday and February. M

Les Neige d'Antan, Località Cret Perreres, Statale 406, Breuil-Cervinia. Tel: 948775. Situated on a mountain this quiet house has only a few rooms, serves typical Valdostana cuisine, and has a fine view of Mt Cervino. Try the *fonduta*. Closed: Monday and 11 September–30 November and 3 May–9 July. Reserve. M

FLORENCE

Enoteca Pinchiorri, Via Ghibellina, 87. Tel: 242777. In the 15th-century Ciofi Palace, with a delightful courtyard for dining in the open air. Superb nouvelle cuisine, with an impressive wine collection (almost 60,000 bottles). Closed: Sunday, Monday lunch and August. Reservations necessary. L

La Loggia, Piazzale Michelangelo. Tel: 287032. The beautiful view of Florence will bewitch you. Serves international or Italian delicacies. Good service. Closed: Wednesday and 1–15 August. M

13 Gobbi, Via del Porcellana, 12r. Tel: 2398769. Beer-house style, but the cooking is Tuscan and first-class. Closed: Sunday, Monday and August. Make reservations. M

Otello, Via degli Orti Oricellari, 36r. Tel: 215819. Typical Florentine restaurant. Closed: Tuesday and August. Reserve. M

Dino, Via Ghibellina, 51r. Tel: 241452. Former wine store. Regional atmosphere and cooking. Closed: Sunday night, Monday and August. M

Omero Via Pian de' Giullari, 11r. Tel: 220053. Also an old store, now transformed into a rustic *trattoria* with outside tables in summer. Splendid view. Closed: Tuesday and August. Reserve. I–M

Cantinone del Gallo Nero, Via S. Spirito, 6r. Tel: 218898. Always crowded, the restaurant is located in a 15th-century wine cellar, very informal. The speciality is its Chianti wine collection (about 300 kinds) and the Tuscan peasant dishes, such as *crostoni, ribollita, pinzimonio*. Closed: Monday and August. I

TUSCANY

Sergio, Lungarno Pacinotti, 1, Pisa. Tel: 48245. Elegant decor with excellent regional cuisine. Closed: Sunday, Monday lunch and January. E

Tullio ai Tre Cristi, Vicolo Provenzano, 1/7, Siena. Tel: 280608. A 19th-century *trattoria* attached to a shrine representing the Crucifixion. The restaurant has been managed for 40 years by the same family. Try the *pici*, a kind of hand-made spaghetti. Closed: Monday and Sunday night. M

Guido, Vicolo Pier Pettinaio, 7, Siena. Tel: 280042. A 14th-century building, with a big kitchen, good service and traditional regional cooking. Closed: Monday. M

La Cisterna, Piazza della Cisterna, 23, Siena. Tel: 940328, San Gimignano. In a 15th-century monastery, with a wonderful view of the turreted village. Popular among tourists. Reserve. M

Cecco, Corso Italia, 125 Arezzo. Tel: 20986. Closed: Monday and August. Bar and *tavola calda*, but good cooking with no pretensions. Closed: Tuesday, Wednesday lunch and November–February. M

La loggetta, Piazza Peschiera, 3, Cortona. Tel: 603777. Mellow atmosphere, with good regional cooking. Closed: Monday and January. Reserve. M

Da Giulio, Via San Tommaso, 29 Lucca. Tel: 55948. Just plain good food. Closed: Sunday, Monday and August. I

Grotta Santa Caterina, Via della Galluzza, 28, Siena. Tel: 282208. Characteristic tavern. Closed: Monday. I

VENICE

Harry's Bar, Calle Vallaresso, 1323, San Marco. Tel: 5285777. This bar/restaurant was a favourite haunt of Hemingway; now mainly patronised by very wealthy Venetians, expatriates and American tourists. Good home-made pastas at exorbitant prices. Closed: Monday and January to mid-February. L

Antico Martini, Campo San Fantin, 1983 San Marco. Tel: 5237020. Close to the Fenice opera house. Elegant and intimate, serving Venetian and international cuisine. Closed: Tuesday and Wednesday. Reserve. L

Poste Vecie, Mercato del Pesce di Rialto, 1608, San Polo. Tel: 721822. Inviting rustic *trattoria* specialising in fish from the nearby market. Closed: Tuesday and 20 November–20 December. Reserve. E

Da Arturo, Calle degli Assassini, 3656, San Marco. Tel: 5286974. Very small, and unusual for Venice as it does not serve fish. Excellent meat, pasta and salads. Open late. Closed: Sunday, holidays and three weeks in August. E

La Furatola, Calle Lunga San Barnaba, 2870, Dorsoduro. Tel: 208594. Unpretentious restaurant where local gourmets go for fish and seafood. Closed: Wednesday afternoon, Thursday and sometimes Monday, July and August. E

Al Covo, Campiello dell Pescaria, 3968 Castello. Tel: 5223812. Enthusiastically run restaurant serving fish fresh from the lagoon, wild duck (seasonal) and home-made desserts. Closed: Wednesday and Thursday. E

Al Graspo de Ua, San Marco, 5094. Tel: 23647. Calle Bombaseri, close to the Rialto bridge. The restaurant under its old wooden roof, is centuries-old, with a long tradition of excellent cooking. It is a delight for those seeking local colour. National cuisine. Closed: Monday, Tuesday and 20–26 December. M

Antica Bessetta, Calle Savio, 1395, Santa Croce. Tel: 721687. Near San Giacomo dell' Orio, off the beaten track. Authentic family run *trattoria* serving regional cuisine. Good value. Closed: Tuesday, Wednesday and 15 July–16 August. M

Alla Madonna, Calle della Madonna, 594, San Polo. Tel: 5233824. Popular fish and seafood restaurant near the Rialto. Good value for Venice, hence always crowded and the service can be brusque. Closed: Wednesday, August and January. Reserve during the week. M

Da Fiore, Calle del Scaleter, 2202 San Polo. Tel: 721308. Small restaurant near Campo San Polo. Well worth seeking out for good food, wine and elegant ambience. Closed: Sunday and Monday. M

Riviera, Zattere, 1473, Dorsoduro. Tel: 5227621. Good home-made pasta and fish. Weather permitting tables are set outside by the water, overlooking the island of Giudecca. Closed: Sunday afternoon and all day Monday. M

Harry's Dolci, Fondamento San Biagio, Giudecca 773. Tel: 5224844. Similar food to Harry's but a good deal cheaper. Specialities are the *dolci* (cakes), which are served all day. Closed: Tuesday, Wednesday and November to mid-March. M

Alle Colonnete, San Marco 987. Tel: 5237083. Typical Venetian cuisine. Closed: Thursday. M

Ai Due Vescovi, San Marco, 812A. Tel: 5236990. Good Venetian cuisine. Closed: Sunday. Reserve I

San Trovaso, Dorsoduro 1010. Tel: 5203703. Cheap, cheerful taverna serving standard Italian cuisine. Closed: Monday. I

Antica Carbonera, San Marco, 4648. Tel: 25479. Rebuilt, but maintaining its 19th-century ambience, with good Italian cooking. Closed: Tuesday, Wednesday and 15 July–16 August. I

VENETO

12 Apostoli, Vicolo Corticella San Marco, 3, Verona. Tel: 596999. One of the best restaurants in Italy, located in an ancient building decorated with frescoes by Casarini. Closed: Sunday dinner, Monday, Christmas and 12 June–7 July. Reservations necessary. E

Dotto, Via Squarcione, 23, Padova. Tel: 25055. Classic furniture, typical cuisine. Try *pasta e fagioli* (pasta and beans) and *baccalà* (stockfish). Closed: Sunday night, Monday and August Reserve. M

Al Pozzo, Via San Antonio, 1, Vicenza. Tel: 21411. Comfortable *belle-époque* ambience and national and regional cuisine. Closed: Tuesday and Sunday in July and August. M

Marconi, Via Fogge, 4, Verona. Tel: 591910. Elegant, with new furniture; some years ago, it was simply an *osteria*. Regional classic cuisine. Closed: Sunday, Tuesday afternoon and August.

FRIULI-VENEZIA GUILIA

Antica Trattoria Suban, Via Comici, 2, Trieste. Tel: 54368. Friendly and simple, with a summer bower. Good regional cuisine. Closed: Tuesday, August and Christmas. Reserve. M

Alla Vedova, Via Tavagnacco, 9, Udine. Tel: 470291. Very old Friulian restaurant, with outdoor tables in summer. Good traditional cooking. Closed: Sunday dinner, Monday and August. Reserve. M

Buffet Bendetto, Via XXX Ottobre, 19, Trieste. Tel: 61655. Rustic and informal, with traditional cooking. Closed: Monday and August. Reserve. I

TRENTINO-ALTO ALDIGE

Chiesa, Parco San Marco, Trento. Tel: 985577. On the first floor of a 17th-century palace with a cloister. Very elegant and refined. Closed: Sunday dinner and Monday. M

Da Abramo, Piazza Gries, 16, Bolzano. Tel: 30141. In the old town hall. Liberty-style restaurant with garden, serving good regional cuisine. Closed: Sunday dinner and Monday. M

BOLOGNA

Dante, Via Belvedere, 2/B. Tel: 224464. In a 14th-century palace. Very elegant. International cuisine. Closed: Monday, Tuesday lunch and August. E

Osteria Luciano, Via Sauro, 17. Tel: 231249. A classic restaurant where one can sample excellent regional food. Try *tortellini* and *armonie dell'Appennino*. Closed: Wednesday and August. M

Serghei, Via Piella, 12, in the historic centre. Typical small *trattoria* with just a few tables, but good cooking, in a pleasant homey atmosphere. I

Birreria Lamma, Via dei Giudei, 4. Tel: 279422. Regional cuisine, for those who are in a hurry and seek peace and quiet. Closed: Wednesday. I

Da Bertino e figlio, Via delle Lame, 55. Tel: 522230. Funny Emilian *trattoria*, with good cooking. Closed: Sunday and 1–15 August. I

Bacco Villa Orsi, Località Funo di Argelato, at Km. 13. Tel: 862451. In an 18th-century villa with a beautiful porch. Regional and international dishes. Try the roasted meat specialities. Closed: Saturday, Sunday and August. Reservations necessary.

EMILIA-ROMAGNA

Fini, Piazza San Franscesco Modena. Tel: 223314. Classic, elegant, but homely, with traditional regional cuisine. Try *bolliti* (boiled meat). Closed: Monday, Tuesday and August. Reservations required. E

Vecchia Rimini, Piazza Ferrari, 22, Rimini. Tel: 51327. Emphasis is on fish and seafood. Closed: Monday, Tuesday and 1–15 August. M

Vecchia Chitarra, Via Ravenna, 13, Ferrara. Tel: 62204. Informal restaurant with very good cooking. Closed: Monday and second half of July. Reserve. M

La Filoma, Via XX Marzo, 15, Parma. Tel: 34269. Refined, with 17th-century furniture and traditional cooking. Closed: Saturday and Sunday. M

Da Enzo, Via Coltellini, 17, Modena. Tel: 225177. Dating back to 1912, it has been tastefully renovated. Typical Modenese cooking. Closed: Saturday and August. M

Al Gallo, Via Maggiore, 87, Ravenna. Tel: 23775. A wonderful pergola in summer. Good (not exceptional) local food. Closed: Monday night, Tuesday and February. I

Righi-La Taverna, Piazza Libertà San Marino. Tel: 991196. Rustic, but good food. Closed: Monday in winter, and January. I

UMBRIA & THE MARCHES

La Badia, Località la Badia, Orvieto. Tel: 90359. Panorama of the town. International cuisine. Closed: Wednesday, January and February. E

Umbria, Via S. Bonaventura, 13, Todi. Tel: 882737. In a 14th-century building, with a delightful terrace for dining in summer, overlooking the hills. Good local food. Closed: Tuesday and 18 December–9 January. M

Il tartufo, Piazza Garibaldi, 24, Spoleto. Tel: 40236. Quiet and dignified with well-prepared traditional cuisine. The dining room preserves a 4th-century Roman floor. Closed: Wednesday and from 15 July–8 August. Reservations required. M

Tre colonne, Viale Plebiscito, 13, Terni. Tel: 54511. Typically rustic, Umbrian furniture and cuisine. Closed: Monday and 1–20 August. Reserve. M

Morino, Via Garibaldi, 37, Orvieto. Tel: 35152. Modern. Excellent cuisine. Closed: Wednesday and July. Reserve. M

Passetto, Piazza IV Novembre, 1, Ancona. Tel: 33214. Elegant and exquisite. Traditional seafood cuisine. The terrace gives a view of the sea. Closed: Wednesday. Reserve. M

Falchetto, Via Bartolo, 20, Perugia. Tel: 61875. Serves authentic local food using the best ingredients, with no pretence. Closed: Monday. I

Buca di San Francesco, Via Brizi, 1, Assisi. Tel: 812204. In a wine cellar, with a rustic atmosphere and good cooking. In summer, dine outdoors. Closed: Monday and 1–15 July. I

Da Remo, Viale Battisti, 49, Foligno. Tel: 50079. The decor and the menu are simple, but the family that runs the place has a long tradition of fine cooking. Closed: Sunday night and Monday. I

NAPLES

Giuseppone al Mare, Via Ferdinando Russo, 13. Tel: 5766002. At Posillipo, right on the sea in a small port. Great seafood. Closed: Sunday and Christmas. E

La Sacrestia, Via Orazio, 116. Tel: 664186. At Mergellina, with a wonderful view back over the Gulf of Naples, in a building reminiscent of an old monastery. In summer you can enjoy typical Neapolitan food in the garden. Closed: Wednesday and August. Reservations necessary. E

La Bersagliera, Borgo Marinaro 10/11. Tel: 7646016. Old restaurant located in a small port with a view of Castel dell'Ovo. Closed: Monday. E

Zi Teresa, Via Partenope 1. Tel: 7642565. A very old, atmospheric restaurant. Seafood specialities.

La Cantinella, Via Nazario Sauro, 23. Tel: 7648684. Very elegant and expensive with a telephone on every table. Closed: Monday. E

La Fazenda, Via Marechiaro, 58/A. Tel: 5757420. In a farm overlooking the Gulf of Naples and Capri, with fine Mediterranean food. In summer, the terrace-garden is open. Closed: Sunday and 15 August–1 September. Reservations necessary. M

Sbrescia, Rampe San Antonio a Posillipo. Tel: 669140. Beautiful view of the Gulf. Fresh seafood. Closed: Monday and 15 August. Reserve. M

Ciro a Santa Brigida, Via S. Brigida, 71. Tel: 5524072. Classic well-known restaurant, good (not great) Neapolitan cooking. Closed: Sunday and August. Reserve. M

Giovanni, Via Domenico Morelli, 14. Tel: 7643565. Classic, quiet place which offers good fish and meat. Closed: Sunday and August. Reservations advised. M

Dante e Beatrice, Piazza Dante 44. Tel: 349905. Genuine Naples *trattoria*, crowded with Neapolitans. Good Neapolitan cooking. Closed: Wednesday and 20–30 August. I

Ettore, Via Santa Lucia, 56. Tel: 7640498. Just plain good food in a simple *trattoria*. Closed: Sunday and August. I

BAY OF NAPLES

Ai Faraglioni, Via Camerelle, 75, Capri. Tel: 8370320. Elegant dining rooms overlook the *faraglioni* and the country. National and international cuisine. Closed: Sunday. Reserve. E

La Piadina, Via Cozzolino, 10, Capri. Tel: 7717141. Popular among tourists. Traditional cuisine. Closed: Tuesday. M

La Pigna, Via Roma, 30, Capri. Tel: 8370280. The ideal place for a romantic dinner. Elegant, international and local. Dining-room with porch and citrus orchard around it. Patio and fountain. Neapolitan cuisine with personality and flair. Closed: Tuesday and during the winter. M

La Capannina, Via delle Botteghe, 126b, Capri. Tel: 8370732. Fashionable and classic, traditional seafood. Closed: Wednesday. Reserve. M

Gennaro, Via del Porto, 66, Ischia. Tel: 99 2917. Overlooking the port. Traditional fish cooking. Closed: Tuesday. M

La Favorita, Corso Italia, 71, Sorrento. Tel: 8781321. Time-honoured restaurant, filled with strange old furniture, with a beautiful garden. Mainly seafood. Closed: Wednesday in winter. M

Al Gambero, Via Cuomo, 9, Salerno. Tel: 225031. Ship's furniture, regional cooking. Closed: Sunday and August. Reserve. M

La buca, Di Bacco, Via Rampa Teglia, 8, Positano. Tel: 875696. Simple and genuine atmosphere and cuisine. Closed: November–March. I

Da Ciccio Cielo-Mare-Terra, Località Vettica, at Km 3 Via Nazionale to Sorrento. Tel: 871030. Sailors' restaurant, with a splendid view of the Gulf of Amalfi. Seafood. I

Da Gemma, Salita Fra' Gerardo Sasso, 9, Amalfi. Tel: 871345. Plain cooking, summer tables on the street. Good seafood. Closed: Thursday. Reserve. I

Nettuno, Via Principi di Piemonte, 1, Paestum. Tel: 811028. Good view of the temples, good Italian cooking. Closed: Monday in winter. Reserve. I

Pascalucci, Contrada Piano Cappelle, Benevento. Tel: 24548. Pleasant local atmosphere and cuisine. Closed: Monday. I

Vecchia America, Piano Cappelle, Benevento. Tel: 24394. Plain local cooking. Closed: Friday. I

ABRUZZO & MOLISE

Guerino, Viale della Riviera, 4, Pescara. Tel: 4212056. Modern. Terraces overlooking the sea. Good seafood. Closed: Tuesday only in winter. M

Il Potesta, Via Persichillo, 3, Campobasso. Tel: 311101. An excellent list of local wines accompanies the menu of traditional food with modern slant. Closed: Sunday and August. M

Tre Marie, Via Tre Marie, 3, L'Aquila. Tel: 413191. Old-fashioned restaurant with a 17th-century fireplace and homey atmosphere. Traditional local cuisine. Try *ciufolotti* (as *primo*) and *mischietto* (as *secondo*). Closed: Monday. Reserve. M

Duomo, via Stazio, 9, Teramo. Tel: 241774. Modern, but old-fashioned local cooking. Closed: Monday. Reserve. I

Venturini, Via de Lollis, 10, Chieti. Tel: 65863. Traditional atmosphere with a terrace. Special roast game. Closed: Tuesday and July. Reserve. I

SARDINIA

Dal Corsaro, Via Regina Margherita, 28, Cagliari. Tel: 664310. During the summer, it is better to go to the restaurant of the same name located at Marina Piccola-Poetto. Tel: 370295, Serves great Sardinian cuisine, elegant, romantic atmosphere. Closed: Tuesday and Christmas. M

Da Franco, Via Capo d'Orso, 1, Palau. Tel: 709310. The right place for a business meeting: refined service, terrace overlooking the little port. Mainly seafood. M

Da Nicola, Lungomare Vespucci, 37, S. Antioco. Tel: 83286. Modern, along the seaside, traditional cooking. Closed: Tuesday in winter and October. I

La Fattoria, Golfo Pevero, Porto Cervo. Tel: 92214. Rustic farmhouse, wooden furniture, huge fireplace where meat is roasted on spits; typical Sardinian cooking. Closed: Monday except in summer.

SICILY

Charleston, Piazza Ungheria, 30, Palermo. Tel: 321366 in the winter or Via Regina Elena, Mondello, tel: 450171 during the summer. Liberty-style atmosphere, excellent service. Sicilian and classic cuisine. Reservations necessary. L

La Scuderia, Viale de Fante, 9, Palermo. Tel: 520323. In the green park of "Favorita", with a summer garden in the Moorish manner. National and Sicilian cuisine. Closed: Sunday night. M

Spanò, Via Messina Marina, 20/c, Palermo. Along the seaside. Tel: 470025. Traditional seafood cooking. Closed: Monday. I

Luraleo, Via Croce, 27, Taormina. Tel: 24279. Friendly, rustic, with lobsters and mussels. There is also a barbecue. Sicilian cooking, especially fish. Closed: Tuesday. Reserve. M

La Siciliana, Via M. Polo, 52/A, Catania. Tel: 376400. Elegant and classic, with a long family tradition of cooks. Offers a summer garden and good Sicilian cooking. Closed: Sunday dinner, Monday. M

Arlecchino, Largo Empedocle, 8, Siracusa. Tel: 66386. Modern, first-rate service, regional cuisine; try *pasta con le sarde*. Closed: Monday and August. Reserve.

Villa Fortugno, road to Marina di Ragusa, 4 km (2½ miles). Tel: 28656. Old country farm with summer garden and good regional cooking. Closed: Monday and August. M

La Botte, Contrada Lenzitti, 416, Monreale. Tel: 414051. Farmhouse-style furniture with old barrels and classic atmosphere and cooking. Closed: Monday and August–September. M

Jolly Hotel, Via C. Altacura. Tel: 81446. Modern, belongs to the hotel bearing the same name. At Piazza Armerina. International cuisine. Closed: during the winter. M

Trieste, Via Napoli, 17, Noto. Tel: 835485. Classic and homely. Also a bar and *rosticceria* (grill). Closed: Monday and 10–30 October. I

El Vigneto, Via Cavaleri Magazzeni, 11, Agrigento. Tel: 414319. Overlooking the Valle dei Templi. The vineyard which gives a name to the restaurant covers part of the terrace. Excellent *caponata*. Closed: Tuesday and October. I

Chez Pierrot, Via Marco Polo, 108, Selinunte. Porch overlooking the Gulf. Speciality is seafood. Closed: January–February.

Tre Fontane, at Castello di Donnafugata, Ragusa. Tel: 45555. In a 19th-century castle in the country. Closed: Friday. I

BASILICATA & CALABRIA

Da Mario, Via XX Settembre, 14, Matera. Tel: 10336491. Inside an old silo; the rustic furniture makes the place look like the inside of a big barrel. The cuisine is typical of Basilicata; try *orecchiette* (the ear-shaped pasta) with *rape* (turnip-tops). Closed: Sunday and August. M

Bonaccorso, Via Bixio, 5, Reggiodi, Calabria. Tel: 96048. Elegant and intimate, old-fashioned atmosphere, the owner is the chef, and also happens to be an artist. Traditional cuisine, with variations. Closed: Sunday and August. Reserve. M

La Calavrisela, Via De Rada, 11a, Cosenza. Tel: 28012. Comfortable. Calabrian cuisine, heavy and spicy. Closed: Saturday night and Sunday. I

APULIA

Cicolella, Viale XXIV Maggio, 60, Foggia. Tel: 3880. Elegant, with a summer terrace. The restaurant is attached to a hotel dating back half a century. Mostly regional cuisine, ear-shaped pasta (*orecchiette*) and fish-soup among the best dishes. Closed: Friday night. Sunday and August. Reserve. E

Bacco, Via Sipontina, 10, Barletta. Tel: 571000. Intimate atmosphere, very good service, national cuisine. Special fish dishes. Closed: Saturday and Sunday. Reserve. E

Al Gambero, Via del Ponte, 4, Taranto. Tel: 4711191. Big and well-lit, overlooking the Marc Piccolo, with the best crawfish in Puglia. Closed: Monday and November. M

Al porto da Michele, Piazza della Libertà, 3, Manfredonia. Tel: 21800. Classic *trattoria* with good seafood. Closed: Monday. M

La Lanterna, Via Tarantini, 14, Brindisi. Tel: 524950. Between the colonno and the cathedral, it uses local specialities for new recipes. Closed: Sunday and August. M

Ostello di Federico, Castel del Monte. Tel: 83043. Close to Frederick II's famous castle, with a beautiful terrace-garden. Regional cooking. Closed: Monday. Reserve. M

Plaza, Via 140° Reg. Fanteria, 10, Lecce. Tel: 25093. Good Pugliese cooking including *ovecchiette*. Closed: Sunday. I

Dal Moro, Via Kennedy, 3, Otranto. Tel: 81325. On the seashore offering a good complete meal at reasonable prices. Closed: Friday. Reserve. I

La Darsena, Via Statuti Marittimi, Trani. Tel: 47333. Excellent value, traditional restaurant, specialising in seafood. Closed: Monday. Reserve. I

BARI

La Pignata, Via Melo, 9. Tel: 5232481. A chic restaurant specialising in seafood and meat dishes. Closed: Wednesday and August. Reserve. E

Miovo Vecchia Bari, Via Dante, 47. Tel: 216496. A local institution serving excellent Puglian specialities. Closed: Friday, Sunday and August. E

Ai due Ghiottoni, Via Putignani, 11. Tel: 5232240. A smart restaurant with excellent food complemented by a good wine list. Closed: Sunday and August. M

GENOA & LIGURIA

Giannino, Corso Trento e Trieste, 23. Tel: 70843. Very comfortable, high-class cooking. At San Remo. Closed: Sunday, Monday lunch, 1–15 July, 15–30 December. Reserve. L

Il Pitosforo, Molo Umberto I, 9, Portofino. Tel: 69020. Modern atmosphere, meeting-place for yachtsmen. International cooking. Closed: Tuesday and 1 January–28 February. Reserve. L

Antica Osteria del Bai, at Genova-Quarto, Via Quarto, 12. Tel: 387478. An historic restaurant where Pope Pius VII and Garibaldi once ate, inside a fortress overlooking the sea. Typical Genoese cuisine. Closed: Monday and 20 July–12 August. E

Gran Gotto, Via Fiume, 11/E. Tel: 564344, near Stazione Birgnole. Classic and elegant, with a rustic atmosphere and regional cooking. Try the *Trenette al pesto*. Closed: Sunday and August. Reserve. M

Zeffirino, Via XX Settembre, 20. Tel: 591990. In the centre of the city; modern furniture, mixed cuisine. Closed: Wednesday. Reserve. M

La Pergola, Via Casaregis, 52r. Tel: 546543. Comfortable atmosphere, regional cooking. Closed: Sunday night, Tuesday and 15 August–15 Sept. M

Da Rina, Mura di via S. Agnese, 59r. Tel: 294900. Traditional *trattoria*, good cooking. Closed: Monday, Christmas, Easter and August. Reserve. M

Del Porto da Nicò, Piazza Brescia, 9. Tel: 84144. The classic *trattoria* of the port, with good seafood. At Sanremo. Closed: Thursday and 1 November–20 December. Reserve. M

Stella, Molo Umberto I, 3, Portofino. Tel: 69007. Marine atmosphere, regional cooking. Closed: Wednesday and 6 January–3 March. Reserve. M

Gambero Rosso, Piazza Marconi, Vernazza (5 Terre). Tel: 812265. Close to the port. A small *osteria* noted for its seafood. Closed: Monday and 7 November–12 December. M

Conchiglia, Piazza del molo, 3, Lerici. Along the seaside, with especially fresh fish. Closed: Wednesday and 20 December–10 January.

Piro, Salita Bertora, 5/R, zona Struppa. Tel: 802304. From the high vantage point of this restaurant you can admire beautiful Genoa spread beneath you. This is a typical simple *trattoria*, with pretty good food. Genoese cooking. Closed: Monday and 15 August–15 September. I

THINGS TO DO

NATIONAL PARKS

As it is impossible to list every tourist attraction offered by Italian travel agencies, we will mention only the National Park areas in Italy:

Parco Nazionale del Gran Paradiso: Home of the last steinbocks and chamois in Italy, this park is the oldest in the country and is 72,000 hectares (178,000 acres) wide. Located in the Alpine zone, it is a must for nature lovers. Tel: 01-659-5704.

Parco Nazionale dello Stelvio: The biggest park in Italy (135,000 hectares or 333,600 acres), near Switzerland, rich in forests and animals. The mountains are wonderful. There are plenty of hotels. Tel: 03-429-01582 or 04-737-0447.

Parco Nazionale dell'Abruzzo: Here the last brown bear in Italy lives in remote splendour in one of the highest sections of the Apennines. For information write to Parco Nazionale d'Abruzzo, Via del Curato, 6, Roma. Tel: 06-654-3584.

If you would like to go hiking in the mountains, pick up the *GTA* (Great Trekking of the Alps), detailing a network of walking paths, with more than 80 overnight areas with shelters. Paths are marked with numerous red signs and distinctive small flags. Every stage calls for 5–7 hours of hiking time at an average of about 1,000 metres in altitude.

At the overnight rest areas there are shelters with double-decker bunks, essential services and a kitchen. The shelters are generally situated in inhabited localities, where it is possible to buy food, phone home, rest for a day, visit historical-ethnographic museums, chat with the inhabitants and also, last but not least, eat a good meal at an inn.

An itinerary can last a month, a week or a day. From the Maritime Alps to Lake Maggiore, a route stretching for 650 km (400 miles) that crosses five provinces, the hiker crosses many splendid parks, such as the Gran Paradiso, the Orsiera-Rocciavrè, the Alta Val Pesio and the Argentera.

All the areas are open to the public from July–September. For detailed information, call the GTA Information Office, Via Barbaroux 1, Torino. Tel: 011 514-477.

CULTURE PLUS

Italy has such a long recorded history that the biggest problem facing the traveller is to choose among the nation's endless cultural attractions. All main centres, most of the provincial cities and many quite small towns have museums. The theatres, galleries, concert halls and book-stores offer something for every interest.

MUSEUMS

Most museums house special exhibitions in addition to their permanent collections. Information about floating exhibitions can be obtained by calling the museum or checking the newspaper.

The museums listed below are some of the most important in Italy, but there are many others, both in the cities listed and elsewhere. Admission prices vary frequently; seldom are they free, but they are usually cheap. Take note: if in Turin, don't miss the **Egyptian Museum** at Via Accademia delle Scienze, 6 and the **Car Museum** at corso Unità d'Italia, 40.

ROME

The Vatican Museum, Viale Vaticano. Tel: 6983333. Almost always very crowded, the Museum offers papal robes, tomb inscriptions and old maps together with the Raphael rooms, the tapestry gallery, the classical statuary, and the works of some of the most important painters of the Italian Middle Ages and Renaissance (such as Giotto, Fra Angelico, and Filippo Lippi). Don't miss the Sistine Chapel, and be sure to buy a catalogue. Open: Monday–Saturday 9am–2pm and the last Sunday of every month. From July–September it is open 9am–4pm.
National Gallery of Ancient Art (Galleria Nazionale d'Arte antica), at Palazzo Barberini, via IV Fontane, 13 and at Palazzo Corsini, via della Lungara, 10. Works from the 13th to the 18th century. Open: Tuesday–Saturday 9am–2pm, Sunday 9am–1pm.
Modern Art Gallery (Galleria Nazionale d'Arte Moderna), Via delle Belle Arti, 131. Paintings by 19th and 20th-century artists, mostly Italian. Open: Tuesday–Saturday 9am–2pm, Sunday 9am–1pm.
National Museum of Oriental Art (Museo Nazionale d'Arte Orientale), Via Merulana, 248. Bronzes, stone, pottery and wooden sculpture of the oriental civilisations. Open: Tuesday–Saturday 9am–2pm, Sunday 9am–1pm.

Museo Nazionale Etrusco di Villa Giulia, Piazza di Villa Giulia, 9. Etruscan Art collection. Open in the summer: Tuesday–Sunday 9am– 2pm, Wednesday 3–7.30pm; in the winter: Tuesday–Sunday 9am– 2pm, Wednesday 9am–6.30pm.
Roman Museum (Museo Nazionale Romano), Piazza dei Cinquecento, Archaeological collections. Open: Tuesday–Saturday 9am–1.45pm, Sunday 9am–1pm.
Museo and Galleria Borghese, Piazza Scipione Borghese, 3 at Villa Borghese. Collections of painting and sculpture, including pieces by Caravaggio and works of Titian, Raphael and Bernini. Open: Tuesday–Saturday 9am–2pm, Sunday 9am–1pm.

FLORENCE

Galleria degli Uffizi, Loggiato degli Uffizi, 6. Best of Italian museums. You can see masterpieces by Botticelli, Leonardo, Raphael, Piero della Francesca, Caravaggio, Giotto and almost every other Italian and foreign artist of importance. Open: Tuesday–Saturday 9am–7pm, Sunday and public holidays 9am–1pm.
Galleria dell'Accademia, Via Ricasoli, 60. Michelangelo's works. Open: Tuesday–Saturday 9am– 2pm, Sunday 9am–1pm.
Museo Archeologico, Via della Colonna, 36. Etruscan, Greek and Roman art. Open: Tuesday–Saturday 9am–2pm, Sunday 9am–1pm.
Museo di San Marco, Piazza San Marco, 1. Frescoes and paintings. Open: Tuesday–Saturday 9am–2pm, Sunday 9am–1pm.

MILAN

Galleria d'Arte Moderna, Via Palestro, 16. Paintings, sculptures and works of the 19th and 20th century. Open: 9.30am–noon, 2.30–5.30pm. Closed: Tuesday.
Museo Archeologico. The Greek, Etruscan and Roman section is in Corso Magenta, 15. Open: 9.30am–12.30pm and 2.30–5.30pm. Closed: Tuesday. Prehistoric and Egyptian art are housed at Castello Sforzesco. Open: 9.30am–12.30pm and 2.30–5.30pm. Closed: Monday.
Museo del Risorgimento, Via Borgonuovo, 23. Documents, relics, paintings, sculptures and prints of the Risorgimento movement. Open: 9.30am– 12.30pm and 2.30–5.30pm. Closed: Monday.
Pinacoteca Ambrosiana, Piazza Pio XI, 2. Paintings from the 14th to the 19th century. Open 9.30am–5pm. Closed: Saturday.
Pinacoteca di Brera, Via Brera 28. Paintings from the 15th to the 20th century. Open: 9am–1.30pm in summer; October–March 9am–2pm, Sunday 9am– 1pm. Closed: Monday.

VENICE

Accademia. This museum offers the cream of Venetian paintings, from the superb Bellini *Madonna* to Giorgione's *Tempest* and Tintoretto's magnificent cycle about the life of St Mark. Open: Tuesday–Saturday 9am–2pm, Sunday 9am–1pm; and Monday in the summer season.

Collezione Peggy Guggenheim in a palazzo near S. Maria della Salute. All the major names of modern art are here. Open: April–October 10am–6pm, Saturday 6–9pm. Closed: Tuesday.

Museum of Dipinti Sacri Bizantini, Ponte dei Greci. The museum features paintings from the Byzantine period. Open: 9am–1pm and 2–5pm.

THEATRES

Italian theatre consists mainly of revivals of the classics, though there are a few avant-garde groups that perform in the big cities. For information on shows, ask the city's EPT (Ente Provinciale del Turismo) or check the local newspaper.

Ticket prices vary depending on the show and venue. If you would like to see an Italian play, the principal theatres are: in Rome, **Teatro Sistina**, Via Sistina, 129. Tel: 4756841 (mainly a music hall), **Teatro Valle**, Via Teatro Valle, 23. Tel: 6543794 and **Teatro Goldoni**, Vicolo de'Soldati, 3. Tel: 6561156.

In Milan, you can go to the **Piccolo Teatro**, Via Rovello, 2, tel: 877663 and to **L'Odeon**, Via Radegonda, 8, tel: 876320; for experimental theatre, try **Teatro dell'Elfo**, Via Menotti, II, tel: 712405 and the **Centro Ricerca Teatro**, Via Dini, 7, tel: 8466592.

If in Florence, you can take in an Italian production at the **Teatro Comunale**, Corso Italia, 12, tel: 2779236, **Teatro della Pergola**, Via della Pergola, 12–32, tel: 2479652, or at **Teatro Verdi**, Via Ghibellina, 101, tel: 213220 and **Teatro Niccolini** Via Ricasoli 3, tel: 213 282. In Naples there are three theatres worth visiting: the **Mercadante Piazza Municipio**, tel: 5524214, a small but beautiful theatre rebuilt in the 1940s; the **Bellini** Via Conte di Ruvo, tel: 5491266, a very old, recently restored venue and the **Politeama Theatre** Via Monte di Dio 80, tel: 7644294.

CONCERTS

Classical music lovers will find themselves at home in Italy. Noteworthy concerts occur all year almost all over the country.

The opera season in Rome is from December–June at the **Teatro dell'Opera**, tel: 4742595 and outdoors at the **Terme** (Baths) **of Caracalla** in July and August. From October–May, the **Auditorium of the National Academy of Santa Cecilia** on Via della Conciliazione and the **Sala dei Concerti** on Via dei Greci offer first-class concerts, tel: 6790389. During the summer, there is an outdoor season at the **Basilica di Massenzio**. Concerts are held also at the **University Auditorium of S. Leone Magno**, tel: 3964777, and at the **Roman Philharmonic Academy** on Via Flaminia, 118.

In Florence, the most important musical event is the International Music Festival, **Maggio Musicale Florentino**, which takes place in May and June at the Teatro Comunale, the principal opera house and concert hall. Open air concerts are held in the Boboli Gardens and in the cloisters of the Badia Fiesolana on July and August evenings. Another younger but important summer festival is **Estate Fiesolana**, which lasts from June till August. This event fills the ancient Roman theatre in Fiesole and several churches in Florence with opera, concerts, theatre, ballet and movies.

The very famous **La Scala** in Milan is a must for every opera fan. The opening evening (usually 7 December) is the city's main cultural event. Ballets and concerts are also held here, tel: 807041.

During the summer, parks are crowded with people enjoying a variety of outdoor cultural events sponsored by the city.

The **Teatro la Fenice** in Venice, tel: 5210161, offers fine programmes of music, ballet and opera in European languages, performed by guest artists. There are many other concert halls in town.

In Turin, classical music is at its peak from late August until the end of September, when **Settembre Musica**, an international music festival, takes over the town, featuring the best national and international performers.

Naples boasts the largest opera house in Italy, **San Carlo**, tel: 7972111, its perfect acoustics draw performers and audiences throughout the year. Bari's **Teatro Petruzzelli** is another fine music hall in the south.

NIGHTLIFE

Nightlife in Italy follows the American and English fashions. There are many nightclubs and discos where young people gather to listen to music, dance and talk. Many of these places go in and out of popularity (or in and out of business) in the space of a few months, so check details in local newspapers.

In recent years, Milan and Florence were tops for hip nightlife: Milan for its rock and discos, Florence for its clubs, while Naples has elegant and stylish nightclubs for the smart set.

In Rome, jazz is very fashionable, while blues music is popular in Naples. Venice is not a city for nightlife and many people prefer sitting in cafés and walking through the beautiful, labyrinthine streets. Below is a list of only the more up-to-date clubs.

ROME

Alibi, Via di Monte Testaccio. It is a gay disco on Tuesday nights only. On other nights it is open to all and there is a theme for dancing. New music.

Yellow Flag, Via della Purificazione, 41. Tel: 465951. White new wave, including the English psychedelic music.

Black Out. Fashionable only on Fridays, when you can meet post-modern and graffiti artists.

Folk Studio, Via Sacchi, 3. At Trastevere. Tel: 6798269. A folk music-hall with a preference for Irish songs. Also true American country music.

Mississippi Jazz Club, Borgo Angelico, 16. Tel: 6540348. An intimate club with the best Roman big or little jazz bands. Famous groups are Maurizio Gianmarco & C., Enrico Pierannunzi, Bruno Biriaco.

La Macumba, Via degli Olimpionici, 19. Refuge for African, Caribbean and Latin music lovers. The rhythms are wild, with the music of Fela Kuti, Dibango and Prince.

Smania, Via S. Onofrio. Offers Brazilian music, but not only samba. More fashionable is the swing of the Yemaia and of the Serpiente Latina every night.

El Trauco, Via Fonte dell'Olio, 5. Is a classic place for Brazilian music.

Manuia in Trastevere, vicolo del Cinque, 56. Is a restaurant as well as a piano bar that sometimes has live Brazilian music.

Il Bagaglino al Salone Margherita, Via due Macelli, 75. Offers cabaret in Italian.

Much More, Via Luciani, 52. Is a disco preferred by the younger set. These days it's a little bit "out".

MILAN

Plastic. The disc jockey Nicola Guiducci chooses music for all tastes.

Capolinea. All big-name be-bop bands meet here. It is possible to eat while listening to the music.

Le Scimmie. Traditional good jazz. Navigli area.

Acqua Sporca. Performances of 1940s-style big bands, every night. Navigli area.

La Budineria. A place for new and unknown Italian singers.

Magia. Rock groups from all over Northern Italy come here to play. Live music, but no dancing.

Rolling Stones, Corso XXII Marzo, 32. Tel: 733172. A "pure" disco, where big-name foreign rock singers may be seen.

Odissea, Via Forze Armate, 42. Tel: 4075653. Another top disco.

FLORENCE

Space électronic, Via Palazzuolo, 37. Tel: 293082. One of the most popular discos.

Caffè Strozzi, Piazza Strozzi. This is a refined meeting-place popular for drinks.

Caffè Voltaire, Via degli Alfani, 26r. Open every night. A meeting-place for friends, recorded music.

Yab Yum, Via Sassetti, 5r. Tel: 282018. Is a very popular disco in a central position.

Caffè Tornabuoni, Lungarno Corsini, 12 - 14/R. Tel: 210751. An elegant piano bar on the banks of the Arno.

NAPLES

City Hall, Corso Vittorio Emanuele. Good jazz; fusion-style; here you can rub elbows with all the great Neapolitan musicians, including Bennato, De Piscopo and Esposito.

La Mela, Via Dei Mille 50, and **Chez Moi**, Via del Parco Marghertia 20, are the most elegant night-clubs in Naples.

Kiss-Kiss, Via Tito Lucresio Caro 6. Tel: 5466566. Large disco with restaurant and cabaret attached.

Virgilio Sports Club, Via Tito Lucresio Caro 6. Tel: 5755261. A smart piano bar with a sea view from the terrace.

TURIN

The Big Club, Corso Brescia, 28. New-wave disco, rock and jazz concerts.

Il Santincielo at Superga. Tel: 890835. Large and popular young disco.

SHOPPING

SHOPPING AREAS

ROME

The best shopping district is around the bottom of the Spanish Steps, with the elegant **Via Condotti** lined with the most exclusive shops (Gucci, Ferragamo and Bulgari).

Other fashionable streets run parallel to Via Condotti, such as **Via Borgognona** (shops of Fendi, Gianfranco Ferrè, Gucci, and Missoni); **Via delle Carrozze** or **Via Frattina** (for ceramics, lingerie and costume jewellery); **Via Vittoria** (where the boutique of Laura Biagiotti lies) and **Via della Croce**. Most of these streets are closed to traffic. For antiques, go window shopping along **Via del Babuino** (do not miss the boutique of Giorgio Armani there) or along **Via Margutta** or **Via Giulia**.

Another fine shopping section is marked by Via del Corso between Piazza del Popolo and Largo Chigi, where **Via del Tritone** begins.

Less expensive and more popular shopping streets are **Via Nazionale**, near the railway station, where Fiorucci (funky and young sportswear and shoes) has his greatest shops, and **Via Cola di Rienzo**.

"The other face of fashion" is represented by the open markets, such as the one in **Via del Sannio** which sells new and second-hand clothes and, of course, the famous one at **Porta Portese**, open only on Sunday, where you can find almost everything. The reign of "Armani-style" secondhand clothes has become *Così è se vi pare* in the last few years, in **Via delle Carrozze**.

MILAN

More than Rome, Milan is the centre for international fashion and manufactured products of Italy. For those with expensive tastes, the most chic and elegant streets for shopping are: **Via Montenapoleone**, **Via Spiga** and **Via S Andrea**, all near the Duomo and La Scala. These streets feature such fine stores as Krizia, Giò Moretti, Trussardi, Kenzo, Sanlorenzo, Giorgio Armani and Ferragamo. Only high-fashion women's and men's clothing are sold here.

FLORENCE

The whole centre of Florence could be considered a huge shop, always crowded with tourists and well-dressed local people. Handicrafts are disappearing, leaving the place to smart and strange fashion shops. Even if it is difficult to make a choice, the most fashionable streets remain **Via Calzaiuoli**, **Via Roma** (absolutely "in" is Luisa), **Via Tornabuoni** (Gucci and Céline), **Via della Vigna Nuova** and **Via Strozzi** (Neuber, Principe, Diavolo Rosa).

Ponte Vecchio is famous almost all over the world for gold and silver jewellery and some antique shops.

The area near the church of Santa Croce is full of top-quality leather goods, while for other handicrafts you can check out the city's two open markets, sprawling **San Lorenzo** and covered **Mercato Nuovo**, near Piazza della Signoria.

VENICE

The most exclusive shopping area in Venice is the **Via XXII Marzo** and the streets around **St Mark's Square**. The best local shopping areas are the Rialto Bridge and San Polo. On the **Lido** on Tuesday morning a market is held, bargains to shop for include shoes, clothes, gifts and fur coats!

NAPLES

The best shopping area is concentrated around the **Piazza Amedeo** to **Piazza Trieste e Trento**: the **Via dei Mille** and **Via Filangieri** have many famous name designer shops. Mariella, one of Italy's most famous and expensive men's wear shops, is located in the same area in **Via Riviera di Chiaia**. Less expensive and more popular shopping streets are the **Via Chiaia** and **Via Roma** near the San Carlo Opera House. Unfortunately all shopping areas in Naples are very crowded and close to the traffic.

SPORTS

SPECTATOR

SOCCER

The national sport in Italy is soccer. Almost every city and village has its own team. The most important national championship is the "Series A" (First Division). The winner of this competition is eligible to play in a kind of European championship, the "Champions' Cup", against the top teams of other European nations.

The "Series A" championship is played from September–May, and each of the 16 teams has to play against each of the other teams twice.

The most successful Italian soccer team is the Juventus FC from Turin, followed by Internazionale from Milan. But many other cities are blessed with successful teams, including Verona, the surprising winner of the 1985 Championship, and Rome.

If you would like to see a game, check the newspaper to find out which team is playing, and where. Remember that it is very difficult to get tickets if the game is an important one. Ticket prices vary according to the importance of the team, the game, and the quality of the seat you want.

MOTOR RACING

The second passion of the Italians is represented by cars and speed. Formula One races attract people interested in the sophisticated technology and the coupling of man and car. This sport attracts mostly a TV audience, because it is expensive to go around the world to see the races. In Italy citizens support the red cars built by Ferrari. There is always a large crowd at the Imola and Monza Grand Prix races.

OTHER SPORTS

Almost every other sport is enjoyed in Italy, including American football. If you are interested in buying tickets for any game, buy the pink *Gazzetta dello Sport* newspaper, where everything under the sun about sports is listed.

USEFUL ADDRESSES

TOURIST INFORMATION

General tourist information is available at the **Ente Nazionale per il Turismo** (ENIT), Via Marghera, 2/6 Rome. Tel: 4971222. The ENIT also has offices on: 15th floor of 630 Fifth Avenue in New York City.

In every chief town you will find the **Ente Provinciale per il Turismo** (EPT) or the **Azienda Autonoma di Soggiorno e Turismo**. For their addresses and phone numbers, check the directory or the *Yellow Pages* under "Enti". Main cities have a sort of "travel tips" together with the directory named *Tutto Città*. Check that too.

Provincial Tourist Offices (EPT) of the main cities are listed below:

ROME

Main headquarters are located in Via Parigi, 5, tel: 463748, but there is an EPT also at the stazione centrale Termini, tel: 465461, and at the airport, tel: 6011255. Main headquarters are open: Monday–Saturday 8.30am–1pm and 2–7pm and provide helpful services from sightseeing suggestions to brochures and maps of Rome and Lazio.

MILAN

EPT offices are located at Stazione Centrale. Tel: 206030. Open in summer: 9am–12.30pm and 2–6.30pm; in winter until 6pm. Closed: Sunday. Also at Piazza del Duomo. Tel: 809662. Open in summer: Monday–Friday 8.45am–6.30pm, Saturday 9am–5pm; in winter: Monday–Friday 8.45am–12.30pm and 1.30–6pm, Saturday till 5pm.

FLORENCE

The EPT office is far from the centre of the city in Via Manzoni, 16. Tel: 23320. Open: Monday–Friday 8.30am–1.30pm and 4–6.30pm, Saturday 8.30am–1pm. More central and efficient is the Azienda Autonoma di Turismo, Provincia-Comune di Firenze, Via Cavoor, 1R. Tel: 2760382. Open: Monday–Saturday 9am–2pm.

VENICE

The EPT office is in San Marco, 71F, tel: 26356, under the arcades of the piazza. Open: Monday–Saturday 9am–12.30pm and 3–7pm, also an office in the station, tel: 715016. Open: daily 8am–7pm.

Almost every town in Italy has a **Touring Club Italiano** (TCI) office, which provides free information about points of interest in the area. Telephone numbers are listed in the local telephone book.

FURTHER READING

Across the River and into the Trees, by Ernest Hemingway.
A Room with a View, by E.M. Forster.
Andreas, by Hugo von Hoffmannsthal. 1930.
The Architecture of the Italian Renaissance, by Peter Murray.
The Aspern Papers, by Henry James.
Autobiography, by Benvenuto Cellini.
Christ Stopped at Eboli, by Carlo Levi.
Le Citta Invisibili, Italo Calvino. Translated as *Invisible Cities*.
The Civilization of the Renaissance in Italy. Jacob Burckhardt.
The Decameron, by Boccaccio.
D.H. ·Lawrence and Italy, by D.H. Lawrence.
The Doge, by A. Palazzeschi.
Etruscan Places, by D.H. Lawrence.
Florence, a Traveller's Companion, by Harold Acton and Edward Chaney.
The Gallery, by John Horne Burns.
Graziella, by Alphonse de Lamartine (AC Mclurg, Chicago).
Il Fuoco, by Gabriele d'Annuncio. Translated as the *Flame of Life*.
Italian Hours, by Henry James.
Italian Journey, by Johann Wolfgang Goethe.
Italian Journeys, by William Dean Howells. 1867.
The Italian Painters of the Renaissance, by Bernard Berenson.
The Italians, by Luigi Barzini.
The Italian World, by John Julius Norwich.
The Last Medici, by Harold Acton.
Lives of the Artists, Vol. 1 & 2, by Giorgio Vasari.
Love and War in the Apenines, by Eric Newby.
The Love of Italy, by Jonathan Keates.
The Mafia, by Clare Sterling (Grafton).
The Mediterranean Passion, by John Pemble.
The Merchant of Prato, by Iris Origo.

Memoirs, by Giacomo Casanova. Translated into many languages.

Naples '44, by Norman Lewis.

Pictures from Italy, by Charles Dickens.

Der Reise, by Bernward Vesper. Translated as *The Journey*.

Renaissance Venice, edited by J.R. Hale.

The Rise and Fall of the House of Medici, by Christopher Hibbert.

Rome, Naples and Florence, by Stendhal (published 1817).

Siren Island, Summer Islands, South Wind and *Old Calabria*, by Norman Douglas.

The Stones of Florence and Venice Observed, by Mary McCarthy.

The Stones of Venice (1851–3), by John Ruskin.

The Story of San Michele, by Axel Munthe.

Those Who Walk Away, by Patricia Highsmith.

Thus Spake Bellavista, by Luciano da Crescenzo.

Der Tod in Venedig, by Thomas Mann. Translated as *Death in Venice*.

A Tramp Abroad, by Mark Twain.

A Venetian Bestiary, by Jan Morris.

Venetian Life, by William Dean Howells. 1866.

Venetian Red, by P.M. Passinetti.

Venice, by Jan Morris.

Venice: A Thousand Years of Culture and Civilisation, by Peter Lauritzen.

Venice and its Lagoon, Giulio Lorenzetti.

Venice for Pleasure, by J.G. Links.

Venice: The Greatness and the Fall, by Mark Twain. 1981.

Venice: The Rise to Empire, by John Julius Norwich.

The Wings of the Dove, by Henry James.

OTHER INSIGHT GUIDES

Other *Insight Guides* which highlight destinations in the region are: Rome, Venice, Florence, Umbria and South Tyrol, and *Insight Pocket Guides* Venice, Rome, Florence Milan and Tuscany.

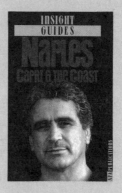

Insight Guide: Tuscany reveals one of the richest and most civilised landscapes on earth, with stunning photography and comprehensive text.

Insight Guide: Bay of Naples does full justice to a fascinating region, including the Amalfi Coast, Pompeii and the islands of Capri and Ischia.

Thoroughly updated and expanded, the best-selling *Insight CityGuide: Rome* lifts the lid on Italy's capital.

Insight Pocket Guide: Venice provides tailor-made tours of one of the most romantic cities in Europe. Perfect for a short break.

ART/PHOTO CREDITS

INDEX

A

Abbazia di Monte Oliveta Maggiore (Benedictine) 261–262
Abruzzo 169–173
Accademia Militare, Modena 237
Acton, Harold 125
Aeolian Islands 333
Agrigento 330
Alassio 202
Alba 200
Albanian College 320
Albanian villages, culture 320
Albenga 202
Alberobello 312–313
Alicudi 333
Alpe di Siussi 228
Amalfi 306
Amalfi Coast 306
Anacapri 304
Andreotti, Giulio 69,73
Aosta 199
Apennine Mountains 169
Apulia (Puglia) 309–315
Apulian Romanesque 309, 312, 321
Arab-Norman architecture 45
Arbatax 335
Arch of Trajan, Benevento 305
Archiginnasio 234
Arco di Augusto, Rimini 240
Arco di Tito 140
Arco Etrusco, Perugia 273
Arno river 254
Arrezzo 271
Arte della Lana (wool guild) 51
Assisi 274
Augustus 38
Avezzano 169

B

Baia 301
Barbagia 334–335
Barberini Mosaic 164
Barcola 233
Bari 309–312
Barletta 309–310
Barzini, Luigi 53, 143
Basilica di San Marco (St Mark's Basilica) 208–209
Basilica di Superga 198–199
Basilicata 321
baths, Roman 146, 153
Battistero, Neoniano 242
Bellini, Giovanni 55, 191, 211, 214, 296

Bellini, Vincenzo 107, 109
Benevento 305
Bergamo 190–191
Berlinguer, Enrico 68–69
Bernini, Gianlorenzo 58, 153, 154, 155, 156
Biblioteca Ambrosiana, Milan 187
Biennale (art exhibition), Venice 216
Black Death 49
Boboli Gardens 253
Boccaccio 255
Bologna 234–237
Bolzano (Bozen) 227
Borromeo, Charles 184
Borromini 58, 152, 154, 155
Botticelli, Sandro 55
Bramante, Donato 56, 188
Bressanone (Brixen) 229
Breughel, Peter 296
Bridge of Sighs 210
Brigata Rossa (Red Brigade) 69
Bronze Age 227, 231
Bronze Warriors 317
Browning, Robert 212
Brunelleschi, Filippo 55, 247, 249, 253
Burano 217
Byron, Lord 25, 141, 203, 207
Byzantine empire 43

C

Ca d'Oro, Venice 212
Caere 165
Caesar, Julius 37
Cagliari 335
Calabria 317–320
Caligula 39
Campi Flegrèi 300
Campo Basso 173
Campo dei Miracoli 267
Canaletto, Antonio 211
Cap d'Orso 334
Capodimonte 291
Caprera 334
Caprese Michelangelo 271
Capri 303–304
Caravaggio, Amerighi da 58, 148, 150, 154, 185, 187
Carbonari 61
Carrara 269
Carthusian monastery (Serra San Bruno) 318–319
Casa di Dante 254
Casa Magna 203
Caserta Vecchia 305
Castel del Monte, Ruvo 312
Castel Sant'Angelo 156
Castel dell'Ovo 291
Castello del Buonconsiglio 230
Castello Estense 239
Castello Sforzesco 185
Castello Ursino 328
Castelvecchio, Adige 223
catacombs 158
Catania 327–328
Cave of the Cumaean Sybil 300
Cavour, Camillo 62–63
Cefalu 333
ceramics 278, 314
ceri (candle) race 280
Certosa di Pavia 187–188

Cerveteri 165
character 79–84
Charlemagne 43–44
Charles I of Anjou 292
Chianti (see wine)
Christianity 40
churches
  Badia Fiorentina, Florence 254
  Basilica di Santo Stefano, Bologna 236
  Basilica di S Zeno, Verona 223
  Basilica di Sant'Andrea, Mantua 190
  Capella degli Scrovegni, Padua 219
  Capello San Severo, Naples 296
  Cattedrale di San Giusto, Friuli 233
  Cattolica (Byzantine) 318
  Chiesa dei Cappuccini, Rome 152
  Chiesa di San Fortunato 277–278
  Chiesa Nuova, Rome 155–156
  Chiesa Russa, San Remo 202
  Gesù Nuovo, Naples 295
  Gesù, Rome 147
  Orsanmichele, Florence 249
  S Giovanni degli Eremiti, Palermo 332 (see also
    Duomo)
  S Giovanni in Laterano, Rome 145
  St Peter's, Rome 156
  San Andrea al Quirinale, Rome 152
  San Andrea della Valle 156
  San Carlino, Rome 152
  San Clemente, Rome 144
  San Filomena (Byzantine) 319
  San Francesco, Arezzo 271
  San Giorgio Maggiore, Venice 209
  San Miniato, Florence 253
  San Nicolò dei Mendicoli, Venice 214
  San Paolo Fuori dei Muri, Rome 147
  San Petronio, Bologna 234
  San Pietro in Vincoli, Rome 153
  San Vitale, Ravenna 241
  Sant'Ambrogio, Milan 186
  Sant'Andrea, Pistoia 269
  Sant'Antimo (abbey church) 262
  Sant'Orso, Aosta 199
  Santa Croce, Florence 253
  Santa Maria dei Miracoli, Venice 215
  Santa Maria del Popolo, Rome 150
  Santa Maria della Salute, Venice 211
  Santa Maria della Vittoria, Rome, 152
  Santa Maria di Castello 201
  Santa Maria Maggiore, Como 194
  Santa Maria Maggiore, Rome 153
  Santa Maria Sopra Minerva, Rome 154
  Santa Sabina, Rome 146
  Trinità del Monte, Rome 151
Cimitero Acattolico 146
Circus Maximus 146
city–states 46
Claudius 39
Codex Purpureus (Greek manuscript) 320–321
Colosseum 144
Columbus, Christopher 200
condottieri (mercenaries) 51–52
Congress of Vienna 61
Conservatorio di Musica 295
Constantine 40
Convent of San Damiano 275–276
Copernicus, Nicolas 236
Corleonesi 73

Correggio, Antonio 190, 238
Cosa Nostra 71–73
Cosenza 320
Costa Smeralda 334
crafts 335
Craxi, Bettino 69
Cremona 188–189
Cristo Velato (Veiled Christ) 296
Crotone 319–320
Cumae 300

D

d'Annunzio, Gabriele 172, 195
d'Este family 164–165, 189–190, 237, 238–239
da Vinci, Leonardo 56, 183, 185–187, 188, 270
Dante Alighieri 46, 195, 203, 237, 242, 254, 309
Due Torre, Bologna 235
della Francesca, Piero 271, 273, 281
Diocletian 40
Donatello 55, 218, 249, 250
Donizetti, Gaetano 107, 109
Douglas, Norman 303, 318–319, 320
Duomo (cathedral)
  Amalfi 306
  Assisi 275
  Bari 311
  Bitonto 312
  Cremona 189
  Ferrara 239
  Florence 247
  Genoa 201
  Gerace 318
  Mantua 190
  Messina 325
  Milan 183–184
  Modena 237
  Monreale 331
  Montepulciano 264
  Naples 295
  Orvieto 278–279
  Padua 219
  Parma 238
  Piazza Armerina 329
  Ravello 306
  Ravenna 242
  Ruvo di Paglia 312
  Salerno 307
  Spoleto 276
  Taranto 313
  Todi 277
  Trani 310
  Trento 230
  Tropea 317
  Turin 197
  Udine 233
  Vicenza 220

E

economic miracle 69
Elba 265
Emilia-Romagna 234–242
Ereno delle Carceri hermitage 276
Esposizione Universale di Roma (EUR) 162–163
Etna, Mount 326–327
Etruscans 31, 32–33, 35, 265–266
Etsch valley 229

F

Farnesina, Rome 158
fashion 89–93, 187
Fellini, Federico 115, 116, 149
Ferrara 238
festivals 335
Fidenza 238
Filicudi 333
film, cinema 113–116
Florence 51–53
Florian's, Venice 210
Fontane delle Novantanove Cannelle 170
food 95–99
  regional/local specialities 96–98, 191, 237, 266, 297, 335
Foresta Umbra 309
Fornovo, Battle of 53
Foro Italico 162
Forster, E.M. 253
Fortuna Primigenia 163
Forum (Rome) 139–140
Fra Angelico 255, 273
Frederick II of Hohenstaufen 309, 315, 320
Friuli-Venezia Giulia 232

G – H

Galilei, Galileo 253
Galleria Vittorio Emanuele (shopping mall) 184
Gallipoli 315
Gardone Riviera 195
Garfagnana nature reserve 268
Garibaldi, Giuseppe 62–63, 71, 334
Genoa 200–201
Gerace 318
ghetto (Rome) 145 (Venice) 215
Ghibellines 46
Ghiberti, Lorenzo 55, 247
Ghirlandaio, Domenico 255
Giardino Hanbury 203
Giardino Zoologico 152
Gibbon, Edward 24
Giotto 55, 219–220, 247, 253, 275
glass (Venice) 217
Goethe, Johann 150, 331, 332
Golfo d'Orosei 335
Gonzaga family 189–190
Gran Sasso d'Italia 171
Grand Canal, Venice 210
Grand Tour 24, 27
Graves, Robert 39
Greek theatre, Paestum 307
  Syracuse 328
  Taormina 326
Greeks 31–33
Gregory I, Pope 43
Grotta Azzurra 304
Grotta di Smeralda 306
Grottadel Cane 301
Grottaglie 314
Grotte Castellana (caves) 313
Gubbio 279
Guelfs 46
Gulf of Castellamare 331
Gulf of La Spezia 203
Hannibal 35
Hawthorne, Nathaniel 12, 148

Hemingway, Ernest 169, 193, 202
Herculaneum 293, 302–303
Holy Roman Empire 45–46
Holy See 121–125
Horace 38
humanism 49

I

Iblei Mountains 329
ice cream 254
Ides of March 37
Ischia 304
Isernia 173
Isole Maddalena 334
Isole Trèmiti 173
Istituto Musicale Donizetti 191
Italian League 52–53
Italians, The 53

J – L

James, Henry 26, 27, 150, 183, 198, 210, 211
Joyce, James 151, 232
Keats, John 23, 25, 146–147, 150
L'Aquila 169
L'Osservatore Romano 121, 123
La Fenice (opera house), Venice 213
La Scala 184
La Trinità (Benedictine abbey) 321
La Verna monastery 270
lace industry 217
Lago di Aveno 301
Lago di Como 193
Lago di Garda 195
Lago Maggiore 193
Lake Kalterer 230
lakes 193–195
language, dialects 81–82
Larino 173
Lateran Treaty 66, 121
Latornia del Paradiso 328–329
Lavarone 231
Lawrence, D.H. 183, 193
Leaning Tower of Pisa 267–268
Lecce 314–315
Lecco 194–195
Lee, Laurie 259
Leonardo (see da Vinci)
Libreria Sansoviniana 209
Lido 217
Liguria 200
Lipari 333
Lippi, Filippo 276
Loggia dei Lanzi 250
Loggia del Consiglio 222
Lombards 43–44
Lucca 268
Luciano, Lucky 72
Luther, Martin 23

M

Machiavelli, Niccolo 53, 251, 253
Mafia 70–73, 79
Malatesta, Sigimondo 240
Manfredonia 309
Mann, Thomas 217

Mannerists 58
Mantegna, Andrea 185, 190, 191
Mantua 189–190
Maratea 321
marble 269
Marches, The 280–281
Marshall Plan 68
Massa Marittima 265
Matera 321
mausoleum of Santa Costanza 158
Mazzini, Joseph 61
Medici family 51, 52–53, 183, 242, 250, 251, 255
Merano 226
Messina 325–326
Messina, Antonello di 326
mezzogiorno 79
Michelangelo Buonarroti 56–57, 153, 156, 185, 249,
    250, 252, 253, 254, 255
Milan 183–187
Modena 237
Monreale 331
Montalcino 262
Monte Cassino 167
Monte Pellegrino 331
Monte Solaro 304
Monte Subasio 274
Montepulciano 263
Monterchi 271
Moro, Aldo 69
Mortorio 334
mosaics 241, 242, 293, 313, 331
museums and galleries
    Accademia Carrara, Begamo 191
    Archeological Museum of Venice 209
    Archeological Museum, Florence 255
    Biblioteca Estense, Modena 237
    Carlo Biscaretti di Ruffia Museo dell Automobile 198
    Centro Marino Marini 269
    Egyptian Museum, Palazzo dell'Accademia delle
        Scienze 198
    Galleria Borghese, Rome 152
    Galleria d'Arte Moderna, Venice 212
    Galleria degli Accademia, Florence 250
    Galleria dell'Accademia, Venice 211–212
    Galleria Doria Pamphili, Rome 148
    Galleria Nazionale d'Arte Moderna, Rome 152
    Galleria Nazionale dell'Umbria 273
    Galleria Nazionale delle Marche 281
    Galleria Nazionale, Rome 151
    Guggenheim Collection, Venice 211
    Museo Archeologico di Antichita, Chieti 172
    Museo Archeologico Nazionale, Naples 291
    Museo Archeologico, Bari 312
    Museo Archeologico, Perugia 274
    Museo Civico di Arte Anchio, Turin 197
    Museo Civico Friuli 233
    Museo Civico, Padua 219
    Museo Civico, Sansepolcro 271
    Museo Civico, Siena 260
    Museo de Arte Sacra, Siena 261
    Museo del Palazzo Venezia, Rome 143
    Museo del Sannio, Benevento 305
    Museo dell'Opera del Duomo, Florence 249
    Museo dell'Opera del Duomo, Siena 261
    Museo della Cattedrale, Chiusi 263
    Museo della Ceramica, Naples 297
    Museo di San Martino, Naples 296
    Museo di Storia ed Arte, Friuli 233
    Museo e Gallerie del Vaticano 157
    Museo Guarnacci (Etruscan remains),Volterra 267
    Museo Jatta, Ruvo 312
    Museo Nazional Etrusco, Chiusi 263
    Museo Nazionale Archeologico Prenestino 164
    Museo Nazionale d'Abruzzo 171
    Museo Nazionale del Melfese 321
    Museo Nazionale della Magna Grecia, Reggio 317
    Museo Nazionale della Scienza e della Tecnica,
        Milan 186
    Museo Nazionale di Villa Giulia, Rome 152
    Museo Nazionale Romano, Rome 153
    Museo Nazionale Tarquinese 167
    Museo Nazionale, Naples 296
    Museo Nazionale, Ravenna 242
    Museo Nazionale, Taranto 313
    Museo Oriental 212
    Museo Pio-Clementino, Rome 157
    Museo Preistorico ed Etnografico (EUR) 163
    Museo Regionale della Sicilia 332
    Museo Teatrale alla Scala 184
    Museo Vetrario (glass museum), Venice 217
    Museum of Cerveteri 166
    Palatine Gallery, Florence 253
    Palazzo Chiericati, Vicenza 221
    Palazzo dei Musei, Modena 237
    Pinacoteca di Brera 185
    Pinacoteca Nazionale, Bologna 236
    Pinacoteca Nazionale, Siena 261
    Pinacoteca Provinciale, Bari 312
    Scuola Grandedi San Rocco, Venice 214
    Vinci Museum 270
Mussolini, Benito 65–68, 71, 114, 162, 195, 225, 227

N

Naples 291–297
Napoleon 61, 265
Necropolis, Tarquinia 167
Nero 39–40
Nervi 202
Norman architecture 331, 333
Normans 44–45
Noto 329

O

Obelisk 144
Odyssey 317
Ogliastra 335
opera 107–111
Orbetello 265
Orti Farnesiani 139
Orto Botanico 332
Orvieto 278–279
Otranto 315

P

Pact of Steel 66
Padua 218–220
Paestum 307
Pagnella mountains 231
Palazzo dei Conservatori, Rome 143
    Bianco, Genoa 201
    Chiaramonte, Palermo 332
    Comunale, Bologna 235
    Davanzati, Florence 254

dei Consoli, Gubbio 280
dei Diamanti, Ferrara 239
del Comune, Ferrara 239
del Comune, Piacenza 238
del Museo Capitolino, Rome 143
della SS Annunziata 172
di Bera 185
di Schifanoia, Ferrara 239
Ducale (Doge's Palace), Venice 209–210
Ducale, Urbino 281
Farnese, Rome 156
Gustinian, Venice 212
Laterano, Rome 145
Reale, Naples 292
Rosso, Genoa 201
Sapienza, Rome 154
Venezia, Rome 143
Palermo 44–45, 331–333
Palio (Siena) 259
Palladio, Andrea 58, 209, 214, 220, 221–222
Panarea 333
Pantheon 154
Parco Archeologico, Baia 301
Parco Naaturale della Maremma 265
Parco Nazionale d'Abruzzo 169
Parma 238
Parmigiano (Parmesan cheese) 237–238
Pasolini, Paolo 113
Pax Romana 38
PCI (Italian Communist Party) 68–69
Peloritani mountains 325
Perugia 273
Pescara 172
Petrarch 23, 203, 236
Petronius 41, 95
Piacenza 238
Piano di Campidano 335
Piazza di Spagna, Rome 150
Piazza Navona, Rome 155
Piazza San Marco, Venice 207–209
Piazza Tre Martiri 240
Pienza 264
pilgrims 23
Pinocchio theme park, Collodi 269
Pisa 267–268
Pisano, Giovanni 269
Pitigliano 266
Pitti Palace 253
pizza 297
Pliny the Younger 193, 194
Plutarch 41
politics, political scandals 80
Pompeii 293, 302
Pompey the Great 36–37
Ponte Vecchio, Florence 252
Pope John Paul II 122
popes, papacy (see Vatican)
Porta del Popolo 149
Porto Cervo 334
Porto Venere 203
Portofino 203
Potenza 321
Pozzuoli 301
Praeneste 163
Prato 269–270
Preti, Mattia 295, 315, 319
Prince, The 53
Procida 304

Puccini, Giacomo 107, 111, 156, 184
Punic Wars 35–36
Pythagoras 319

R

Raphael l51, 148, 150, 155, 156, 158, 185, 199, 236, 252, 281Risorgimento 61–63
Ravello 306–307
Ravenna 241–242
Reggia dei Gonzaga 190
Renaissance 49, 51
Renaissance art and architecture 55–58, 158, 170, 216, 222, 238, 247, 249, 255, 264, 294
Reni, Guido 236
Rialto, Venice 214
Riina, Toto 73
Rimini 239–240
Riviera di Levante 201
Riviera di Ponente 201
Rocca del Albornoz, Spoleto 276
Roger the Norman 291
Roman Arena, Verona 222
Roman Curia 125
Roman Forum, Assisi 275
Roman Forum, Rimini 240
Roman theatre, Aosta 199
Roman theatre, Paestum 307
Romazzino, Sardinia 334
Rome 33, 35–40, 139–158
Romeo and Juliet 223
Roncole 238
Rossano 320–321
Rossellini, Roberto 113, 115–116
Rossini, Giocchino 107, 109
Rubens, Peter Paul 156, 253, 273

S

Sacro Speco (Holy Grotto) 167
St Clare 275–276
St Dominic 237
St Francis 270–271, 275–276
St Mark's Square (see Piazza San Marco)
St Nicholas 311
Salerno 307
Salina 333
San Galgano (Cistercian abbey) 264
San Gimignano 266
San Marco convent 255
San Marino 281
San Remo 202
Santa Maria Capua Vetere amphitheatre 304
Santa Severina 319
Santuario di San Michel 309
Sardinia 334–335
Sarn valley 227
sassi (cave dwellings) 321
Satyricon, The 95
Savonarola, Girolamo 53
Scala Santa 145
Scilla 317
Segesta 331
Selinunte 330
Sforza, Francesco 50–52
Shakespeare, William 218
Shelley, Percy Bysshe 25, 150, 183, 193, 203
Sicily 44–45, 67, 325–333

Sila Piccola 319
"Simulaun Man" 226–227
Sistine Chapel 57, 157
skiing, ski resorts 225, 228
Soffio 334
Solfatara 301
Sopramonte 335
Sorrento 305–306
Sovana 266
spa towns 225, 226, 262, 269
Spanish Steps, Rome 150
Spoleto 276–277
Stendhal 193, 194
Stradivari, Antonio 189
Stromboli 333
Subiaco 167
Suetonius 303
Sulcis 335
Sulmona 171
Swiss Guards 125
Syracuse 328

T

Taormina 326
Taranto 313–314
Tavole Palatine, Metaponto 321
Teatro di Roma 163
Teatro Romano, Verona 223
Teatro San Carlo, Naples 292
Tempio di Apollo, Syracuse 328
Tempio di Athena, Syracuse 328
Tempio di Saturno 141–142
Tempio di Vesta 140–141
Tempio Malatestiano 240
Temple of Bacchus 307
Temple of Neptune 307
Tesoro dell'Archivescado 320
Tiberius 39, 303
Tiberius's Villa 303
Tiepolo, Giambattista 233
Tintoretto, Jacopo 58, 210, 211, 214, 221
Titian 57, 148, 211, 214, 252, 253, 296
Todi 277
Tomba di Dante (Dante's Tomb) 242
Toncello 217
Torre Ghirlandina 237
traminer grapes 230
Trani 310
Trastevere, Rome 154
Treaty of Utrecht 61
Trentino-Alto Adige 225
Trento 230
Trevi Fountain, Rome 149
Triple Alliance 65
Tropea 317
truffles 200
trulli 312–313
Turin 197–198
Turin Shroud 197–198
Tuscany 259–271
Twain, Mark 26–27, 180, 200

U – V

Uccello, Paolo 249, 255
Udine 233
Uffizi Gallery 55, 58, 73, 247, 251
Umbria 273–280
underground churches 310
University of Bologna 236
Urbino 280–281
Valle d'Aosta 197–200
Vasari, Giorgio 153–154, 157–158, 238, 247, 251, 252, 295
Vatican 121–125, 156–157
Velazquez, Diego 149
Venice 207–217
Venosa 321
Ventimiglia 203
Verdi, Giuseppe 184, 189, 213, 238
Verona 222–223
Veronese, Paolo 210, 211
Versilia 268
Vesuvius 291, 303
Via Appia 305
Via Sacra, Rome 140
Via Veneto, Rome 151–152
Viareggio 268
Vicenza 220–221
Victor Emmanuel I 62–63
Victor Emmanuel II 66–67, 184
Vieste 309
Villa Cimbrone 307
Villa d'Este 164–165
Villa Rufolo 306–307
Vinci 270
Virgil 38, 189, 291
Visconti family 50–52, 183,188
Visconti, Luchino 114, 116
Volta, Alessandro 188, 194
Volterra 266–267
Volto Santo (Holy Face) 268
Vulcano 333

W – Y

Wagner, Richard 212, 306
water sports 225
wine, vineyards 101–105, 200, 225, 230, 259, 262, 264, 278, 320
wool trade 51
World War I 65
World War II 66–68
Yeats, W.B. 241

A
B
C
D
E

G
H
I
J
a
b
c
d
e
f
g
h
i
j
k
l